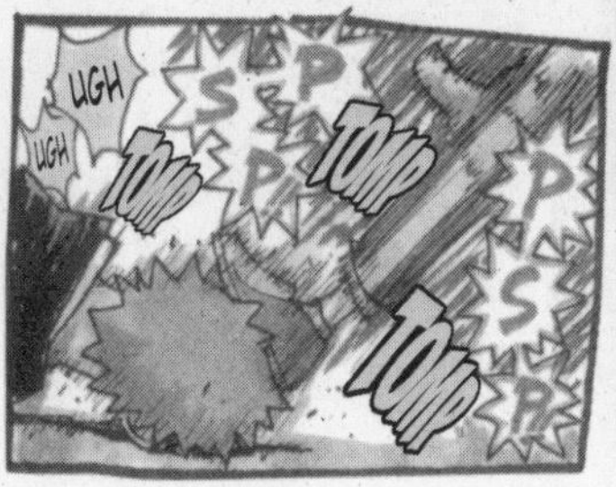
UGH
UGH
TOMP
TOMP
TOMP

The first ever *Bleach* game has been released (it's been out for a while) for the world's most anticipated console, the PSP (PlayStation Portable)! I don't know what to say except that it's really cutting edge. This game is every boy's dream—a fighting game! Naturally, the first time you play, you've gotta be Ichigo. But on my very first go, I got my butt kicked by Orihime! C'mon, Ichigo, you can do better than that.
—Tite Kubo

Bleach is author Tite Kubo's second title. Kubo made his debut with *Zombiepowder.*, a four-volume series for *Weekly Shonen Jump*. To date, *Bleach* has been translated into numerous languages and has also inspired an animated TV series that began airing in the U.S. in 2006. Beginning its serialization in 2001, *Bleach* is still a mainstay in the pages of *Weekly Shonen Jump*. In 2005, *Bleach* was awarded the prestigious Shogakukan Manga Award in the *shonen* (boys) category.

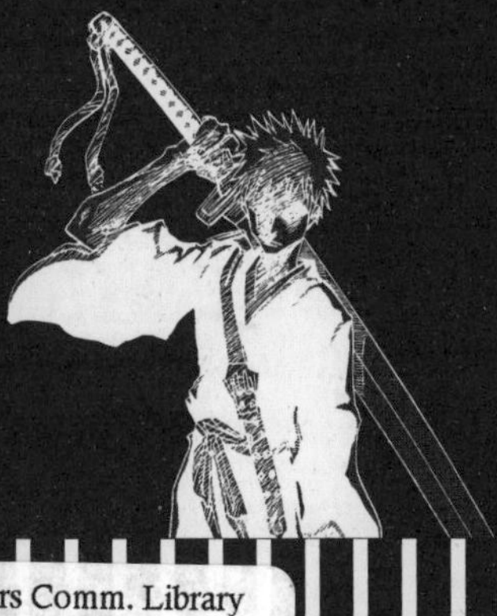

BLEACH
Vol. 17: ROSA RUBICUNDIOR, LILIO CANDIDIOR
The SHONEN JUMP Manga Edition

STORY AND ART BY
TITE KUBO

English Adaptation/Lance Caselman
Translation/Joe Yamazaki
Touch-Up Art & Lettering/Mark McMurray
Design/Sean Lee
Editor/Yuki Takagaki

Editor in Chief, Books/Alvin Lu
Editor in Chief, Magazines/Marc Weidenbaum
VP, Publishing Licensing/Rika Inouye
VP, Sales and product Marketing/Gonzalo Ferreyra
VP, Creative/Linda Espinosa
Publisher/Hyoe Narita

Printed in the U.S.A.

Published by VIZ Media, LLC
P.O. Box 77010
San Francisco, CA 94107

SHONEN JUMP Manga Edition
10 9 8 7 6 5 4
First printing, February 2007
Fourth printing, June 2008

Red like blood
White like bone
Red like solitude
White like silence
Red like the senses of a beast
White like the heart of a god
Red like molten hatred
White like chilling cries of pain
Red like the shadows that feed on the night
Like a sigh piercing the moon
It shines white and scatters red

BLEACH17 ROSA RUBICUNDIOR, LILIO CANDIDIOR

STARS AND

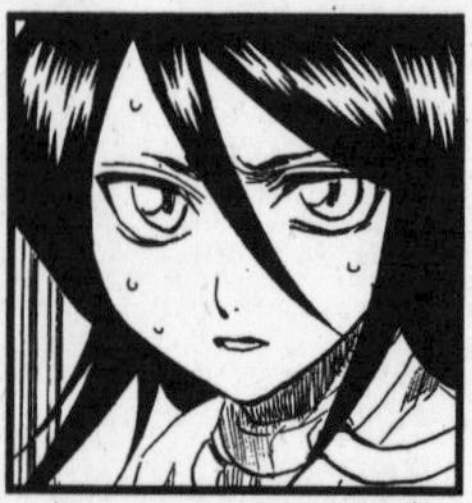

朽木白哉
Byakuya Kuchiki

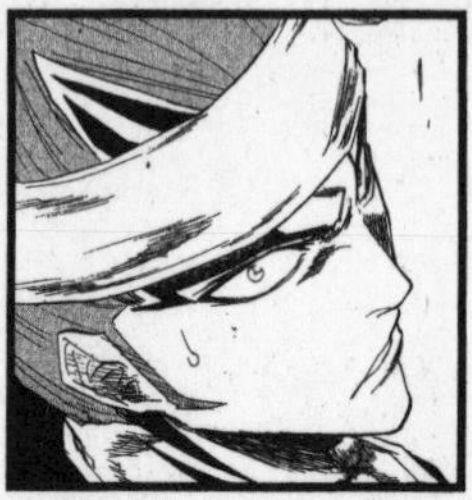

Rukia Kuchiki
朽木ルキア

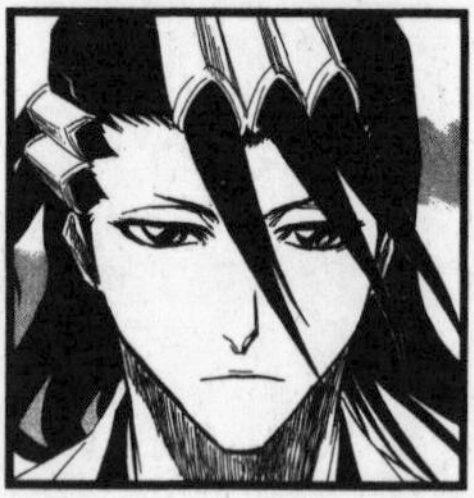

Renji Abarai
阿散井恋次

plot

As Rukia's date with death looms ever nearer, Ichigo struggles desperately to achieve Bankai. Meanwhile, Orihime and the others, lacking a leader, enlist the aid of the fearsome Kenpachi Zaraki. And Renji, fearing that Ichigo will be too late to save Rukia, goes to save her himself, only to be intercepted by the deadly Byakuya Kuchiki!

BLEACH ALL

市丸ギン
Gin Ichimaru

東仙要
Kaname Tôsen

Kenpachi Zaraki
更木剣八

STORIES

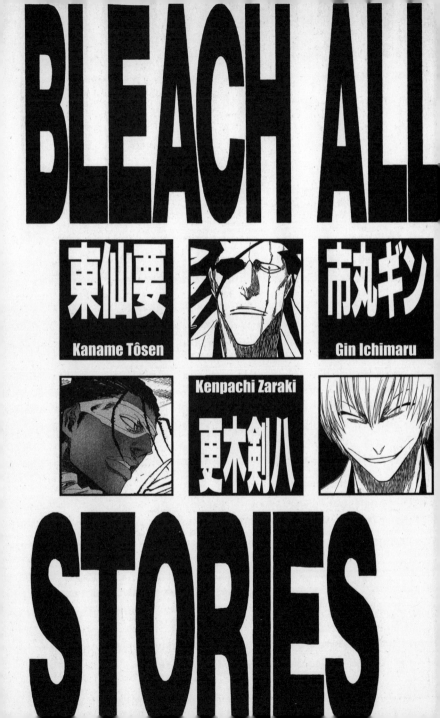

BLEACH17

ROSA RUBICUNDIOR, LILIO CANDIDIOR

Contents

140. Bite at the Moon

I WAS AFRAID...

PRETENDING TO CHASE...
PRETENDING TO SHARPEN MY FANGS...

BUT IN TRUTH, I WAS AFRAID...

...TO EVEN STEP ON YOUR SHADOW.

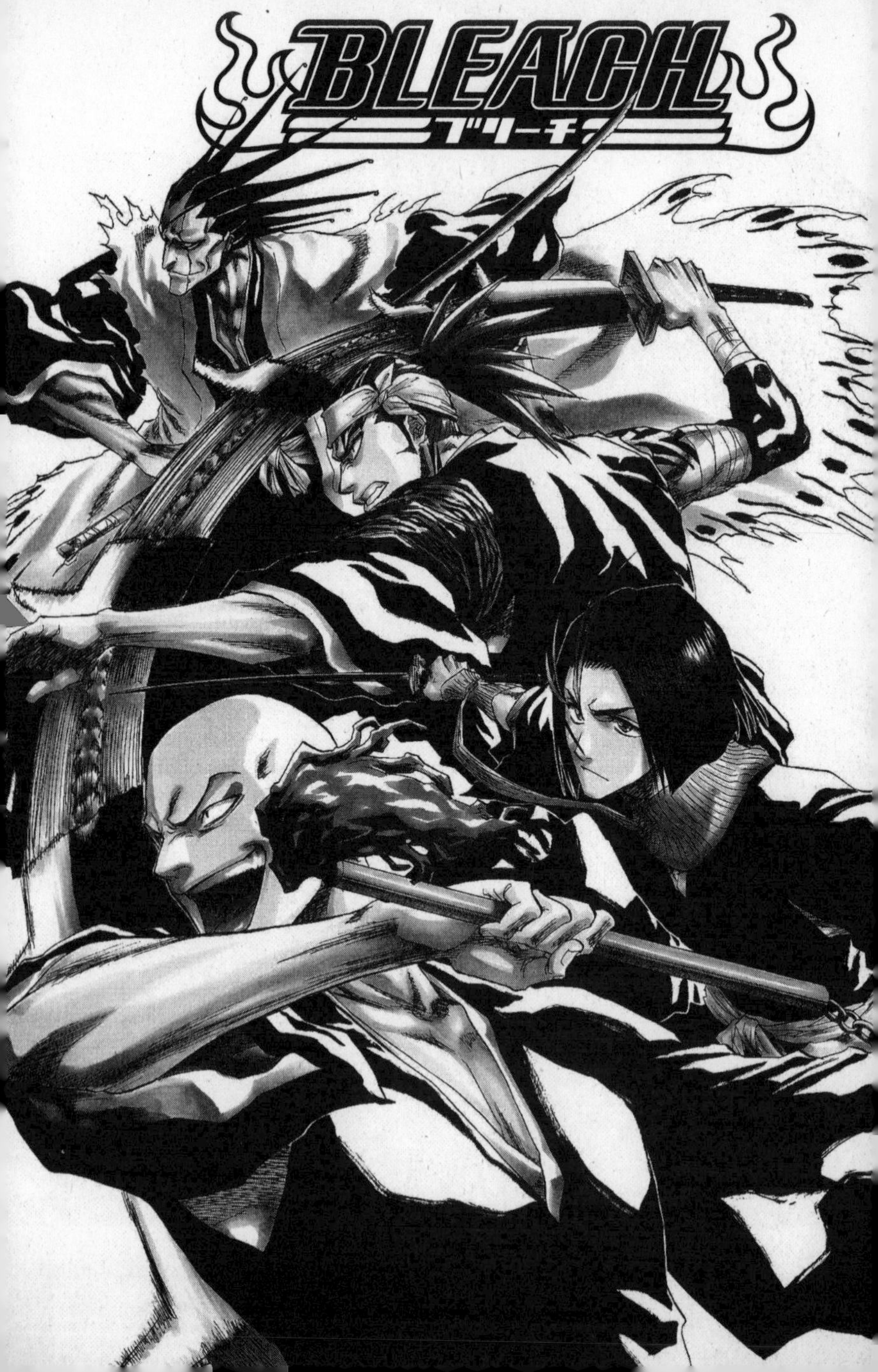
BLEACH

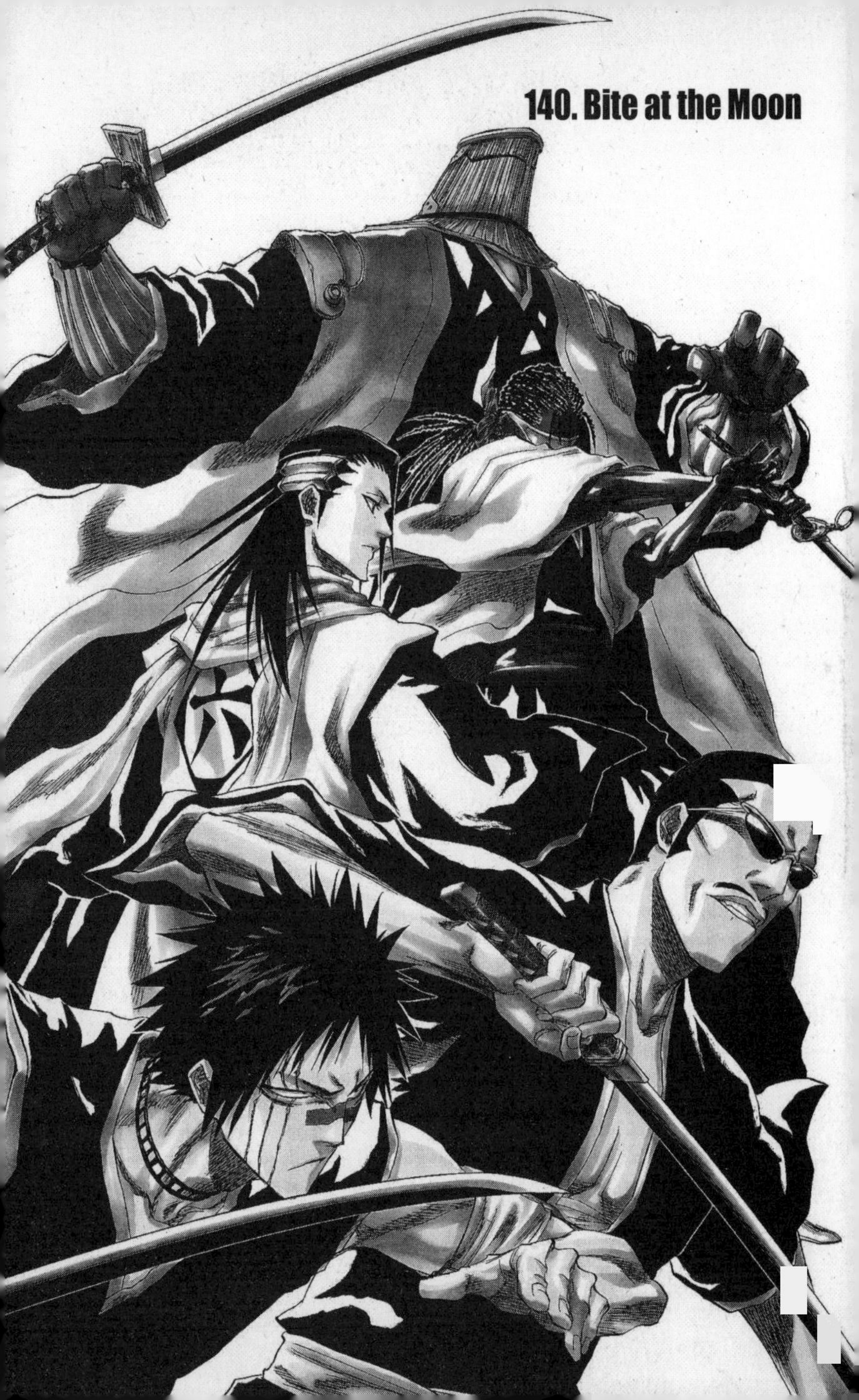
140. Bite at the Moon

BLEACH
ブリーチ

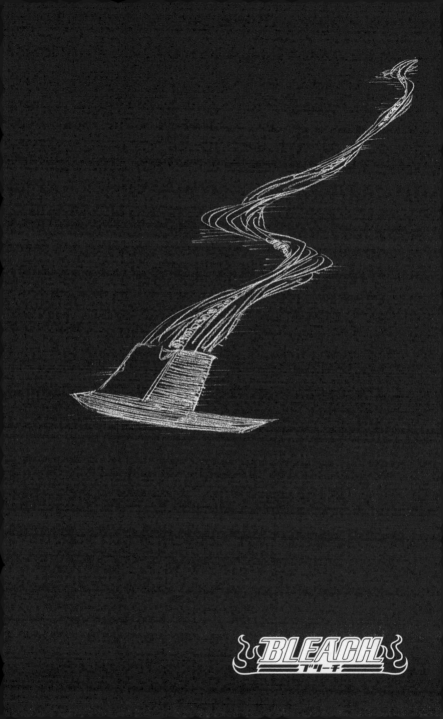

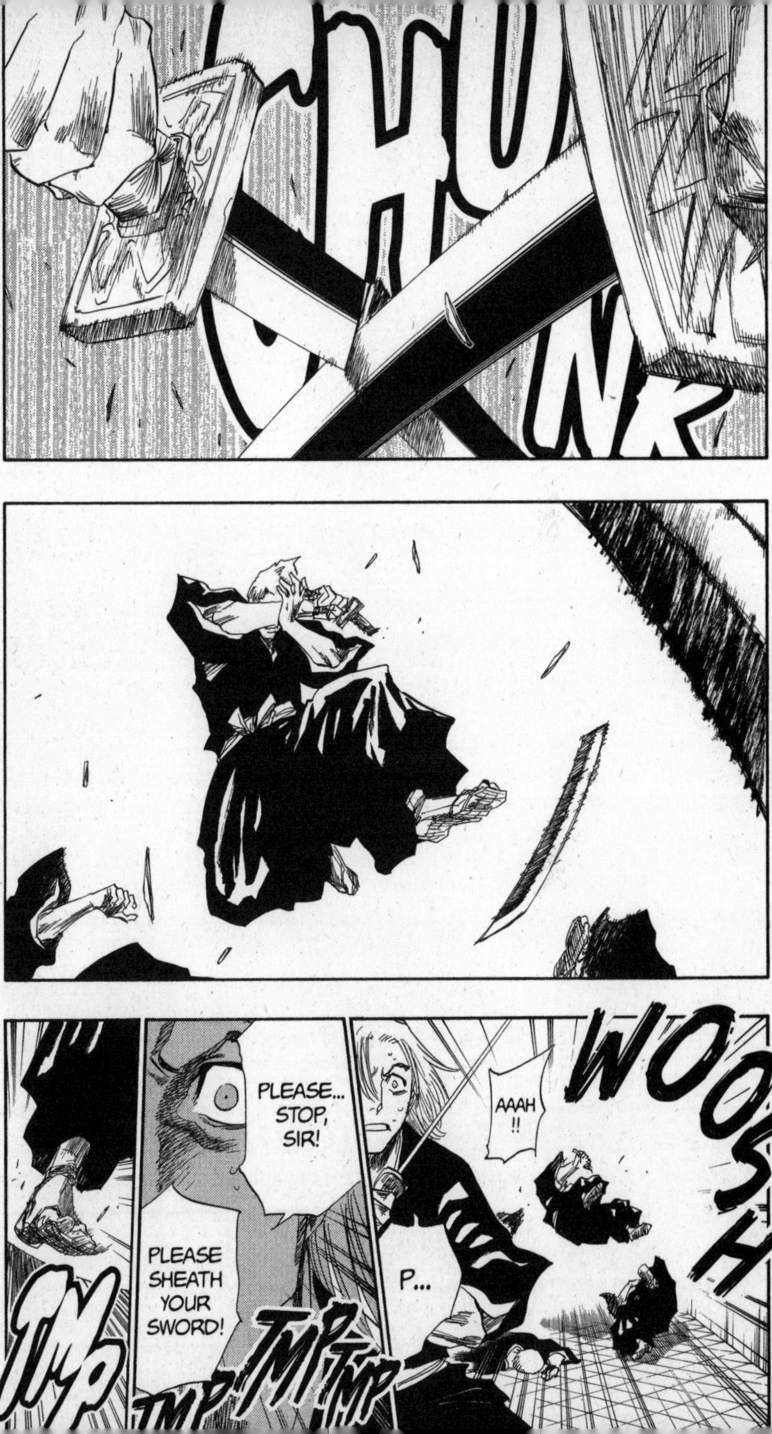
WOOSH
AAAH !!
P...
PLEASE... STOP, SIR!
PLEASE SHEATH YOUR SWORD!
TMP TMP TMP

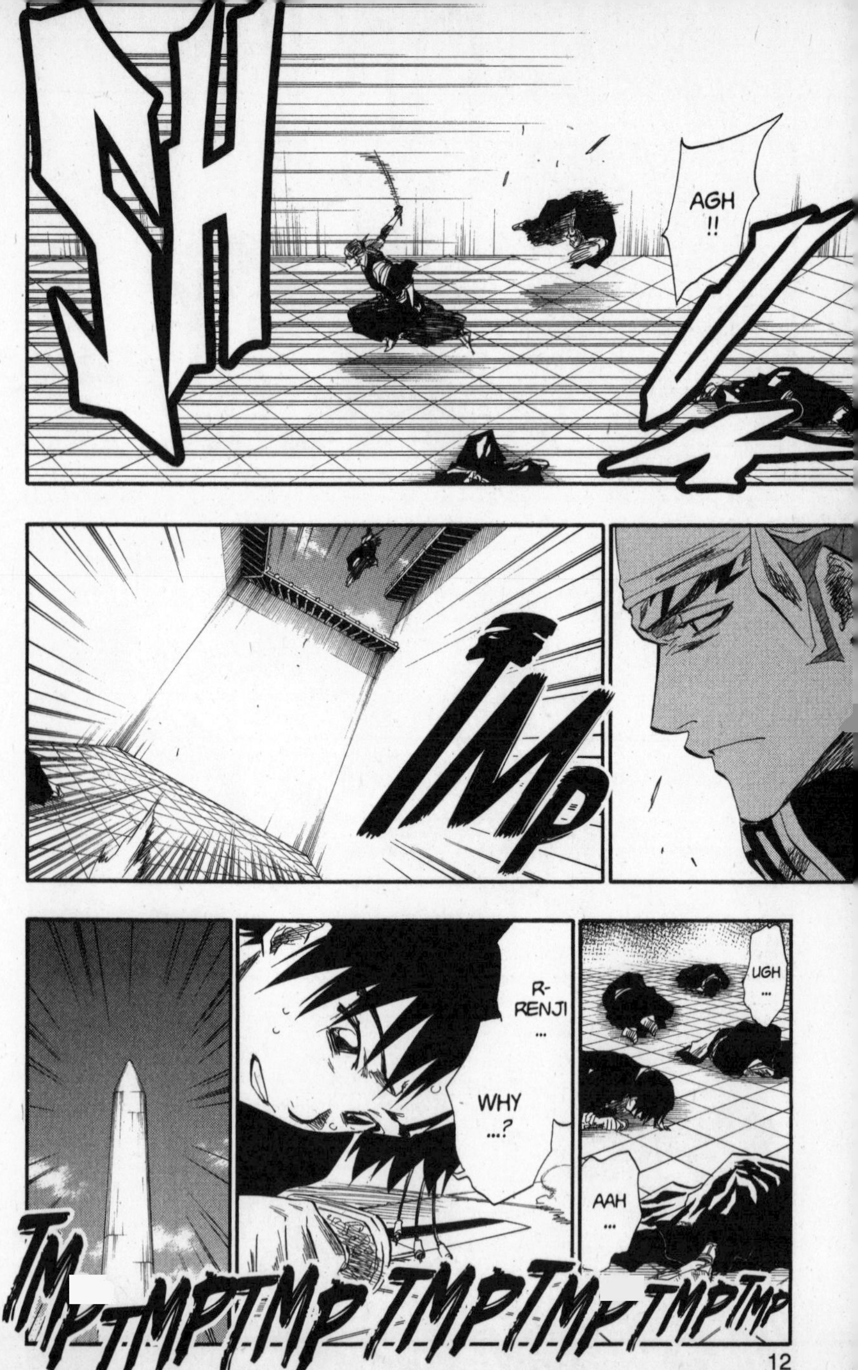
AGH!!
SH
TMP
UGH...
AAH...
R-RENJI...
WHY...?
TMPTMPTMPTMP TMPTMPTMPTMP

READ THIS WAY

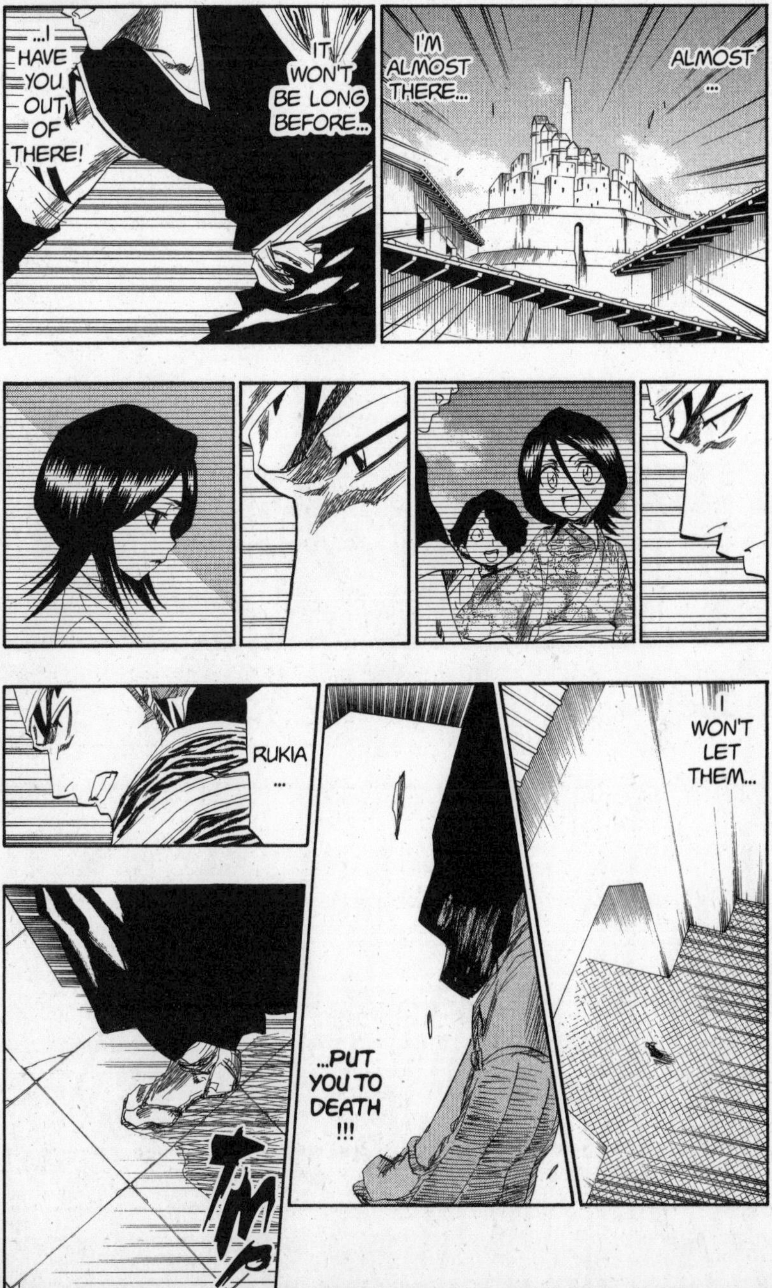
I'M ALMOST THERE...
ALMOST ...
IT WON'T BE LONG BEFORE...
...I HAVE YOU OUT OF THERE!
I WON'T LET THEM...
...PUT YOU TO DEATH !!!
RUKIA ...
TMP

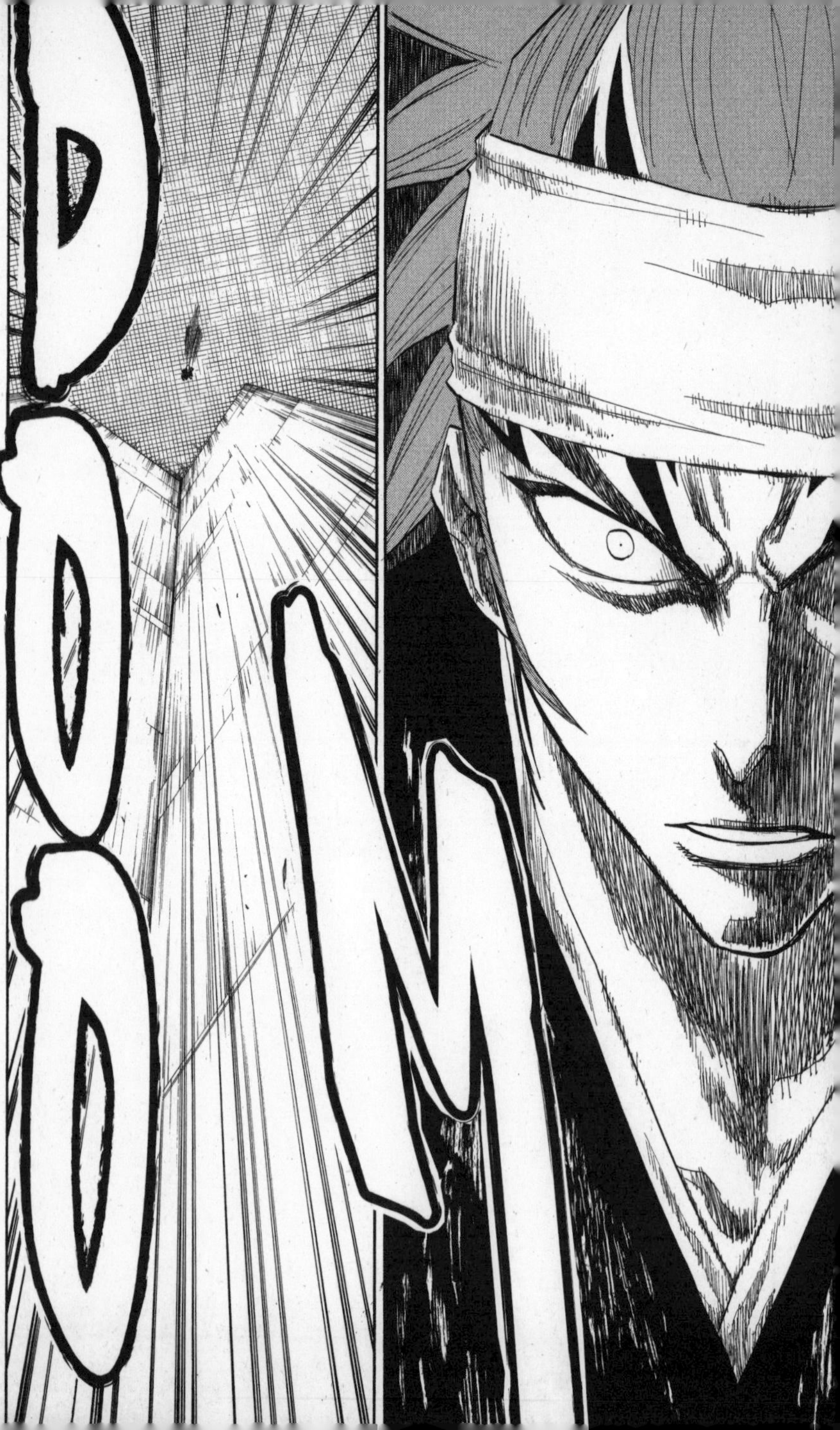
DOOM

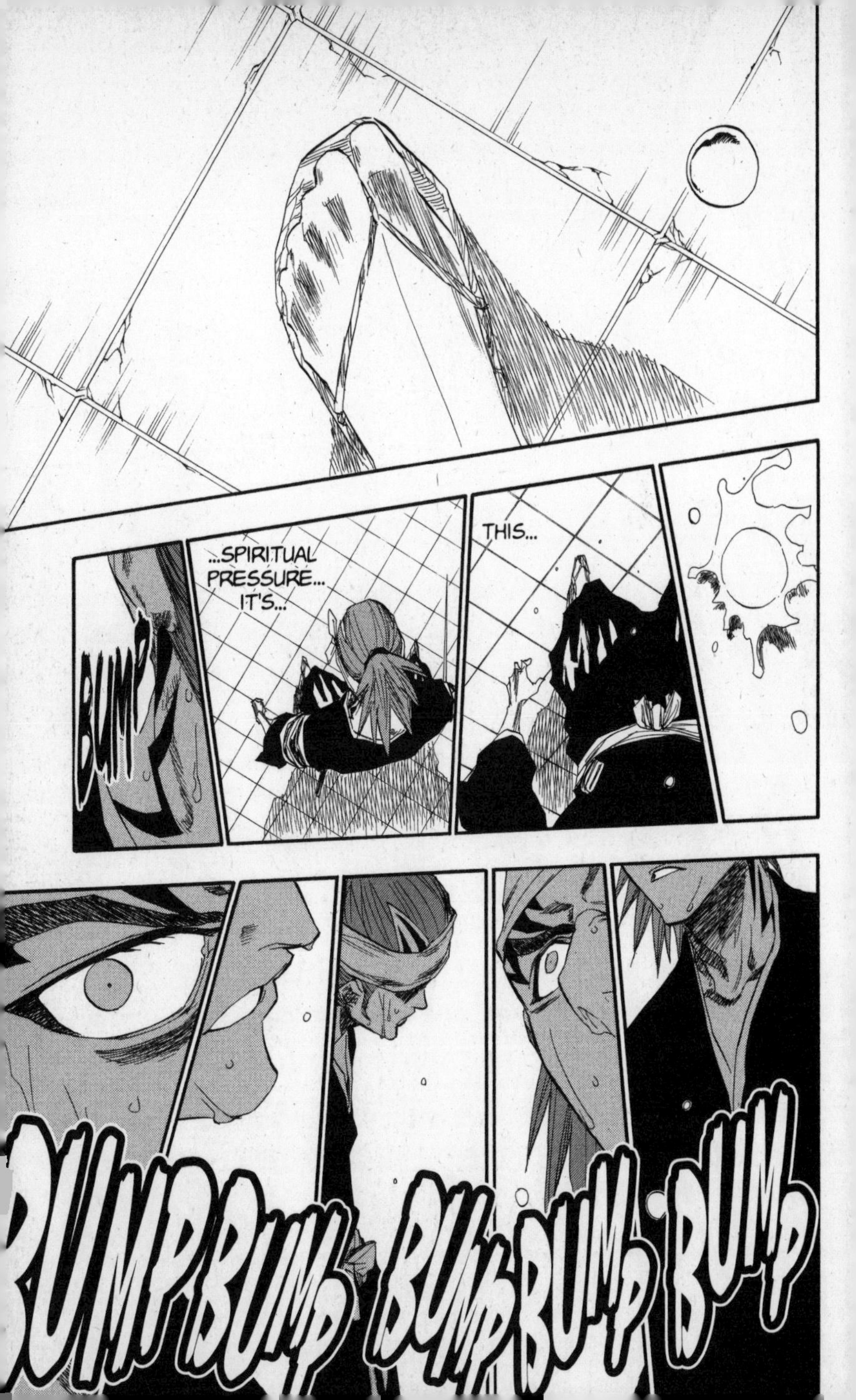
THIS...
...SPIRITUAL PRESSURE... IT'S...
BUMP
BUMP
BUMP
BUMP
BUMP
BUMP

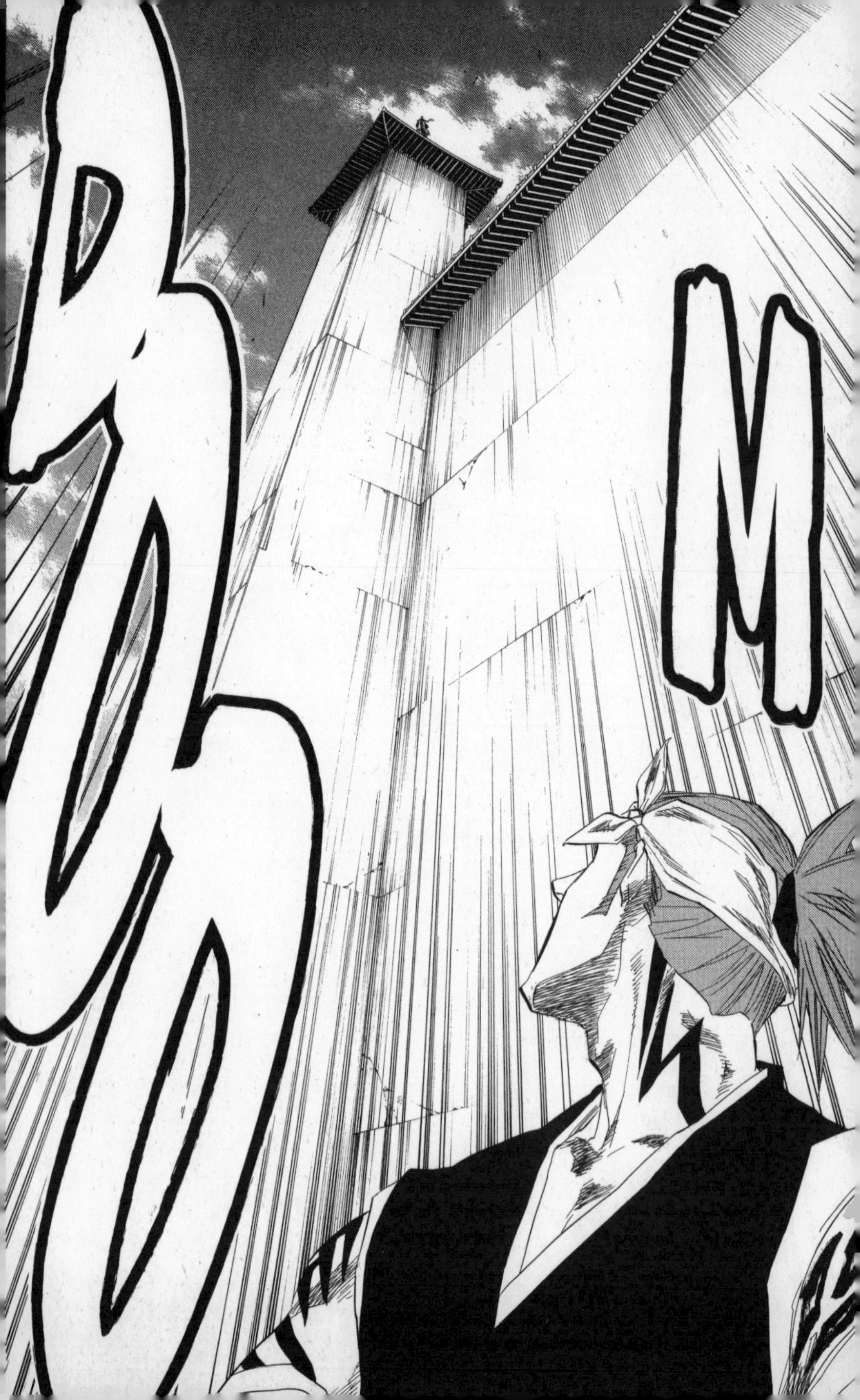
M

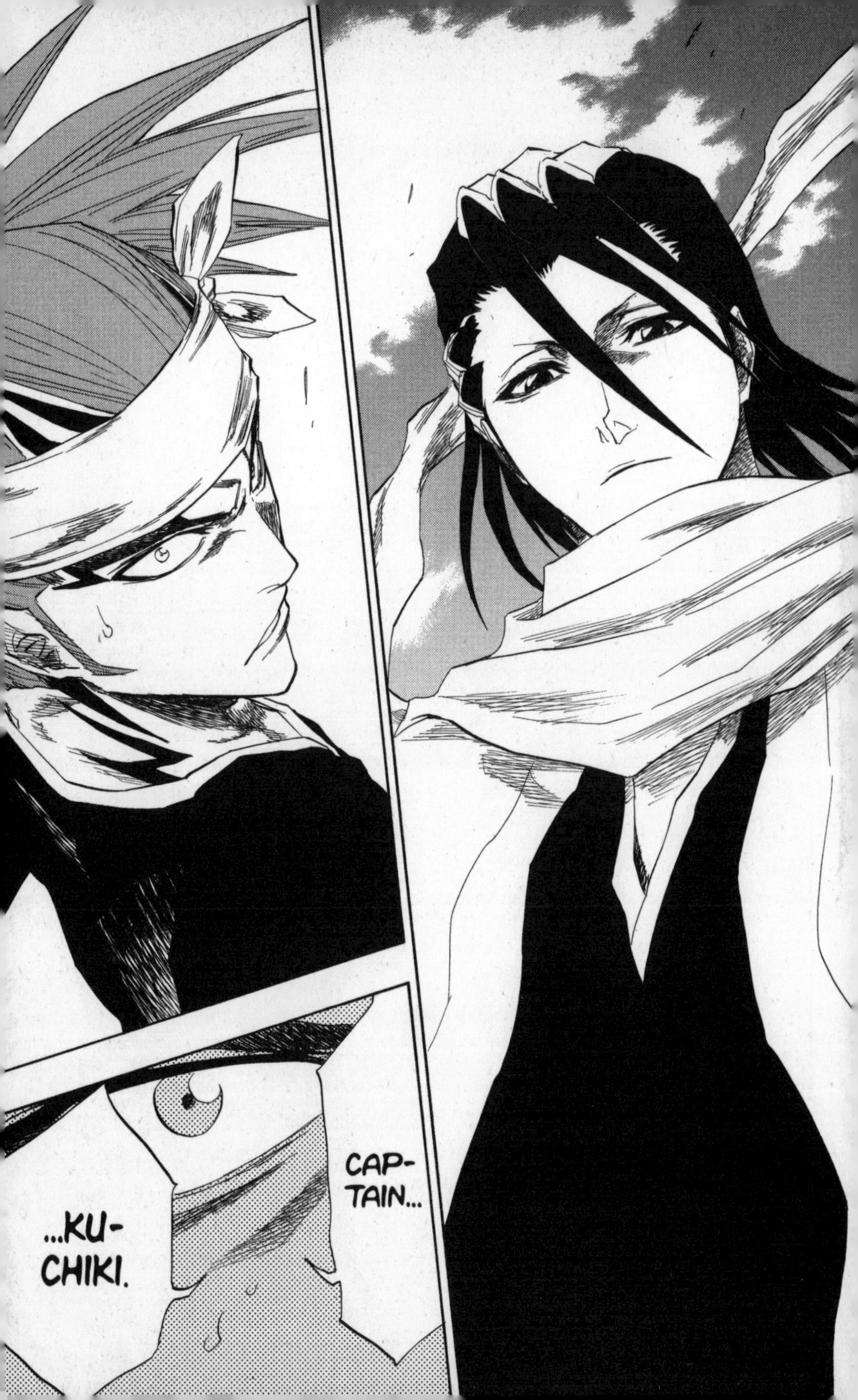
CAP-
TAIN...
...KU-
CHIKI.

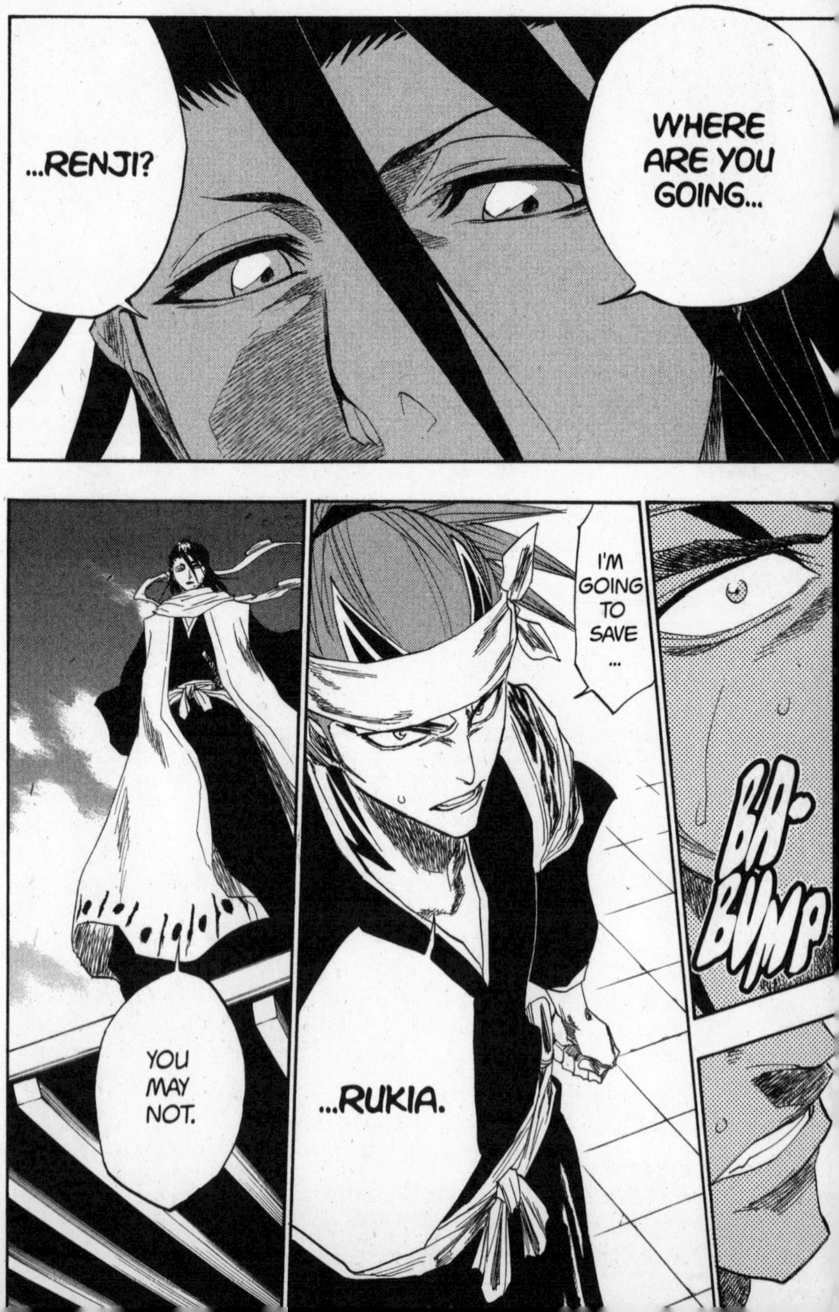
WHERE ARE YOU GOING...
...RENJI?
BA-BUMP
I'M GOING TO SAVE ...
...RUKIA.
YOU MAY NOT.

«READ THIS WAY«

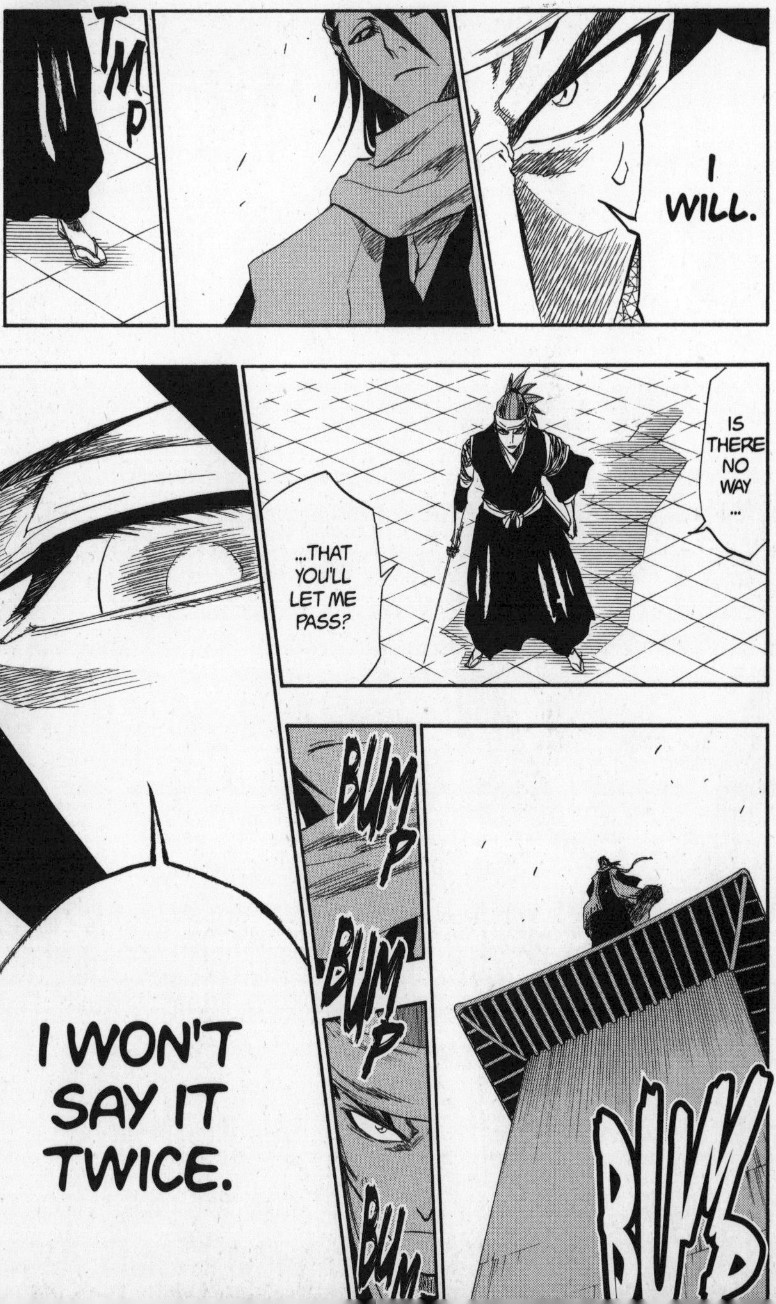

I WILL.
TMP
IS THERE NO WAY ...
...THAT YOU'LL LET ME PASS?
BUMP
BUMP
BUM
I WON'T SAY IT TWICE.

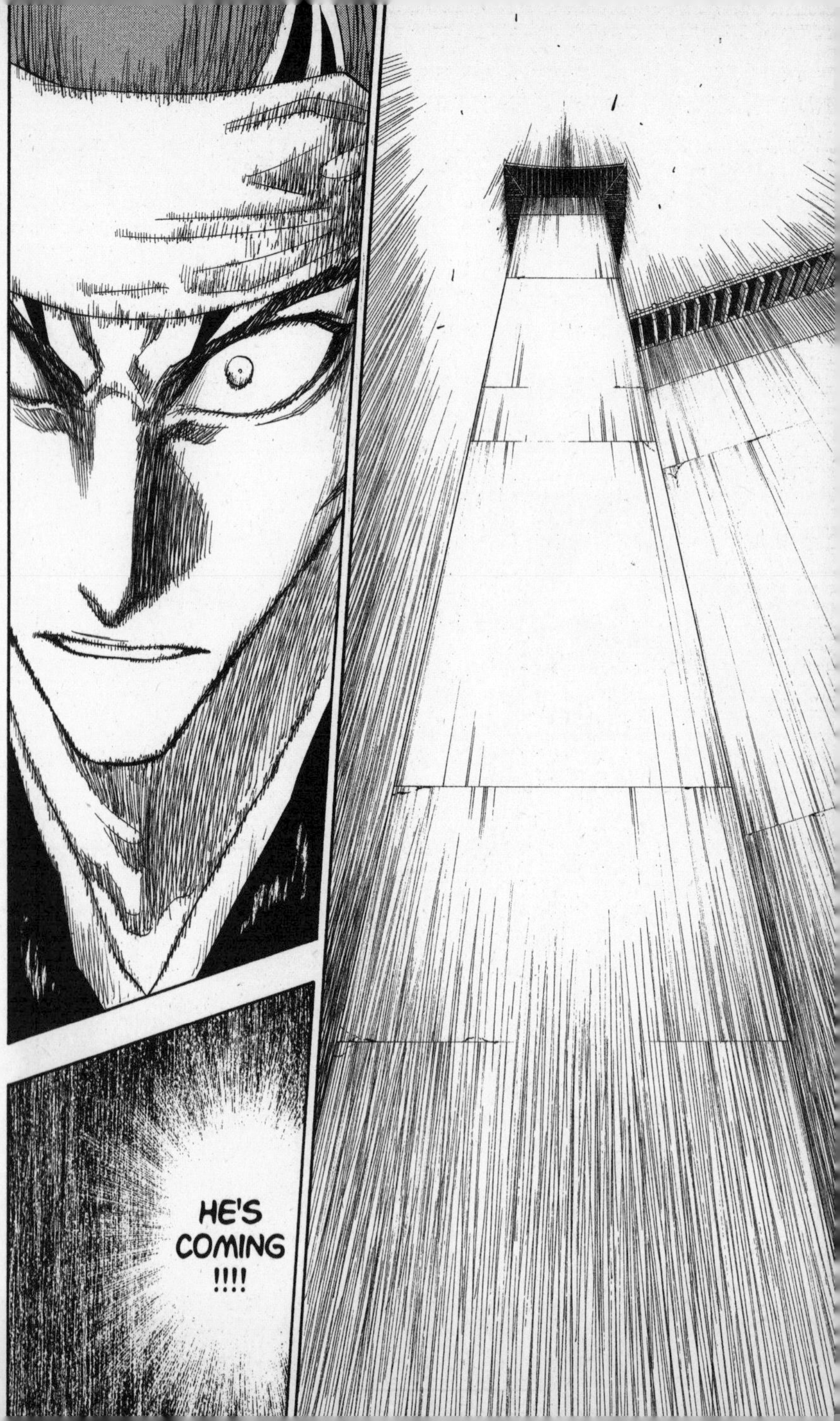
HE'S COMING !!!!

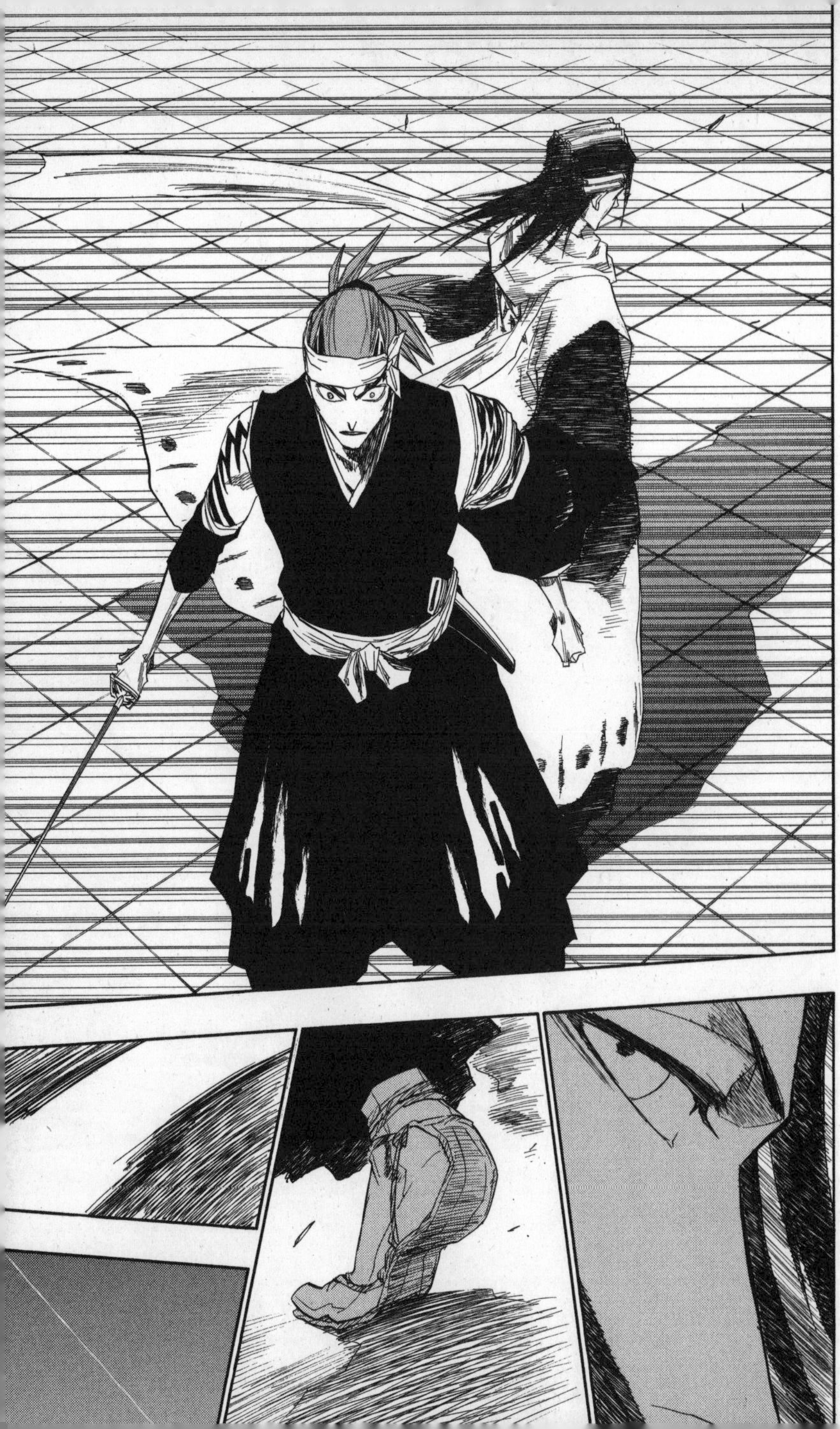

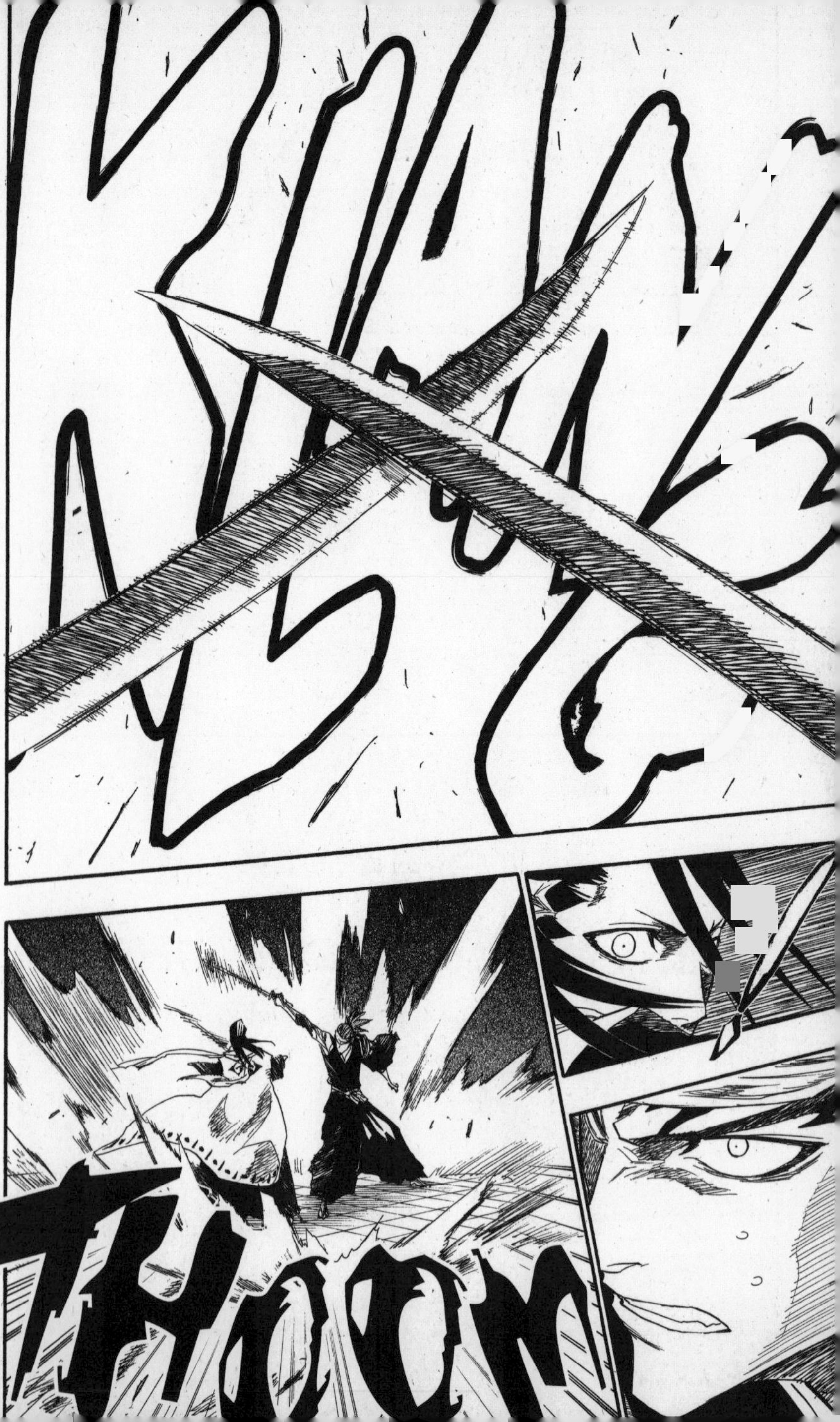
THOOM

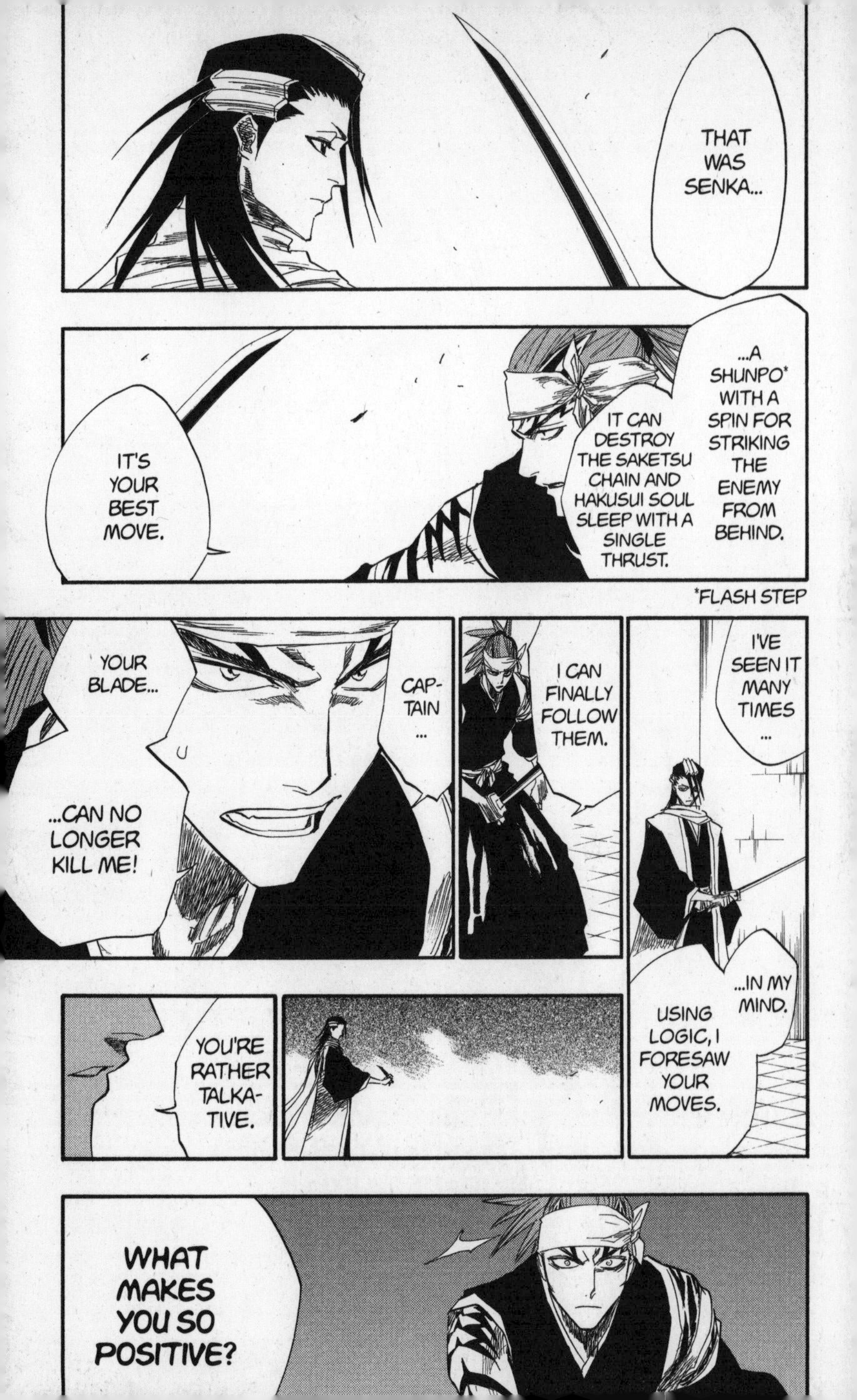
THAT WAS SENKA...
...A SHUNPO* WITH A SPIN FOR STRIKING THE ENEMY FROM BEHIND.
IT CAN DESTROY THE SAKETSU CHAIN AND HAKUSUI SOUL SLEEP WITH A SINGLE THRUST.
IT'S YOUR BEST MOVE.
*FLASH STEP
I'VE SEEN IT MANY TIMES...
...IN MY MIND.
USING LOGIC, I FORESAW YOUR MOVES.
I CAN FINALLY FOLLOW THEM.
CAP-TAIN...
YOUR BLADE...
...CAN NO LONGER KILL ME!
YOU'RE RATHER TALKA-TIVE.
WHAT MAKES YOU SO POSITIVE?

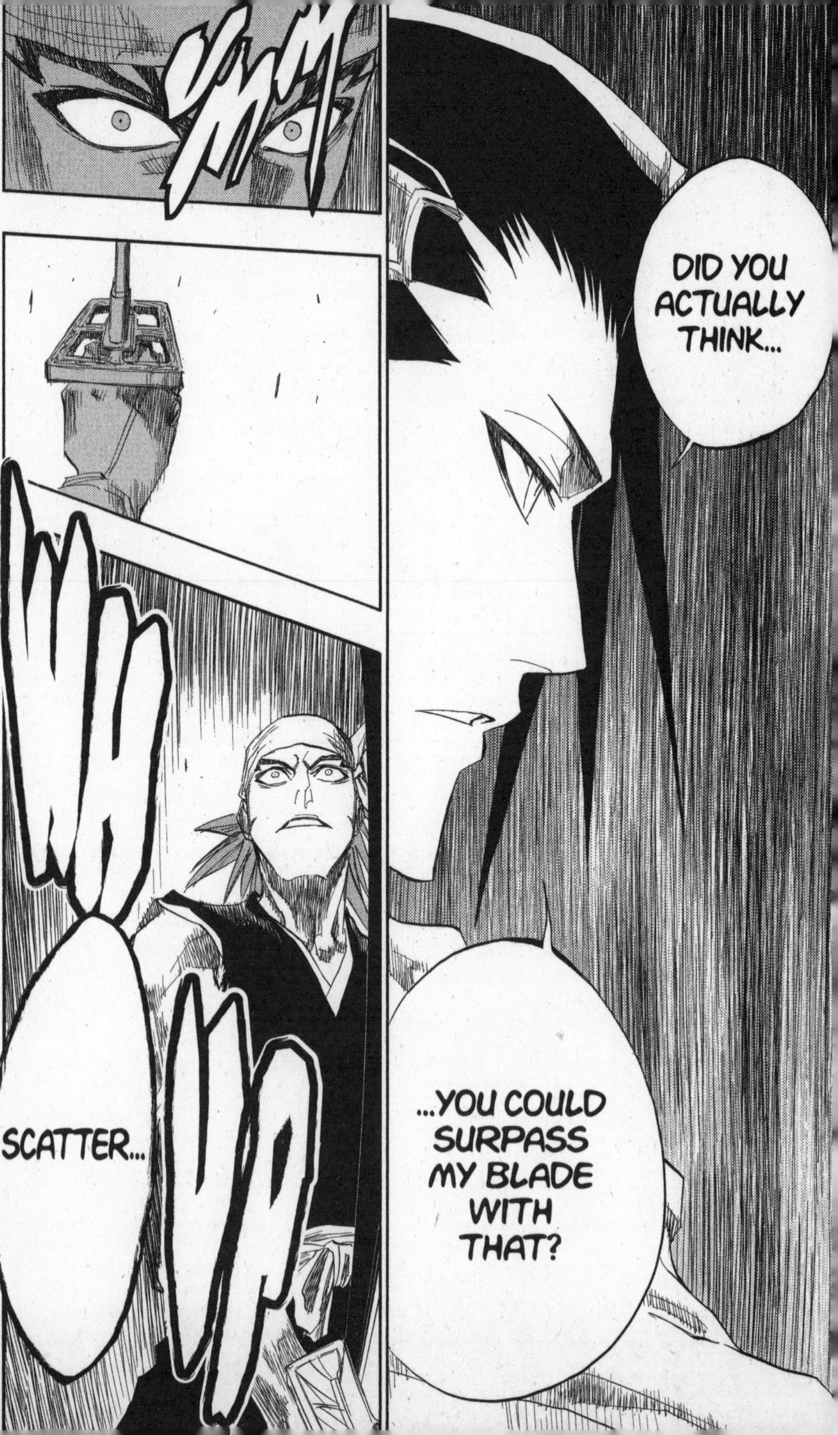
DID YOU ACTUALLY THINK...
...YOU COULD SURPASS MY BLADE WITH THAT?
SCATTER...

READ THIS WAY

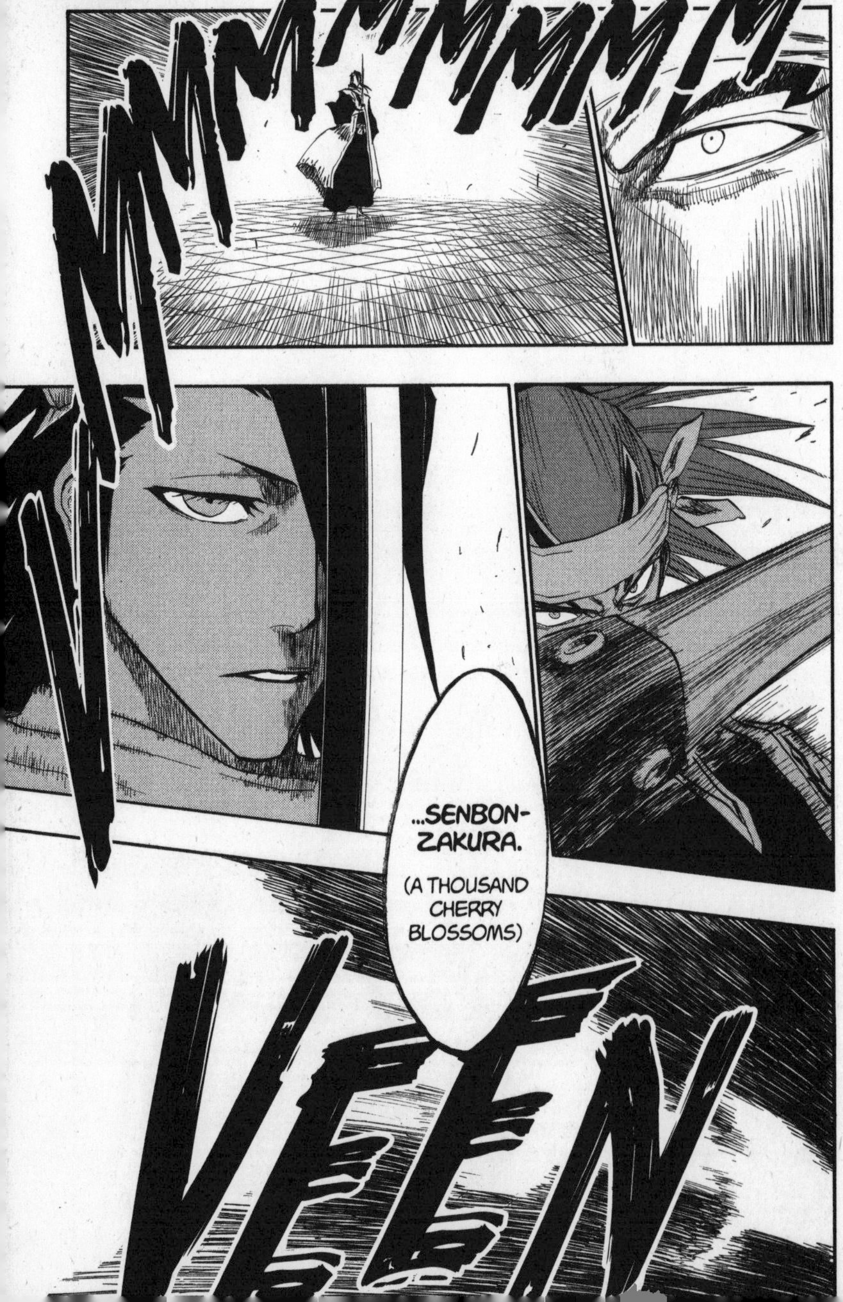
MMMMMMMMMMMM
...SENBON-ZAKURA.
(A THOUSAND CHERRY BLOSSOMS)
VEEN

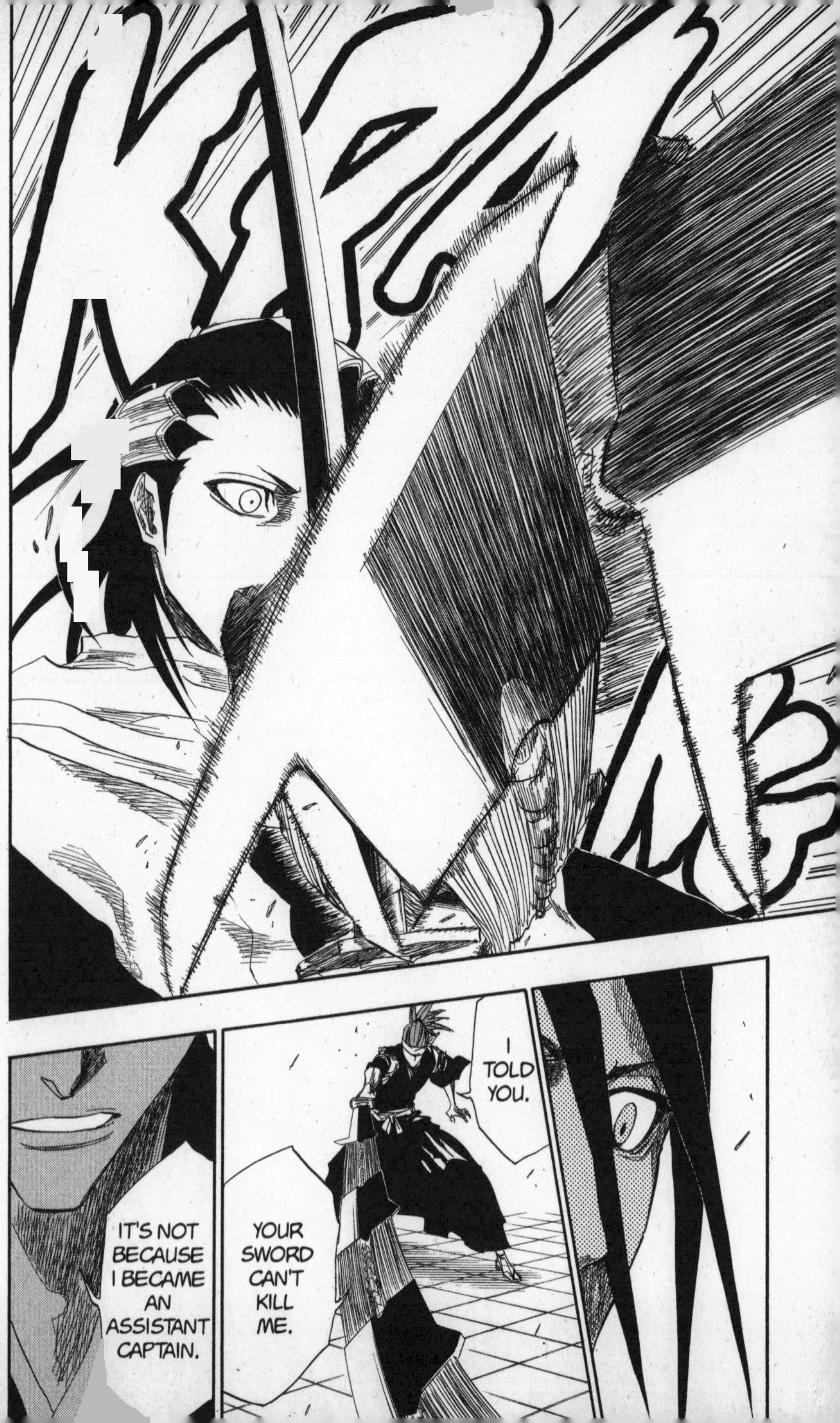
I TOLD YOU.
YOUR SWORD CAN'T KILL ME.
IT'S NOT BECAUSE I BECAME AN ASSISTANT CAPTAIN.

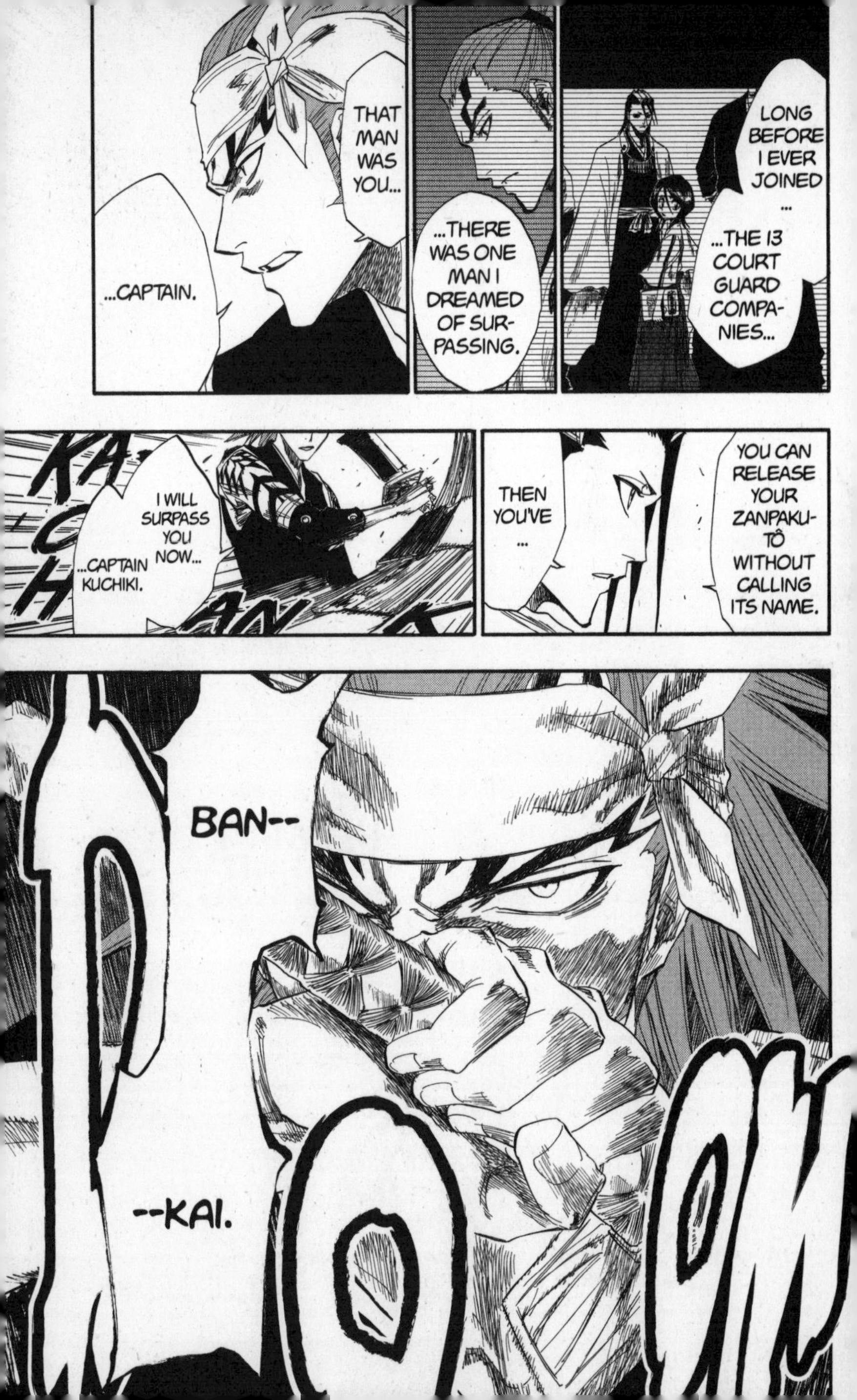
LONG BEFORE I EVER JOINED ...
...THE 13 COURT GUARD COMPANIES...
...THERE WAS ONE MAN I DREAMED OF SURPASSING.
THAT MAN WAS YOU...
...CAPTAIN.
YOU CAN RELEASE YOUR ZANPAKU-TÔ WITHOUT CALLING ITS NAME.
THEN YOU'VE ...
I WILL SURPASS YOU NOW...
...CAPTAIN KUCHIKI.
BAN--
--KAI.

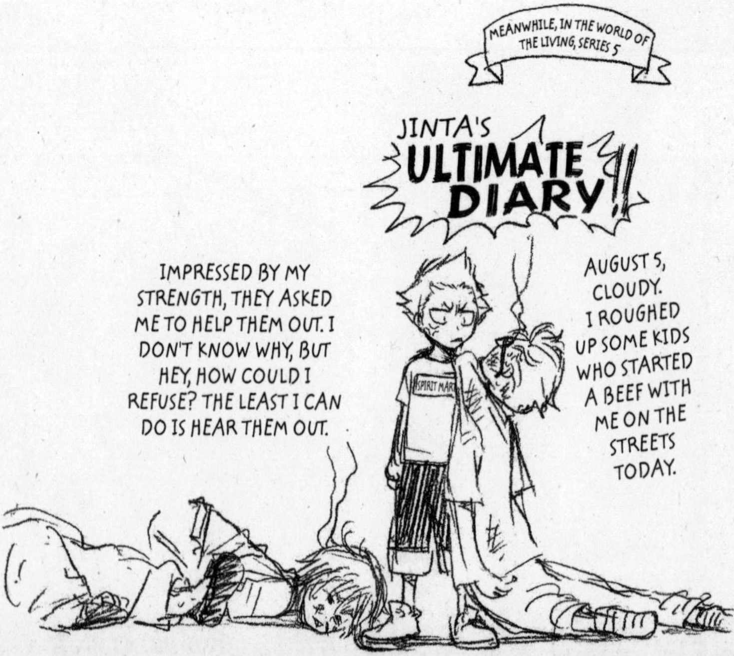
MEANWHILE, IN THE WORLD OF THE LIVING, SERIES 5
JINTA'S ULTIMATE DIARY!!
AUGUST 5, CLOUDY. I ROUGHED UP SOME KIDS WHO STARTED A BEEF WITH ME ON THE STREETS TODAY.
SPIRIT MAR
IMPRESSED BY MY STRENGTH, THEY ASKED ME TO HELP THEM OUT. I DON'T KNOW WHY, BUT HEY, HOW COULD I REFUSE? THE LEAST I CAN DO IS HEAR THEM OUT.

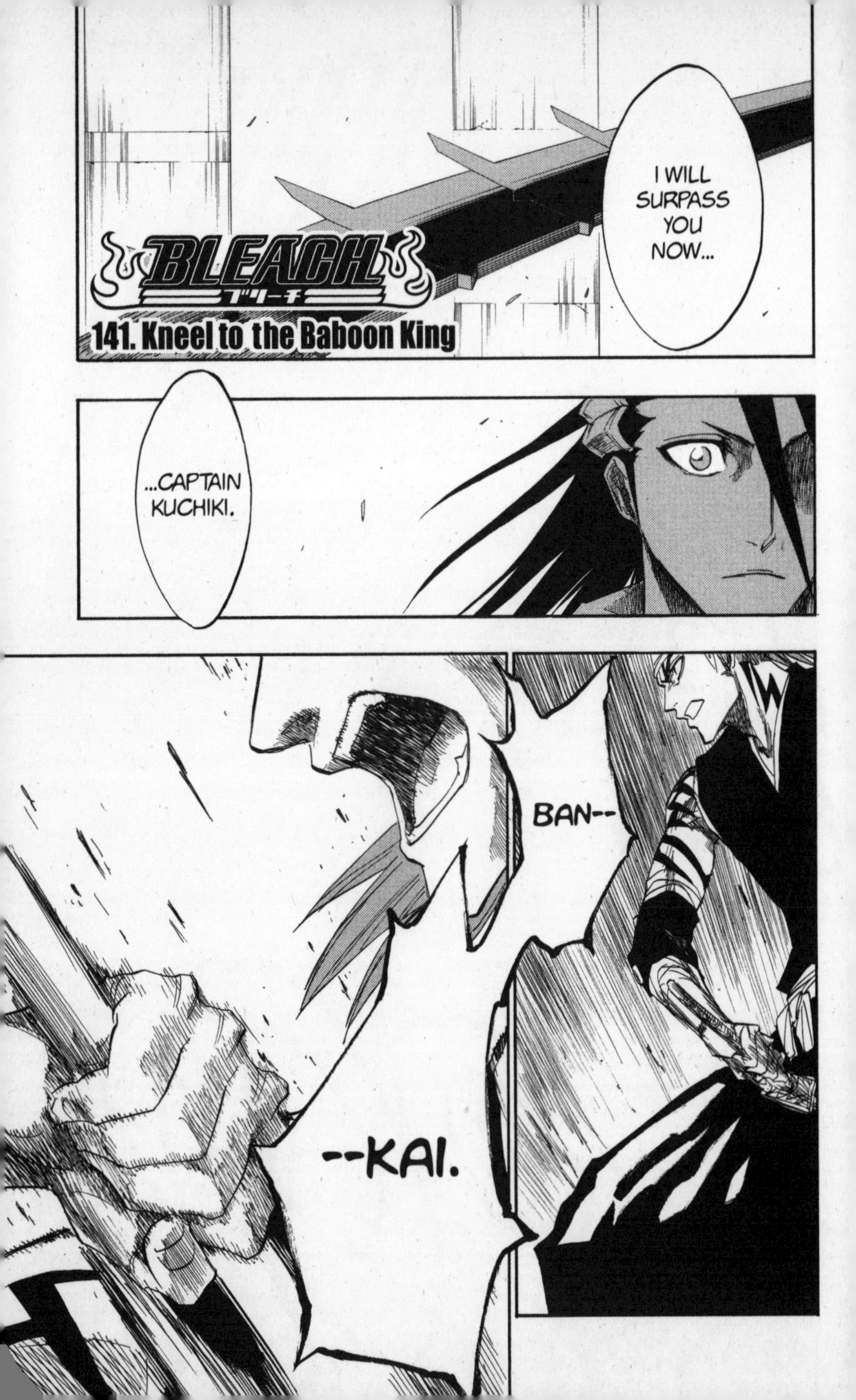
I WILL SURPASS YOU NOW...
BLEACH
ブリーチ
141. Kneel to the Baboon King
...CAPTAIN KUCHIKI.
BAN--
--KAI.

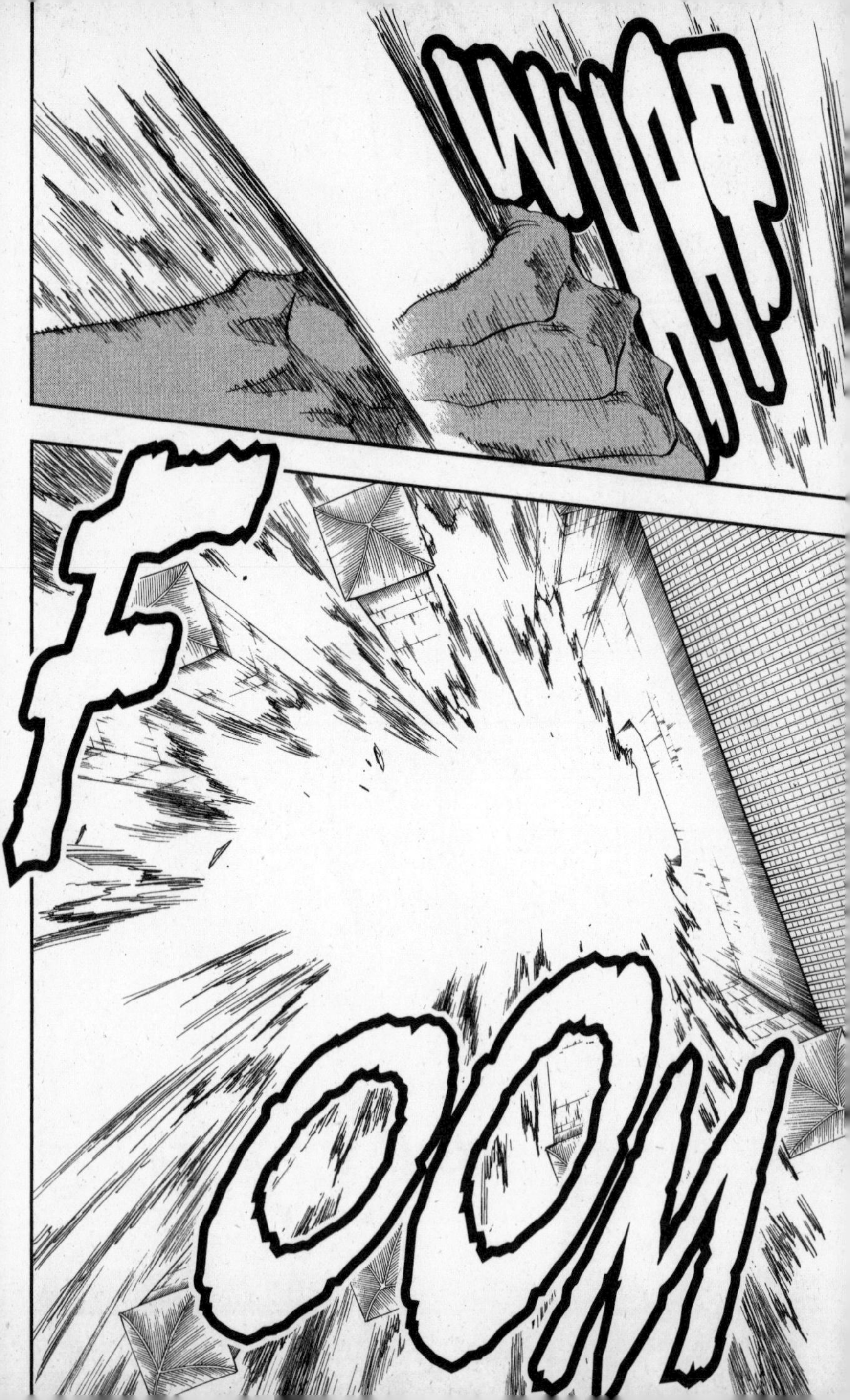
WHAP
FOOM

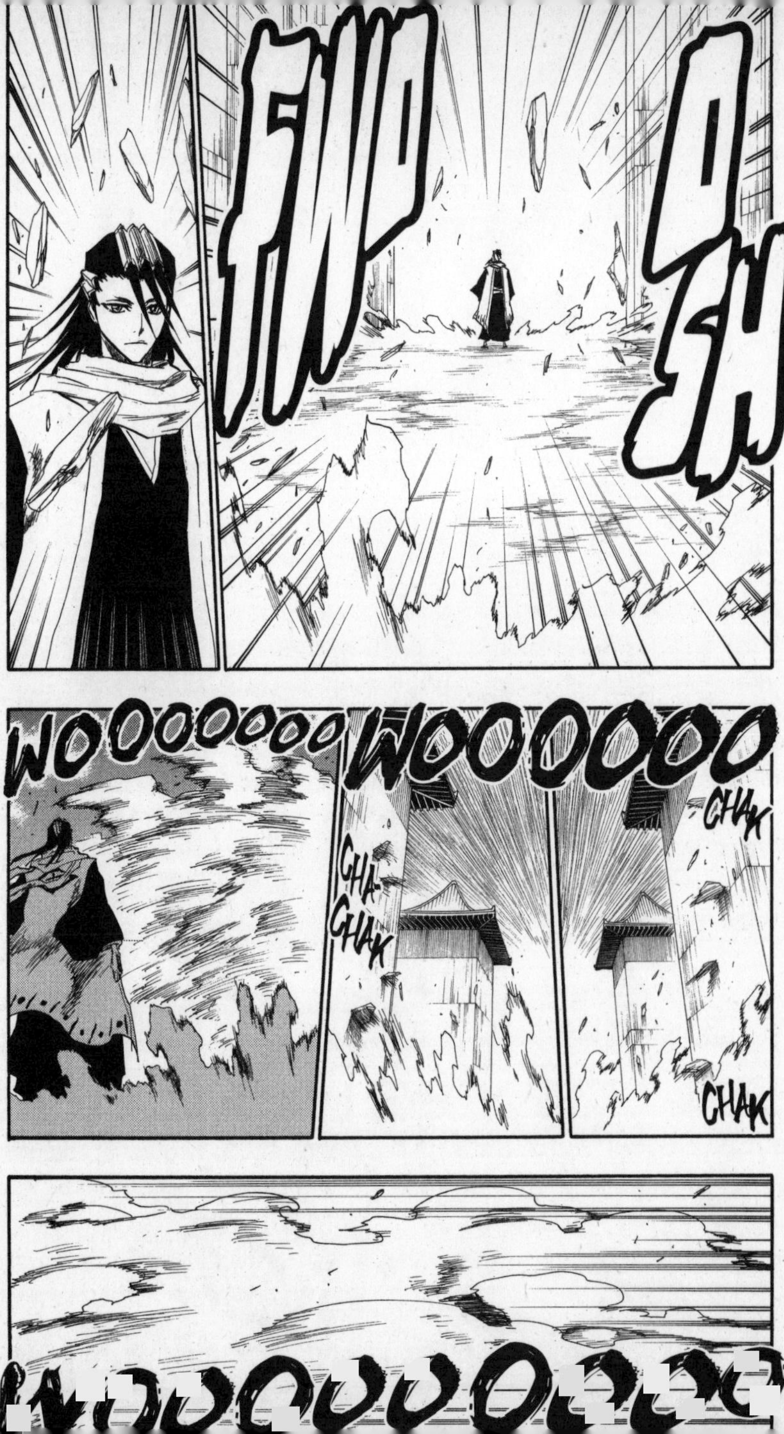
WOOOOOOO
CHAK
CHAK
CHA-CHAK
WOOOOOOO

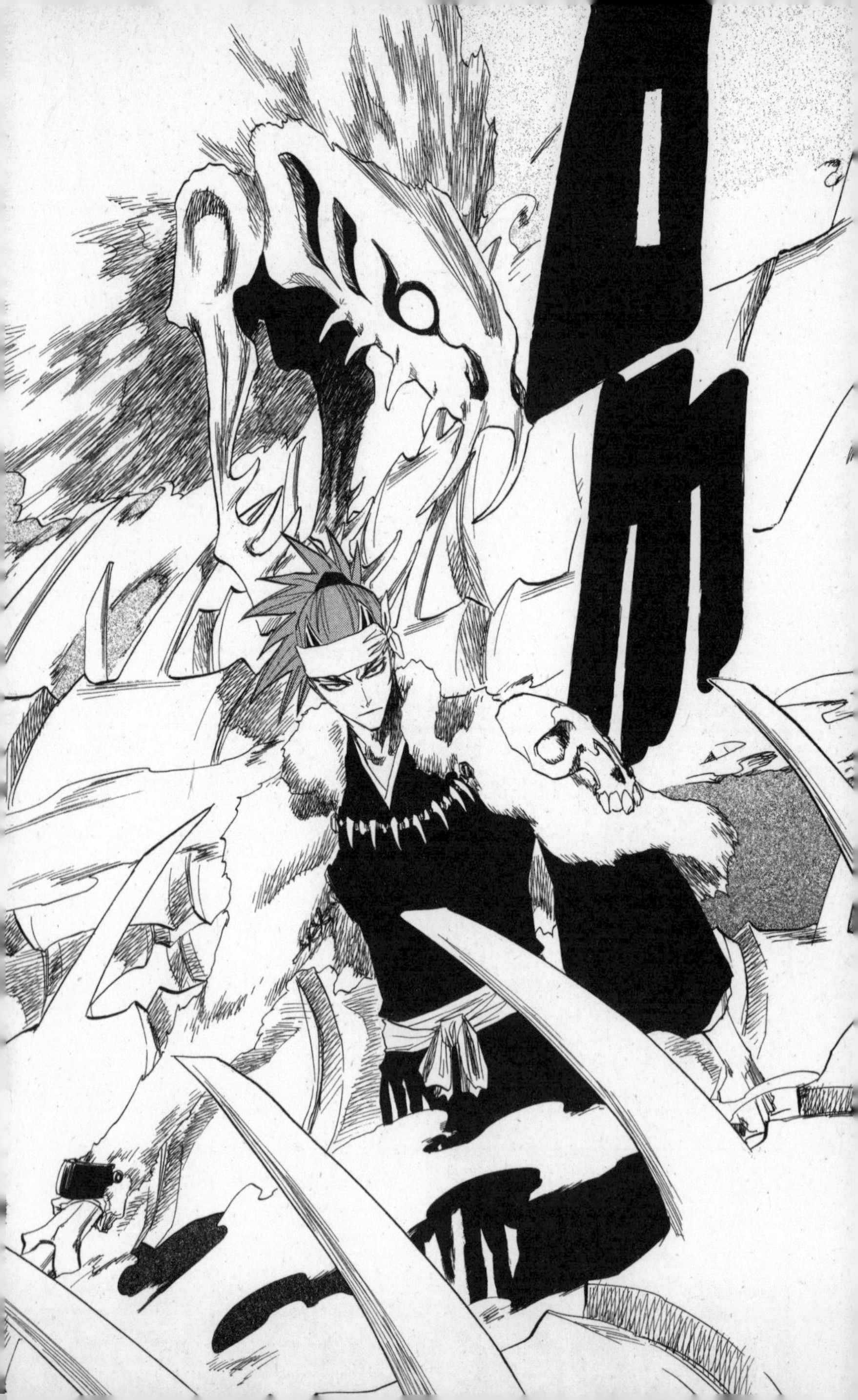

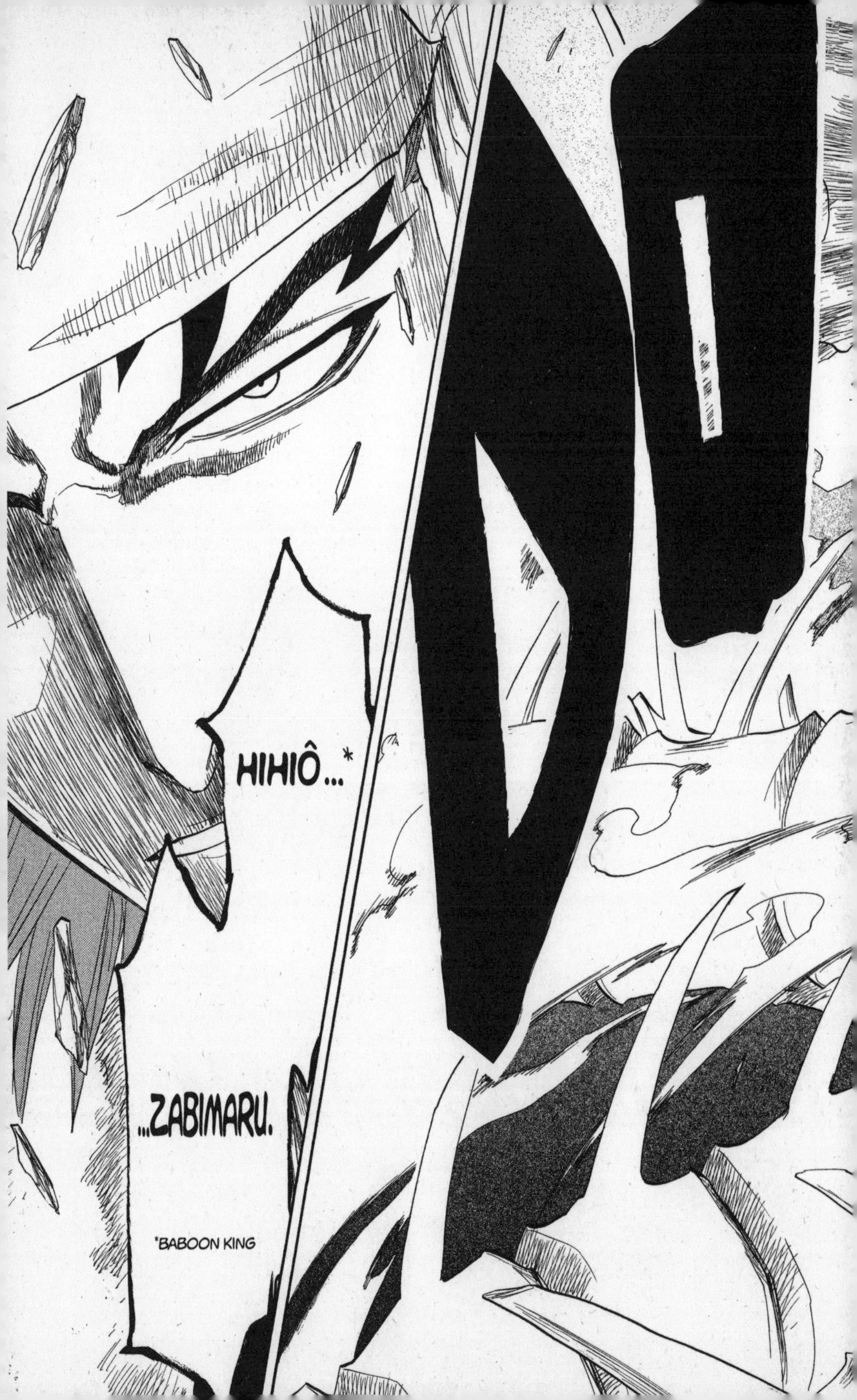
HIHIÔ...*
...ZABIMARU.
*BABOON KING

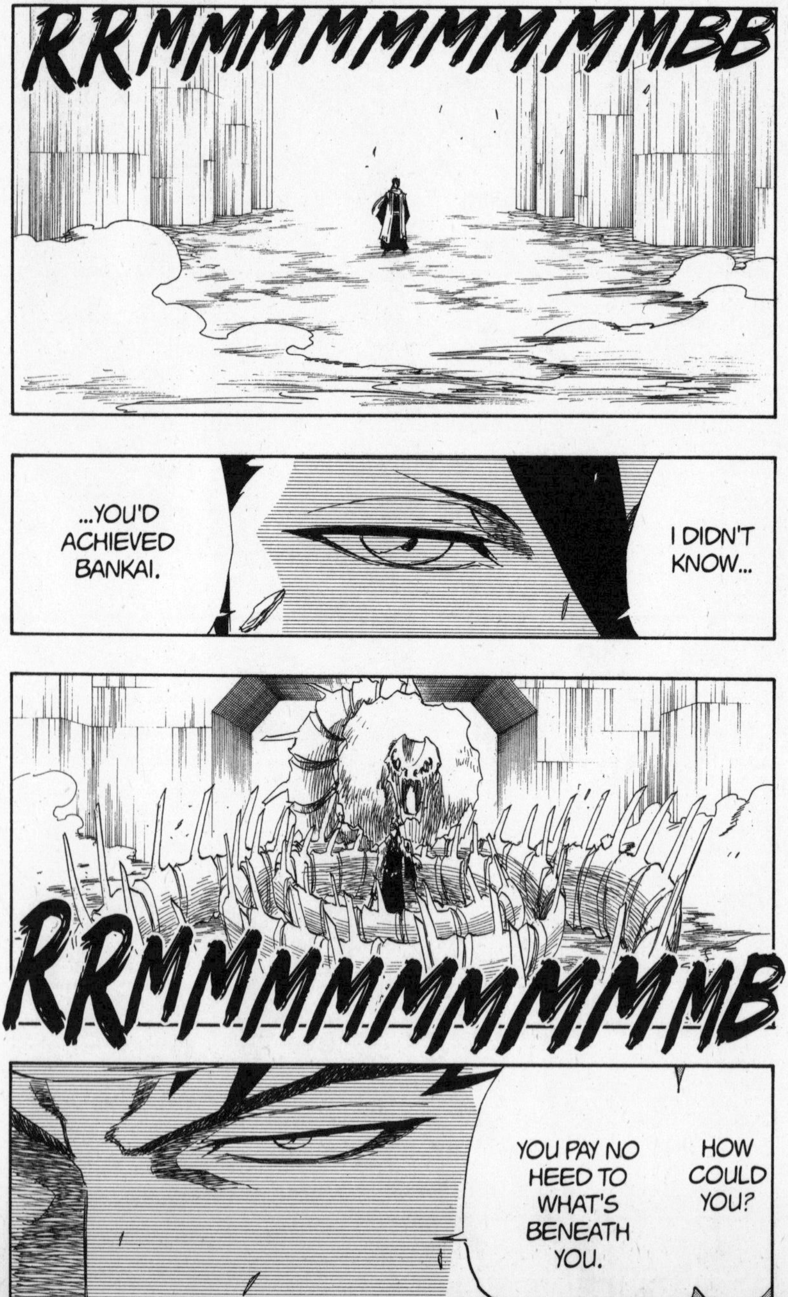
RRMMMMMMMMMMMBB
I DIDN'T KNOW...
...YOU'D ACHIEVED BANKAI.
RRMMMMMMMMMMMB
HOW COULD YOU?
YOU PAY NO HEED TO WHAT'S BENEATH YOU.

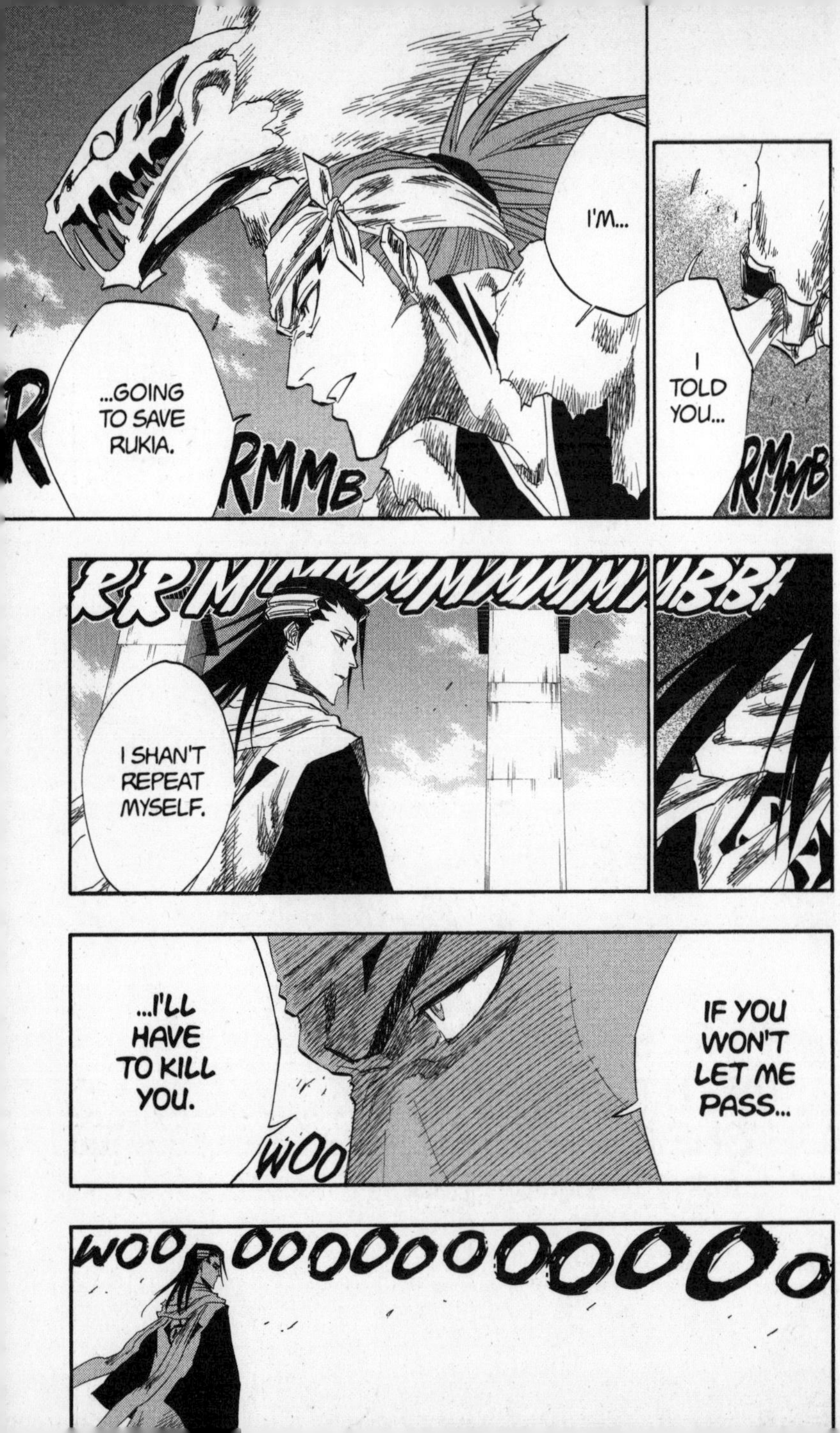
I TOLD YOU...
RMMB
I'M...
...GOING TO SAVE RUKIA.
RMMB
R
RRMMMMMMMMMMMBB
I SHAN'T REPEAT MYSELF.
IF YOU WON'T LET ME PASS...
...I'LL HAVE TO KILL YOU.
WOO
WOO OOOOOOOOOOOO

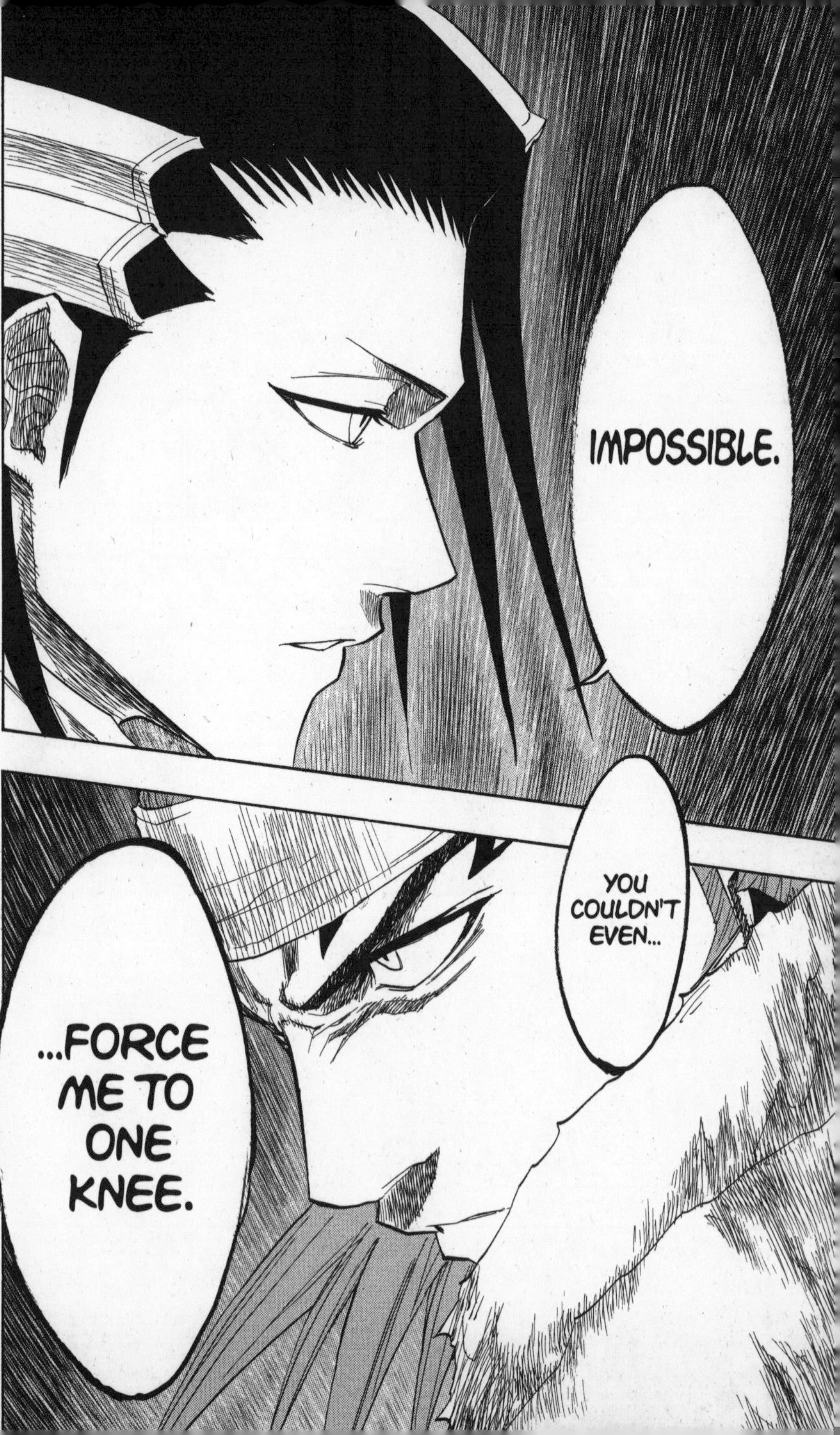
IMPOSSIBLE.
YOU COULDN'T EVEN...
...FORCE ME TO ONE KNEE.

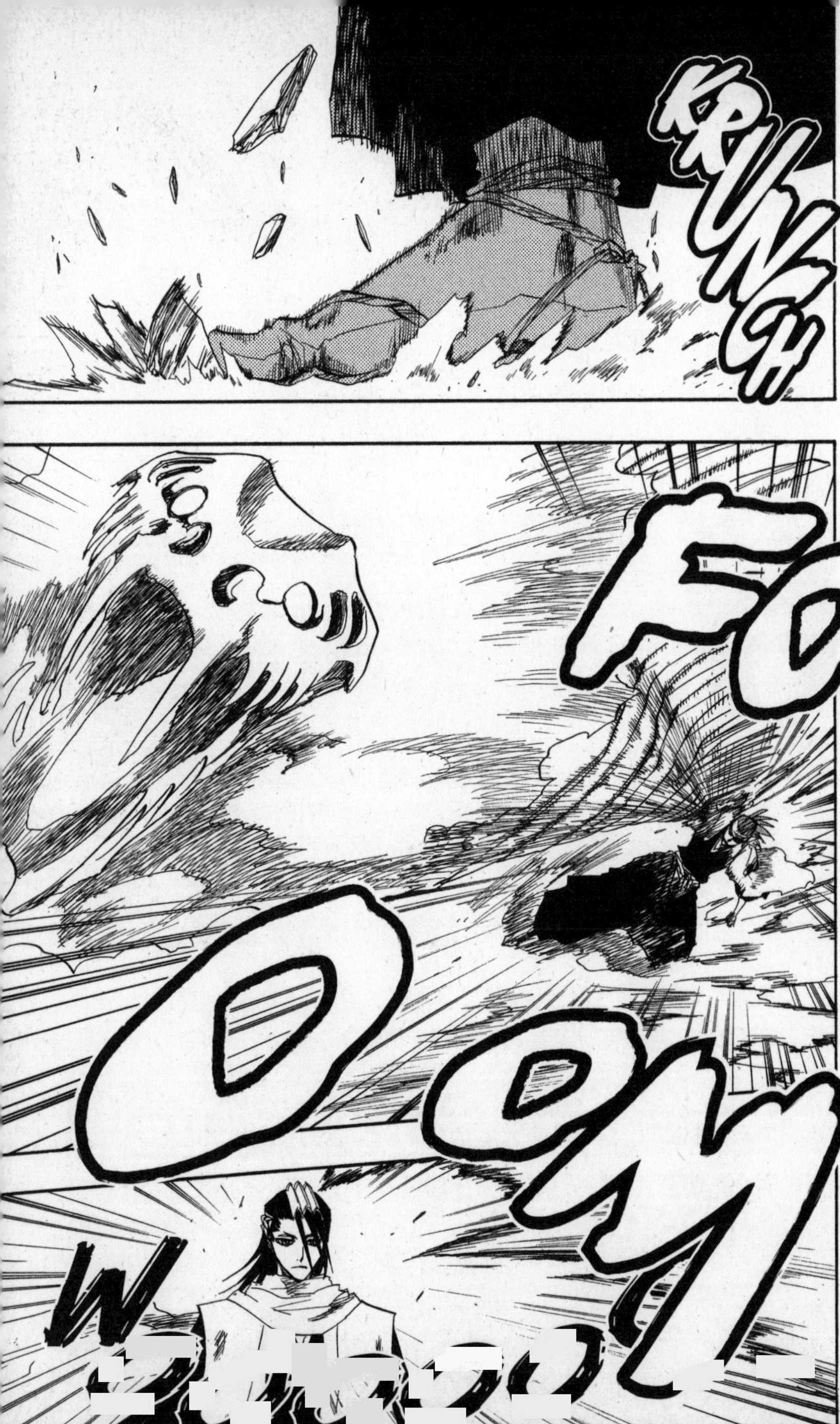
KRUNCH
FOOOM

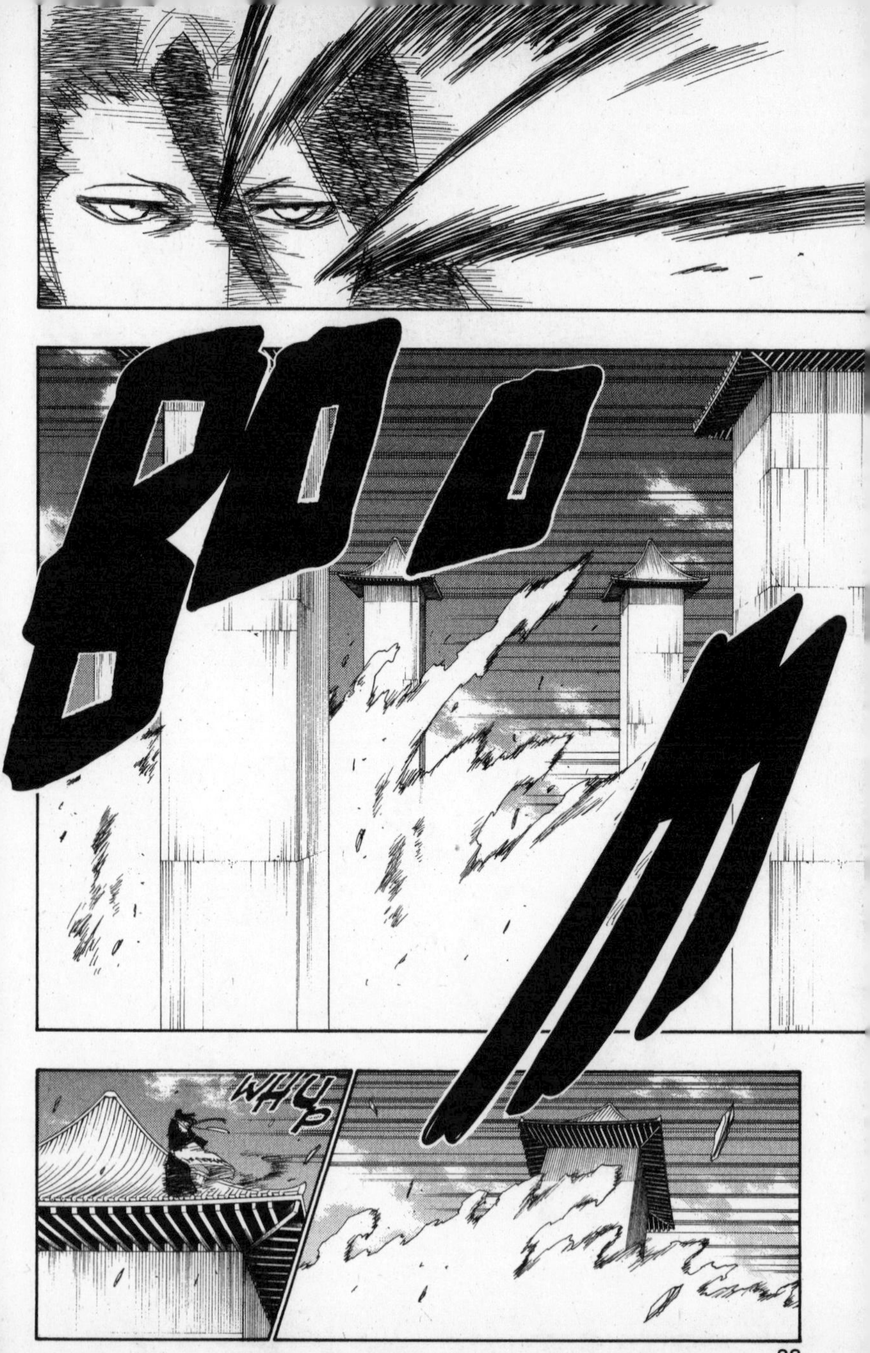
BOOM
WHUP

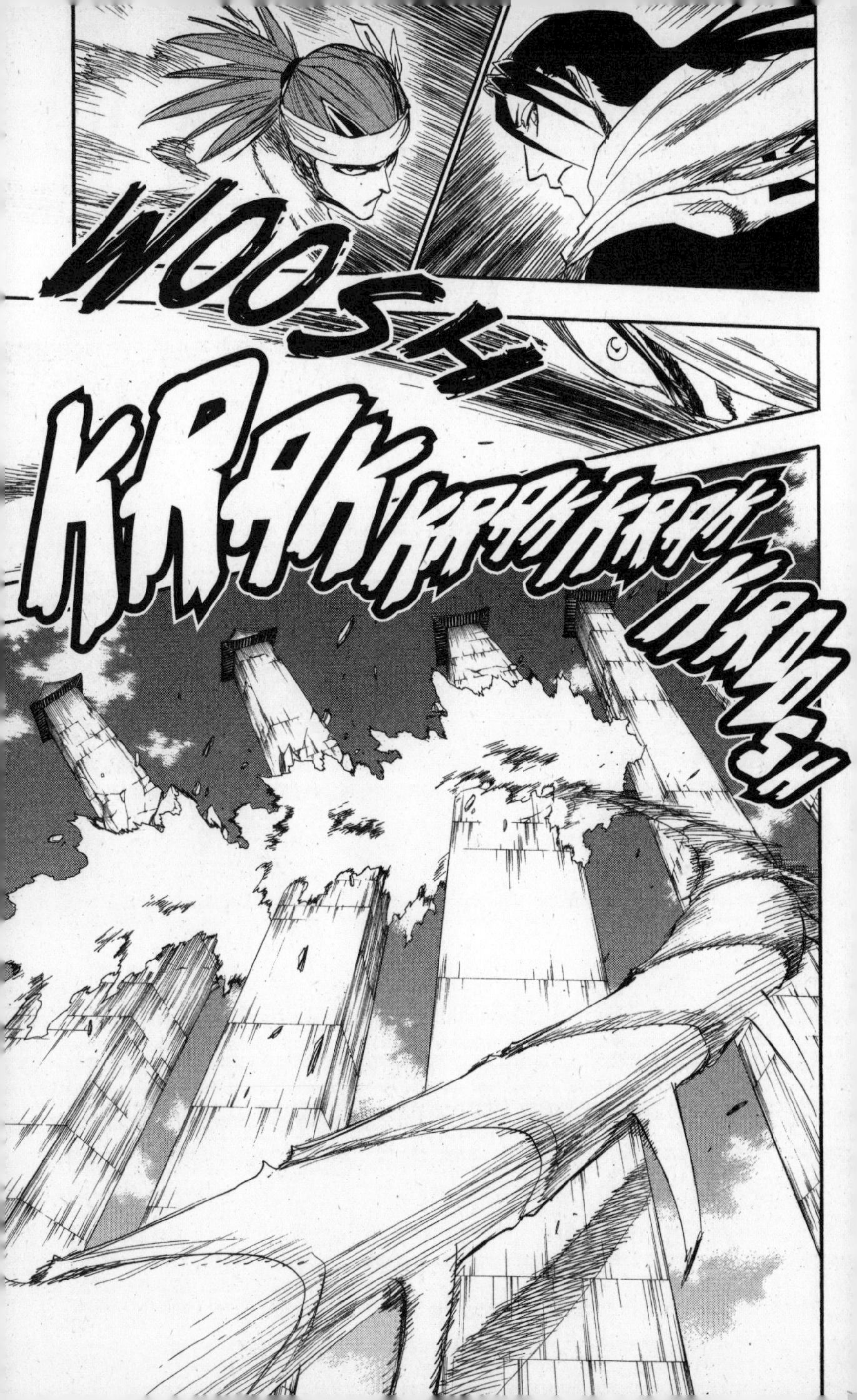
WOOSH
KRAKKRRAKKRRAKKRRAKKRRASH

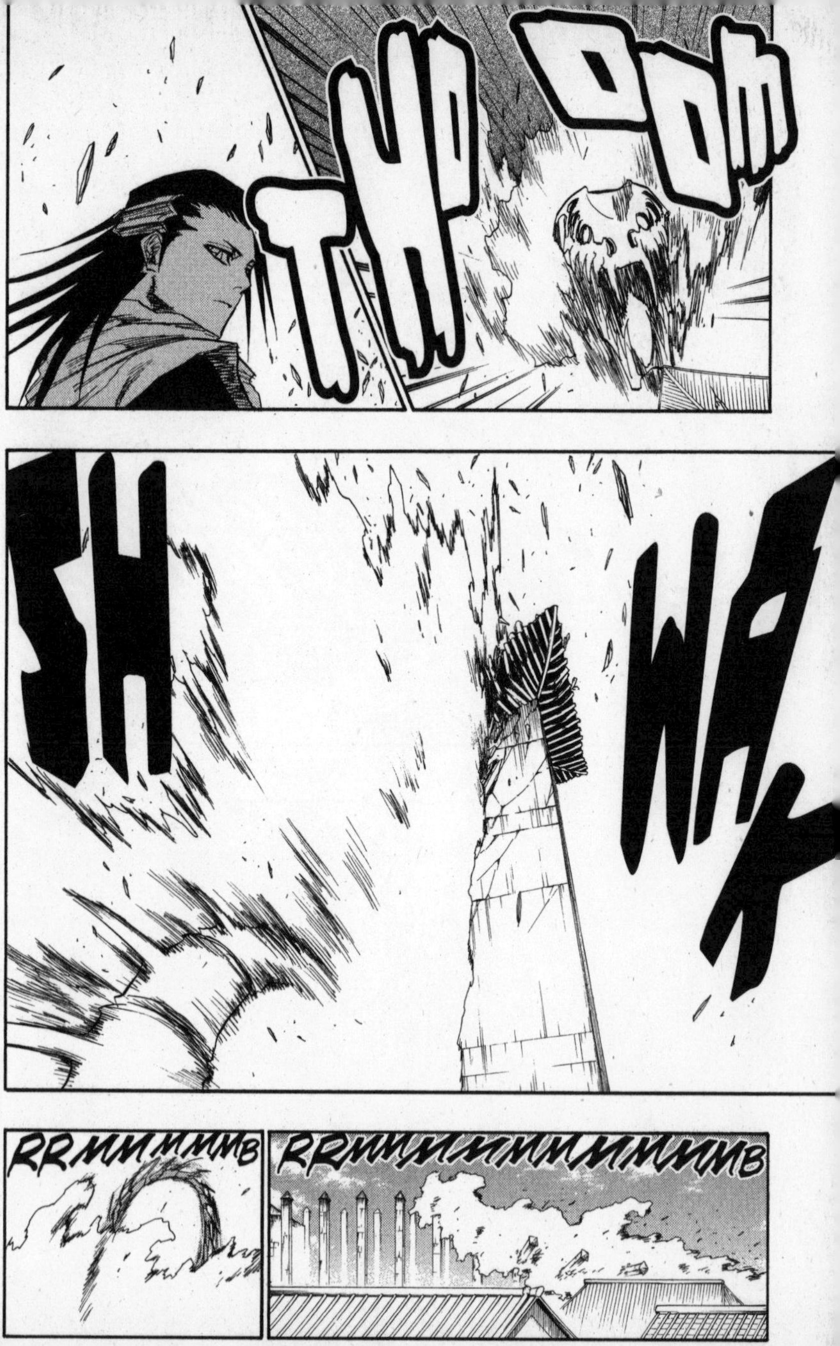
THO OOM
SH WA
RRMMMMMMMMMMMMB
RRMMMMMB

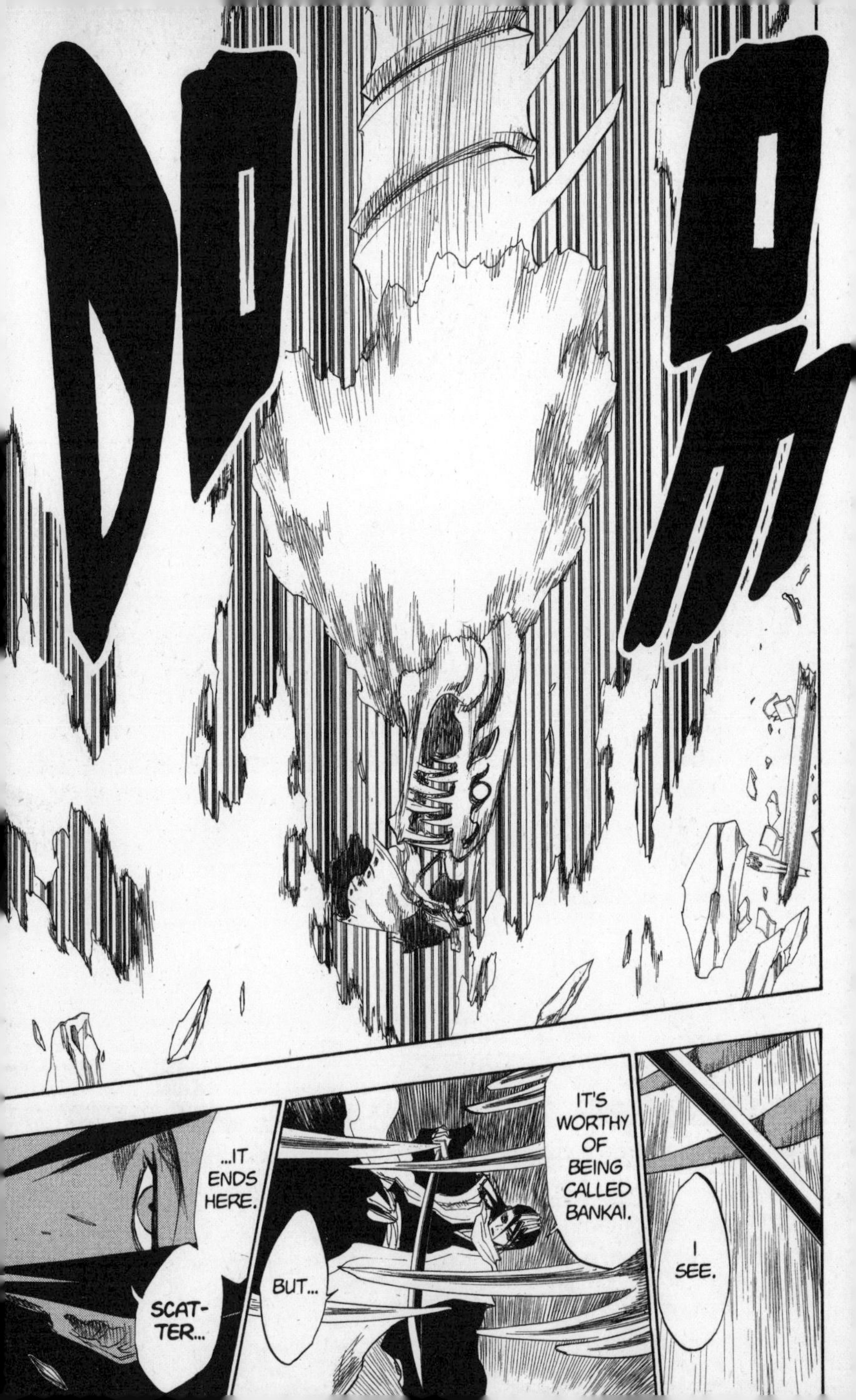
I SEE.
IT'S WORTHY OF BEING CALLED BANKAI.
BUT...
...IT ENDS HERE.
SCAT-TER...

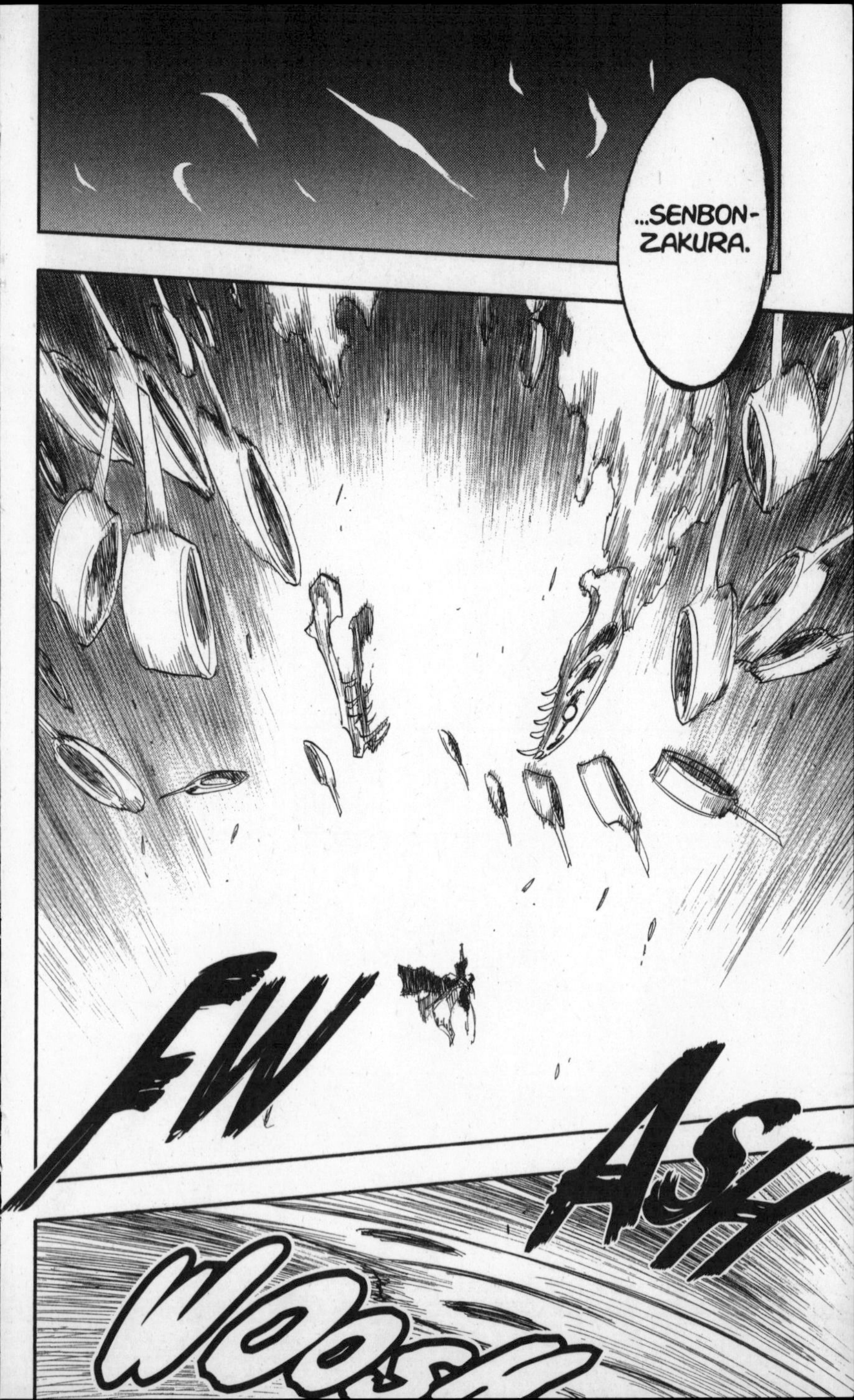
...SENBON-ZAKURA.
FWASH
WOOSH

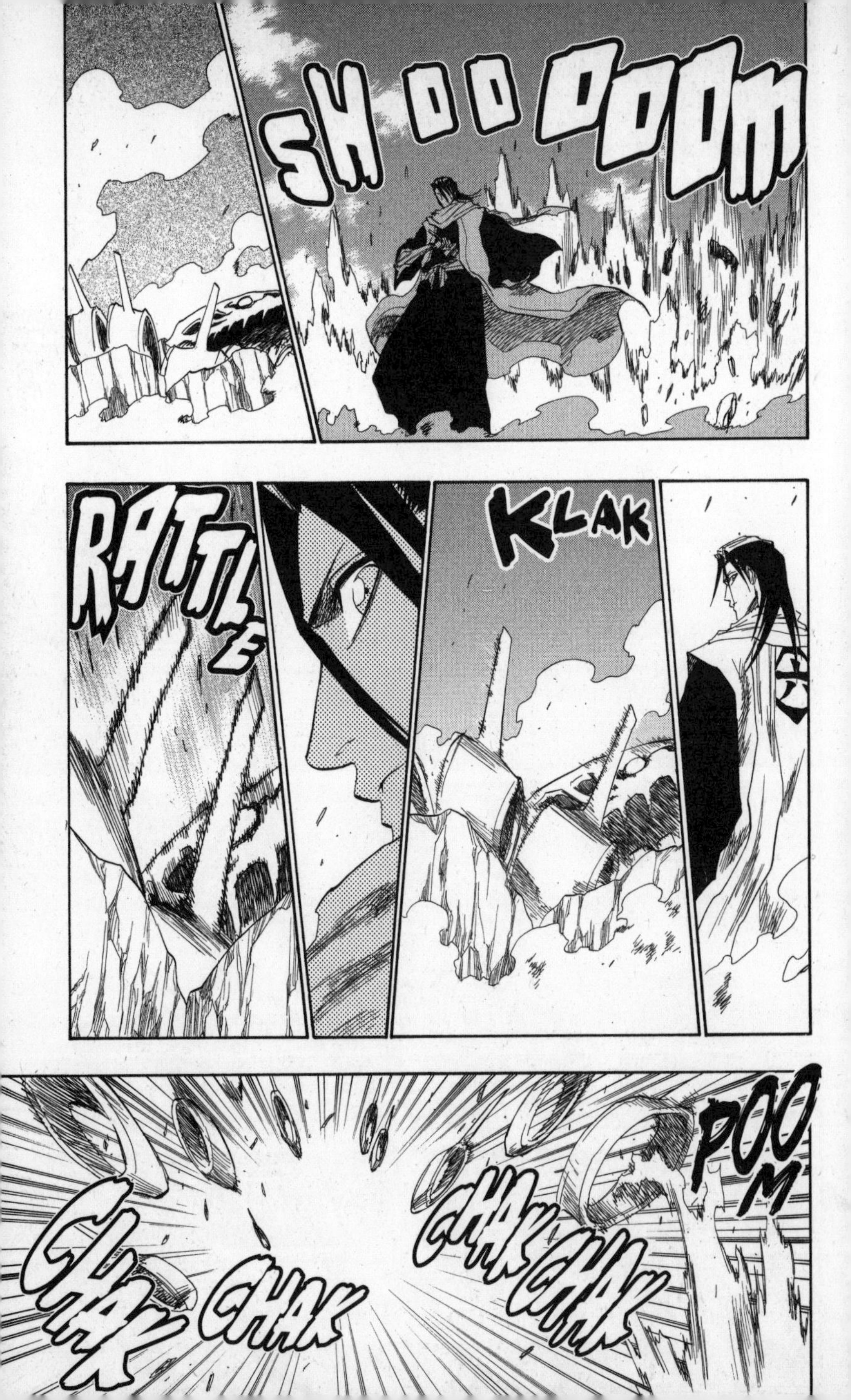
SHOOOOOM
KLAK
RATTLE
POOM
CHAK
CHAK
CHAK
CHAK

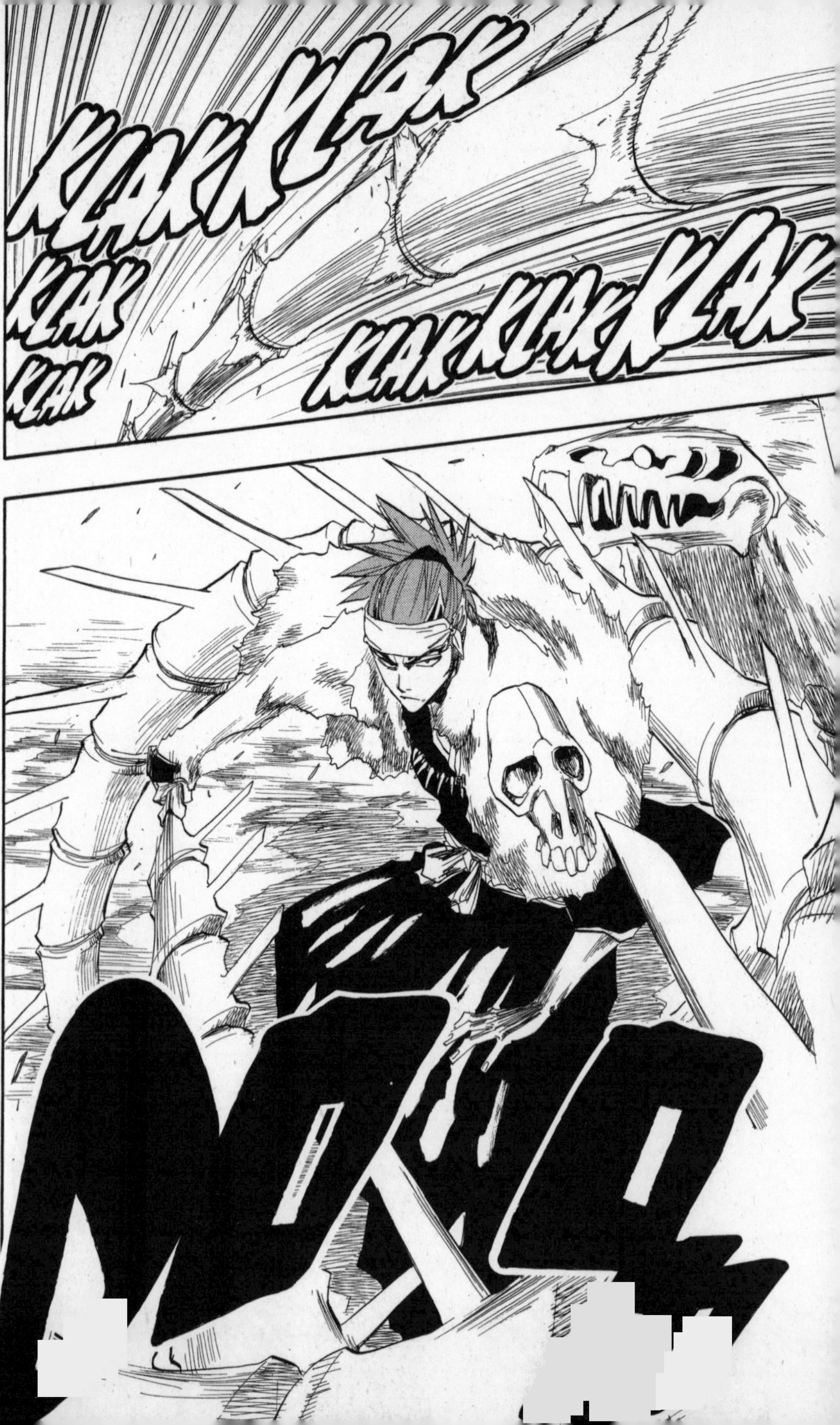
KLAK KLAK
KLAK KLAK KLAK
KLAK KLAK

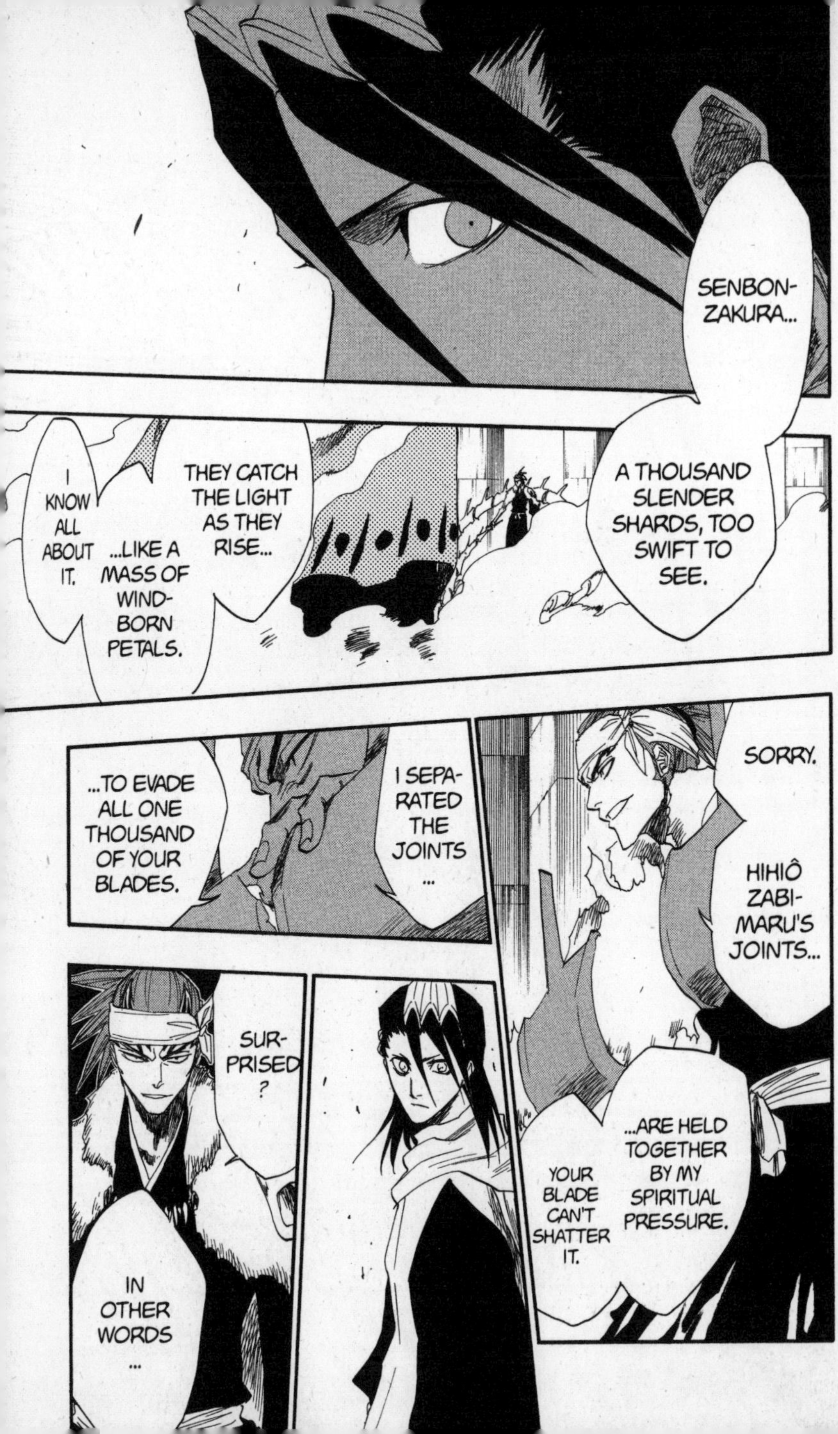
SENBON-ZAKURA...
A THOUSAND SLENDER SHARDS, TOO SWIFT TO SEE.
THEY CATCH THE LIGHT AS THEY RISE...
...LIKE A MASS OF WIND-BORN PETALS.
I KNOW ALL ABOUT IT.
SORRY.
HIHIÔ ZABI-MARU'S JOINTS...
...ARE HELD TOGETHER BY MY SPIRITUAL PRESSURE.
YOUR BLADE CAN'T SHATTER IT.
I SEPA-RATED THE JOINTS...
...TO EVADE ALL ONE THOUSAND OF YOUR BLADES.
SUR-PRISED?
IN OTHER WORDS...

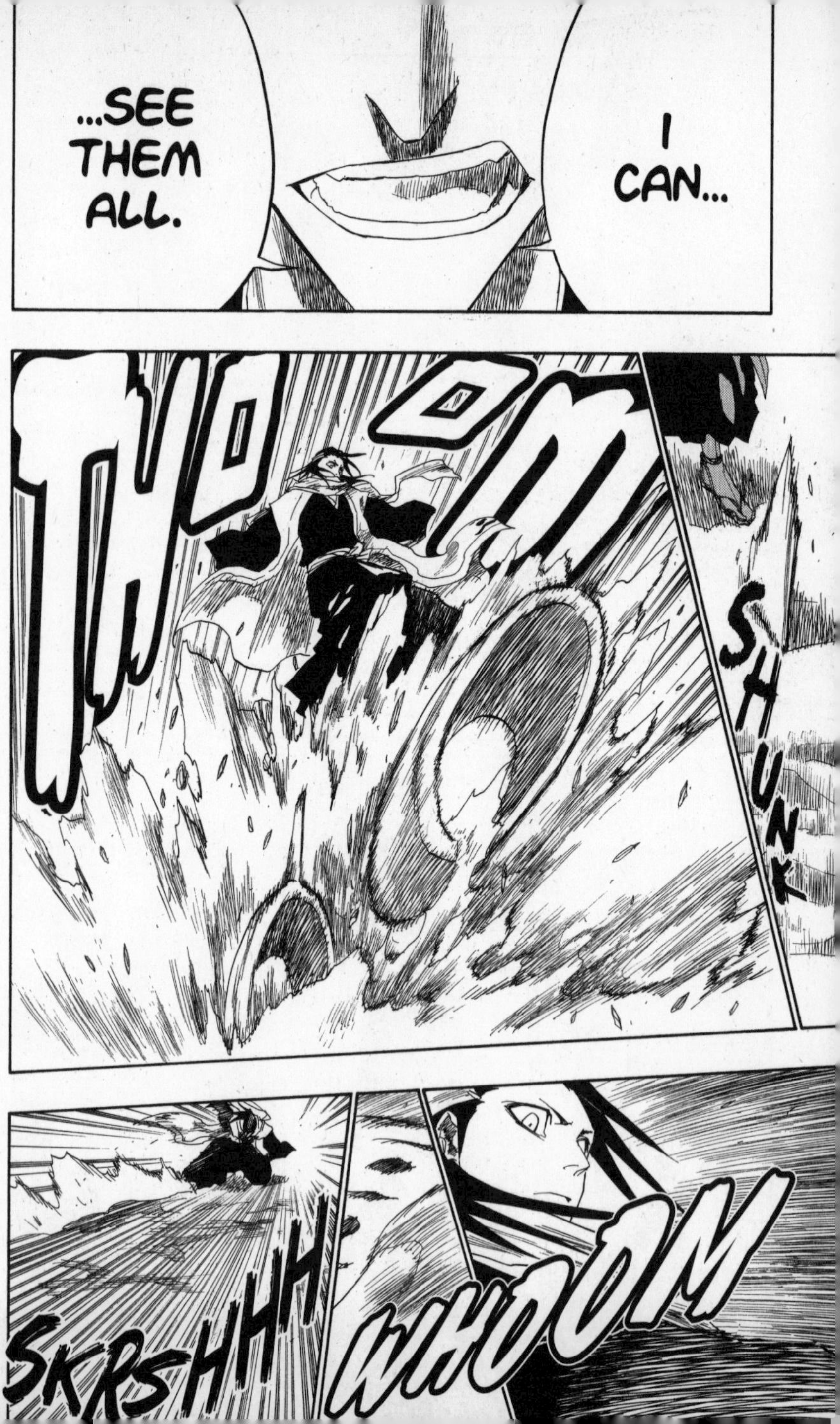
I CAN...
...SEE THEM ALL.
SHUNK
THOOM
WHOOOM
SKRSHHH

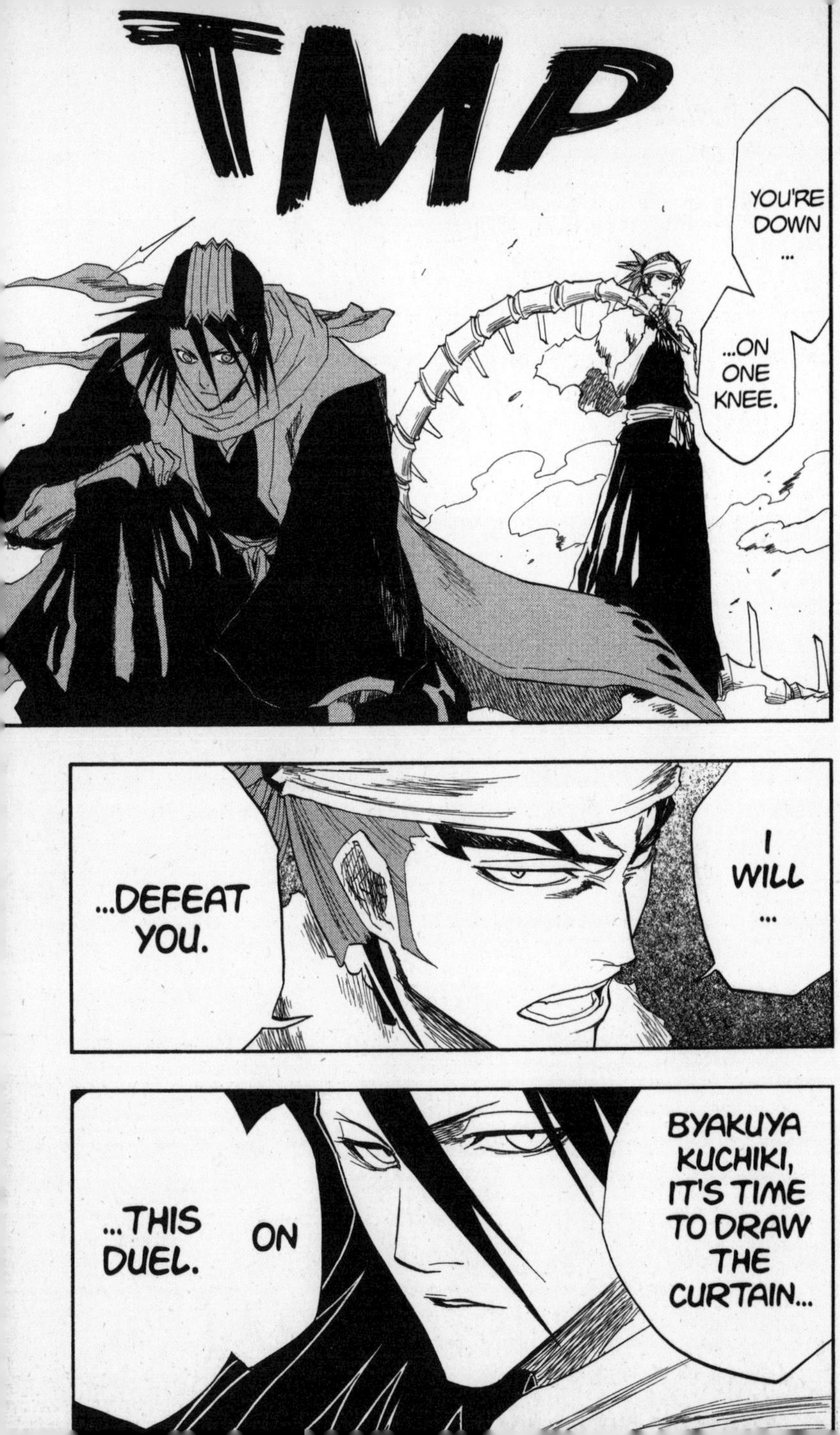
TMP
YOU'RE DOWN ...
...ON ONE KNEE.
I WILL ...
...DEFEAT YOU.
BYAKUYA KUCHIKI, IT'S TIME TO DRAW THE CURTAIN...
ON
...THIS DUEL.

SOCCER'S NOTHING LIKE BASEBALL. THE GUYS WHO PLAY IT ARE KINDA DUMB. WHY DON'T THEY JUST KICK THE CRAP OUT OF THE GUY IN FRONT OF THE NET? THEN THEY COULD SCORE ALL THEY WANT. THIS IS GONNA BE A PIECE O' CAKE.

AUGUST 9, RAINY. TURNS OUT THEY WANTED ME TO PLAY SOCCER FOR THEM. SO I WATCHED A SOCCER VIDEO THEY GAVE ME TO BONE UP.

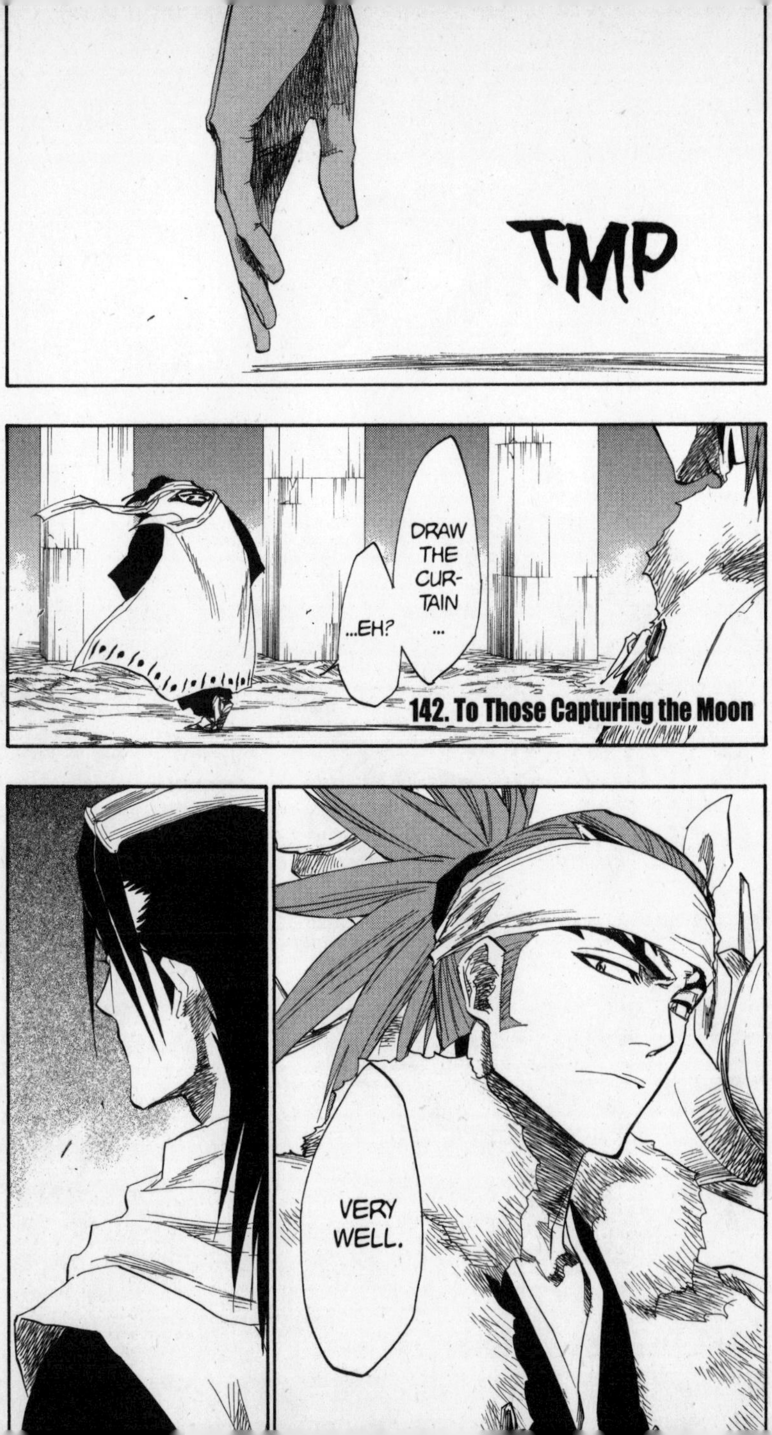
TMP
DRAW THE CURTAIN...
...EH?
142. To Those Capturing the Moon
VERY WELL.

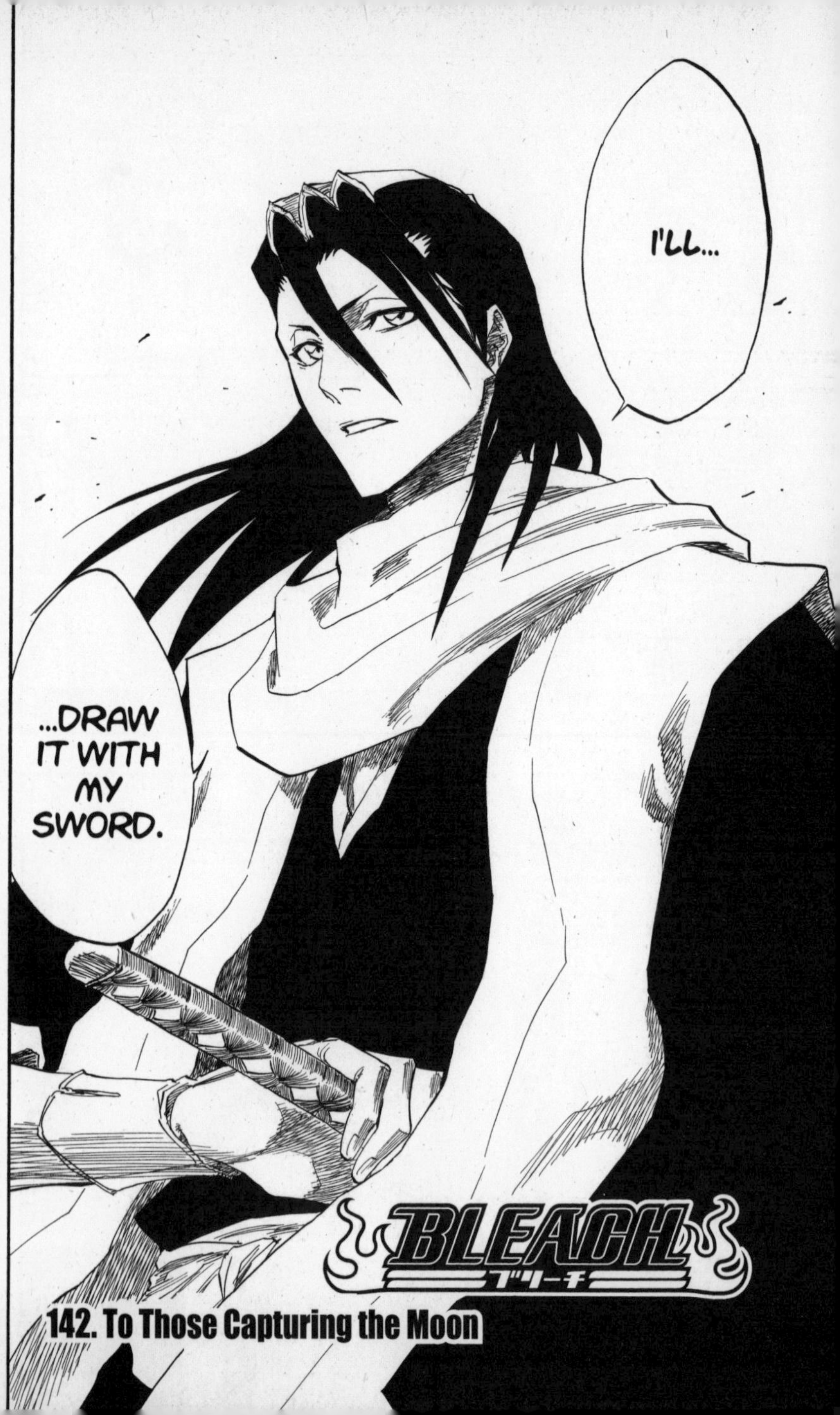
I'LL...
...DRAW IT WITH MY SWORD.
BLEACH
ブリーチ
142. To Those Capturing the Moon

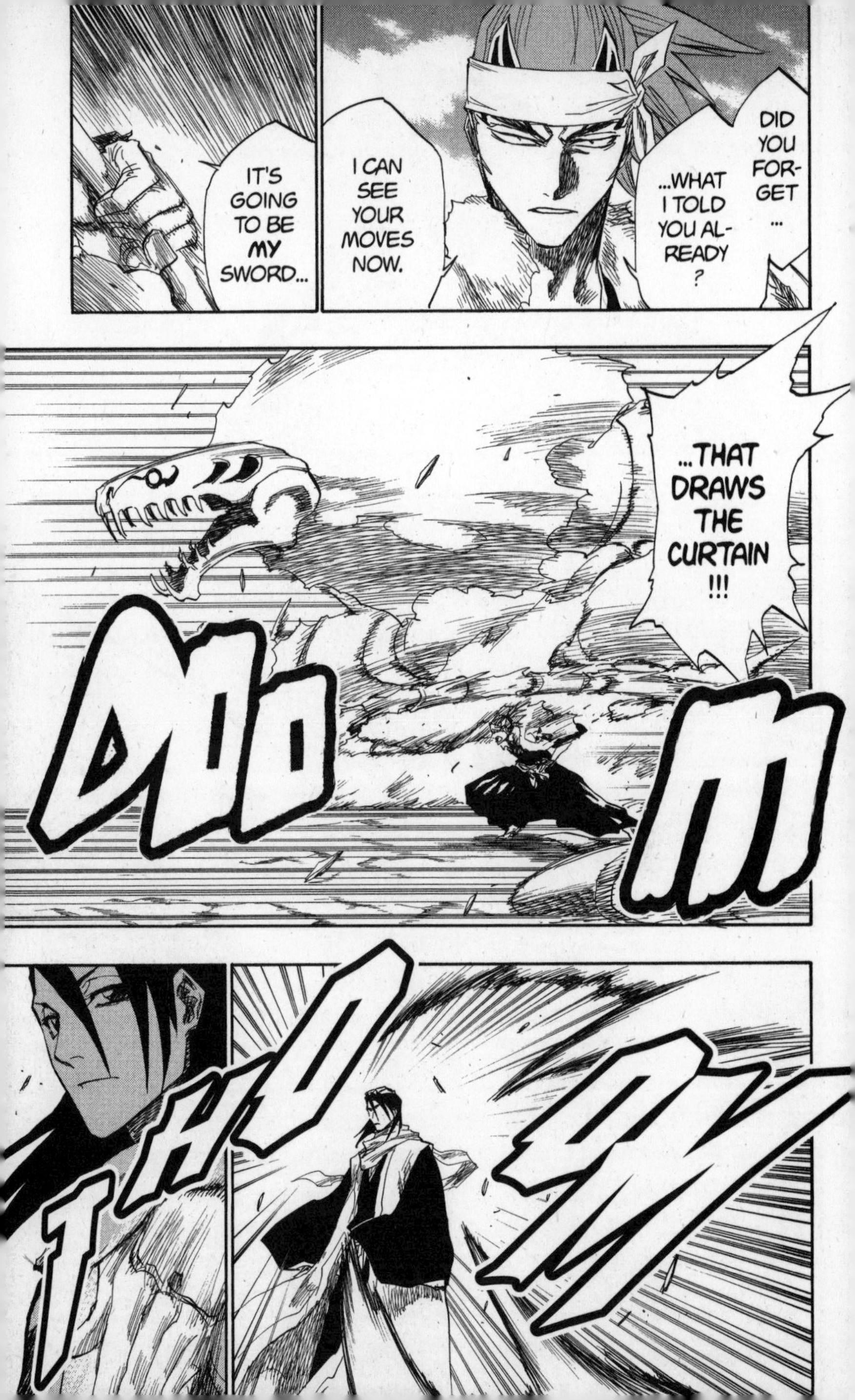
DID YOU FOR-GET ...
...WHAT I TOLD YOU AL-READY ?
I CAN SEE YOUR MOVES NOW.
IT'S GOING TO BE MY SWORD...
...THAT DRAWS THE CURTAIN !!!
DOOM

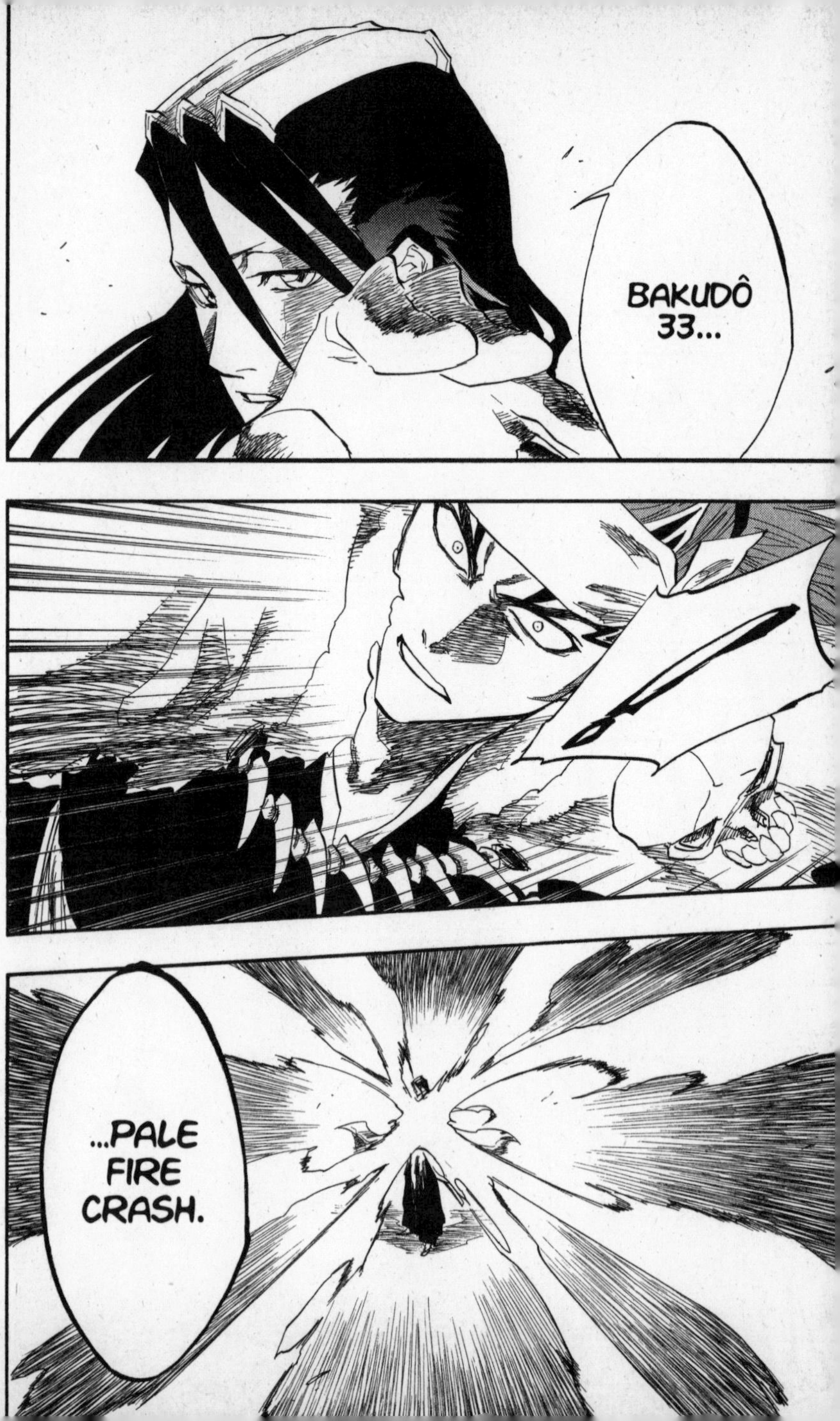
BAKUDÔ 33...
...PALE FIRE CRASH.

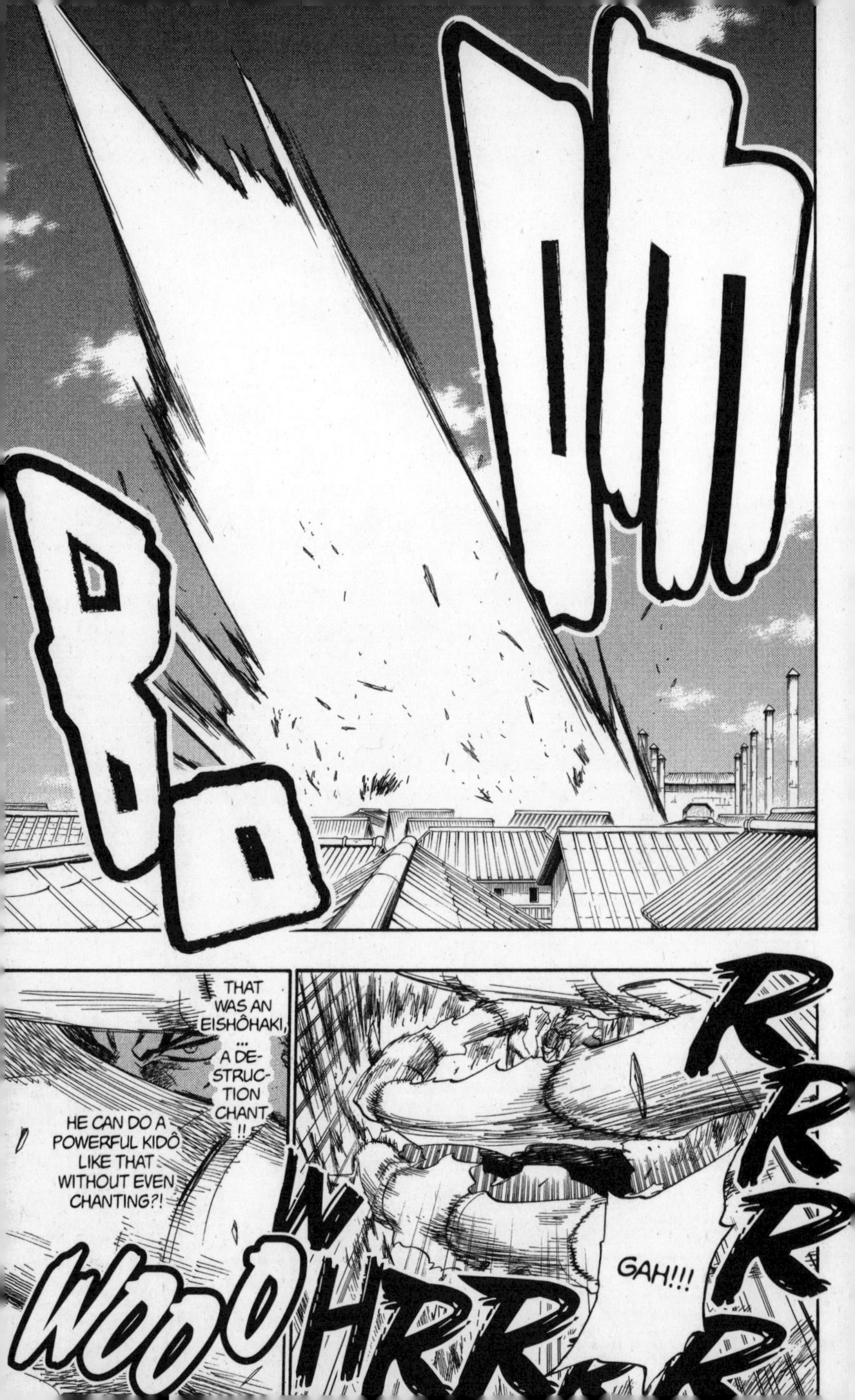
GAH!!!
THAT WAS AN EISHÔHAKI, ... A DE-STRUCTION CHANT !!
HE CAN DO A POWERFUL KIDÔ LIKE THAT WITHOUT EVEN CHANTING?!

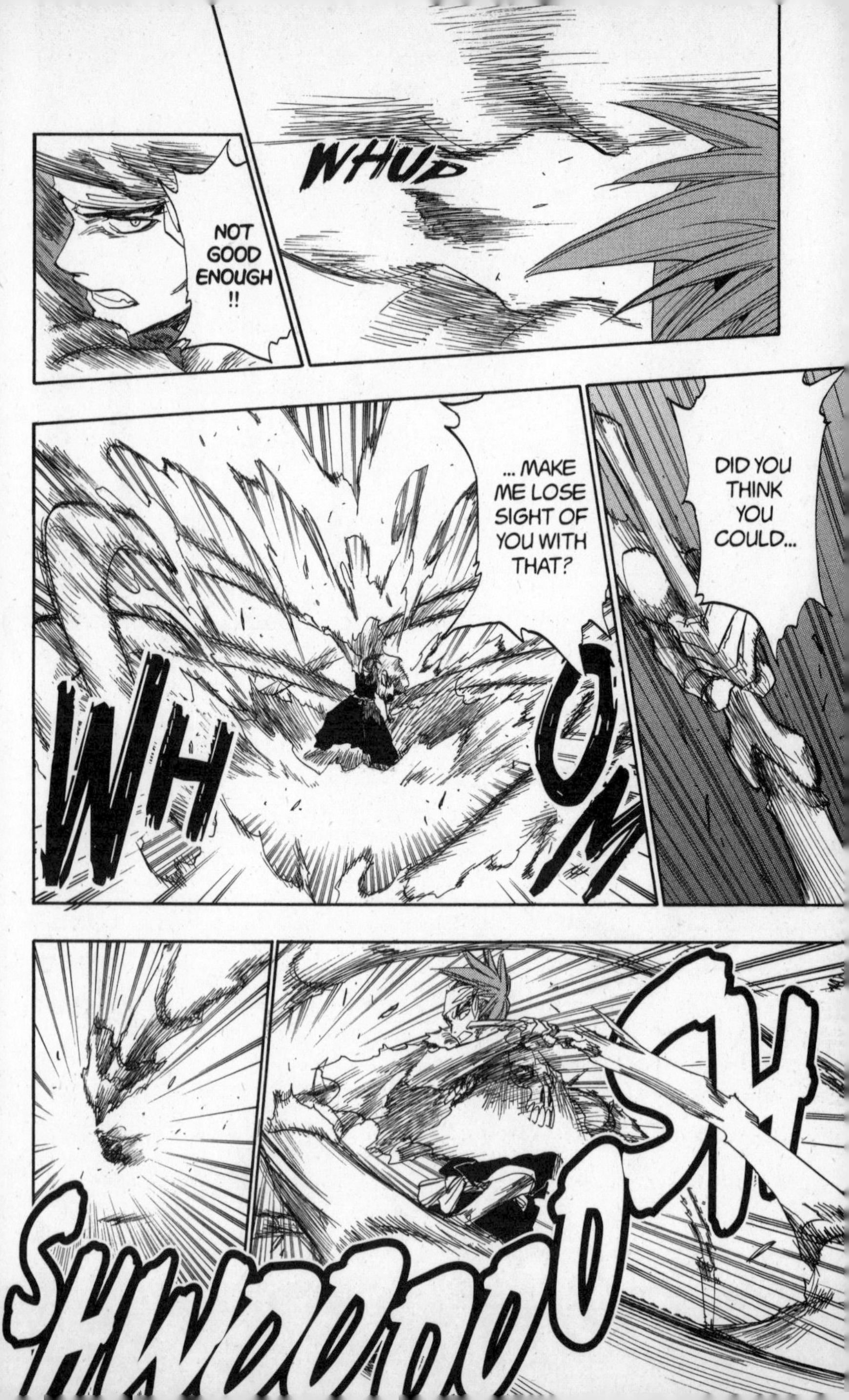
WHUP
NOT GOOD ENOUGH!!
DID YOU THINK YOU COULD...
...MAKE ME LOSE SIGHT OF YOU WITH THAT?
WHOOM
SHWOOOOOOSH

READ THIS WAY

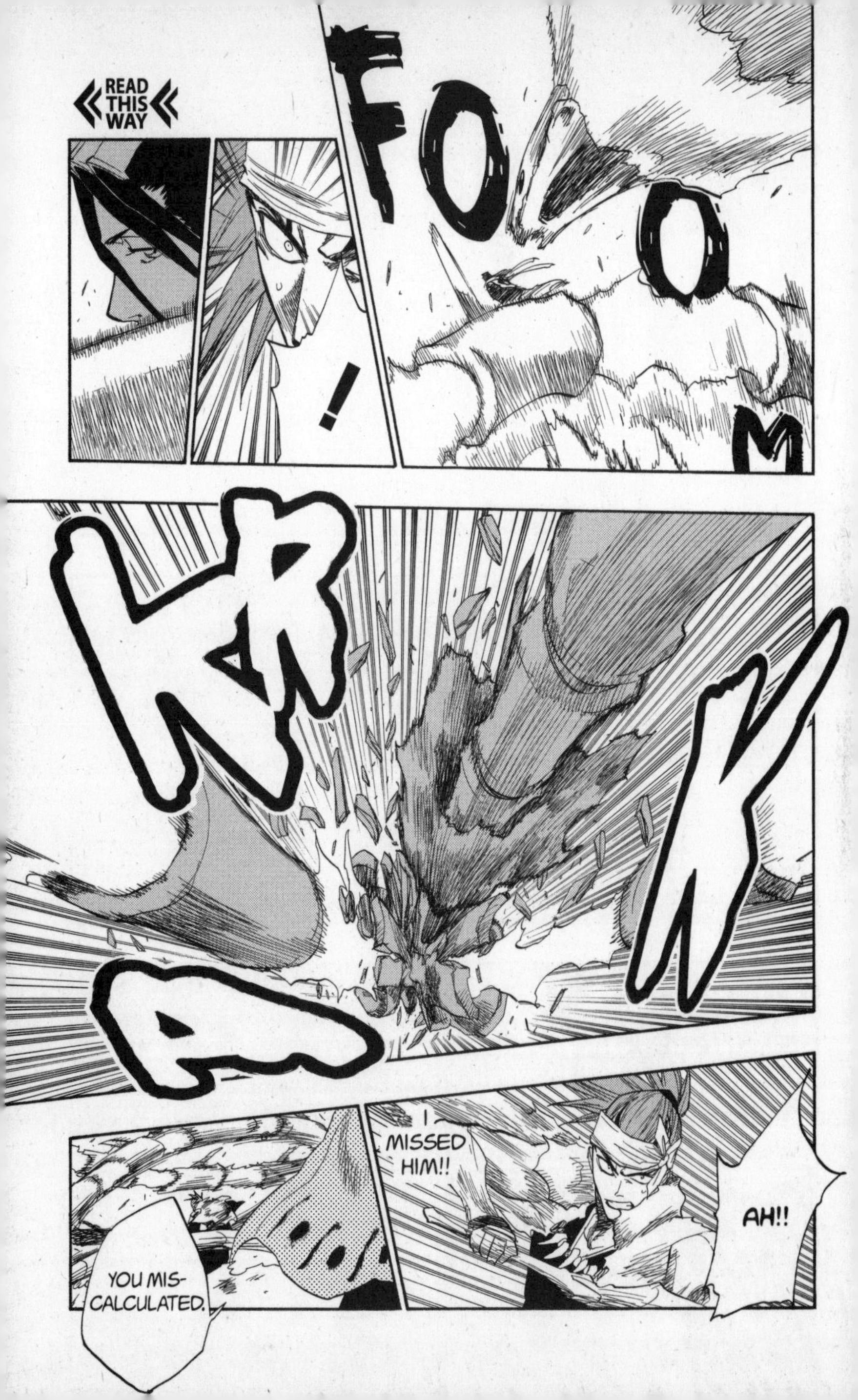
FOOOM
!
KRAK
I MISSED HIM!!
AH!!
YOU MIS-CALCULATED.

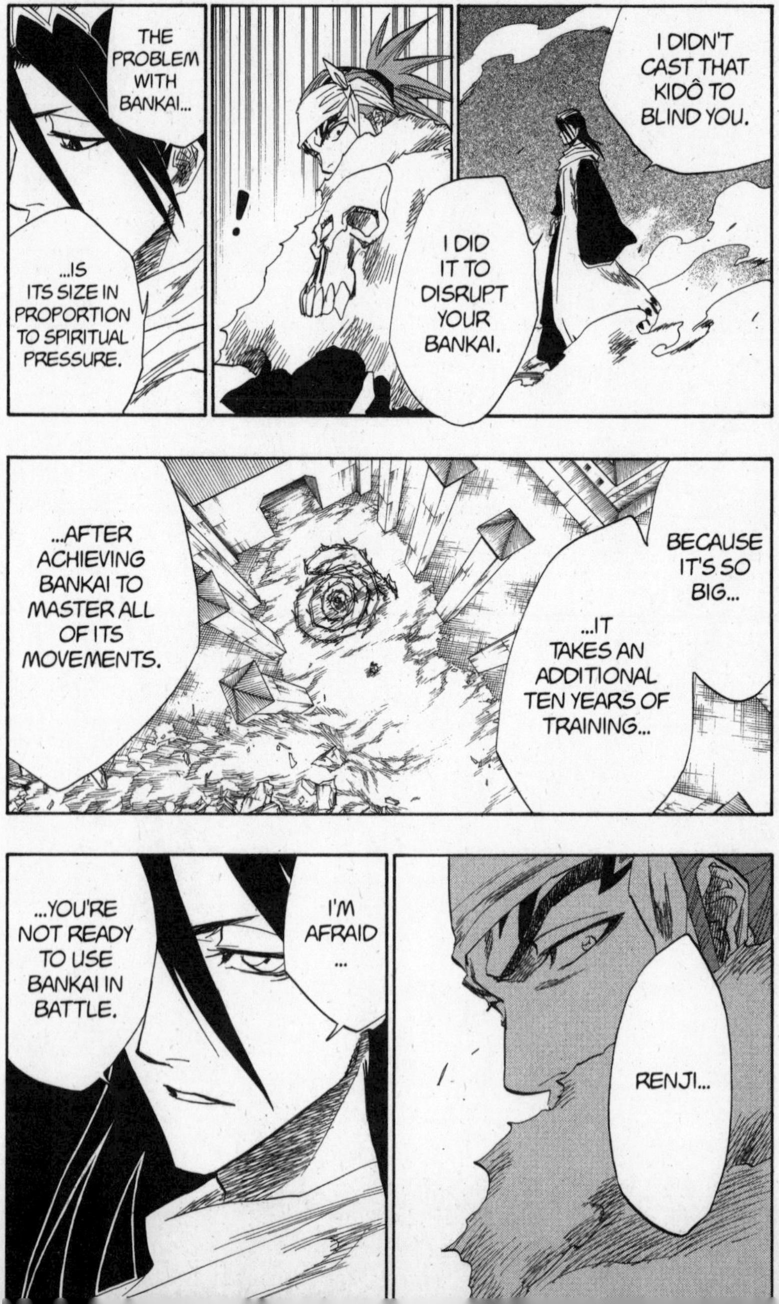
I DIDN'T CAST THAT KIDÔ TO BLIND YOU.
I DID IT TO DISRUPT YOUR BANKAI.
!
THE PROBLEM WITH BANKAI...
...IS ITS SIZE IN PROPORTION TO SPIRITUAL PRESSURE.
BECAUSE IT'S SO BIG...
...IT TAKES AN ADDITIONAL TEN YEARS OF TRAINING...
...AFTER ACHIEVING BANKAI TO MASTER ALL OF ITS MOVEMENTS.
RENJI...
I'M AFRAID ...
...YOU'RE NOT READY TO USE BANKAI IN BATTLE.

READ THIS WAY

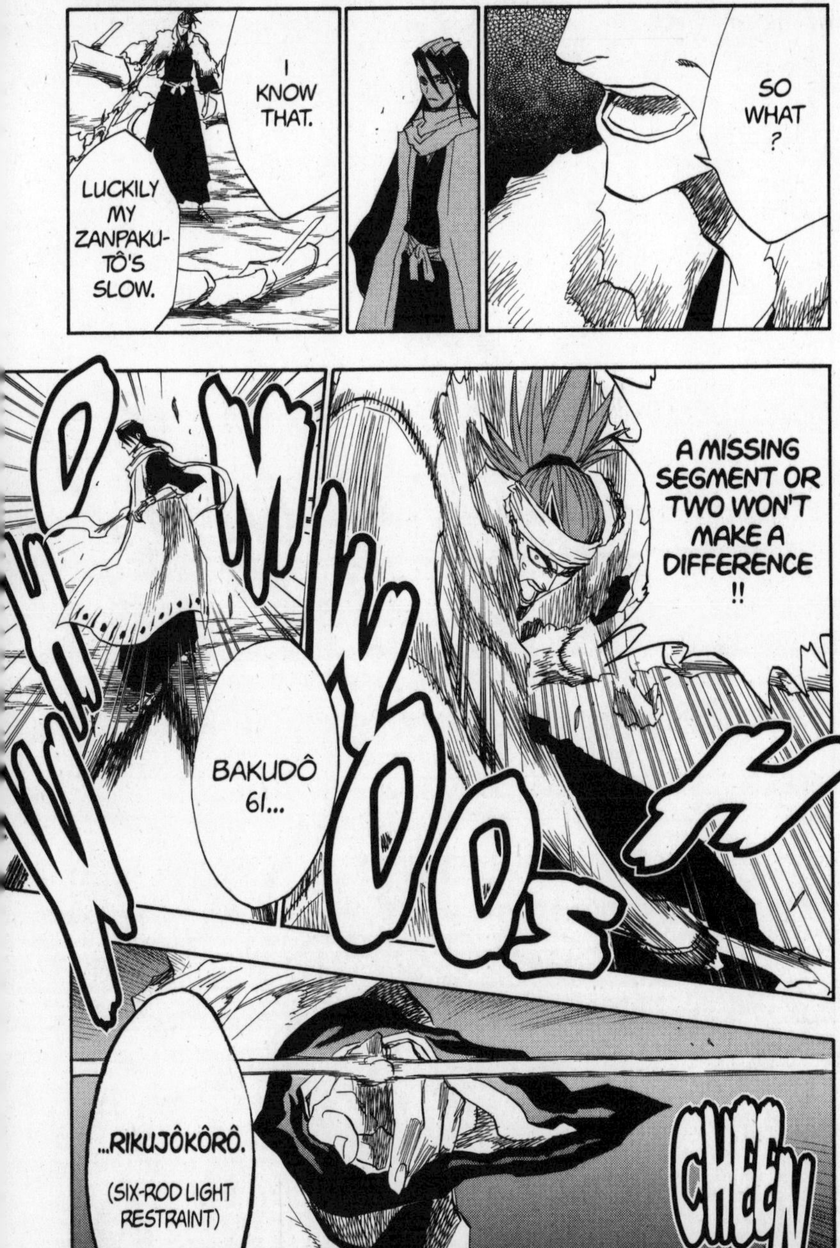
SO WHAT?
I KNOW THAT.
LUCKILY MY ZANPAKU-TÔ'S SLOW.
A MISSING SEGMENT OR TWO WON'T MAKE A DIFFERENCE!!
WHOOOSH
BAKUDÔ 61...
CHEEN
...RIKUJÔKÔRÔ.
(SIX-ROD LIGHT RESTRAINT)

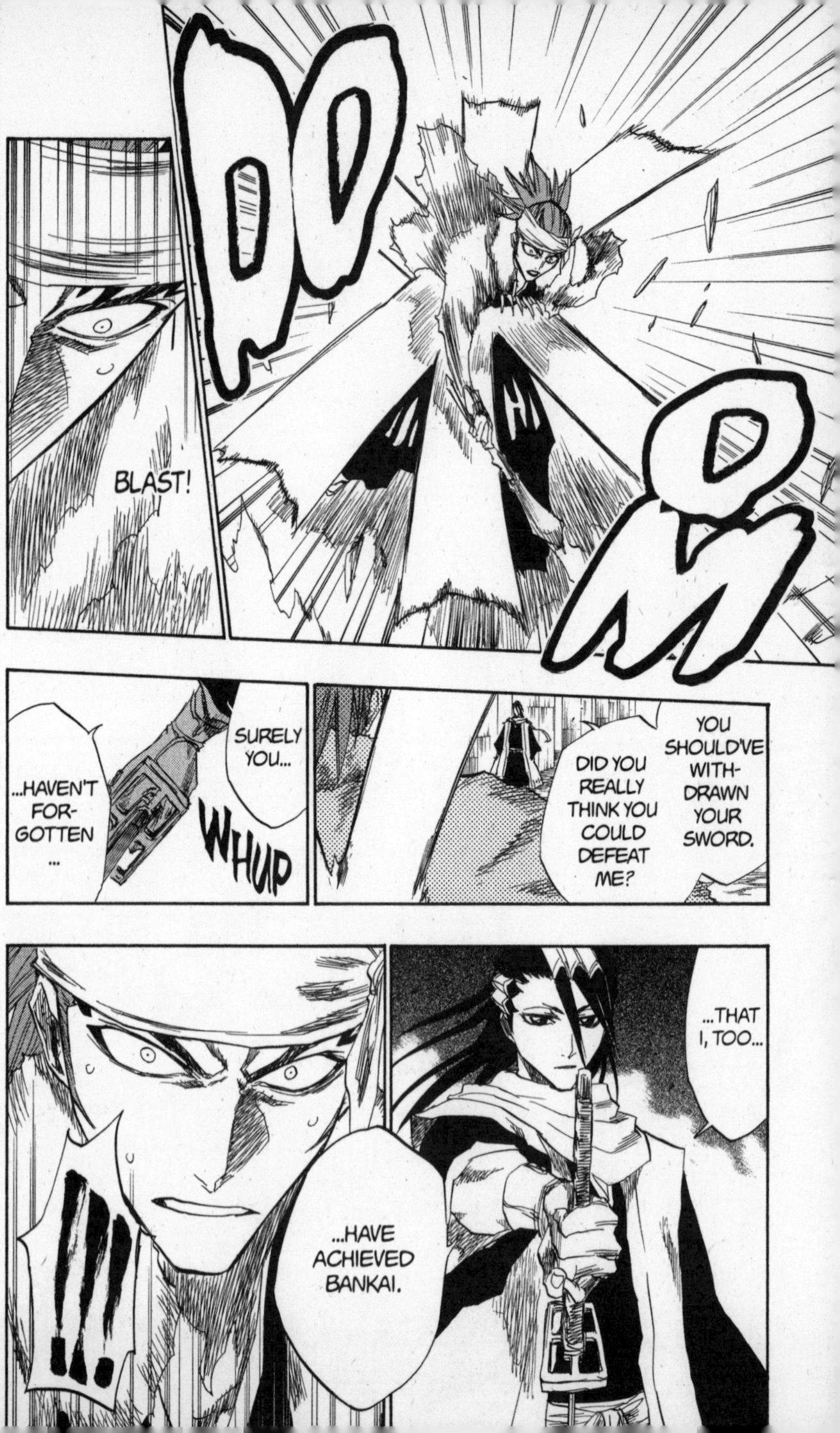
DOOM
BLAST!
YOU SHOULD'VE WITH-DRAWN YOUR SWORD.
DID YOU REALLY THINK YOU COULD DEFEAT ME?
SURELY YOU...
WHUP
...HAVEN'T FOR-GOTTEN ...
...THAT I, TOO...
...HAVE ACHIEVED BANKAI.
!!!

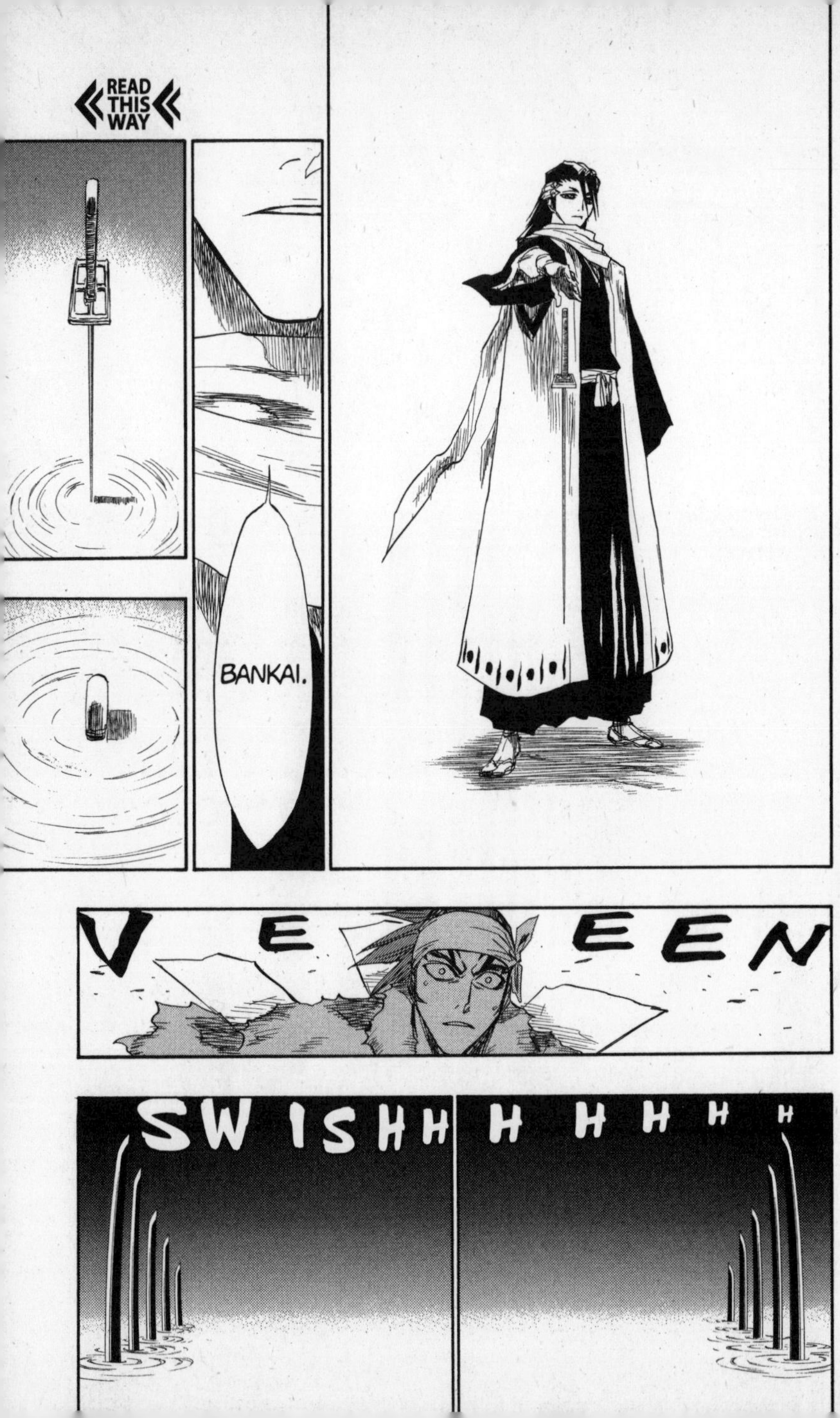
READ THIS WAY
BANKAI.
VEEEN
SWISHHHHHH

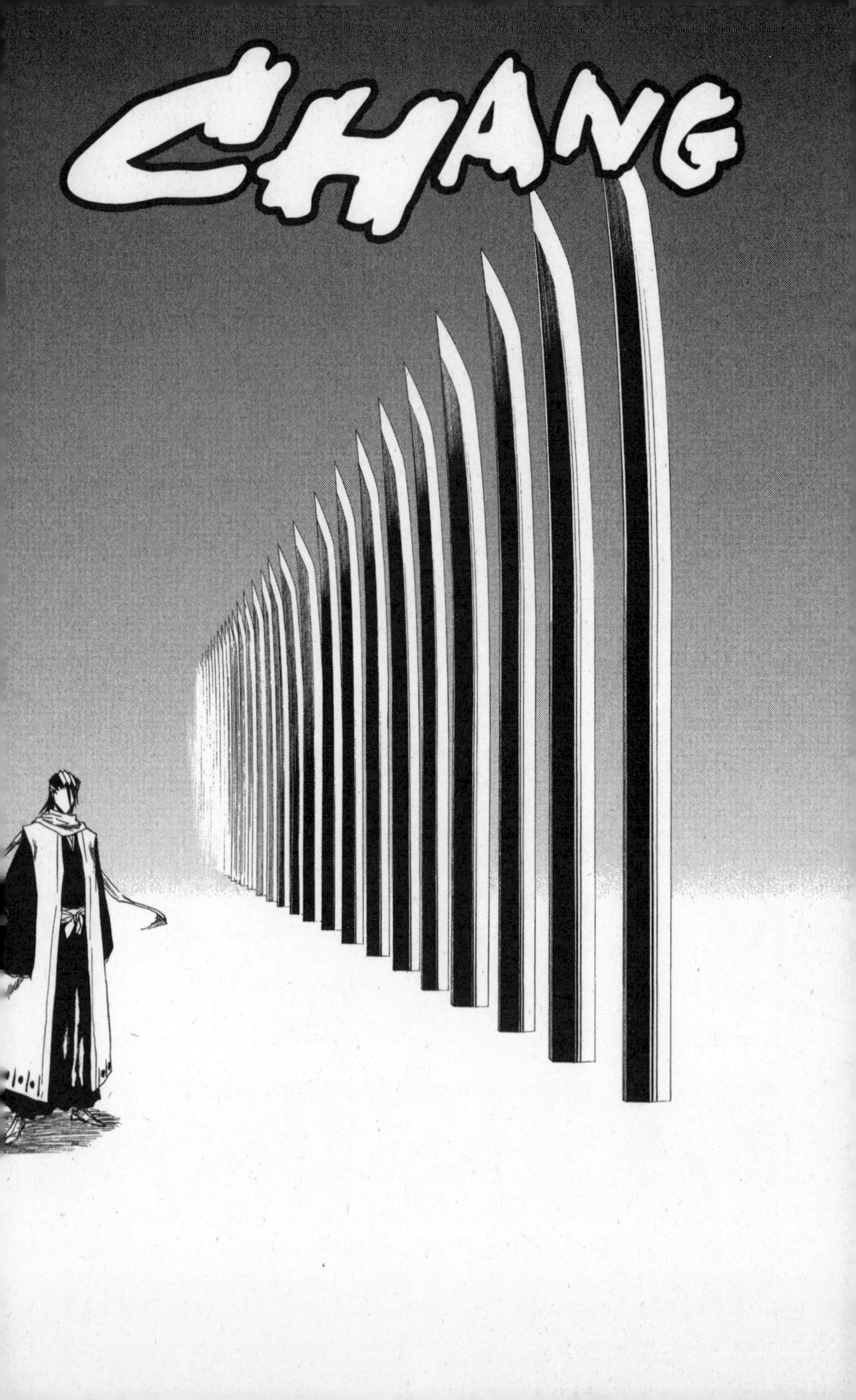
CHANG

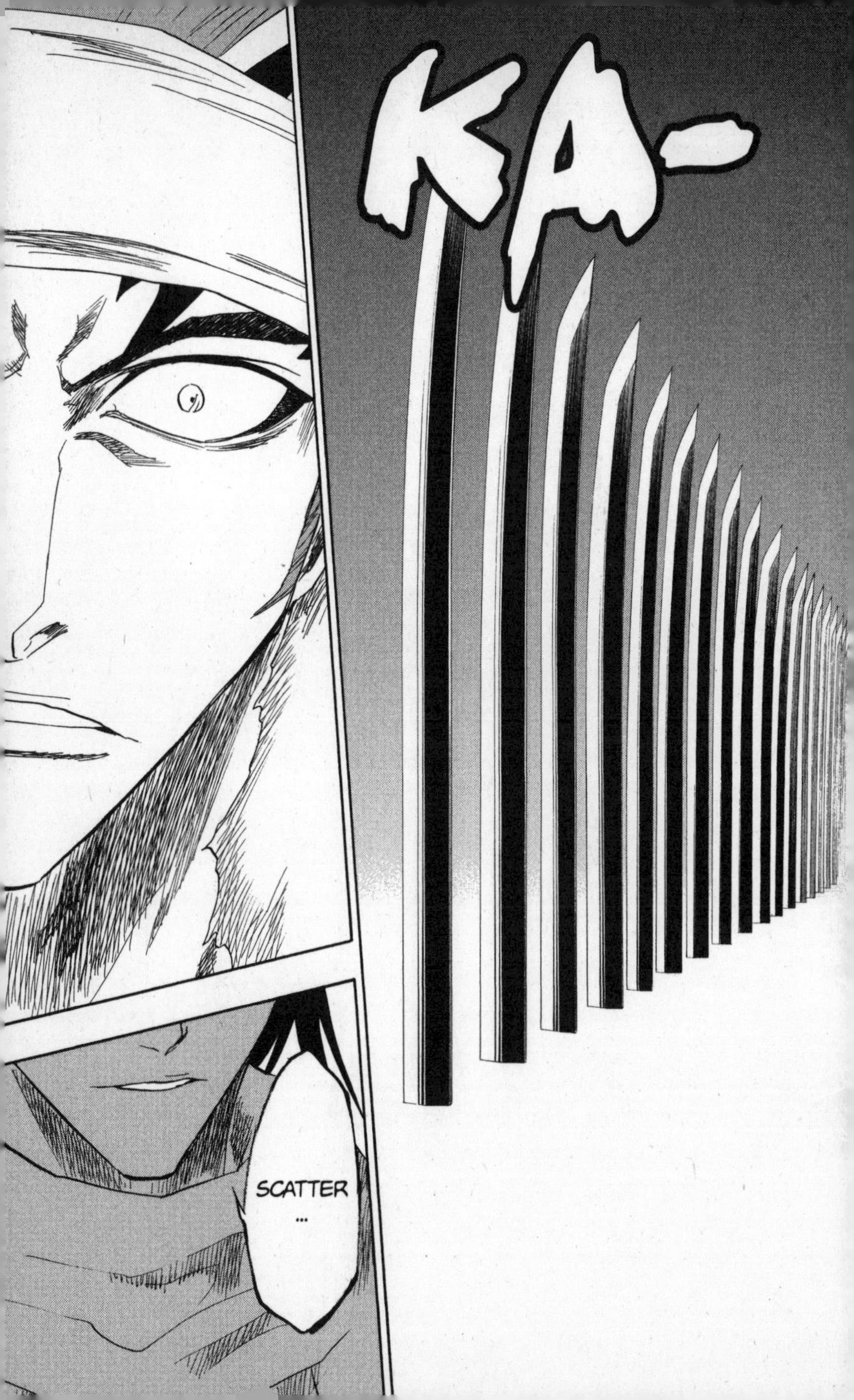
KA-
SCATTER
...

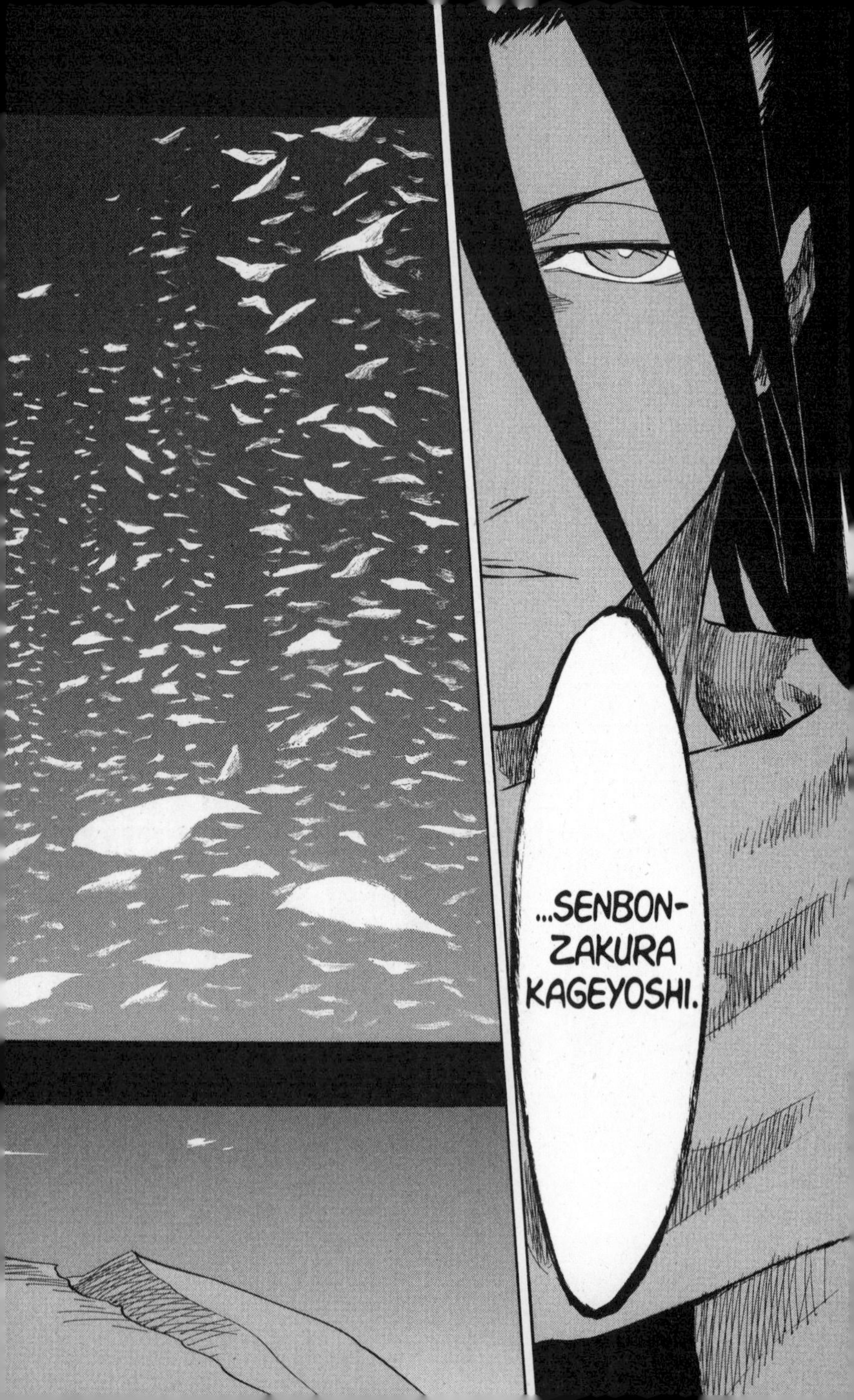
...SENBON-ZAKURA KAGEYOSHI.

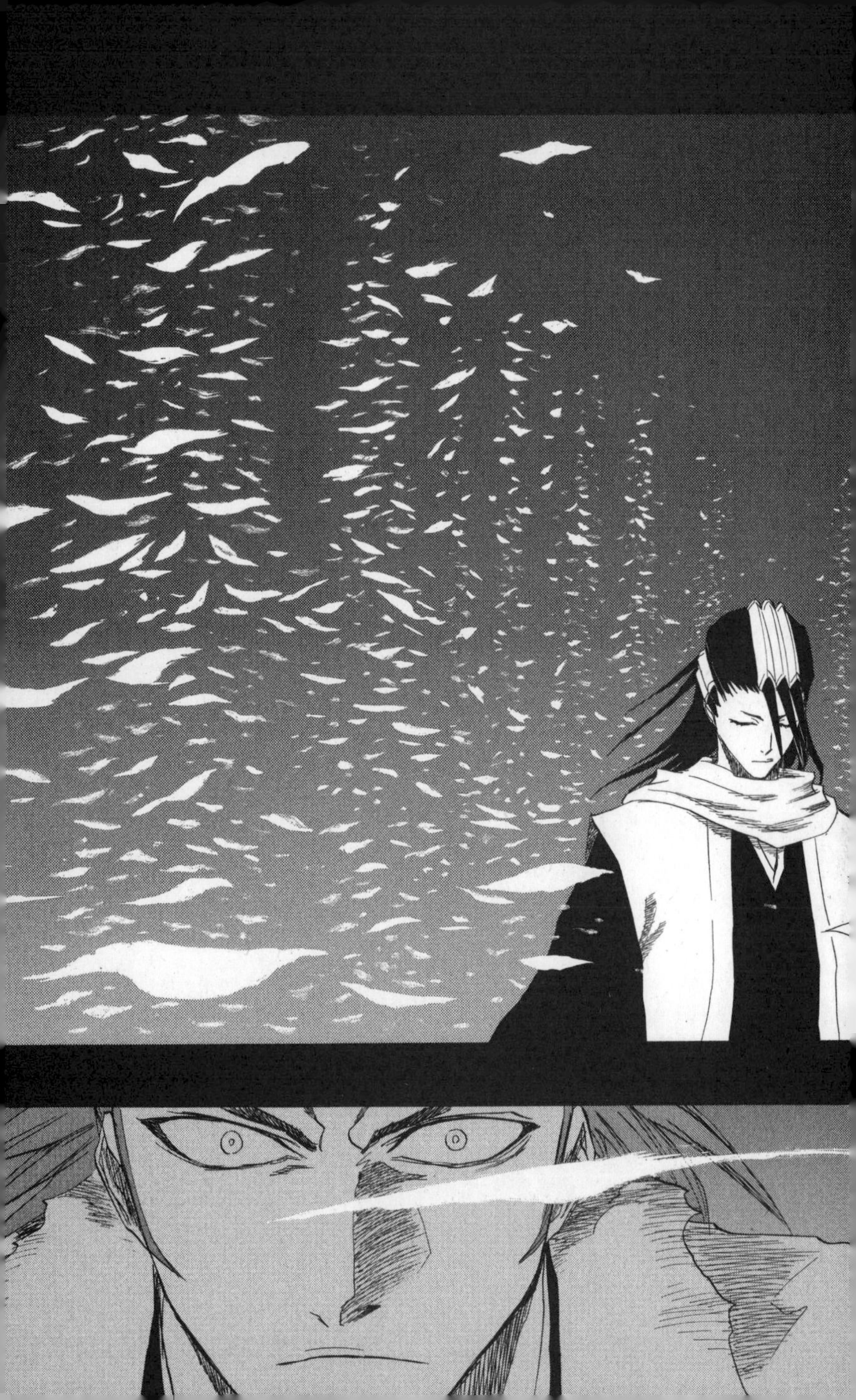

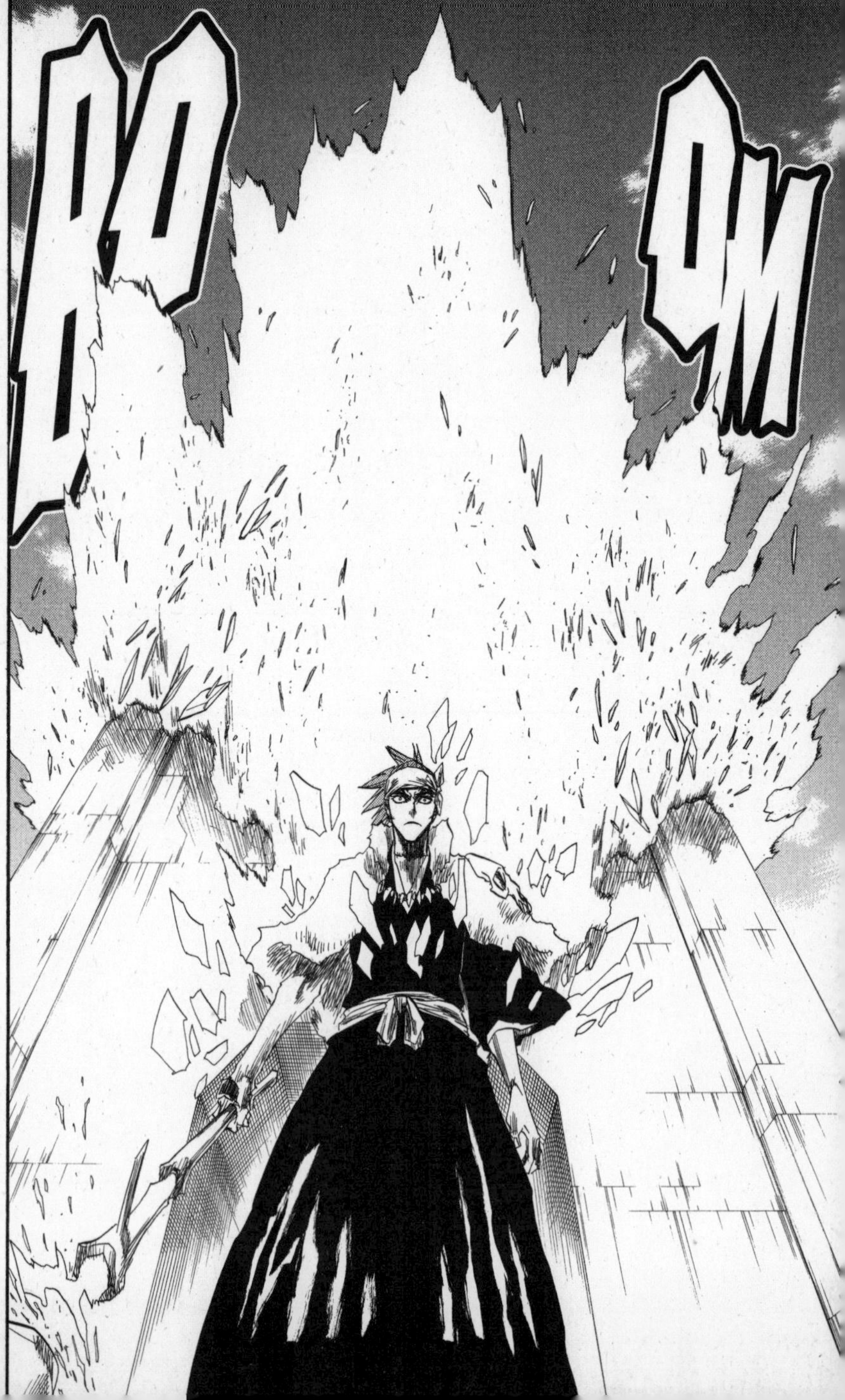
BO
OM

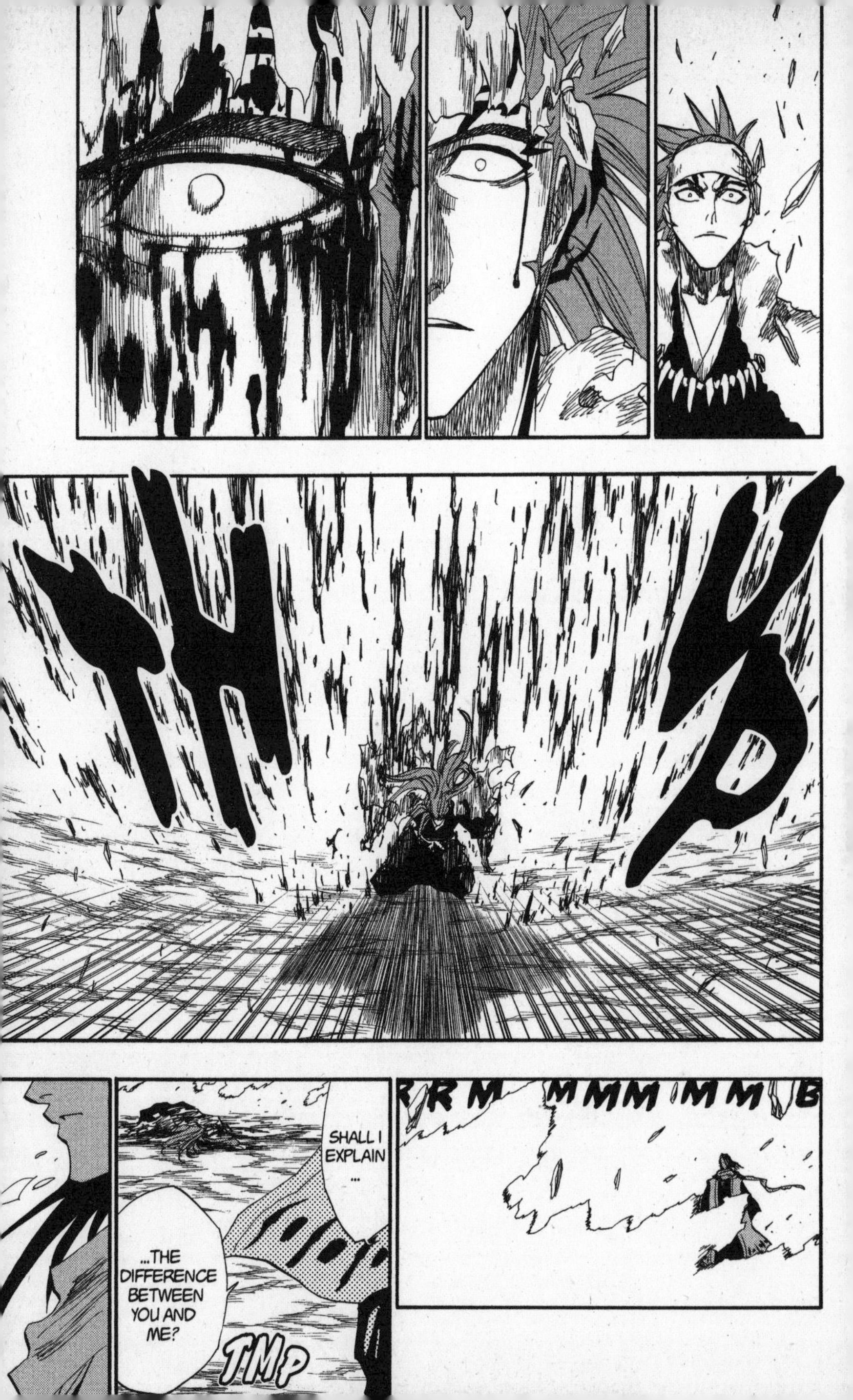
SHALL I EXPLAIN ...
...THE DIFFERENCE BETWEEN YOU AND ME?
TMP

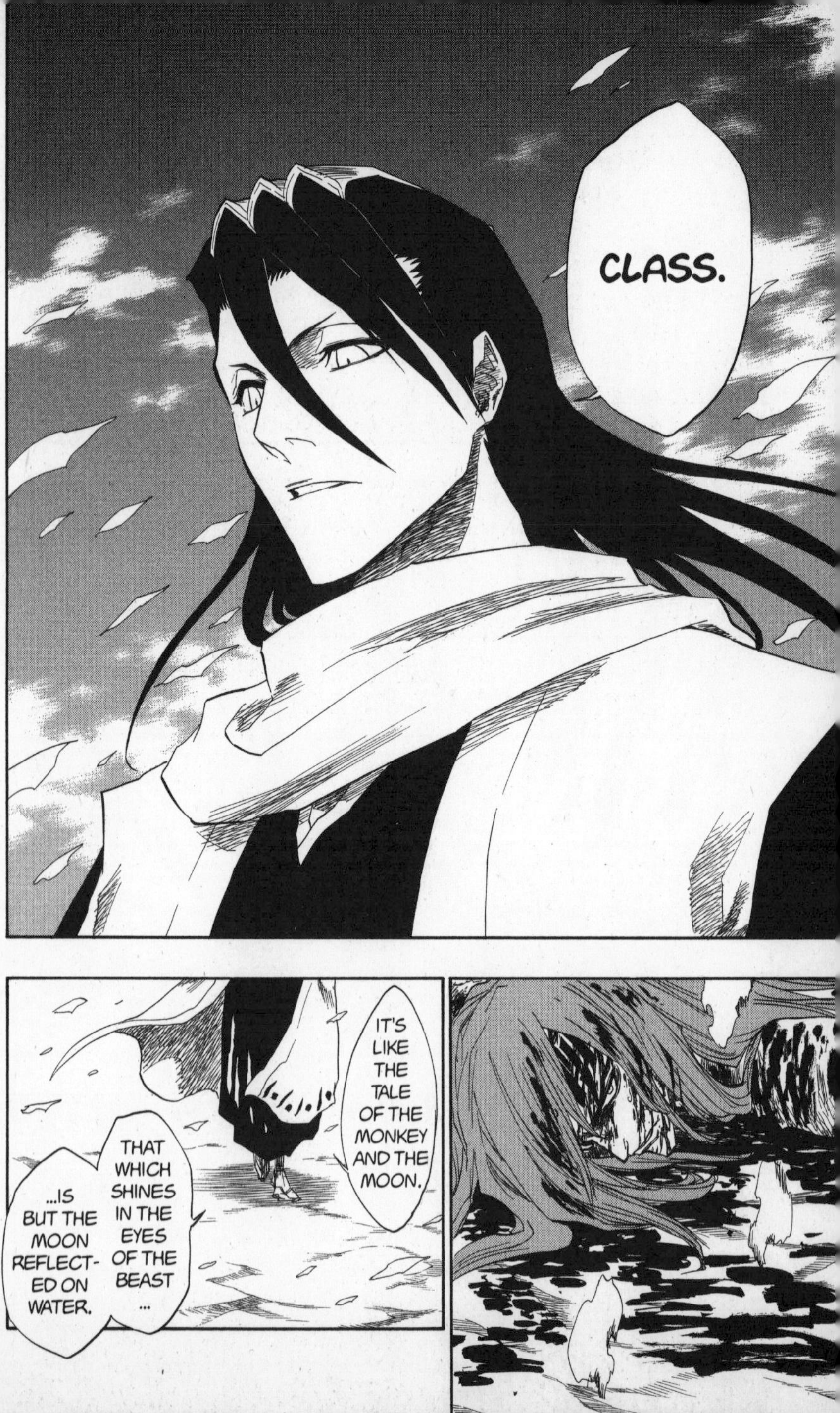
CLASS.
IT'S LIKE THE TALE OF THE MONKEY AND THE MOON.
THAT WHICH SHINES IN THE EYES OF THE BEAST...
...IS BUT THE MOON REFLECTED ON WATER.

READ THIS WAY

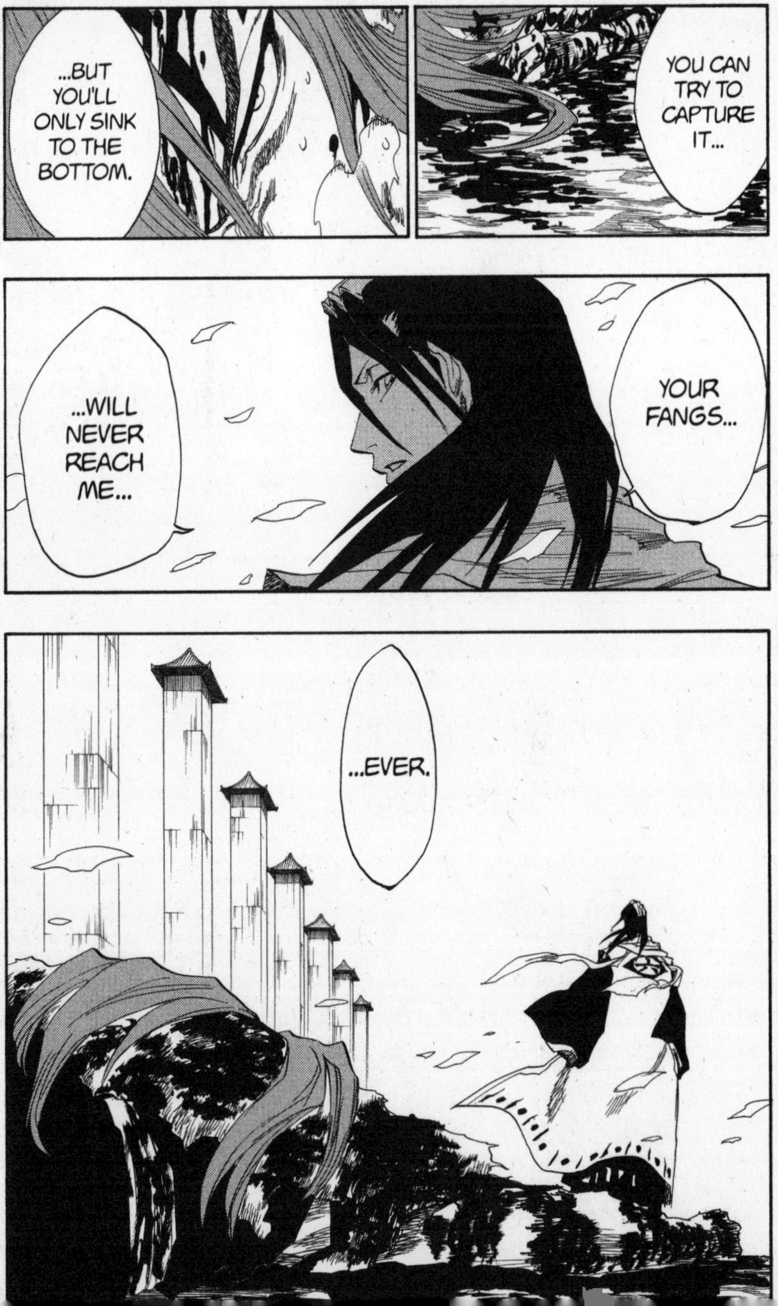
YOU CAN TRY TO CAPTURE IT...
...BUT YOU'LL ONLY SINK TO THE BOTTOM.
YOUR FANGS...
...WILL NEVER REACH ME...
...EVER.

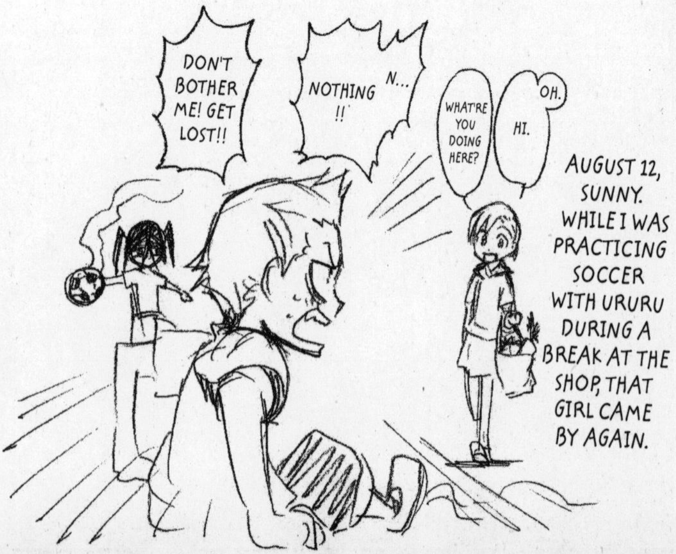
AUGUST 12, SUNNY. WHILE I WAS PRACTICING SOCCER WITH URURU DURING A BREAK AT THE SHOP, THAT GIRL CAME BY AGAIN.
OH.
HI.
WHAT'RE YOU DOING HERE?
N...
NOTHING!!
DON'T BOTHER ME! GET LOST!!

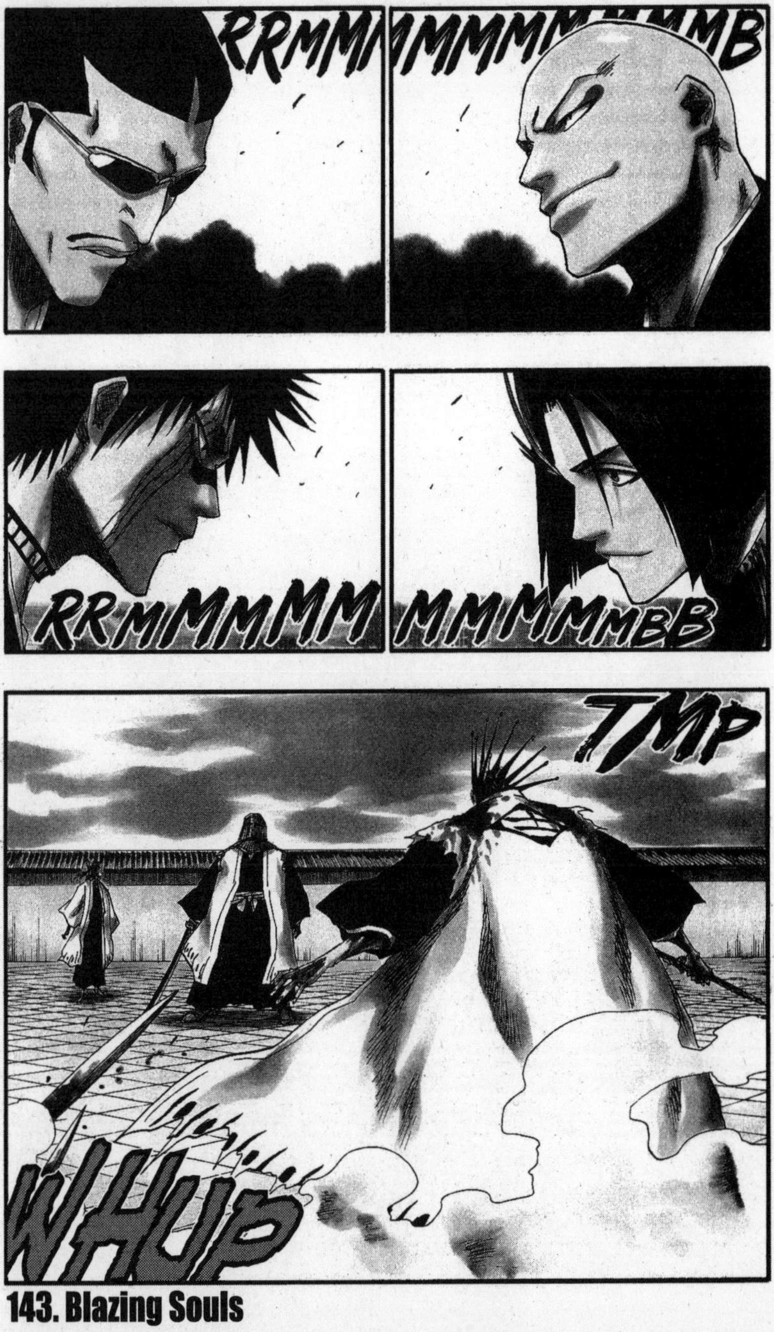
RRMMMMMMMMMMMB
RRMMMMMM
MMMMMMBB
TMP
WHUP

143. Blazing Souls

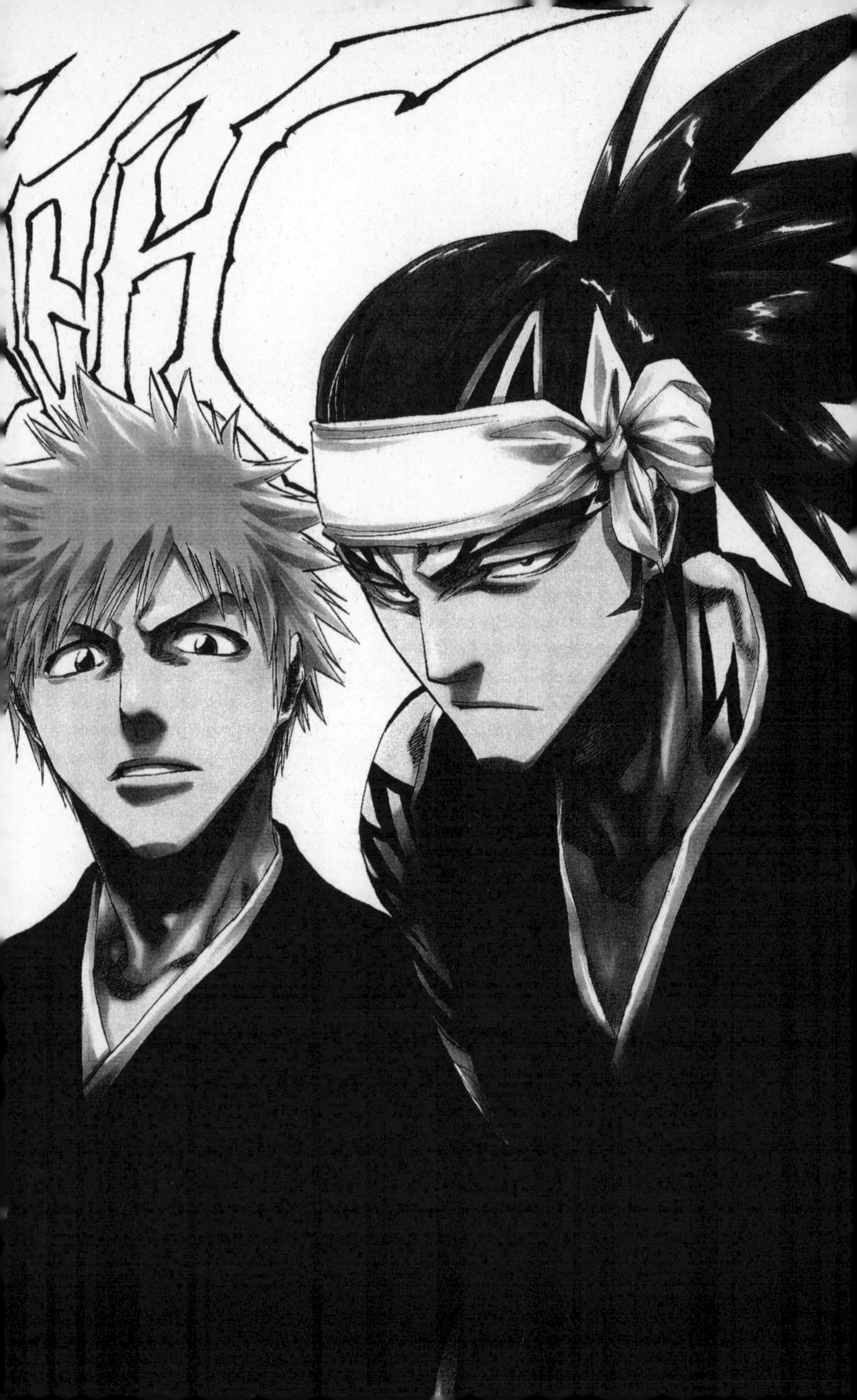

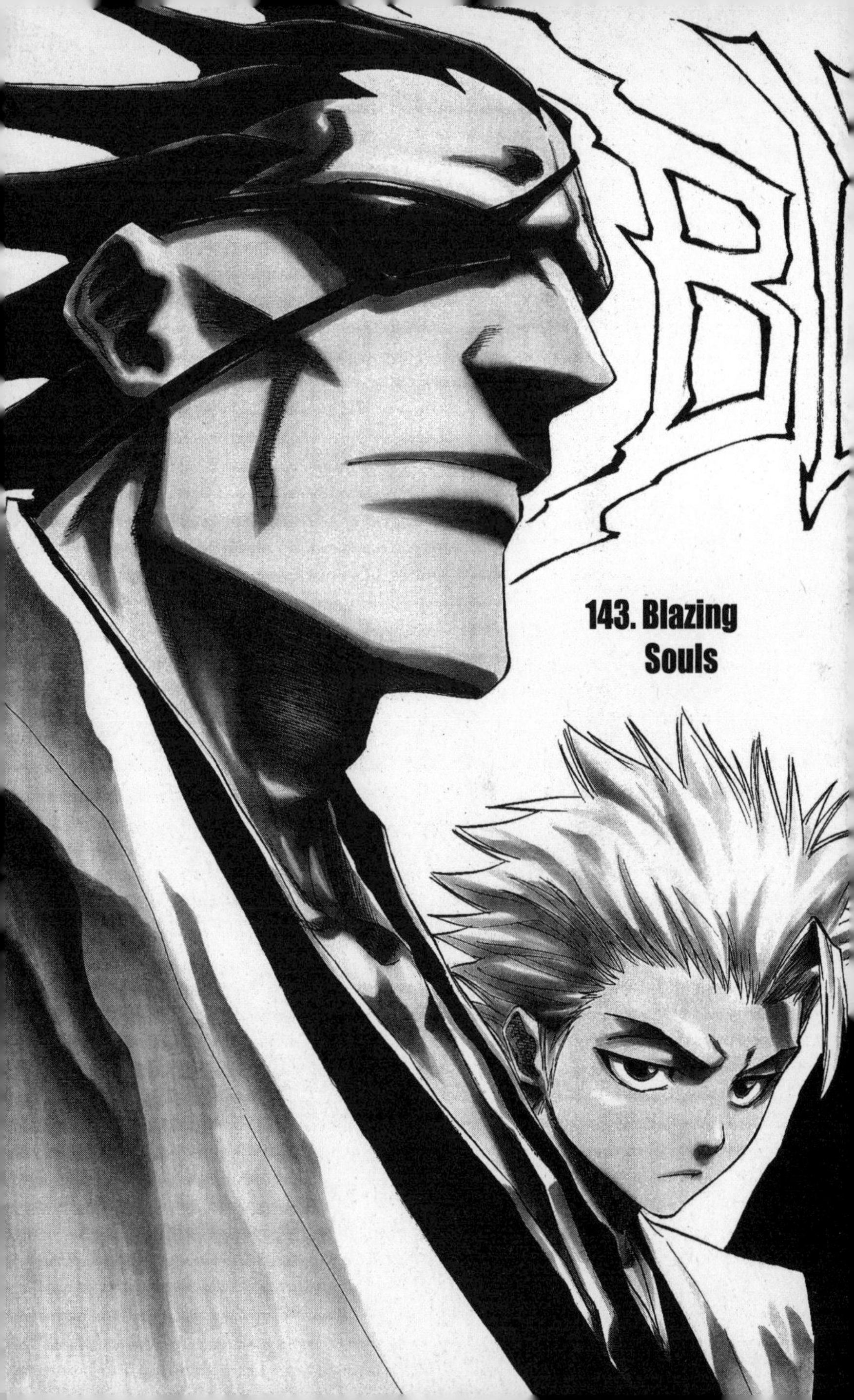
143. Blazing Souls

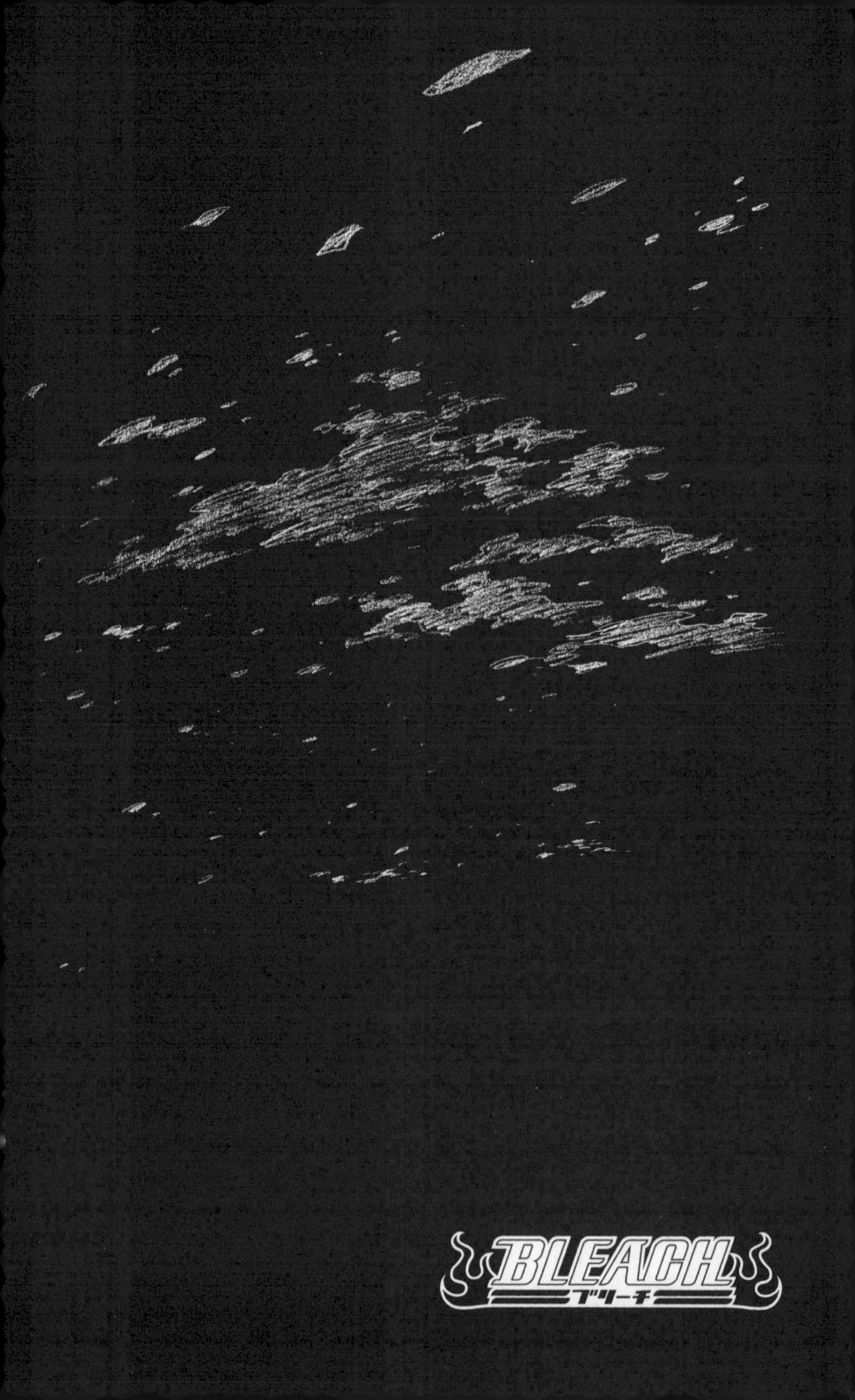
BLEACH
ブリーチ

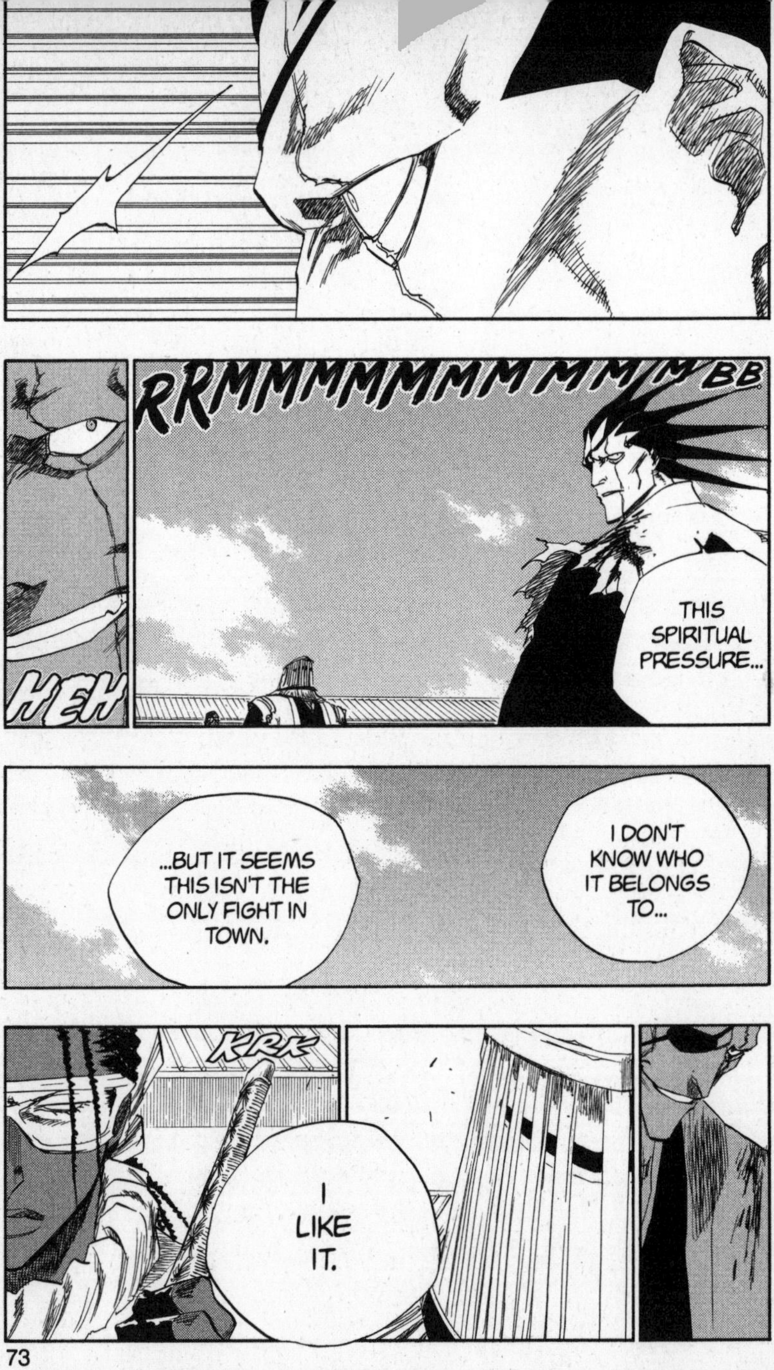
RRMMMMMMMMMMMBB
THIS SPIRITUAL PRESSURE...
HEH
I DON'T KNOW WHO IT BELONGS TO...
...BUT IT SEEMS THIS ISN'T THE ONLY FIGHT IN TOWN.
KRK
I LIKE IT.

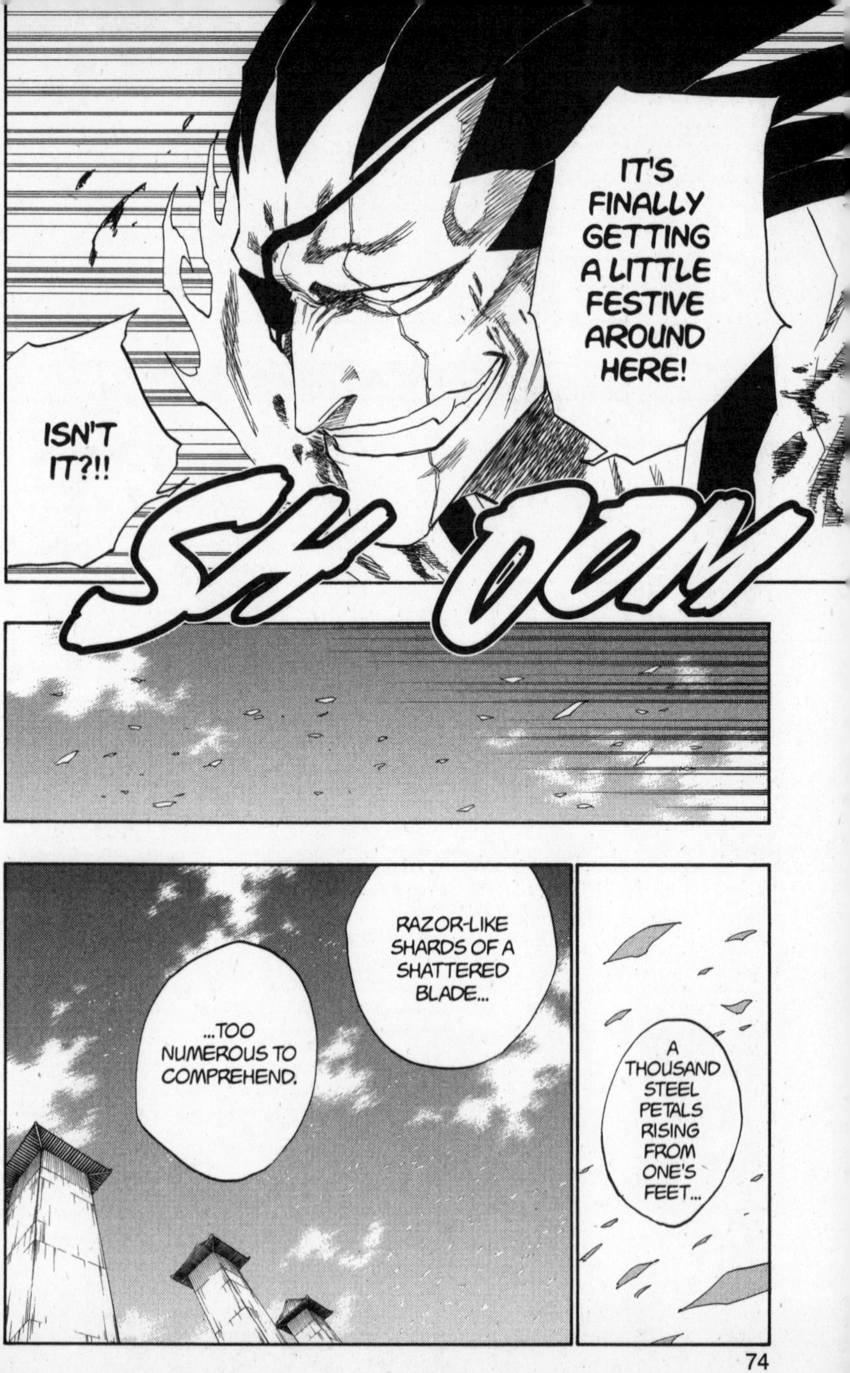
IT'S FINALLY GETTING A LITTLE FESTIVE AROUND HERE!
ISN'T IT?!!
SHOOM
A THOUSAND STEEL PETALS RISING FROM ONE'S FEET...
RAZOR-LIKE SHARDS OF A SHATTERED BLADE...
...TOO NUMEROUS TO COMPREHEND.

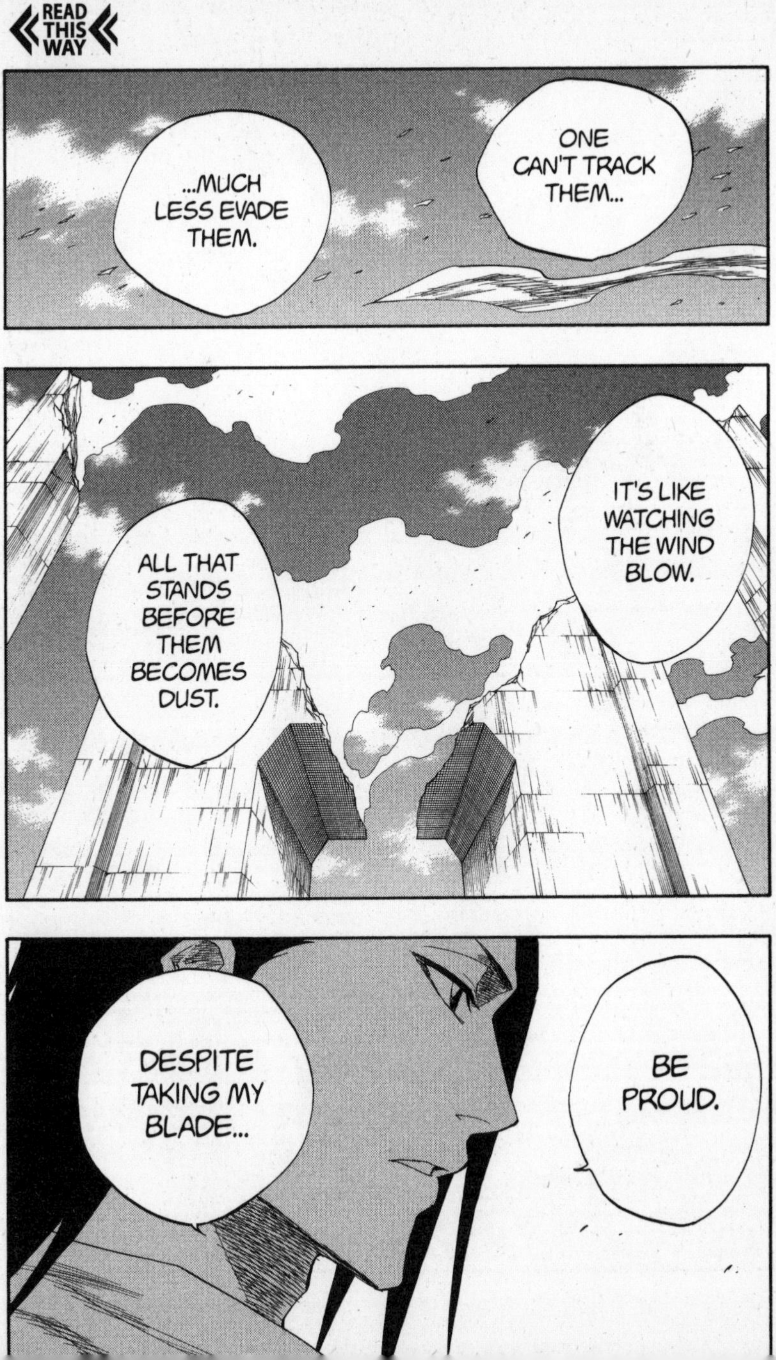
READ THIS WAY
ONE CAN'T TRACK THEM...
...MUCH LESS EVADE THEM.
IT'S LIKE WATCHING THE WIND BLOW.
ALL THAT STANDS BEFORE THEM BECOMES DUST.
BE PROUD.
DESPITE TAKING MY BLADE...

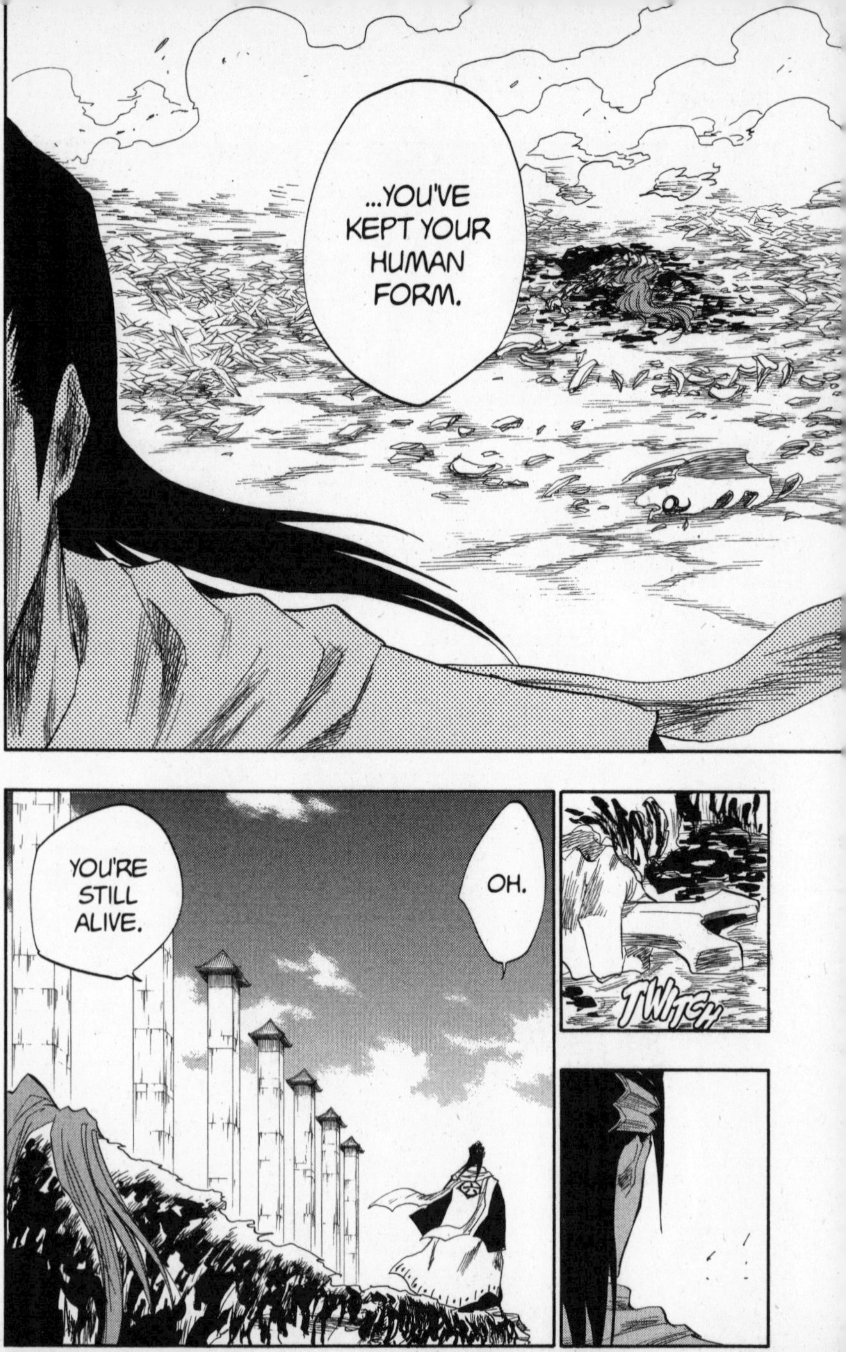
...YOU'VE KEPT YOUR HUMAN FORM.
TWITCH
OH.
YOU'RE STILL ALIVE.

READ THIS WAY

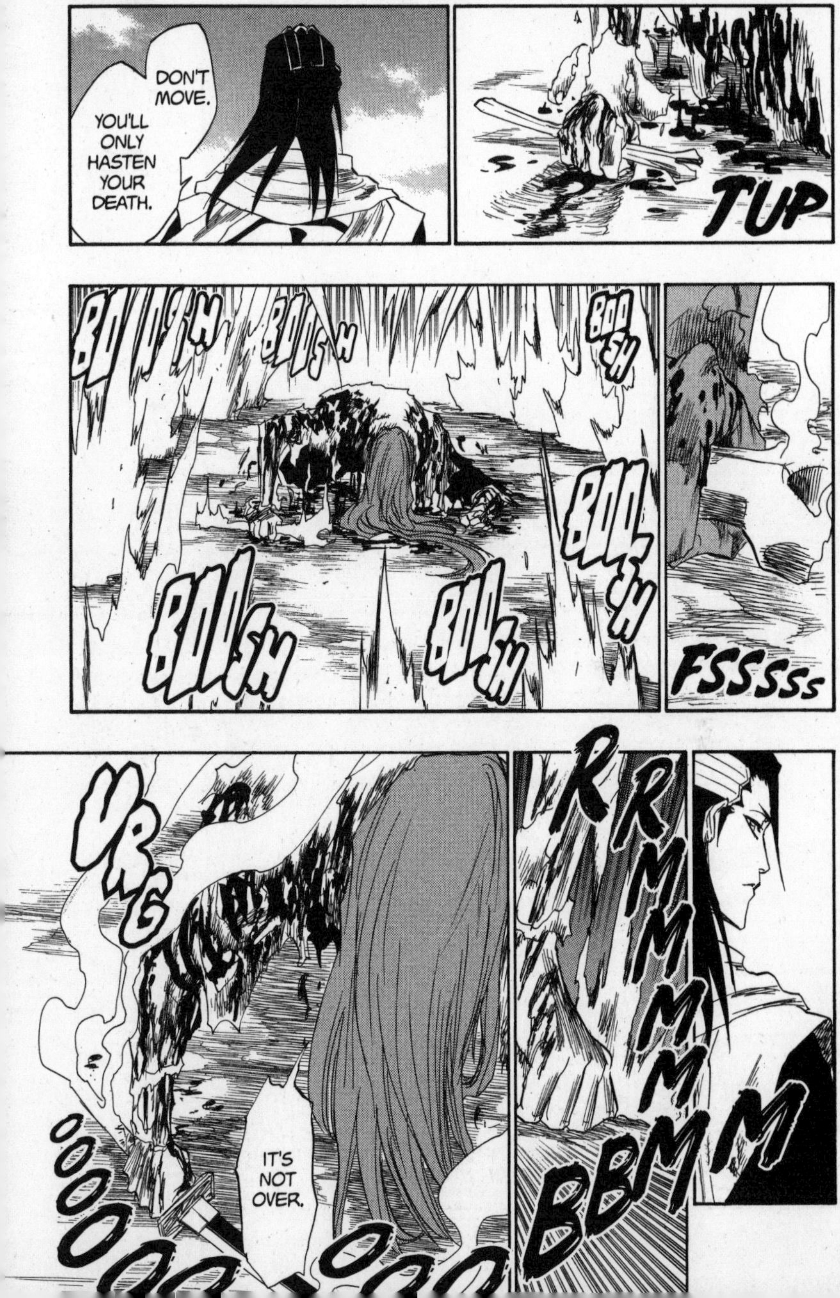
TUP
DON'T MOVE.
YOU'LL ONLY HASTEN YOUR DEATH.
FSSSSS
BOOSH
BOOSH
BOOSH
BOOSH
BOOSH
BOOSH
RRMMMMMM
BBMM
URG
IT'S NOT OVER.
OOOOOOOOO

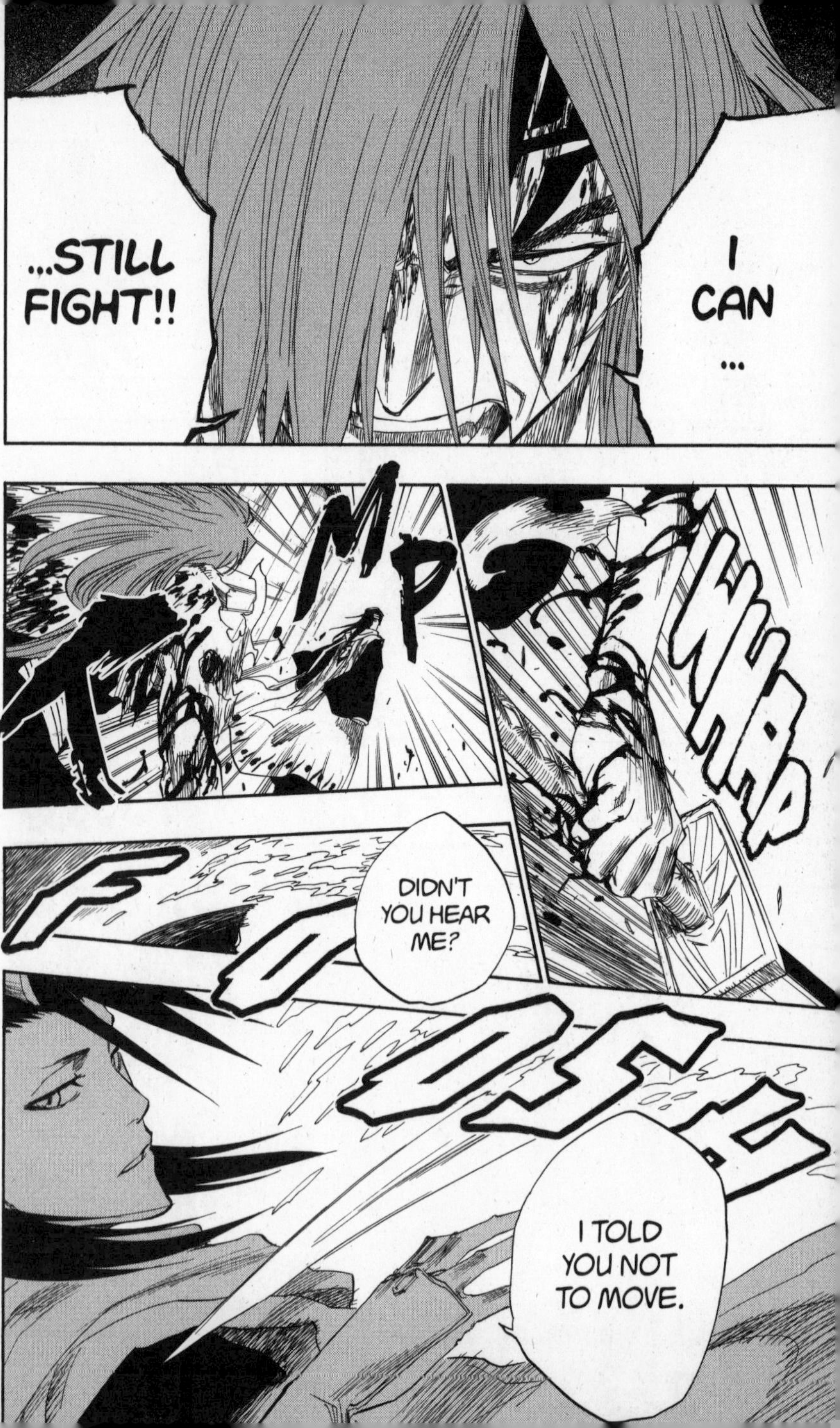
I CAN ...
...STILL FIGHT!!
WHAP
DIDN'T YOU HEAR ME?
I TOLD YOU NOT TO MOVE.

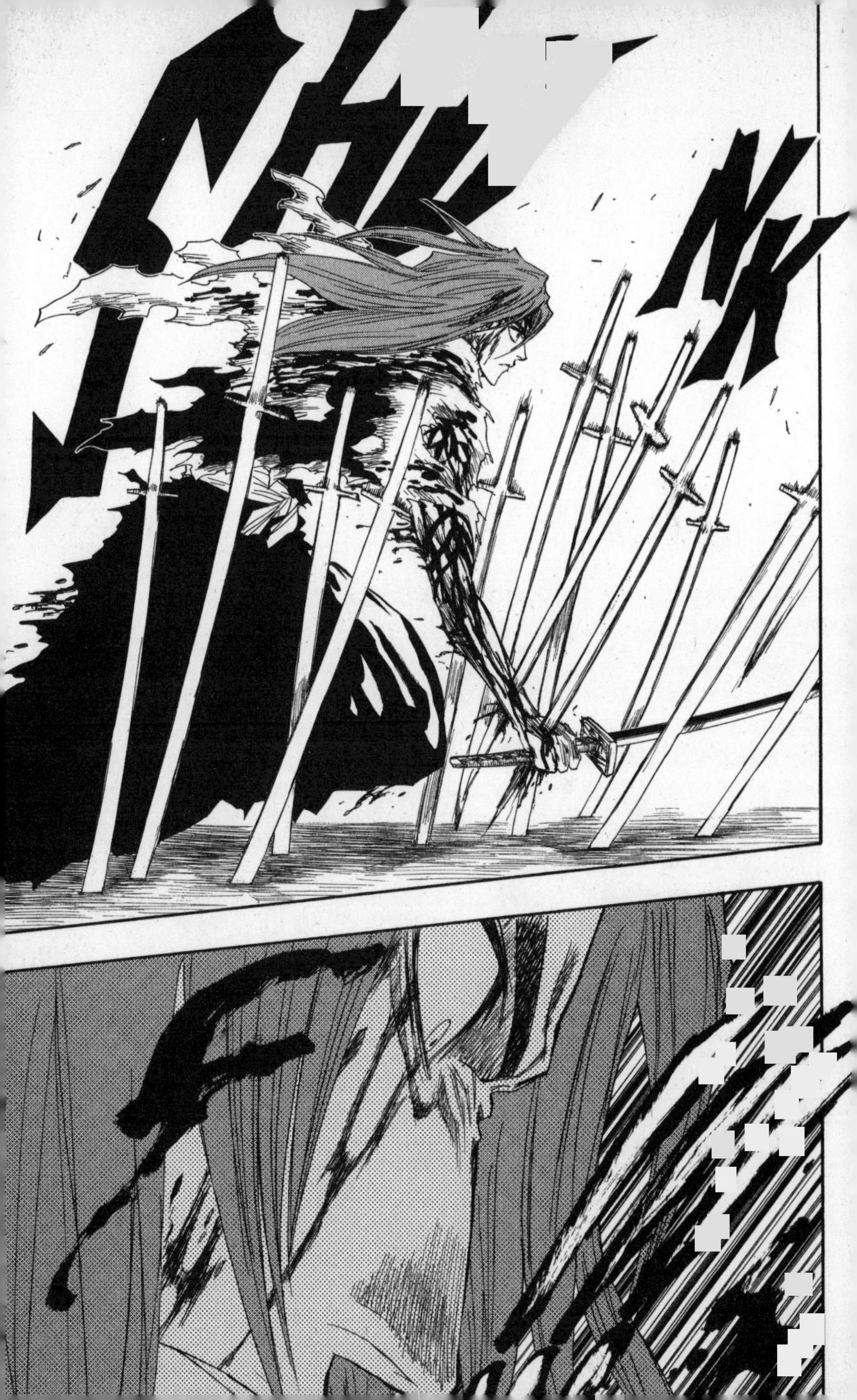

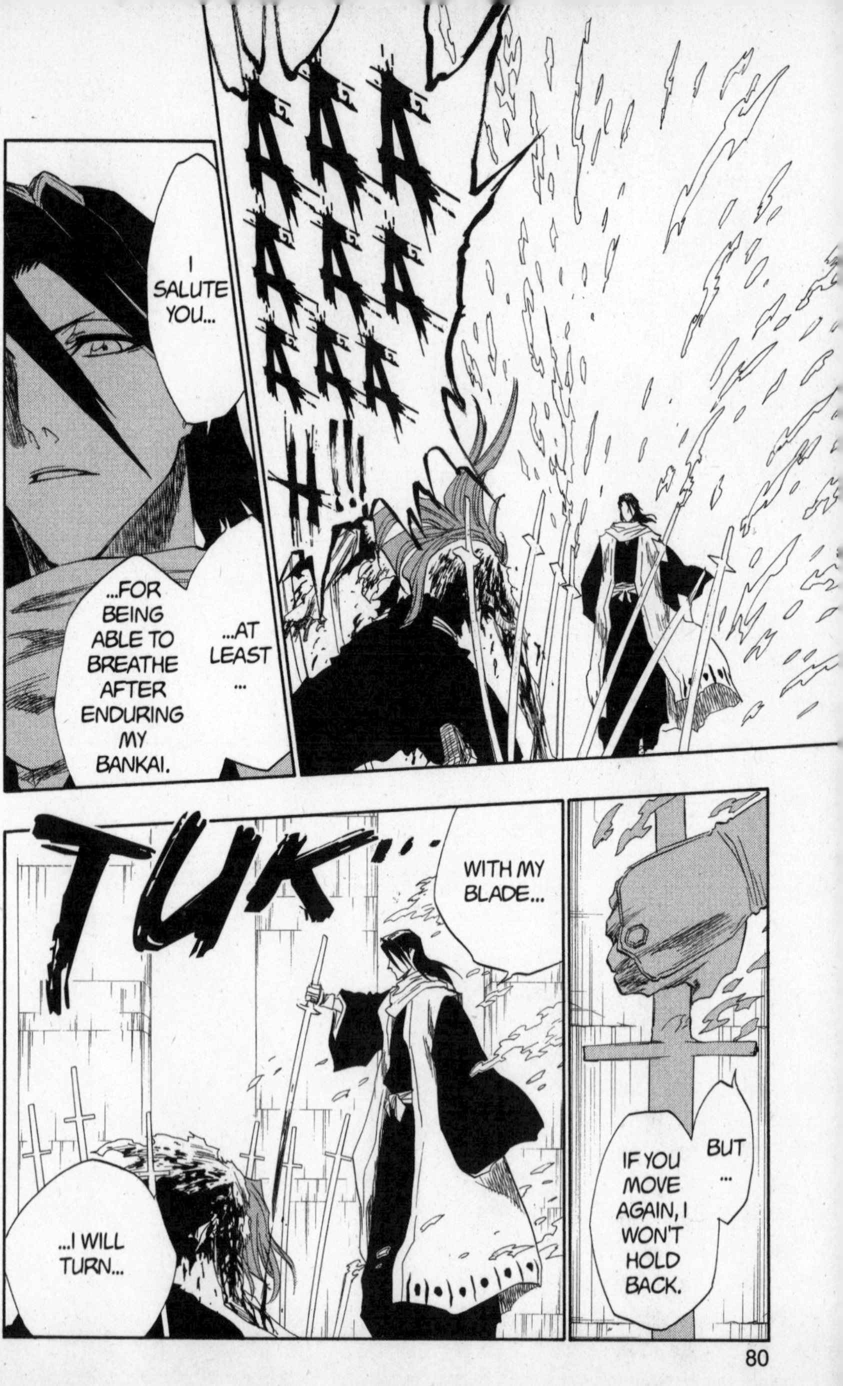
AAAAAAAAAH!!!
I SALUTE YOU...
...AT LEAST...
...FOR BEING ABLE TO BREATHE AFTER ENDURING MY BANKAI.
BUT...
IF YOU MOVE AGAIN, I WON'T HOLD BACK.
WITH MY BLADE...
TUK...
...I WILL TURN...

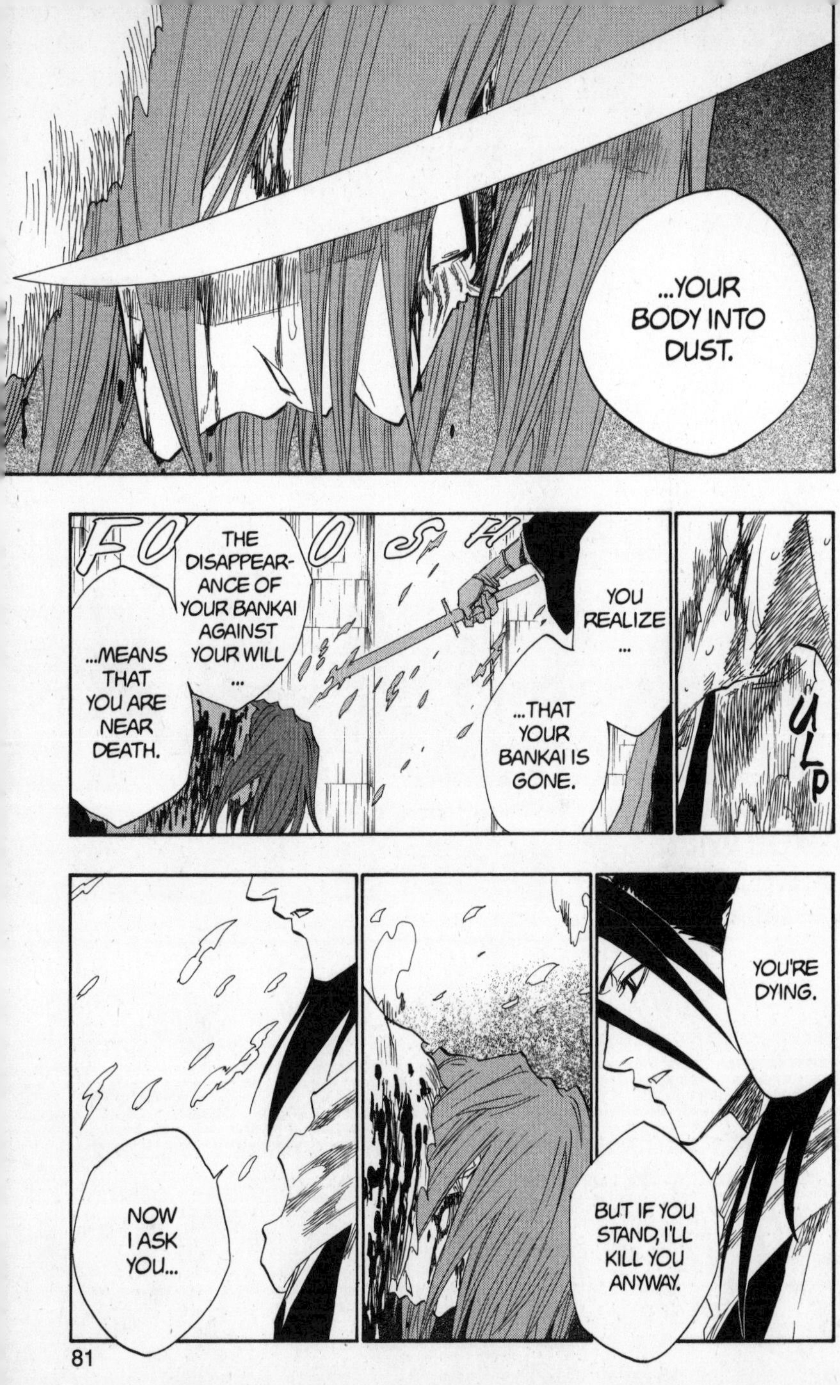
...YOUR BODY INTO DUST.
ULP
YOU REALIZE ...
...THAT YOUR BANKAI IS GONE.
FOOSH
THE DISAPPEARANCE OF YOUR BANKAI AGAINST YOUR WILL ...
...MEANS THAT YOU ARE NEAR DEATH.
YOU'RE DYING.
BUT IF YOU STAND, I'LL KILL YOU ANYWAY.
NOW I ASK YOU...

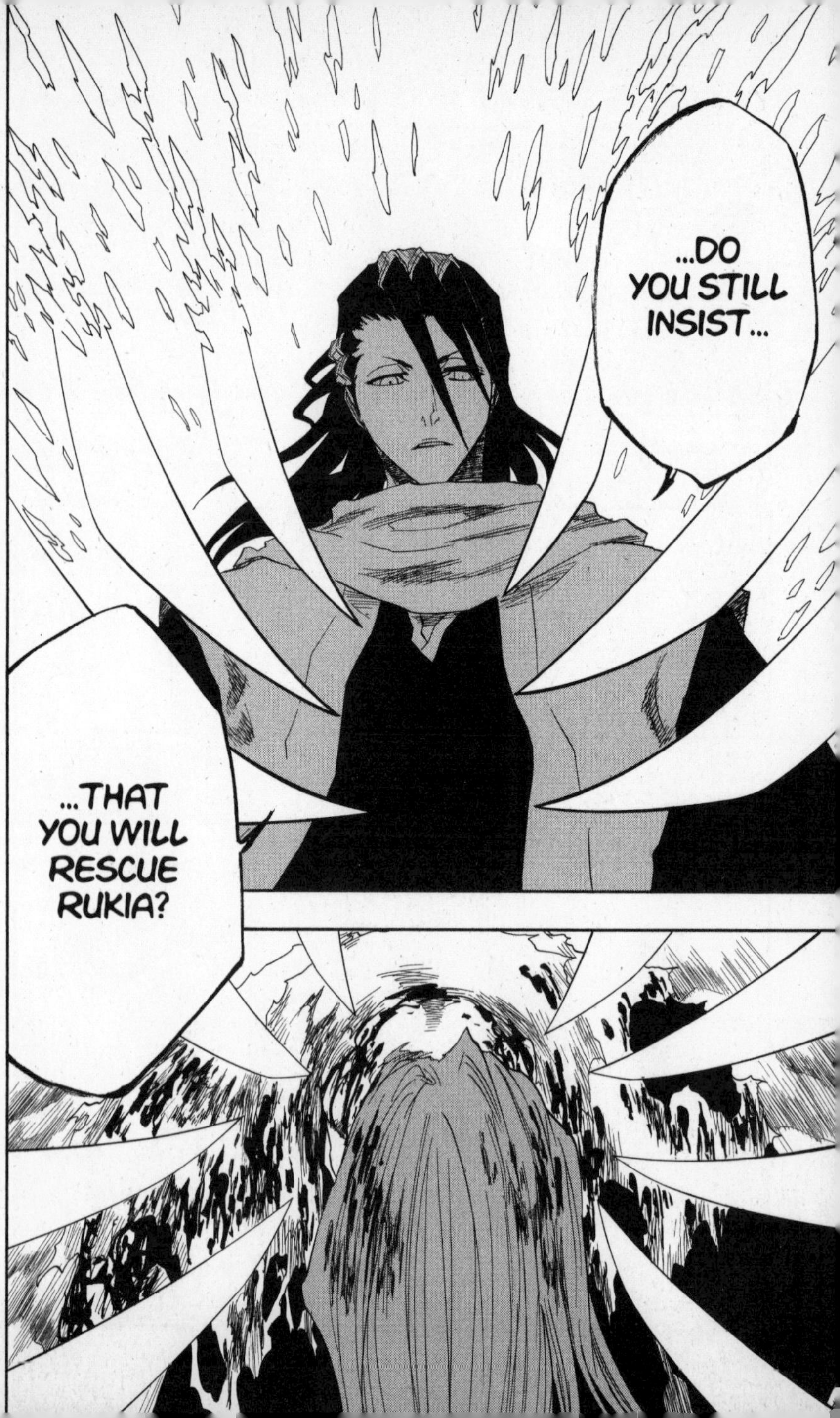
...DO YOU STILL INSIST...
...THAT YOU WILL RESCUE RUKIA?

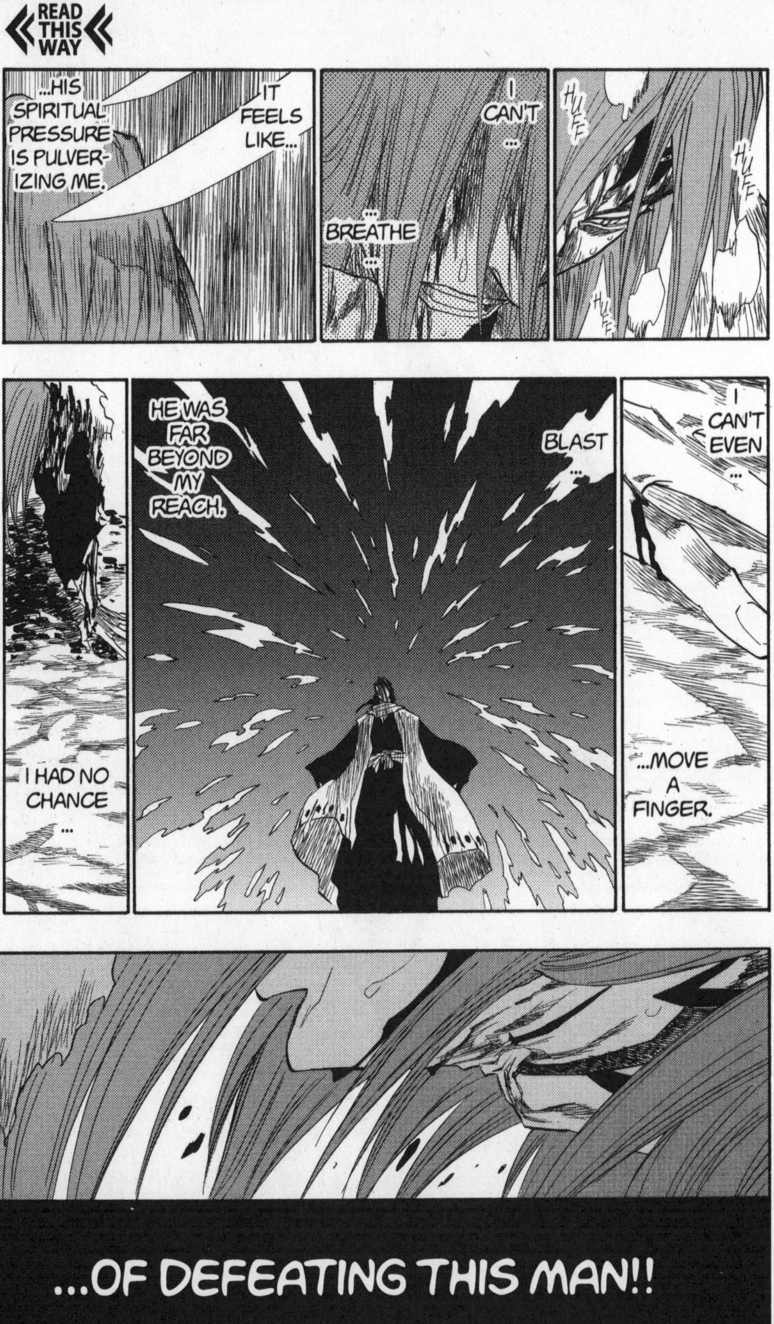
READ THIS WAY
HUFF
HUFF
HUFF
I CAN'T ...
... BREATHE ...
IT FEELS LIKE...
...HIS SPIRITUAL PRESSURE IS PULVER-IZING ME.
I CAN'T EVEN ...
...MOVE A FINGER.
BLAST ...
HE WAS FAR BEYOND MY REACH.
I HAD NO CHANCE ...
...OF DEFEATING THIS MAN!!

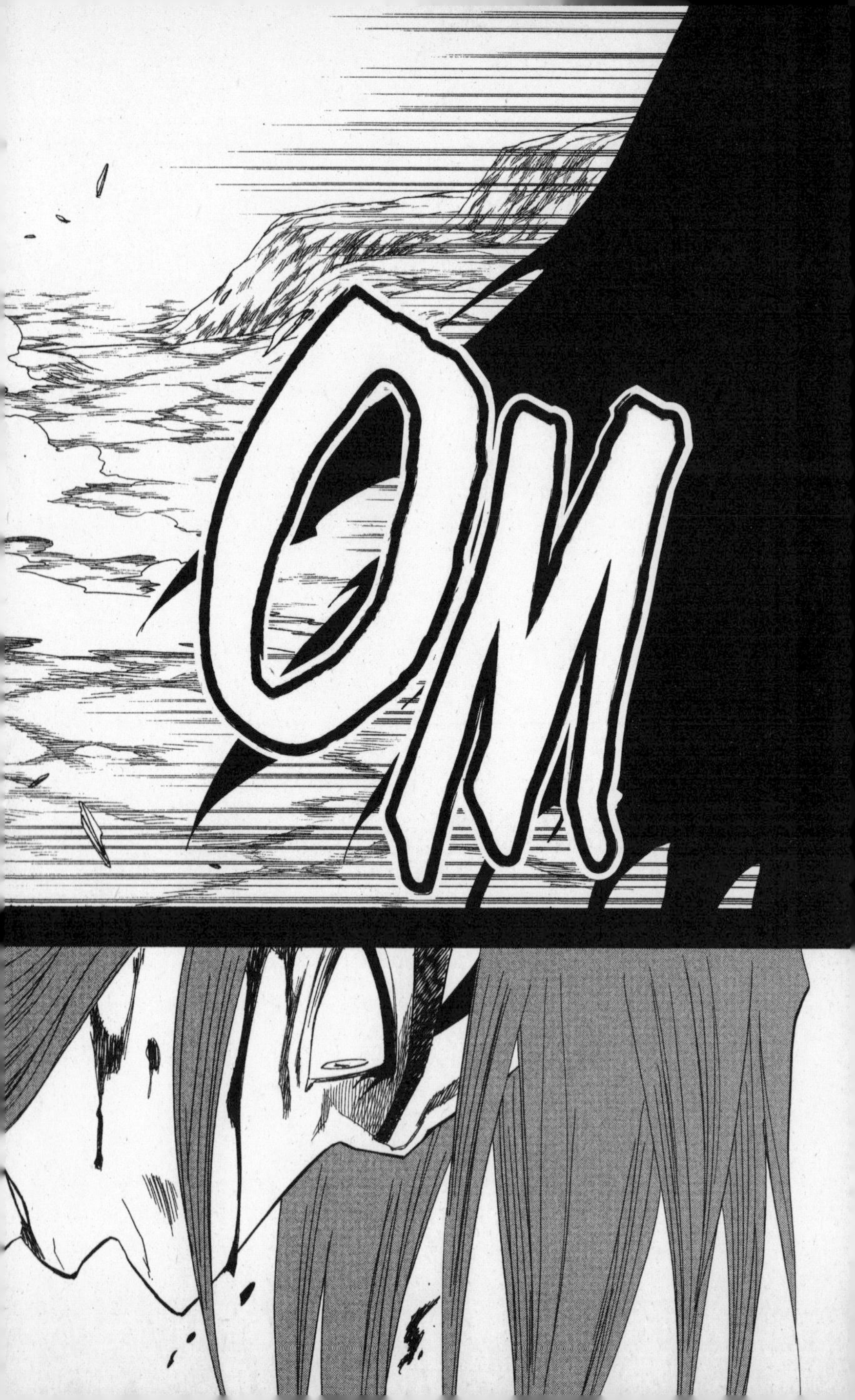
OM

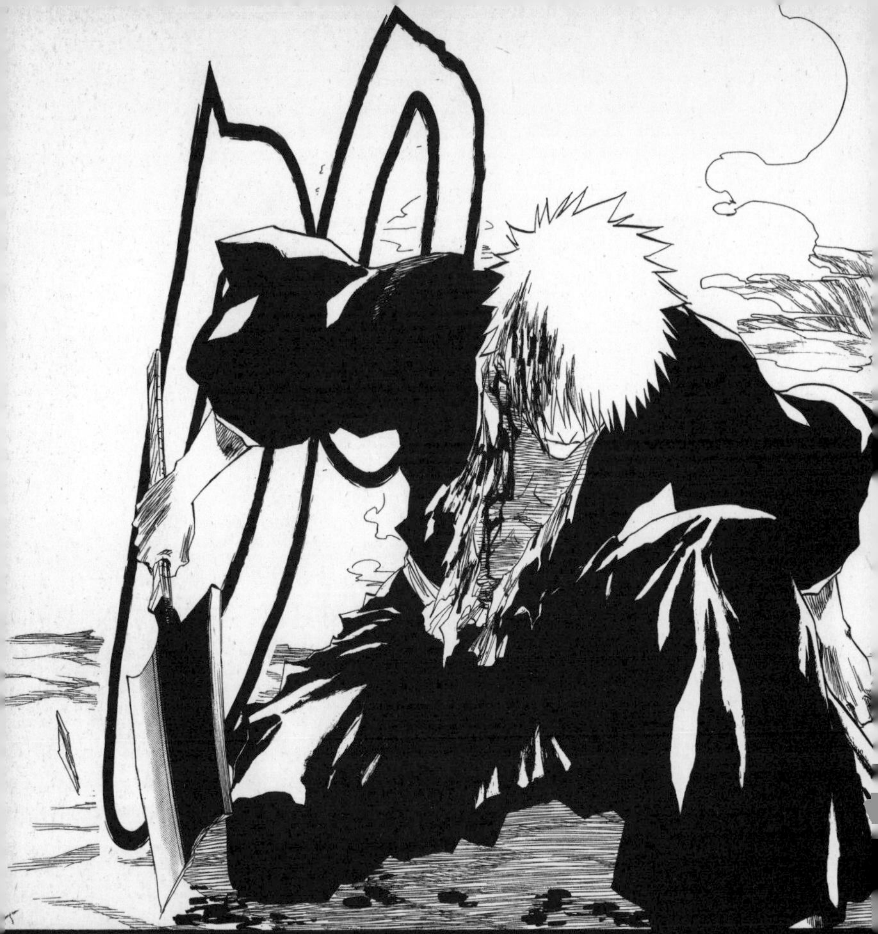
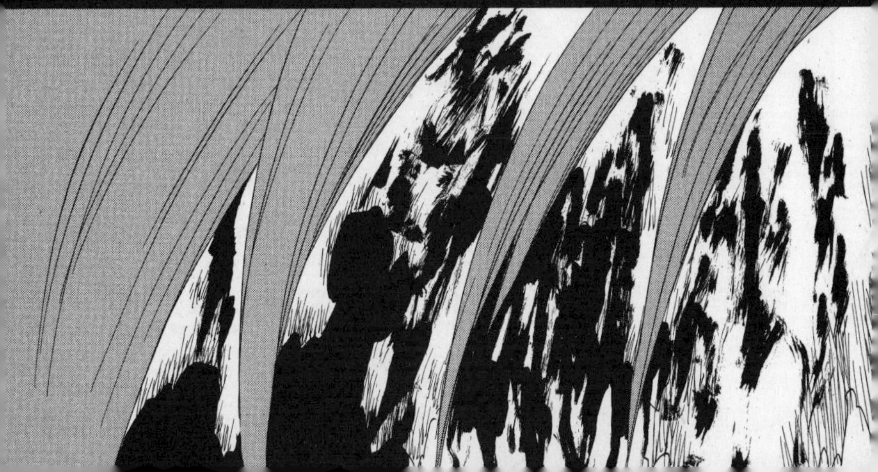

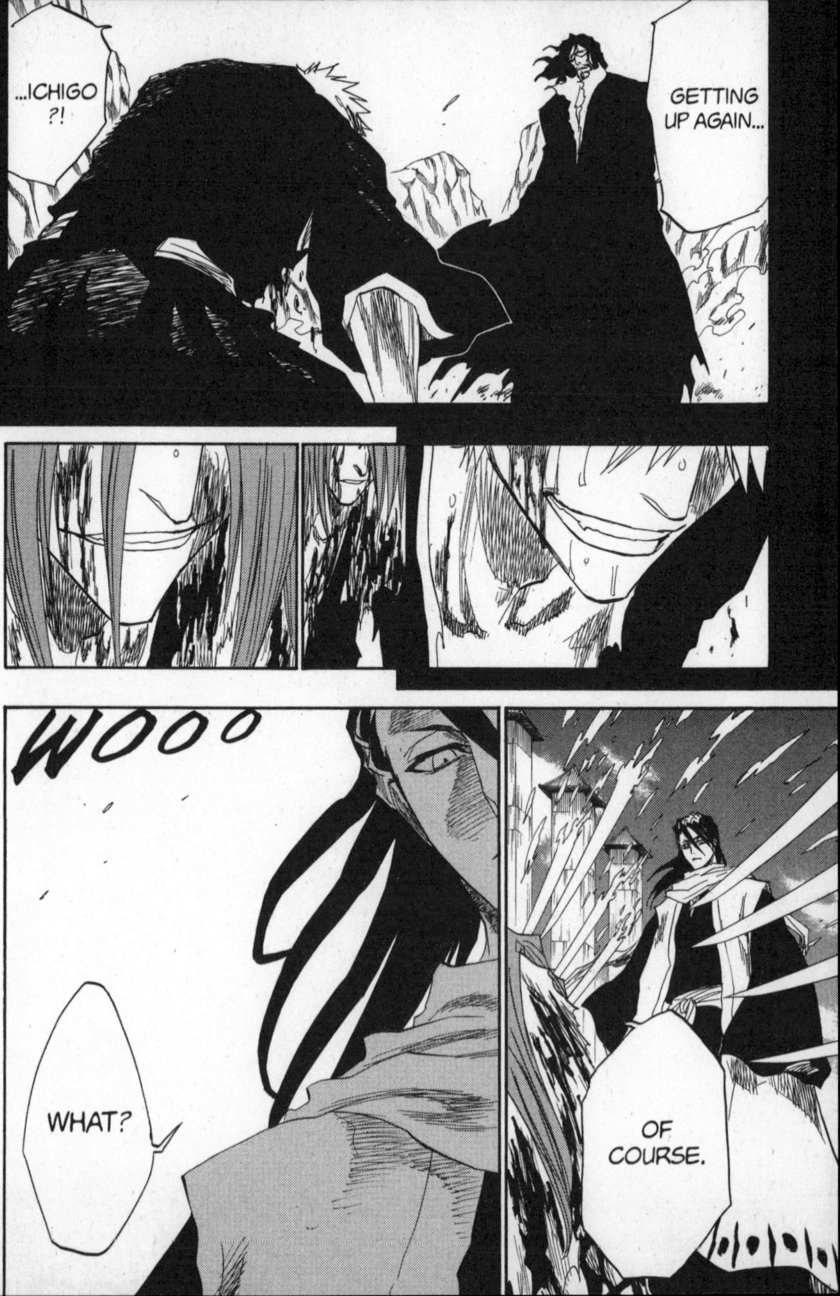
GETTING UP AGAIN...
...ICHIGO ?!
OF COURSE.
WOOO
WHAT?

READ THIS WAY

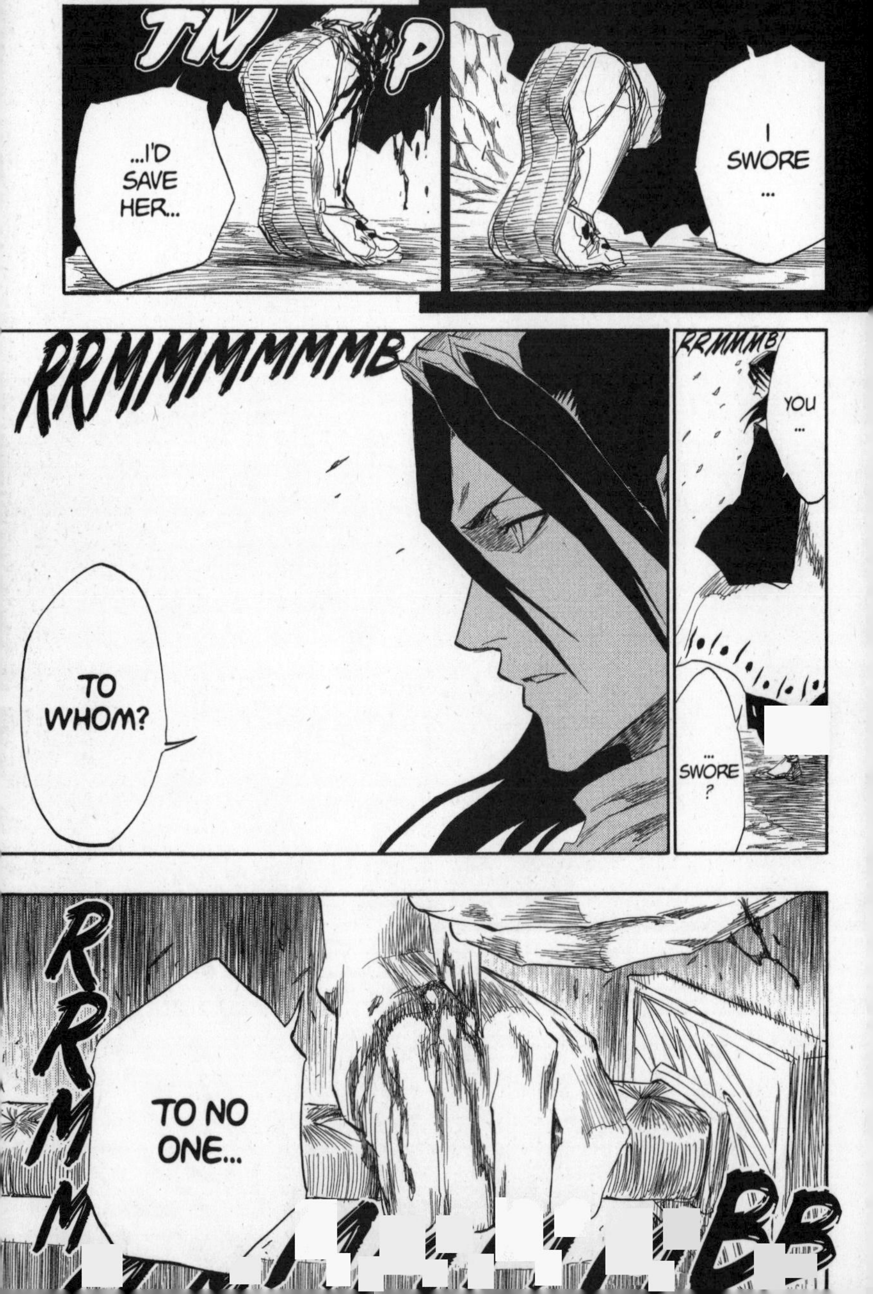
I SWORE ...
...I'D SAVE HER...
RRMMMB
YOU ...
... SWORE ?
RRMMMMMMB
TO WHOM?
TO NO ONE...

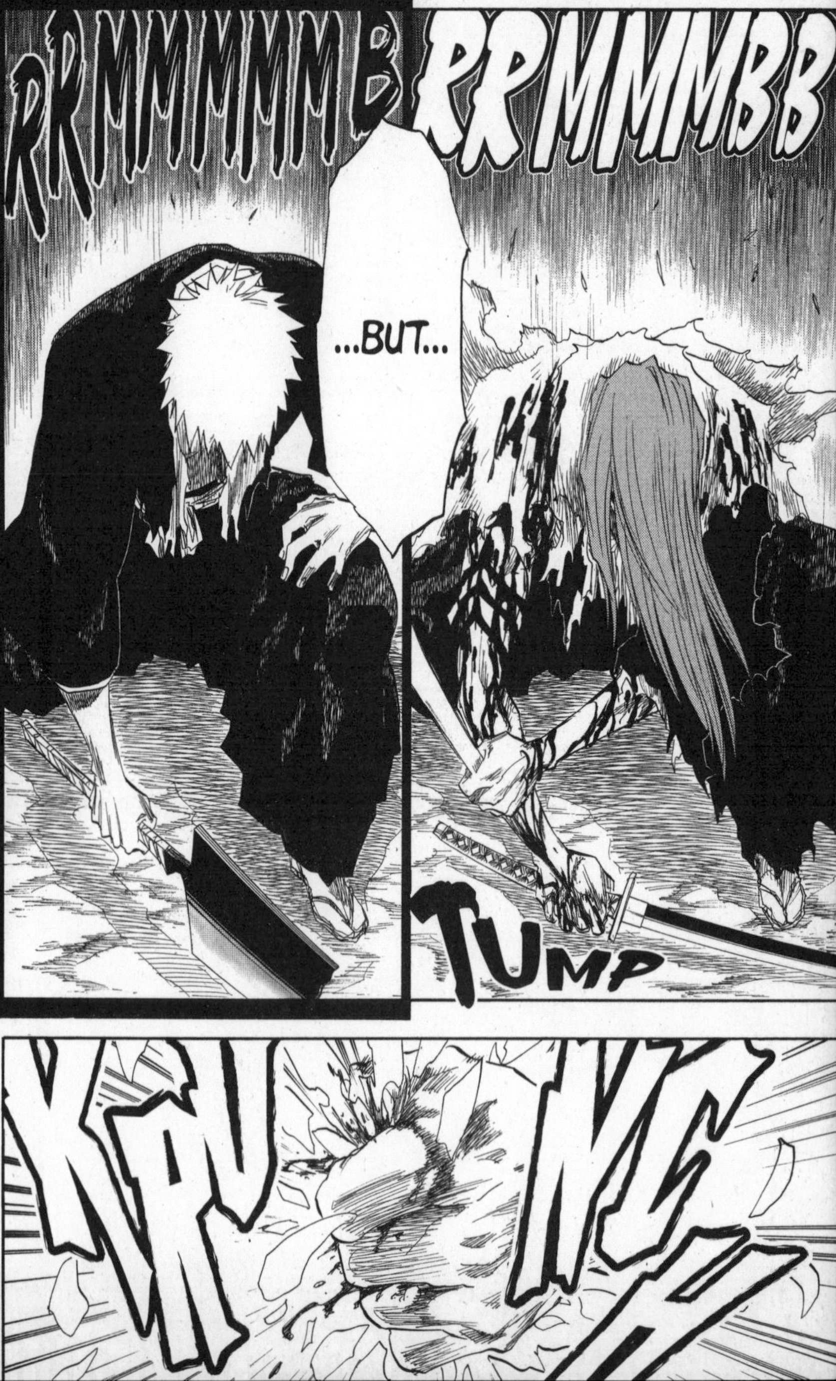
RRMMMBB
TUMP
...BUT...
RRMMMMB

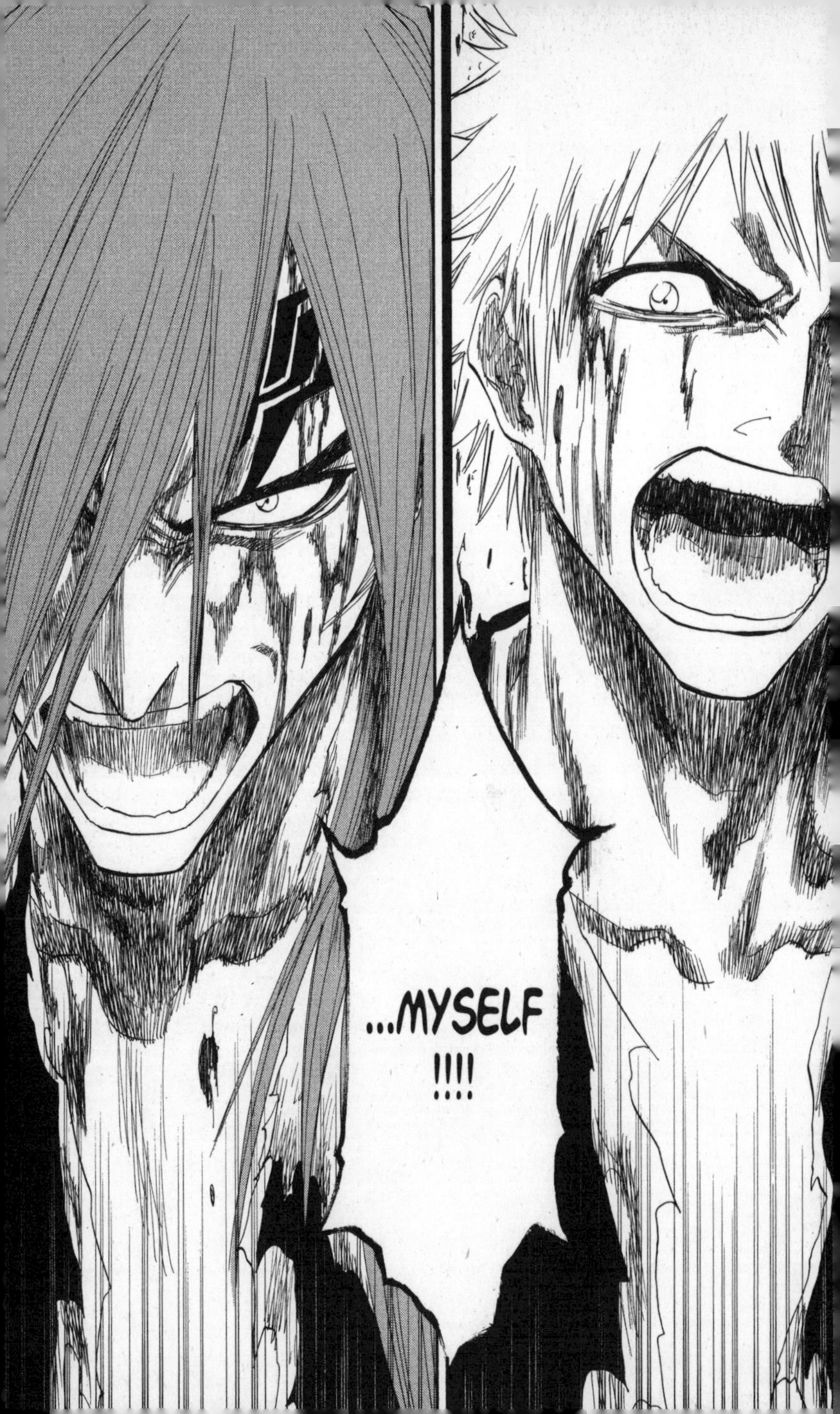
...MYSELF
!!!!

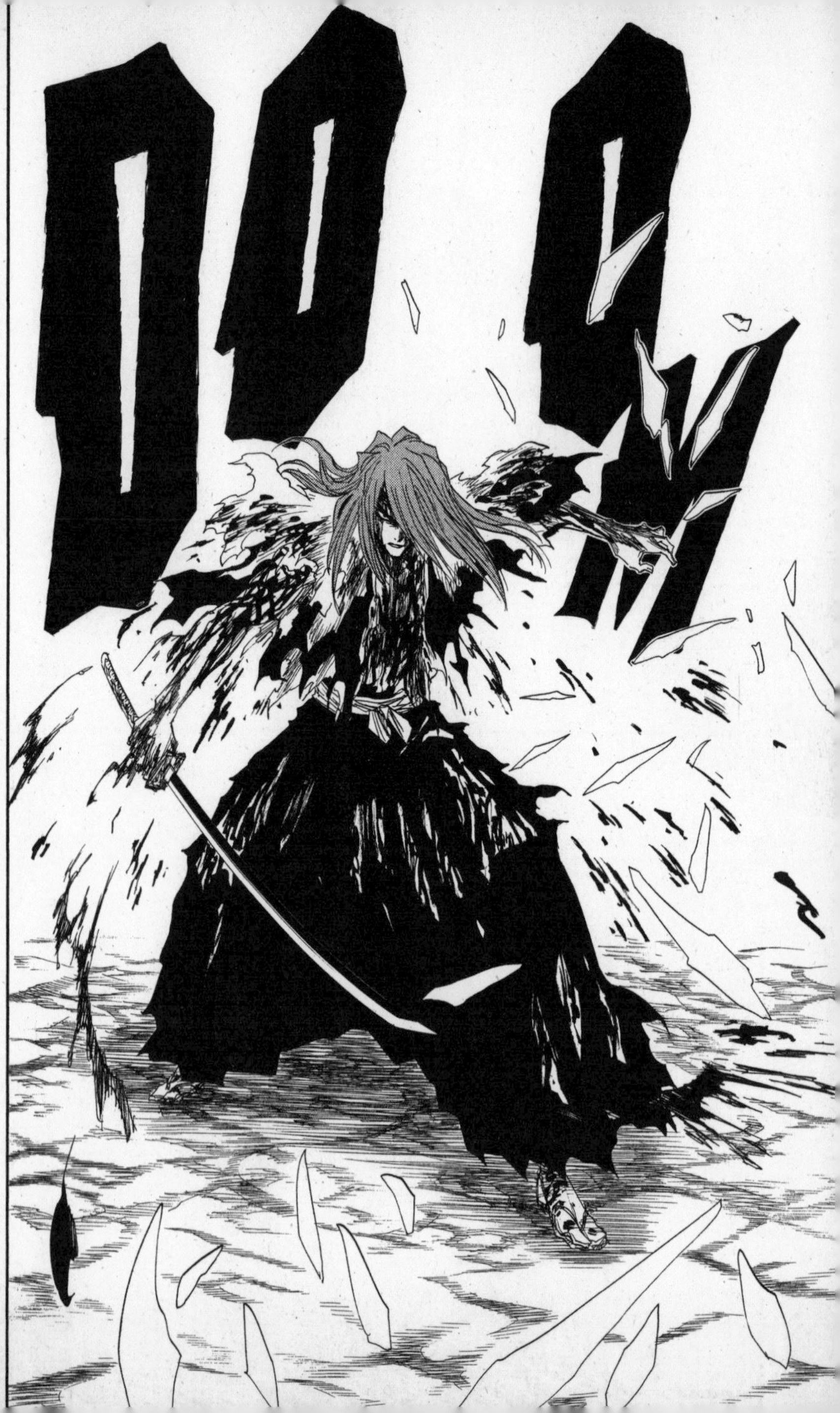
DOOM

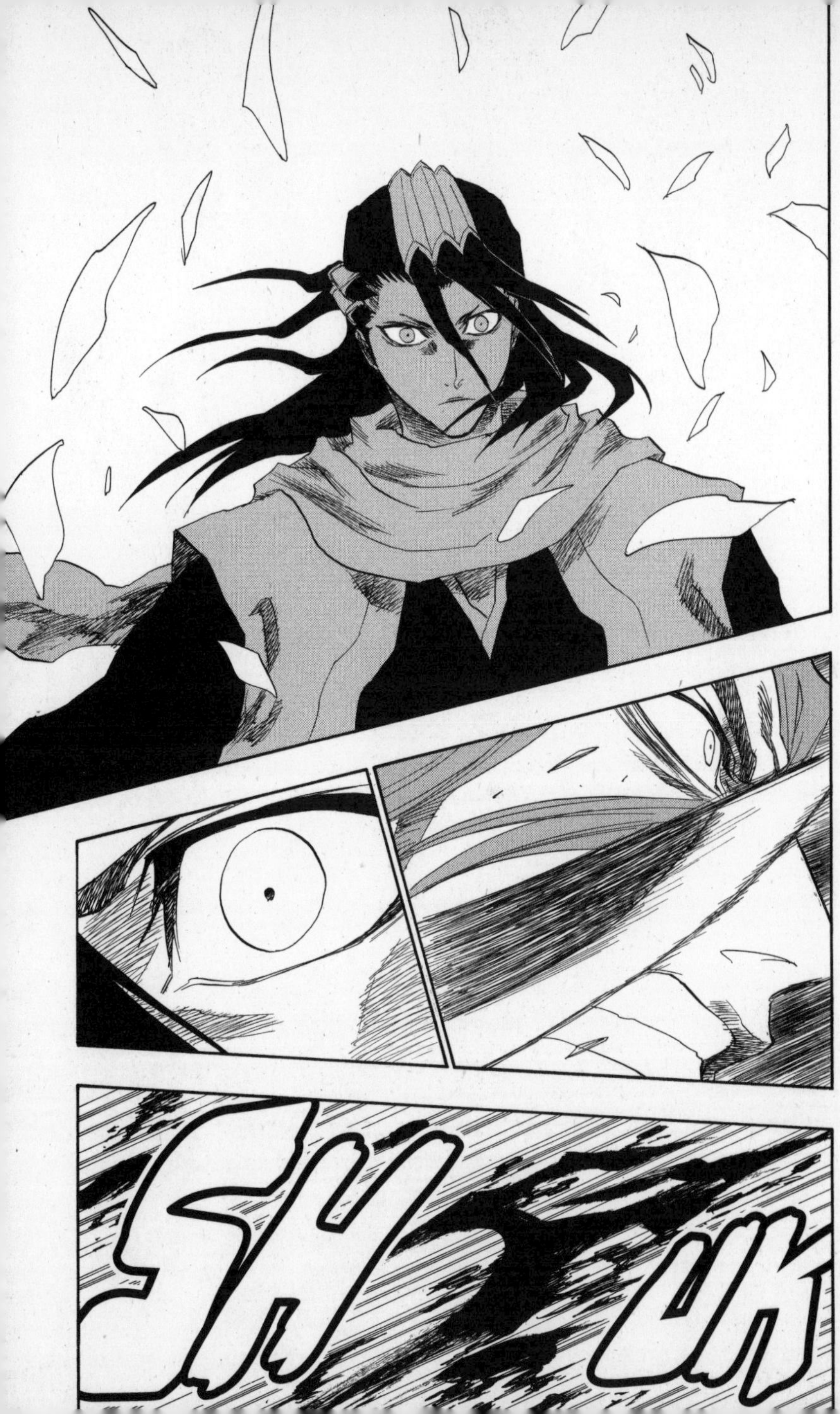

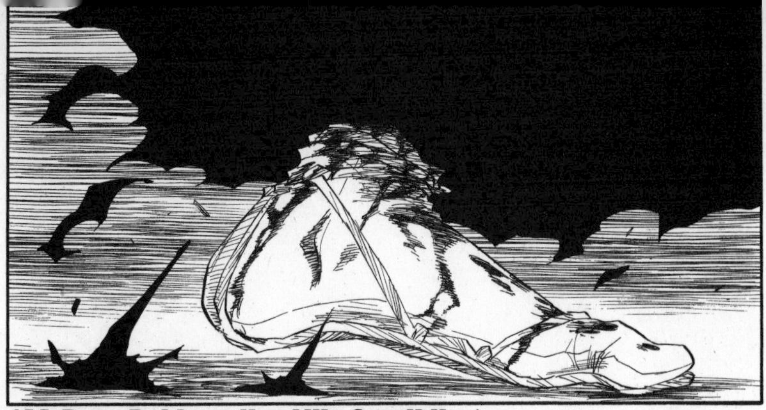

144. Rosa Rubicundior, Lilio Candidior*

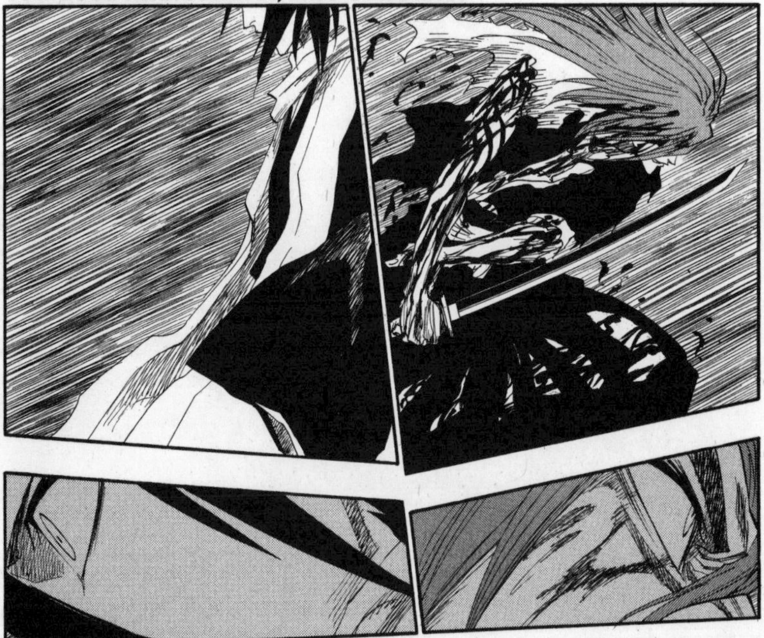

*LATIN FOR "REDDER THAN THE ROSE, WHITER THAN THE LILY"

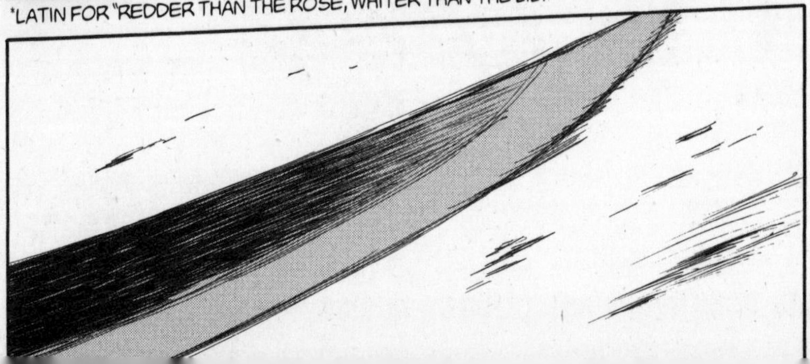

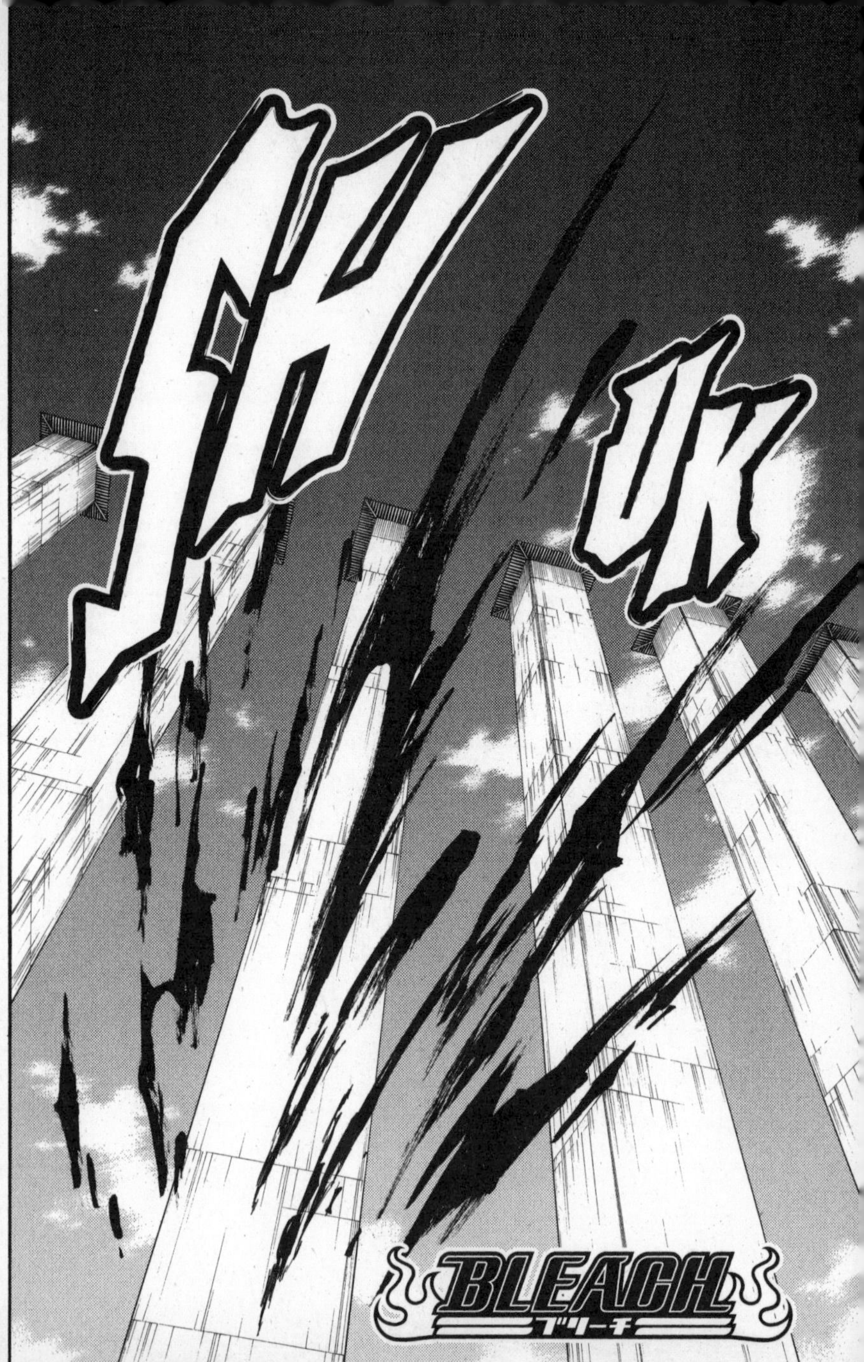
SHUK
BLEACH
ブリーチ

144. Rosa Rubicundior, Lilio Candidior

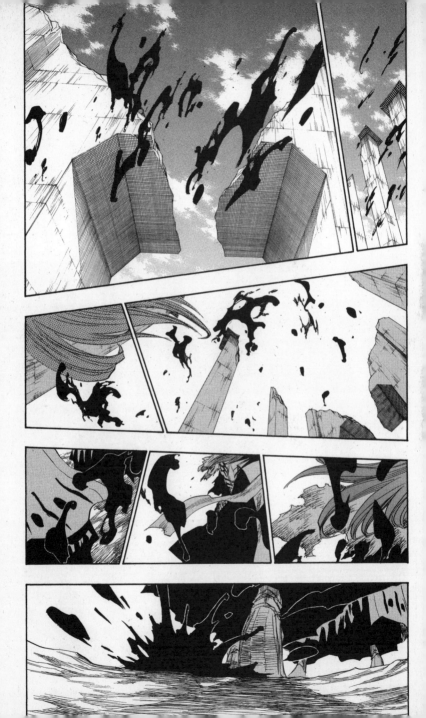

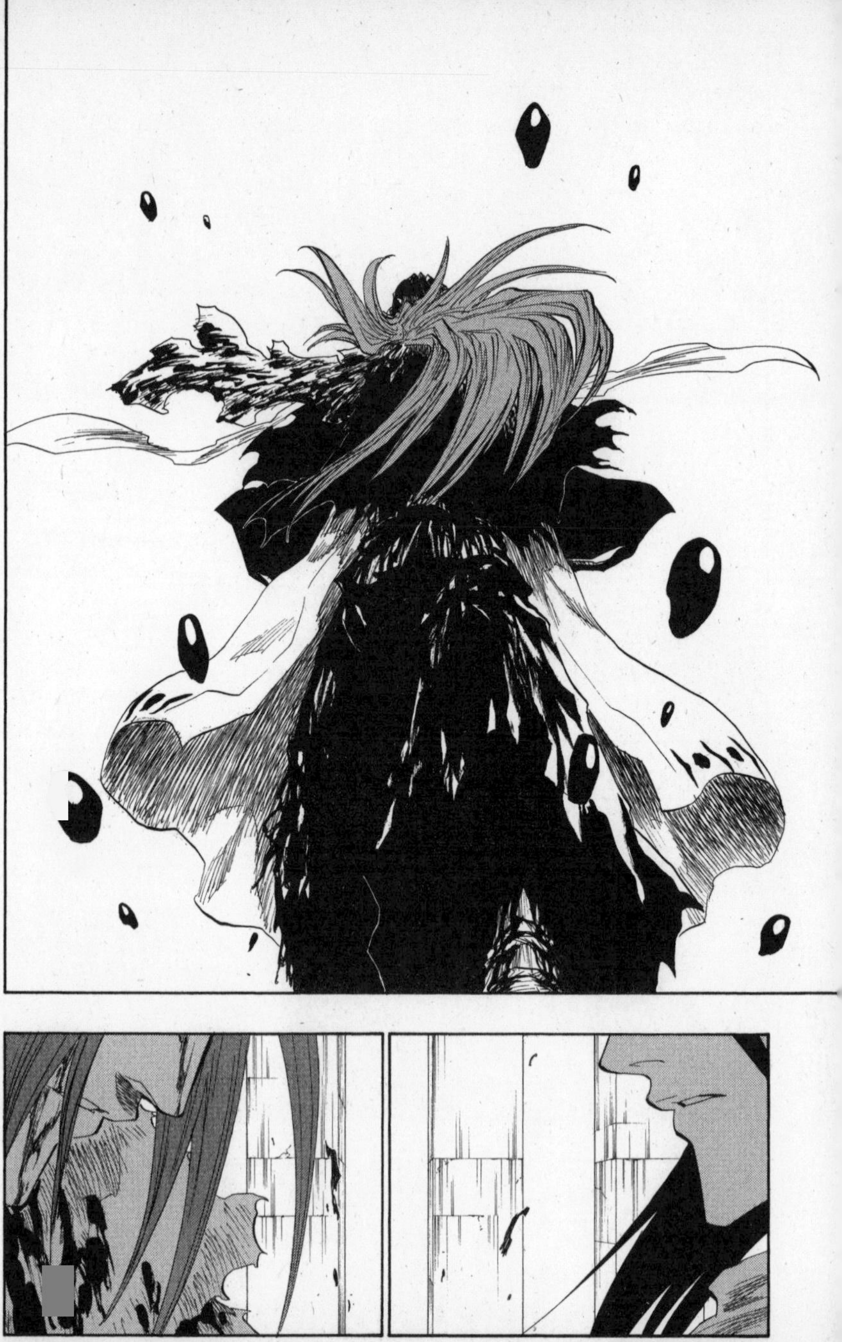

READ THIS WAY

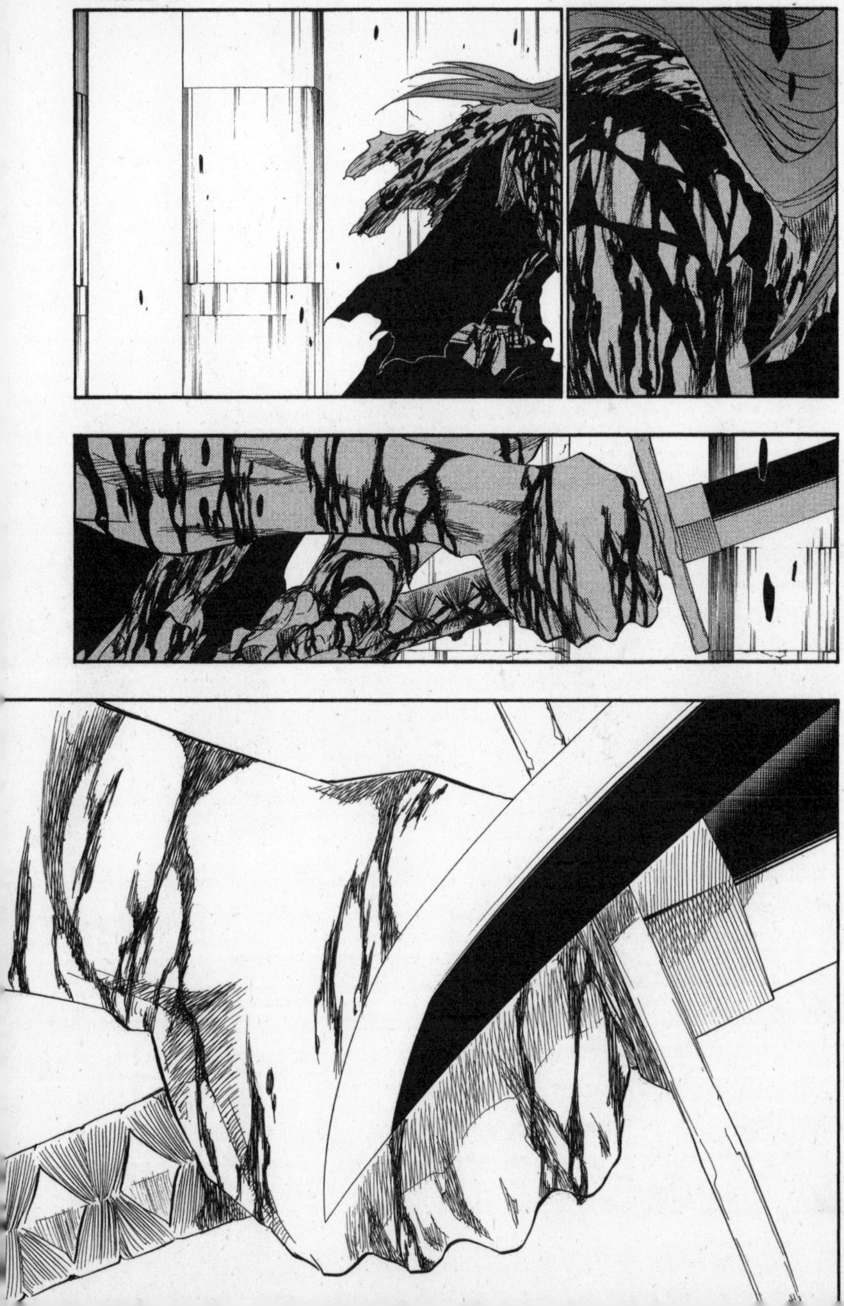

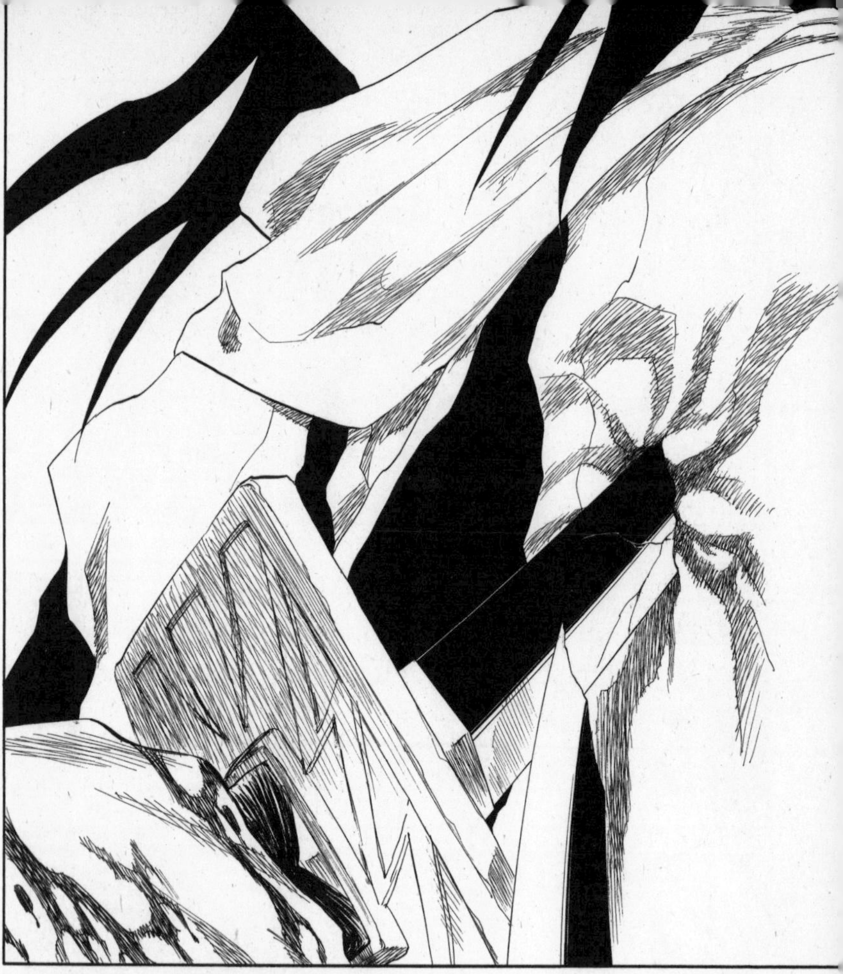

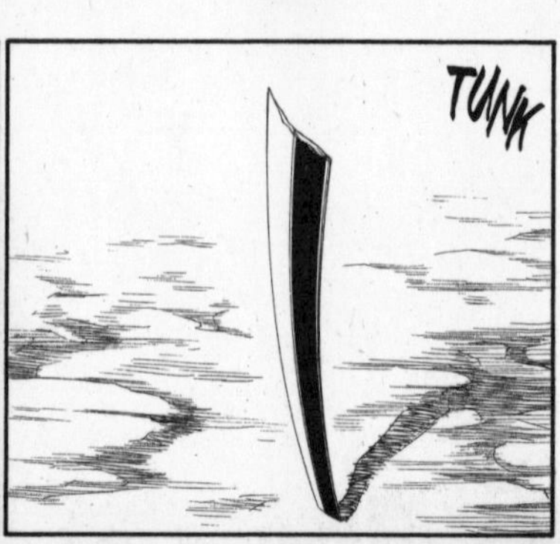
TUNK

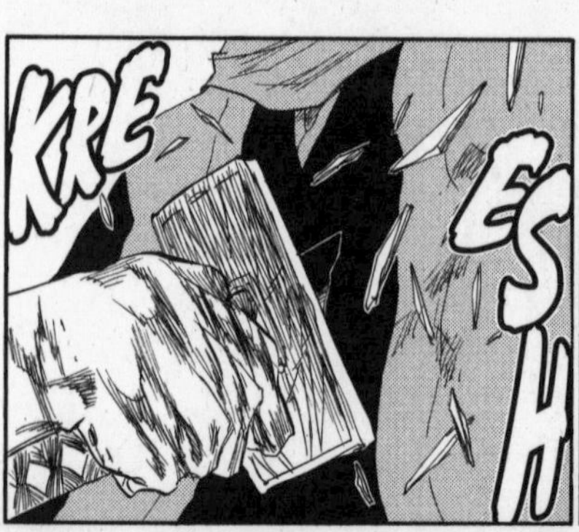
KREESH

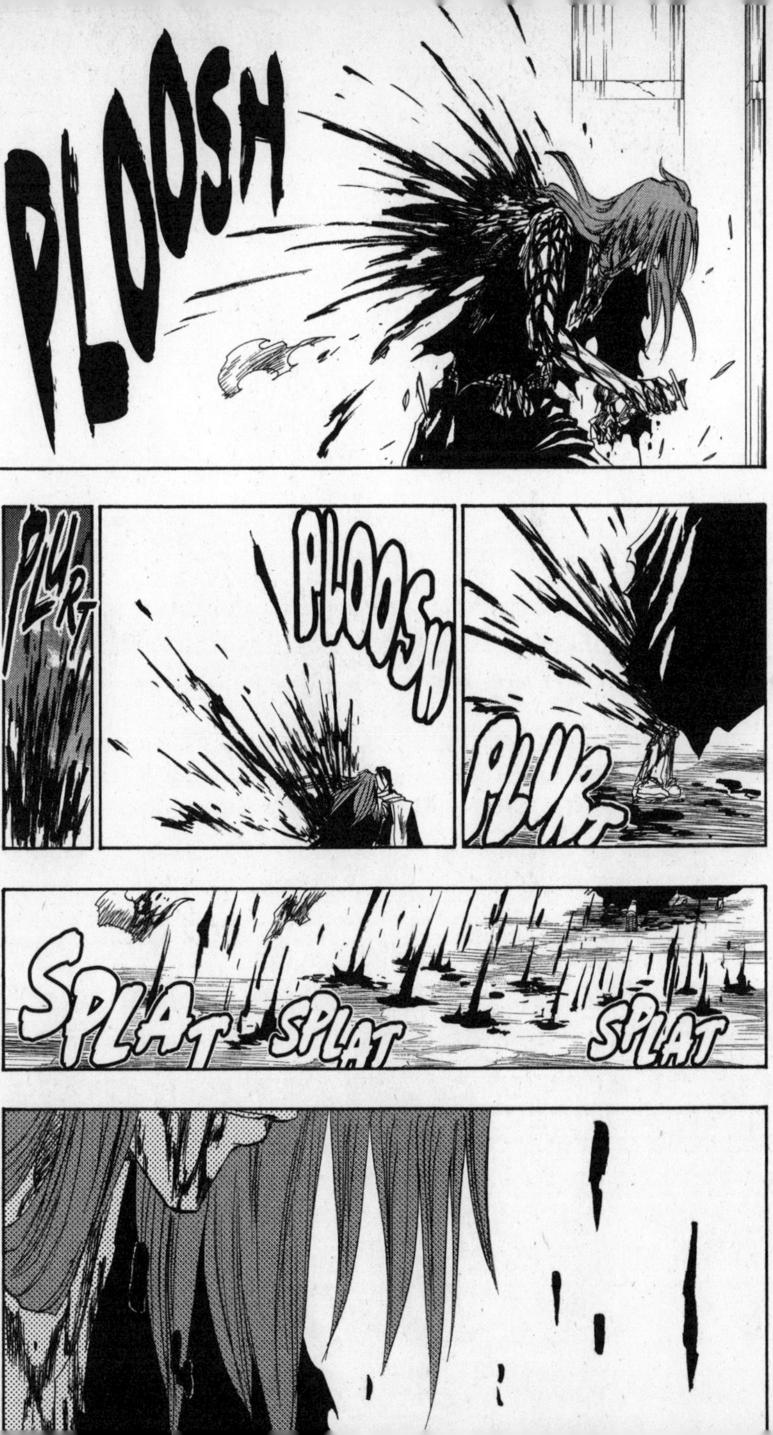
PLOOSH
PLURT
PLOOSH
PLURT
SPLAT
SPLAT
SPLAT

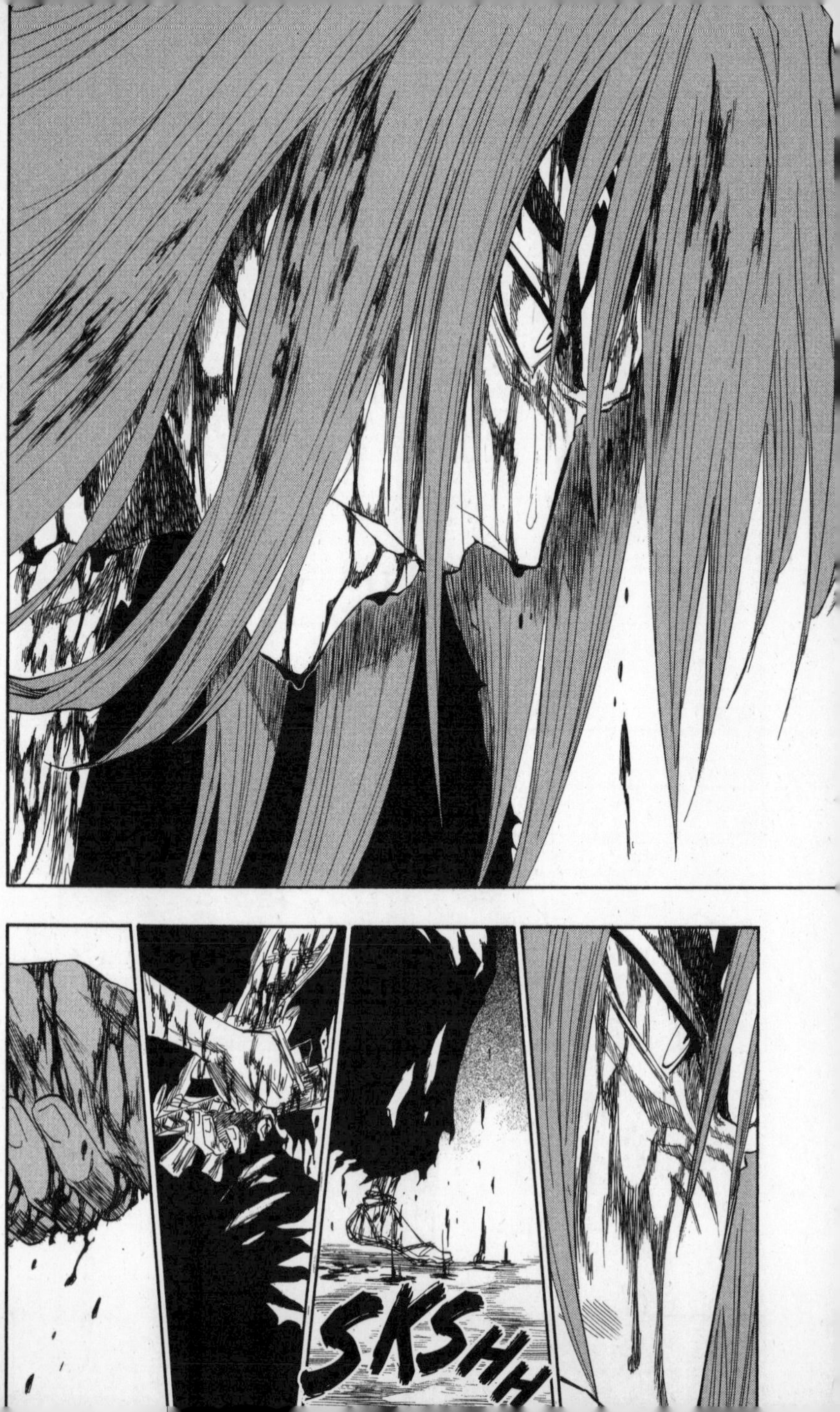
SKSHH

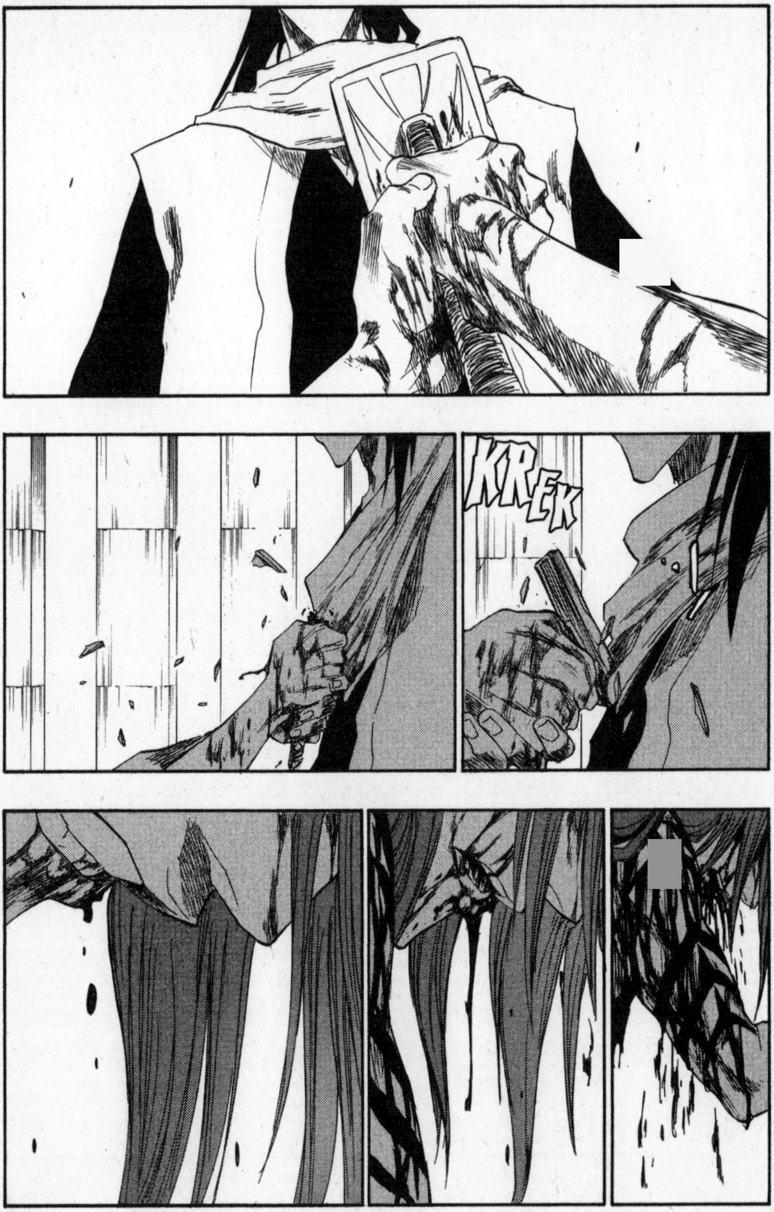
KREK

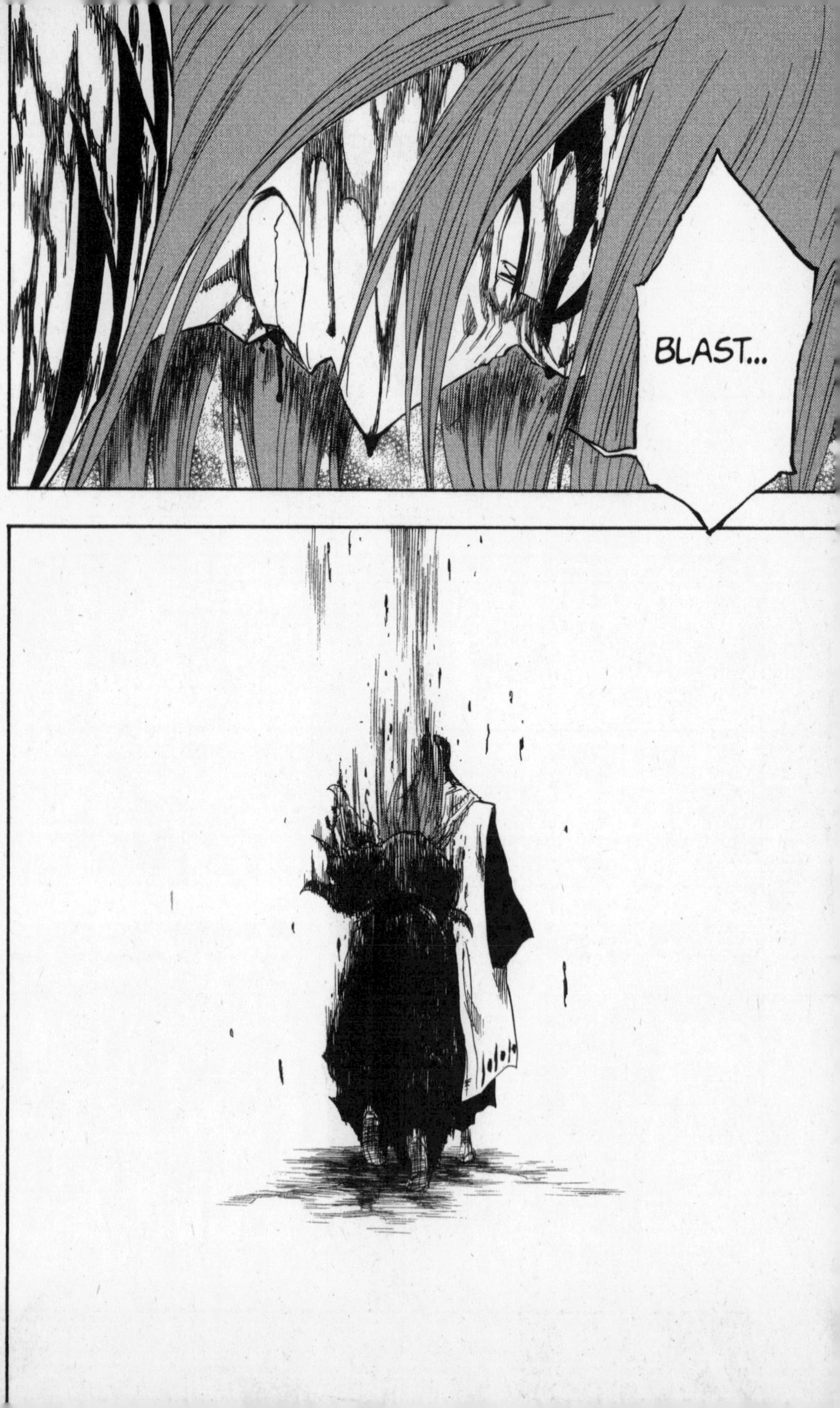
BLAST...

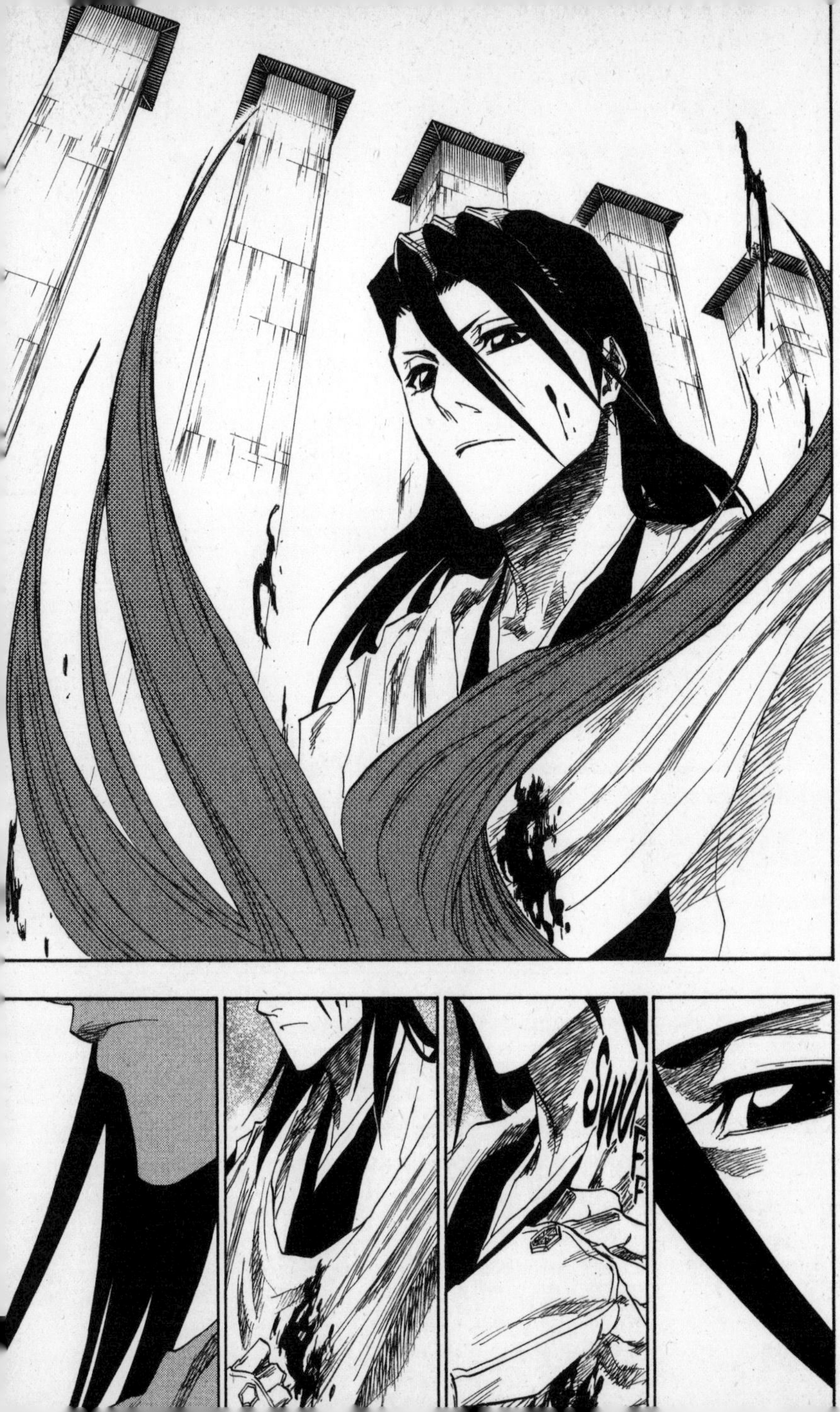
SWUFF

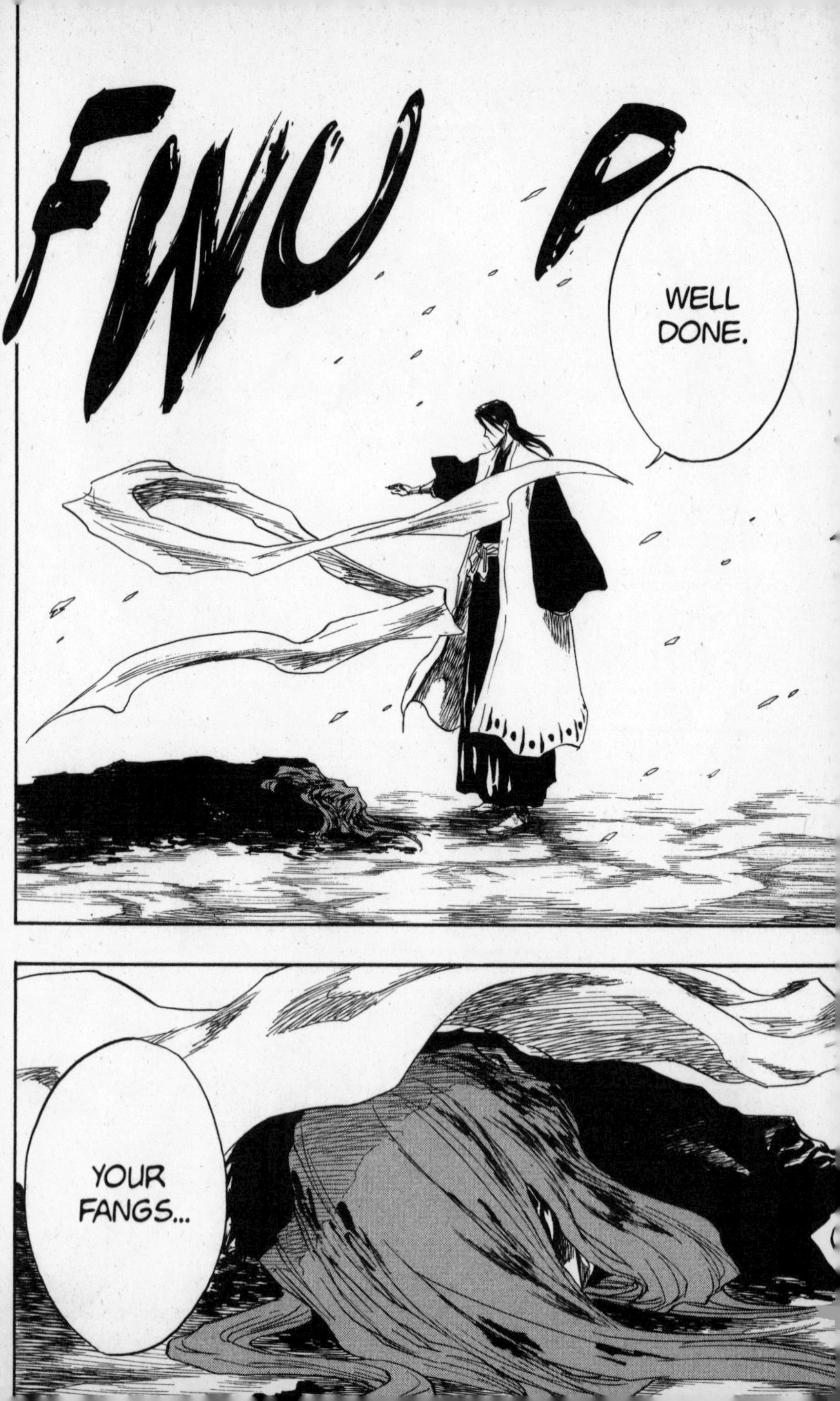
FWUP
WELL DONE.
YOUR FANGS...

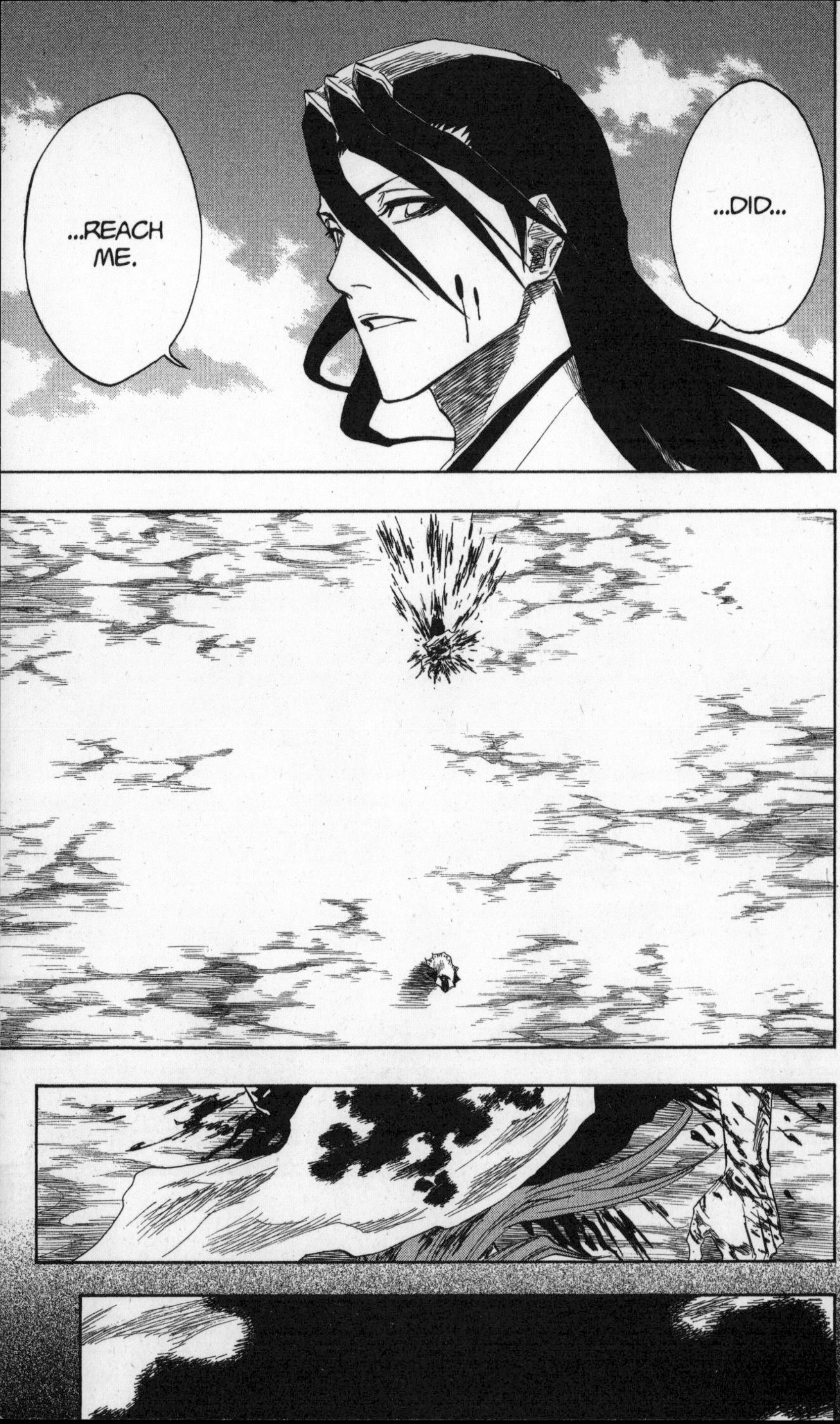
...DID...
...REACH ME.

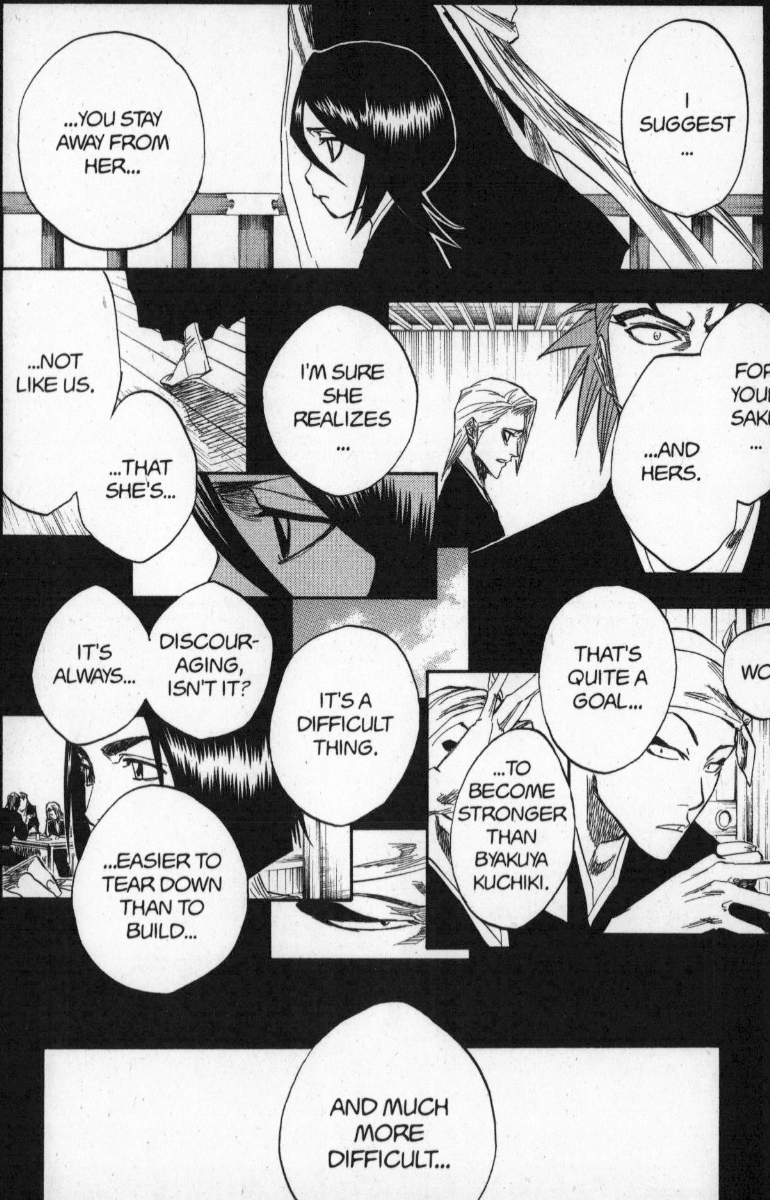
I SUGGEST ...
...YOU STAY AWAY FROM HER...
FOR YOUR SAKE ...
...AND HERS.
I'M SURE SHE REALIZES ...
...THAT SHE'S...
...NOT LIKE US.
WOW.
THAT'S QUITE A GOAL...
...TO BECOME STRONGER THAN BYAKUYA KUCHIKI.
IT'S A DIFFICULT THING.
DISCOURAGING, ISN'T IT?
IT'S ALWAYS...
...EASIER TO TEAR DOWN THAN TO BUILD...
AND MUCH MORE DIFFICULT...

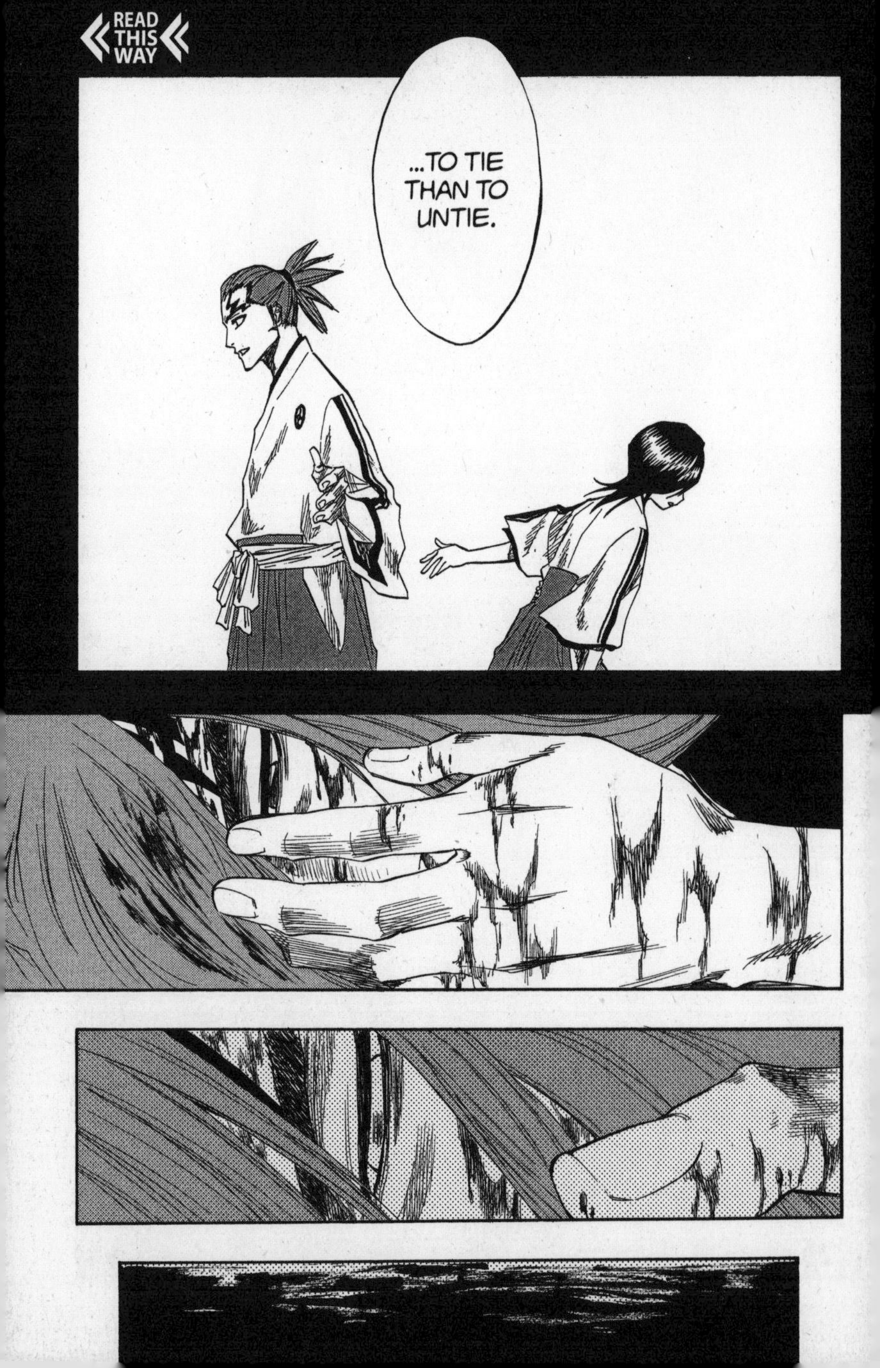
READ THIS WAY
...TO TIE THAN TO UNTIE.

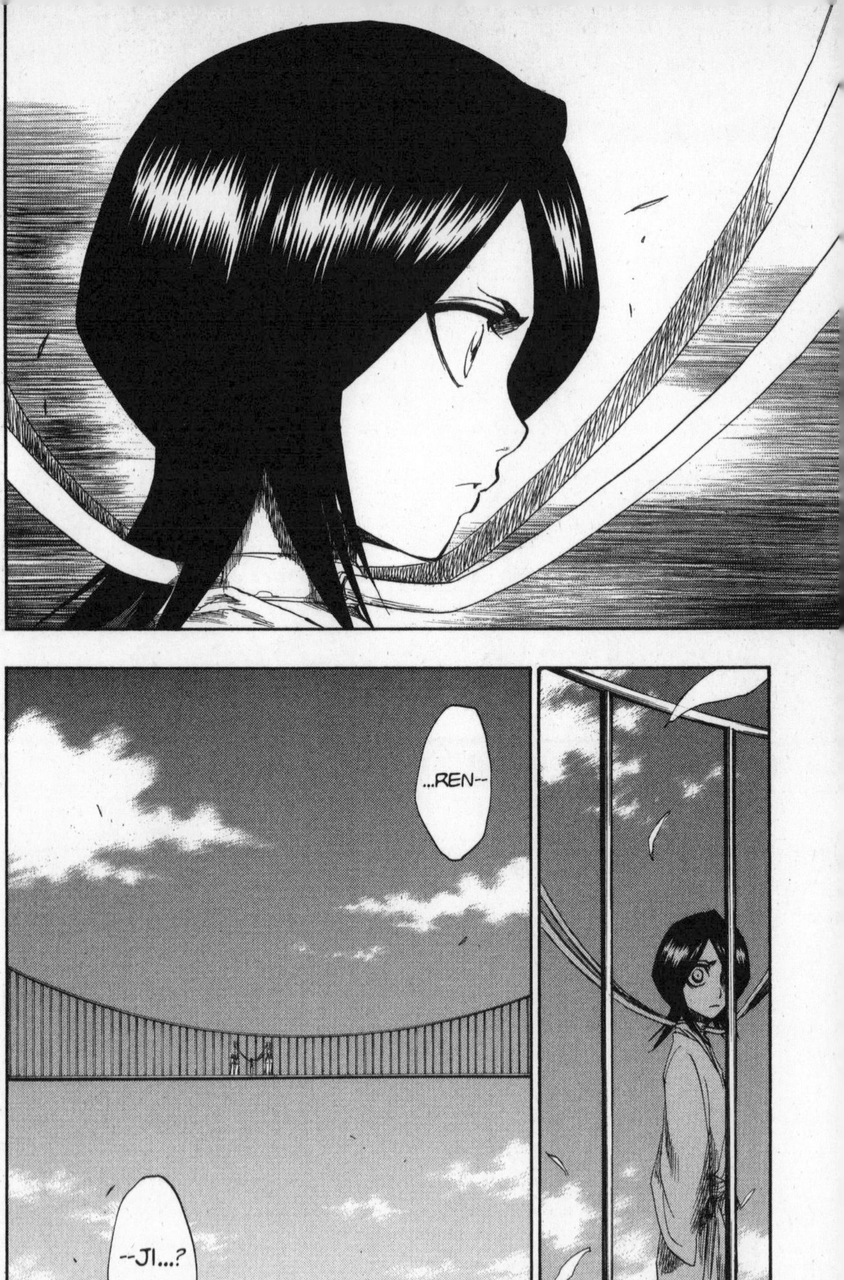
...REN--
--JI...?

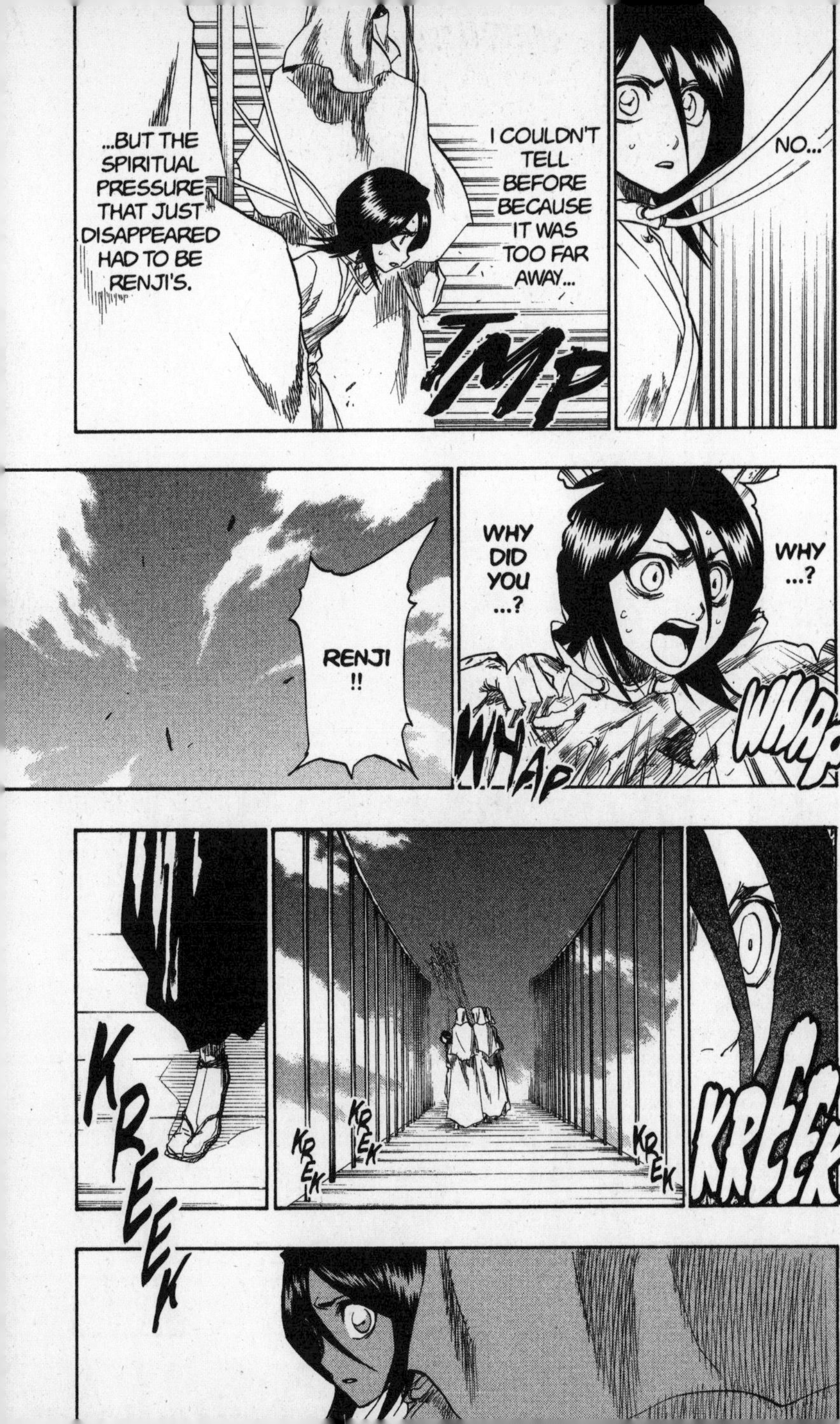
NO...
I COULDN'T TELL BEFORE BECAUSE IT WAS TOO FAR AWAY...
...BUT THE SPIRITUAL PRESSURE THAT JUST DISAPPEARED HAD TO BE RENJI'S.
TMP
WHY ...?
WHY DID YOU ...?
WHAP
WHAP
RENJI !!
KREEK
KREK
KREK
KREK
KREEEK

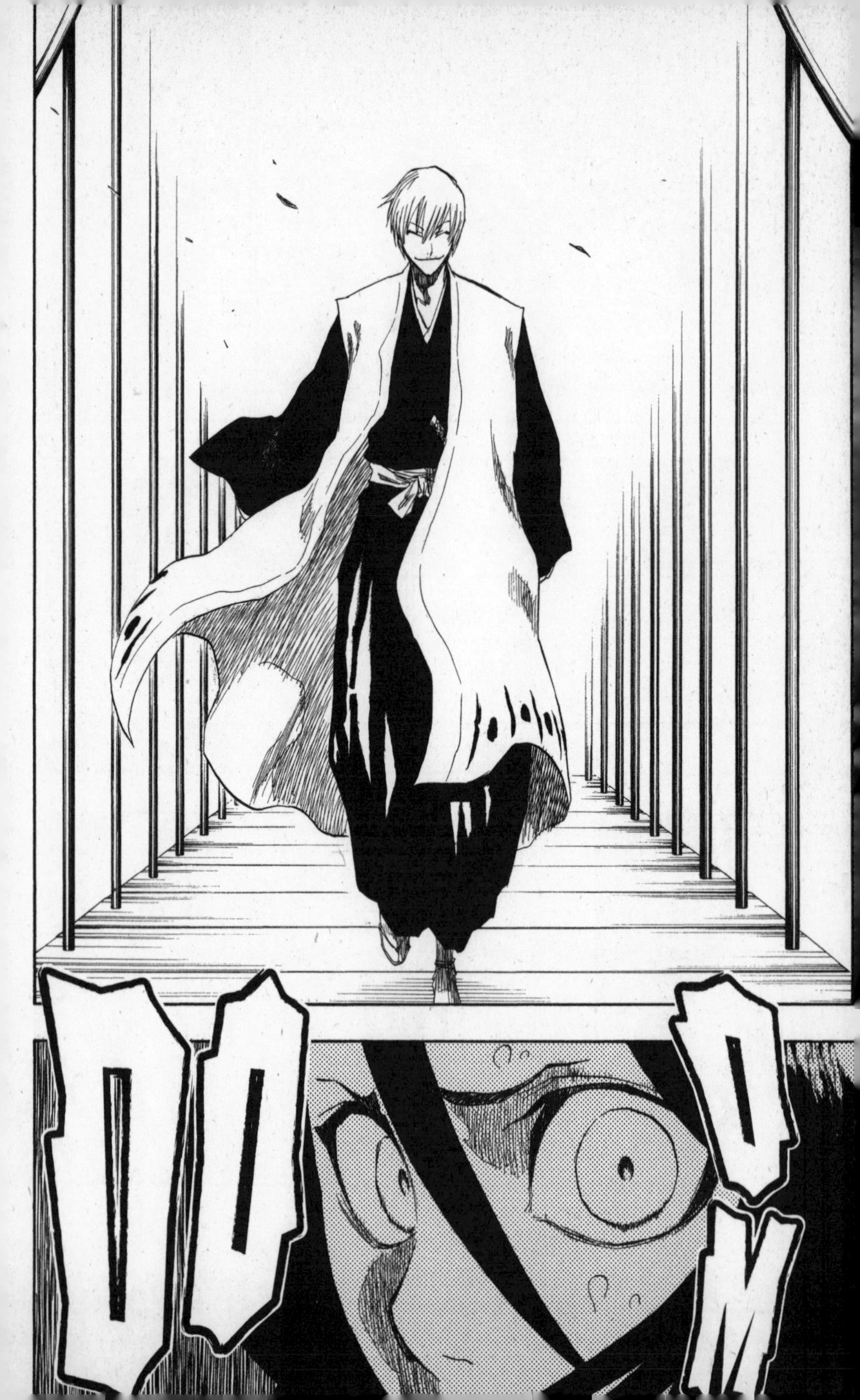
DOOM

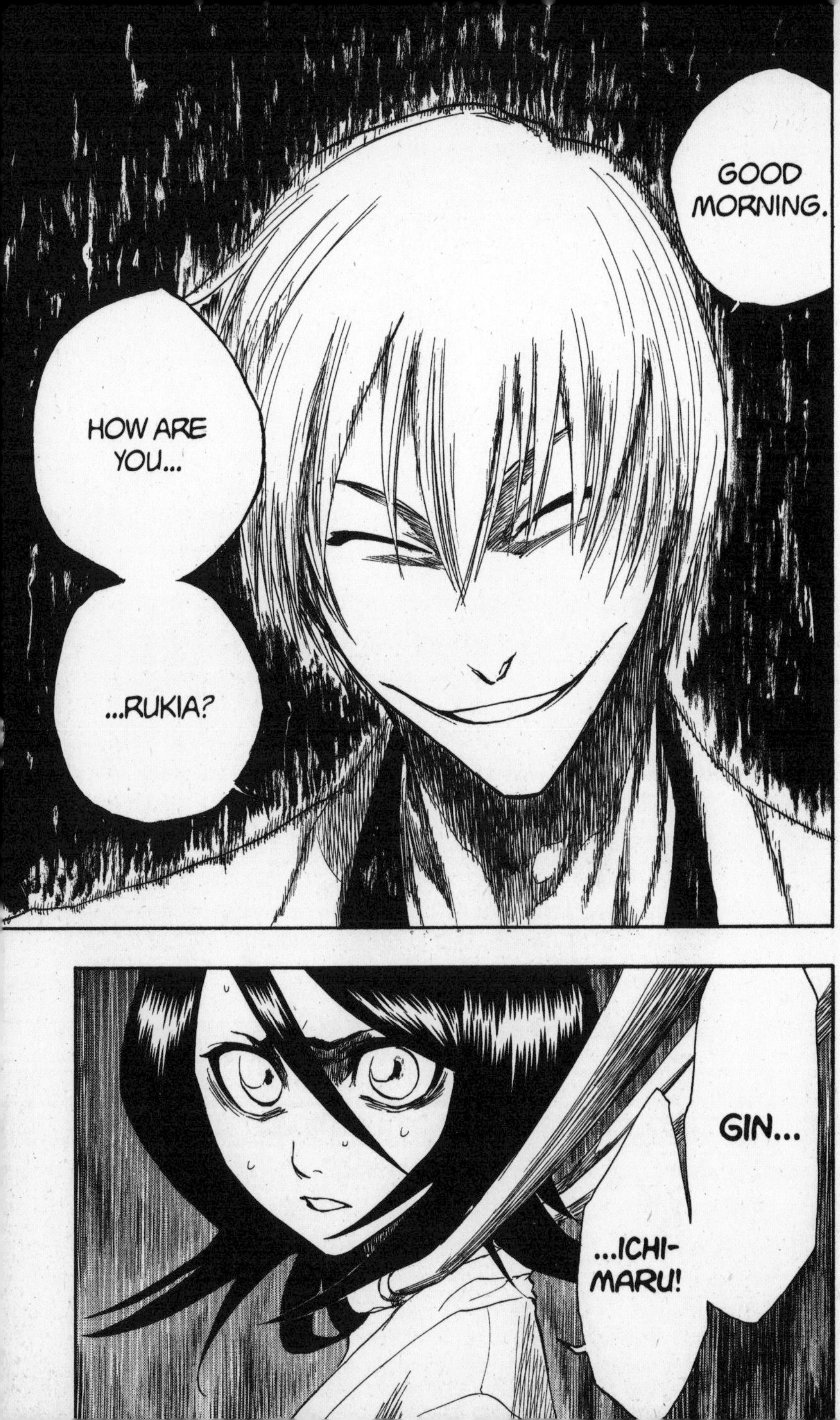
GOOD MORNING.
HOW ARE YOU...
...RUKIA?
GIN...
...ICHI-MARU!

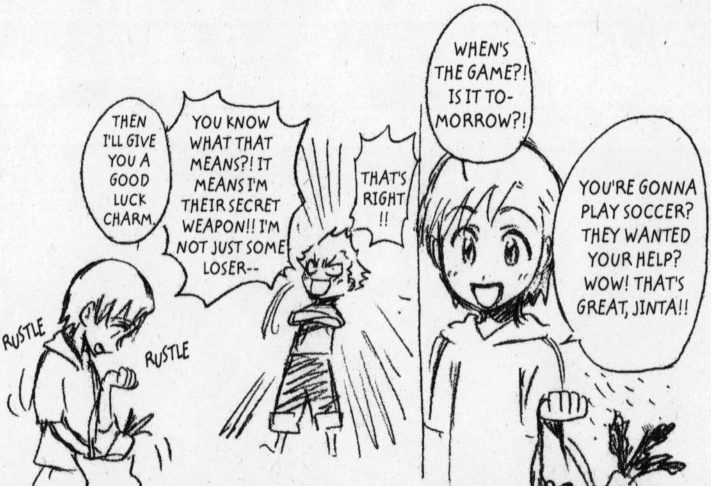
YOU'RE GONNA PLAY SOCCER? THEY WANTED YOUR HELP? WOW! THAT'S GREAT, JINTA!!
WHEN'S THE GAME?! IS IT TO-MORROW?!
THAT'S RIGHT !!
YOU KNOW WHAT THAT MEANS?! IT MEANS I'M THEIR SECRET WEAPON!! I'M NOT JUST SOME LOSER--
THEN I'LL GIVE YOU A GOOD LUCK CHARM.
RUSTLE
RUSTLE

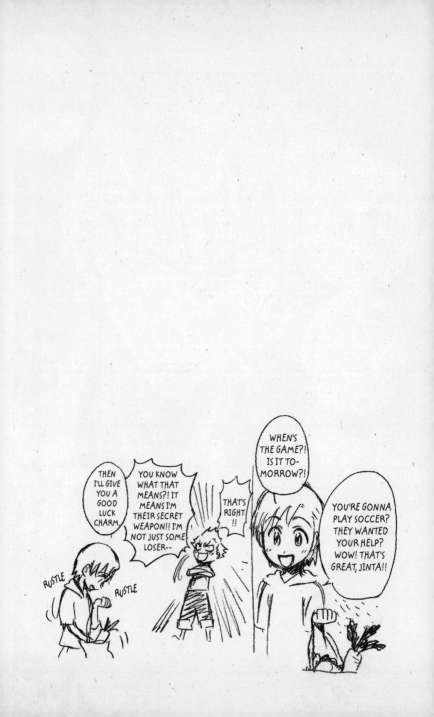

145. Shaken

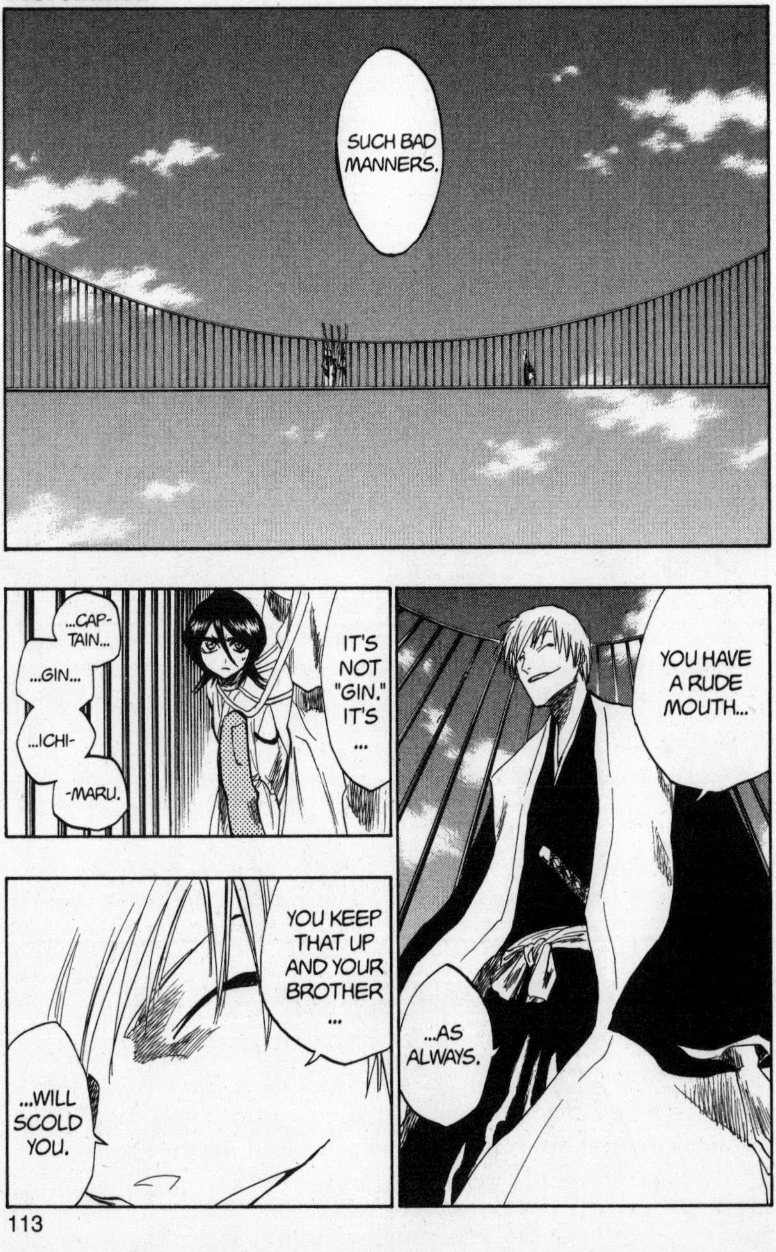
SUCH BAD MANNERS.
YOU HAVE A RUDE MOUTH...
...AS ALWAYS.
IT'S NOT "GIN." IT'S ...
...CAP-TAIN...
...GIN...
...ICHI-
-MARU.
YOU KEEP THAT UP AND YOUR BROTHER ...
...WILL SCOLD YOU.

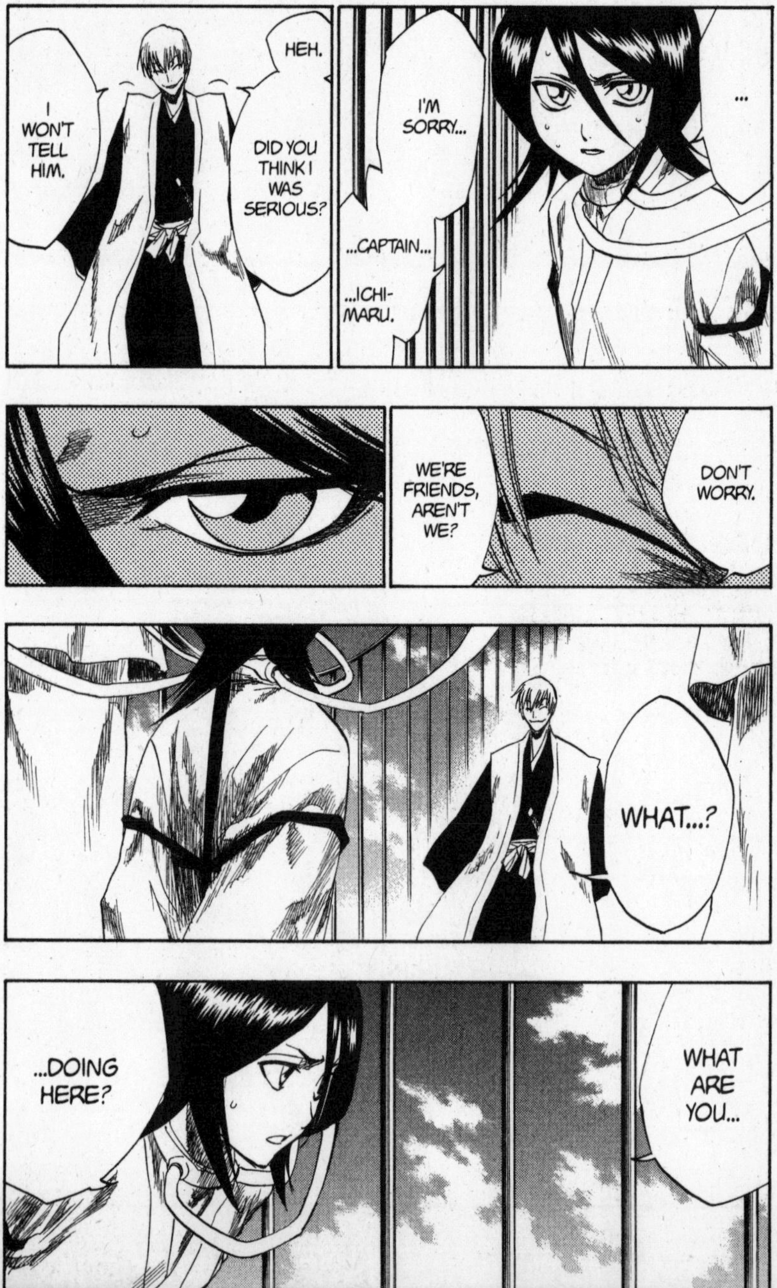
...
I'M SORRY...
...CAPTAIN...
...ICHI-MARU.
HEH.
DID YOU THINK I WAS SERIOUS?
I WON'T TELL HIM.
DON'T WORRY.
WE'RE FRIENDS, AREN'T WE?
WHAT...?
WHAT ARE YOU...
...DOING HERE?

READ THIS WAY

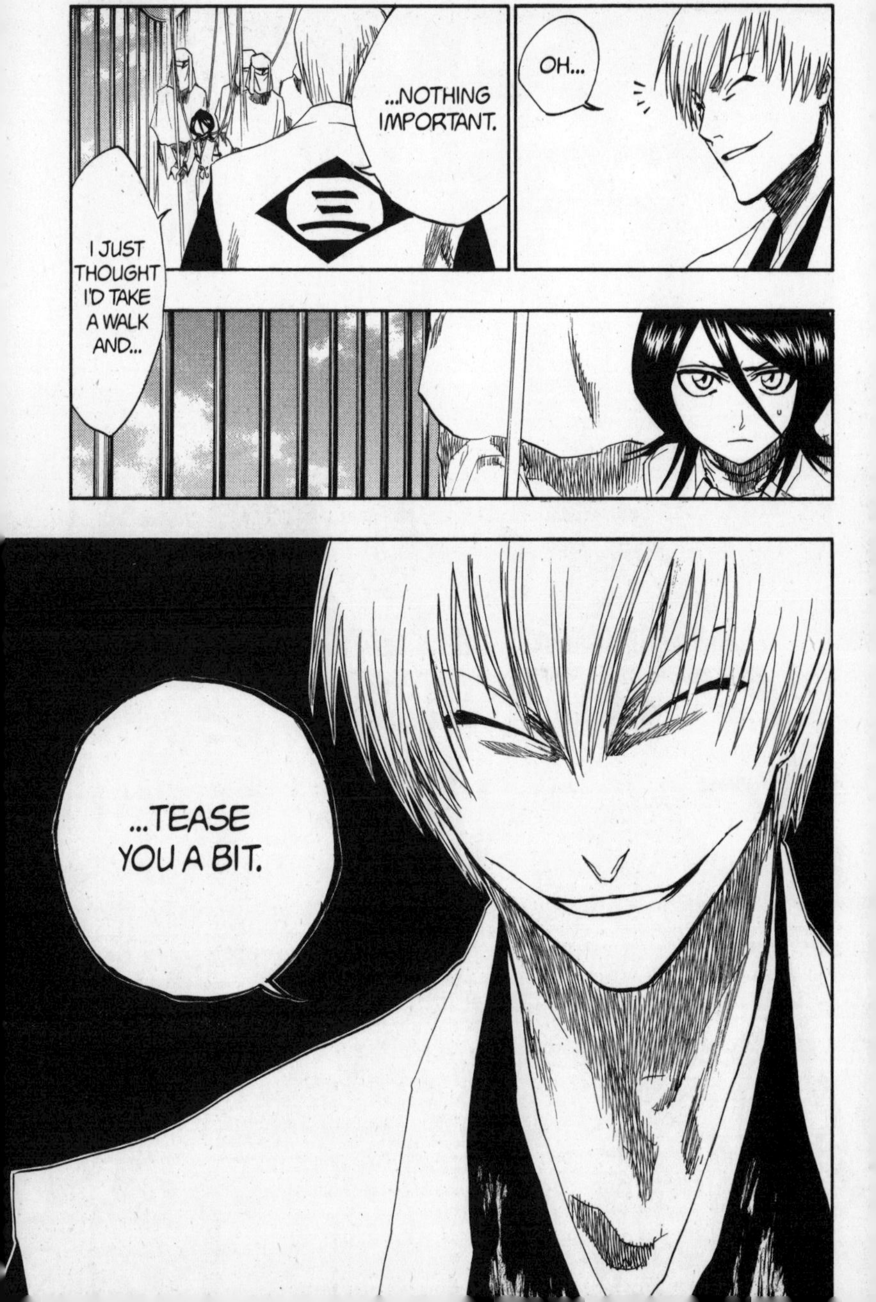
OH...
...NOTHING IMPORTANT.
I JUST THOUGHT I'D TAKE A WALK AND...
...TEASE YOU A BIT.

145. Shaken

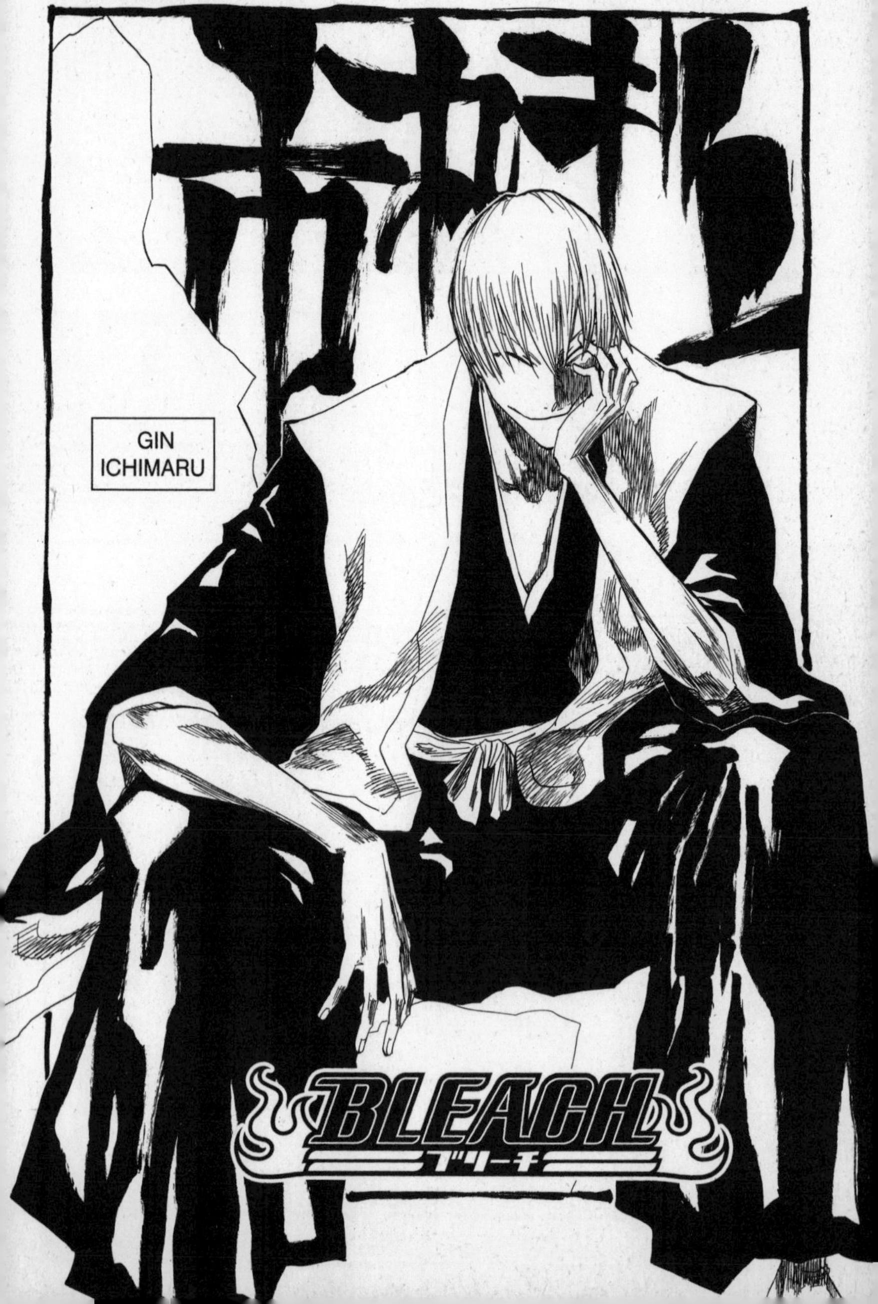
GIN ICHIMARU
BLEACH
ブリーチ

READ THIS WAY

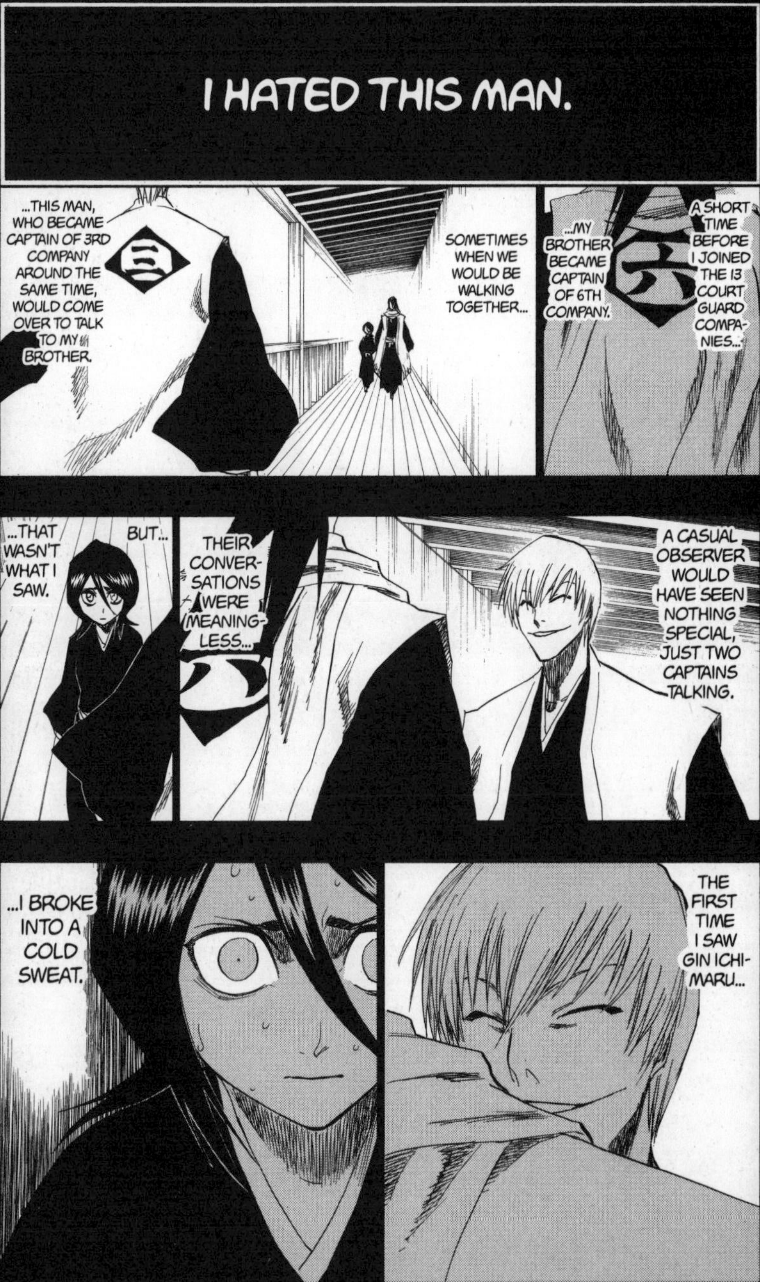
I HATED THIS MAN.
A SHORT TIME BEFORE I JOINED THE 13 COURT GUARD COMPANIES...
...MY BROTHER BECAME CAPTAIN OF 6TH COMPANY.
SOMETIMES WHEN WE WOULD BE WALKING TOGETHER...
...THIS MAN, WHO BECAME CAPTAIN OF 3RD COMPANY AROUND THE SAME TIME, WOULD COME OVER TO TALK TO MY BROTHER.
A CASUAL OBSERVER WOULD HAVE SEEN NOTHING SPECIAL, JUST TWO CAPTAINS TALKING.
THEIR CONVERSATIONS WERE MEANINGLESS...
BUT...
...THAT WASN'T WHAT I SAW.
THE FIRST TIME I SAW GIN ICHIMARU...
...I BROKE INTO A COLD SWEAT.

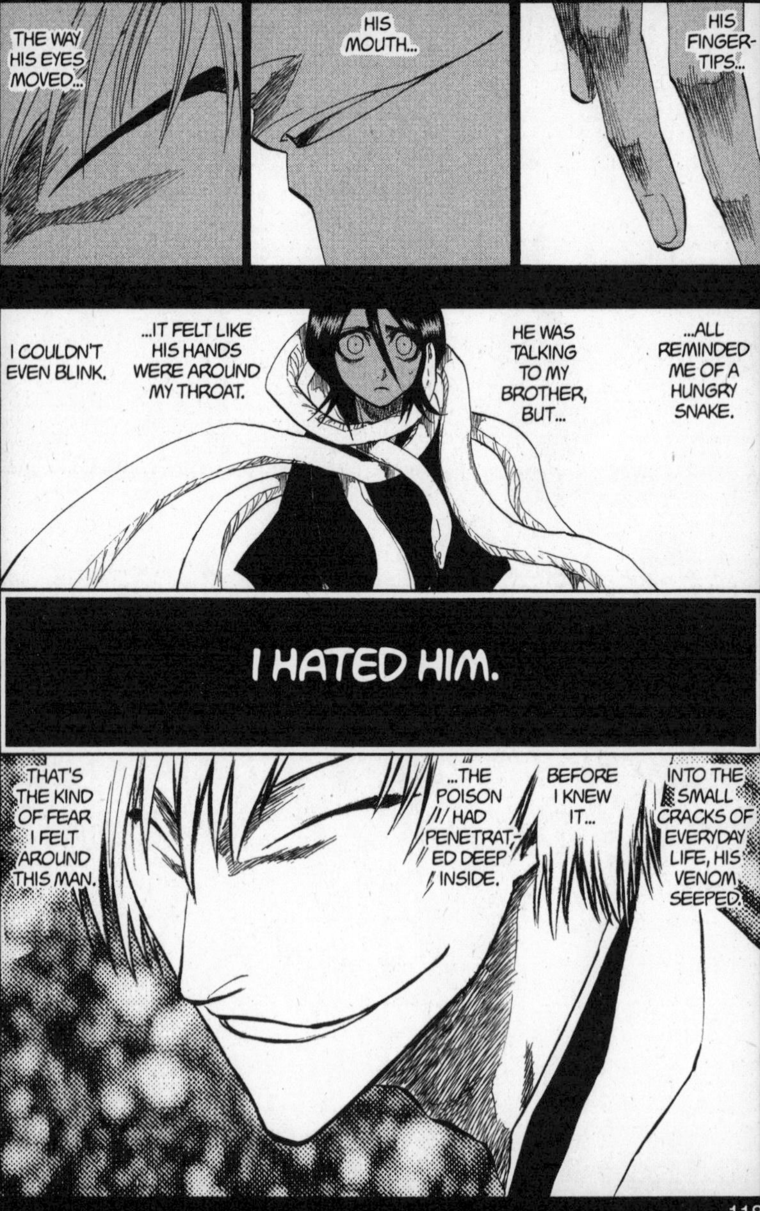
HIS FINGER-TIPS...
HIS MOUTH...
THE WAY HIS EYES MOVED...
...ALL REMINDED ME OF A HUNGRY SNAKE.
HE WAS TALKING TO MY BROTHER, BUT...
...IT FELT LIKE HIS HANDS WERE AROUND MY THROAT.
I COULDN'T EVEN BLINK.
I HATED HIM.
INTO THE SMALL CRACKS OF EVERYDAY LIFE, HIS VENOM SEEPED.
BEFORE I KNEW IT...
...THE POISON HAD PENETRAT-ED DEEP INSIDE.
THAT'S THE KIND OF FEAR I FELT AROUND THIS MAN.

READ THIS WAY

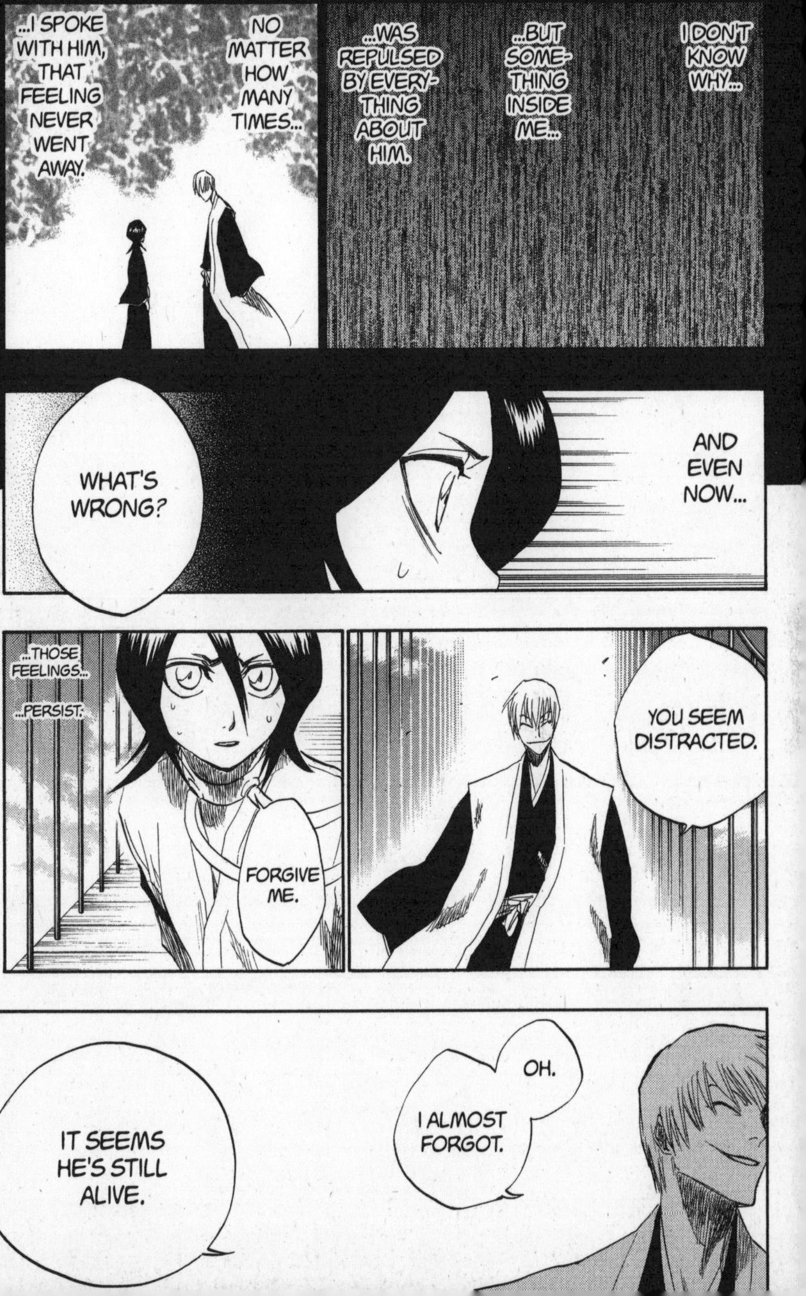
I DON'T KNOW WHY...
...BUT SOMETHING INSIDE ME...
...WAS REPULSED BY EVERYTHING ABOUT HIM.
NO MATTER HOW MANY TIMES...
...I SPOKE WITH HIM, THAT FEELING NEVER WENT AWAY.
AND EVEN NOW...
WHAT'S WRONG?
YOU SEEM DISTRACTED.
...THOSE FEELINGS...
...PERSIST.
FORGIVE ME.
OH.
I ALMOST FORGOT.
IT SEEMS HE'S STILL ALIVE.

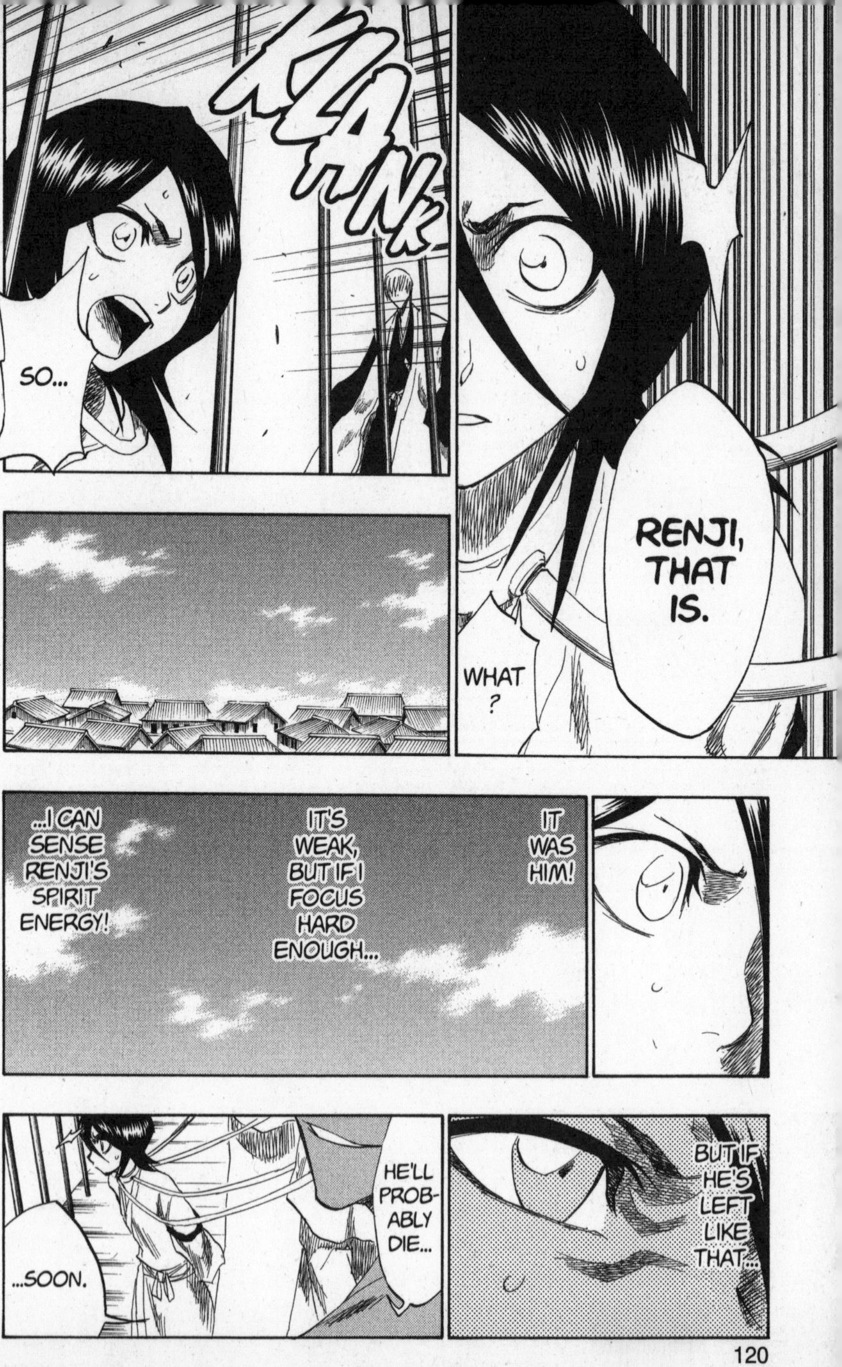
RENJI, THAT IS.
WHAT ?
KLANK
SO...
IT WAS HIM!
IT'S WEAK, BUT IF I FOCUS HARD ENOUGH...
...I CAN SENSE RENJI'S SPIRIT ENERGY!
BUT IF HE'S LEFT LIKE THAT...
HE'LL PROBABLY DIE...
...SOON.

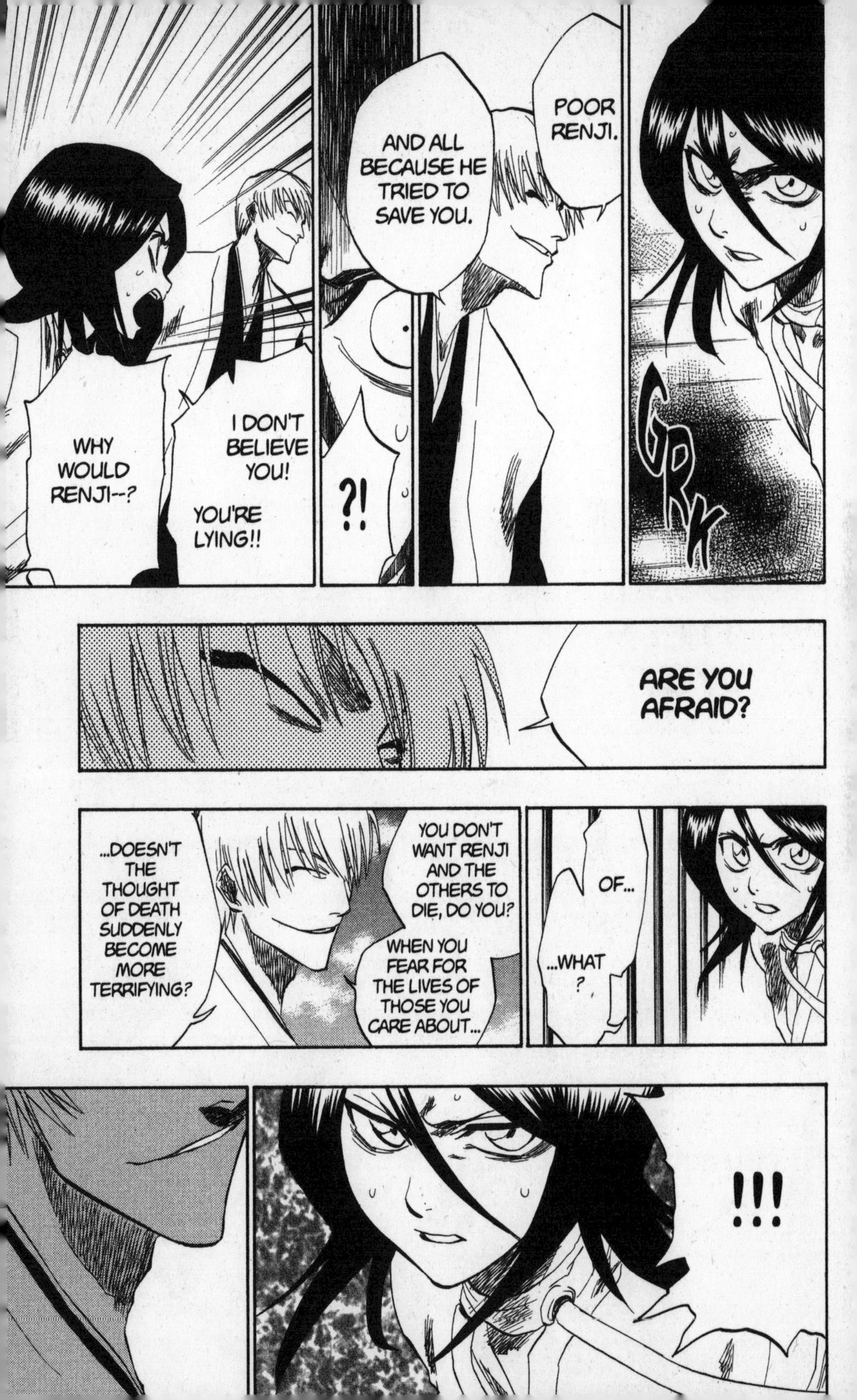
GRK
POOR RENJI.
AND ALL BECAUSE HE TRIED TO SAVE YOU.
?!
I DON'T BELIEVE YOU!
YOU'RE LYING!!
WHY WOULD RENJI--?
ARE YOU AFRAID?
OF...
...WHAT ?
YOU DON'T WANT RENJI AND THE OTHERS TO DIE, DO YOU?
WHEN YOU FEAR FOR THE LIVES OF THOSE YOU CARE ABOUT...
...DOESN'T THE THOUGHT OF DEATH SUDDENLY BECOME MORE TERRIFYING?
!!!

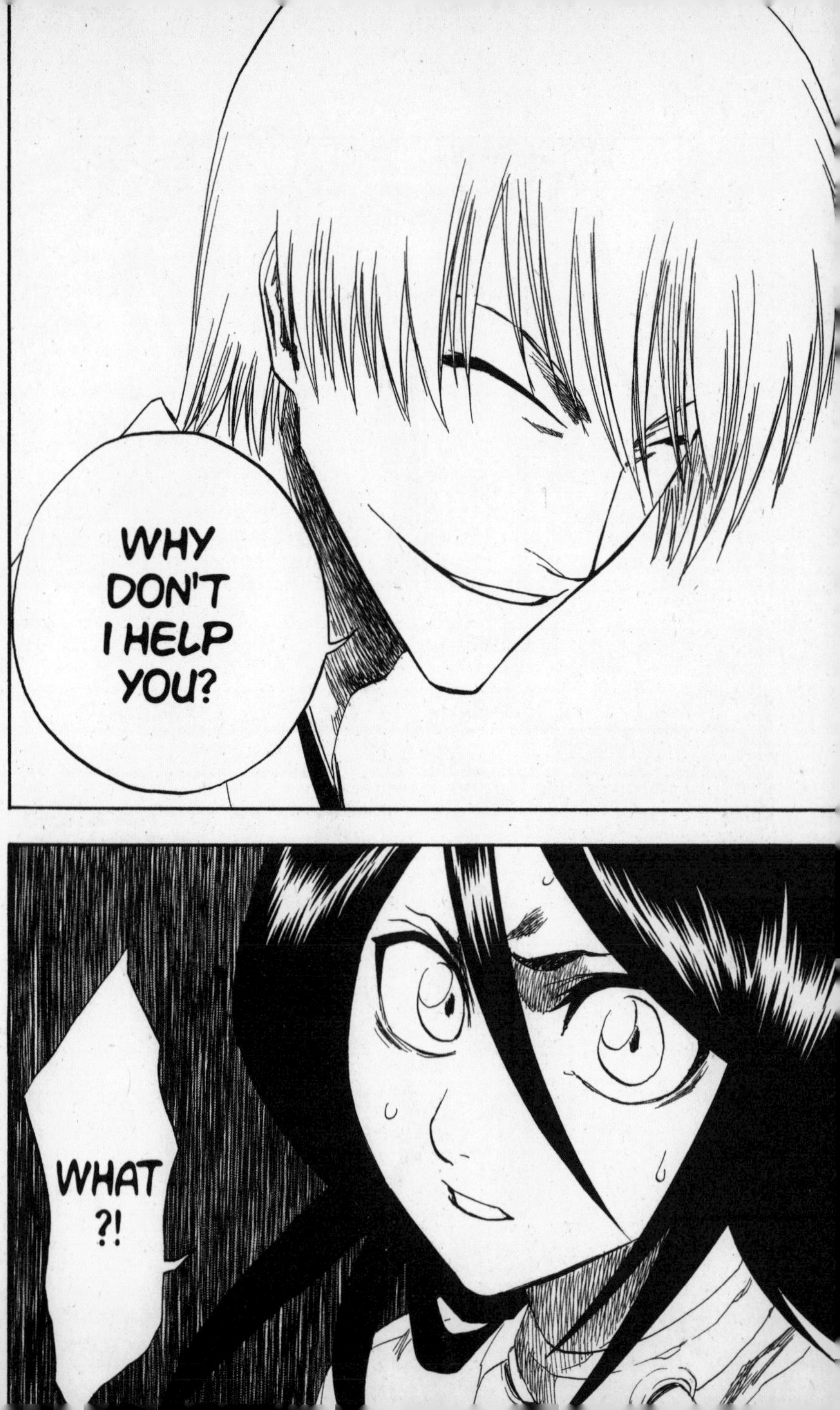
WHY DON'T I HELP YOU?
WHAT ?!

READ THIS WAY

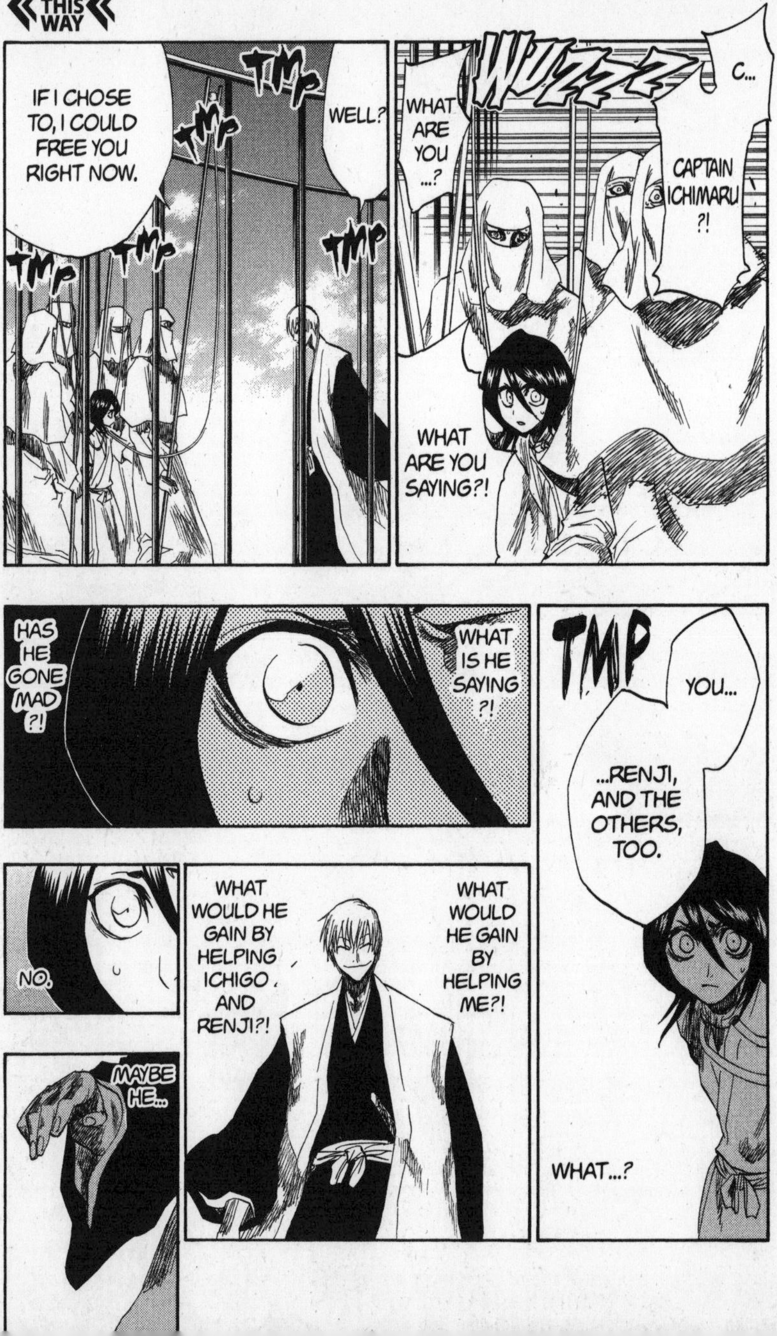
C...
CAPTAIN ICHIMARU?!
WUZZZ
WHAT ARE YOU ...?
WHAT ARE YOU SAYING?!
WELL?
TMP
IF I CHOSE TO, I COULD FREE YOU RIGHT NOW.
TMP
TMP
TMP
TMP
TMP
YOU...
...RENJI, AND THE OTHERS, TOO.
WHAT...?
WHAT IS HE SAYING?!
HAS HE GONE MAD?!
WHAT WOULD HE GAIN BY HELPING ME?!
WHAT WOULD HE GAIN BY HELPING ICHIGO AND RENJI?!
NO.
MAYBE HE...

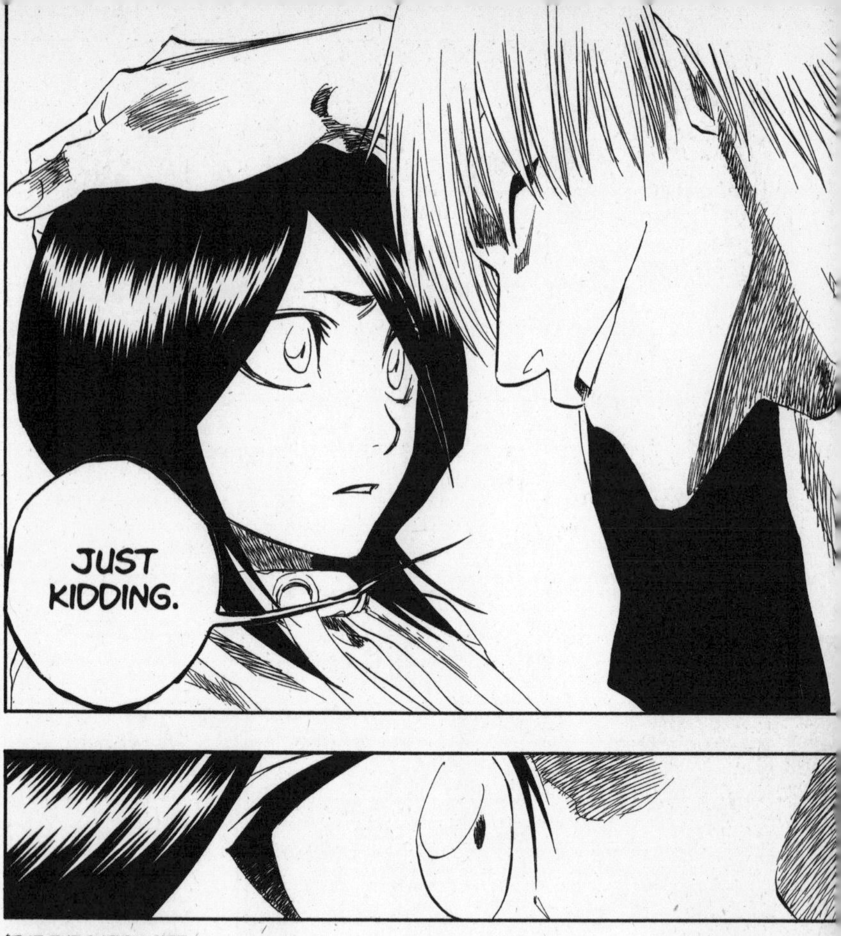
JUST KIDDING.

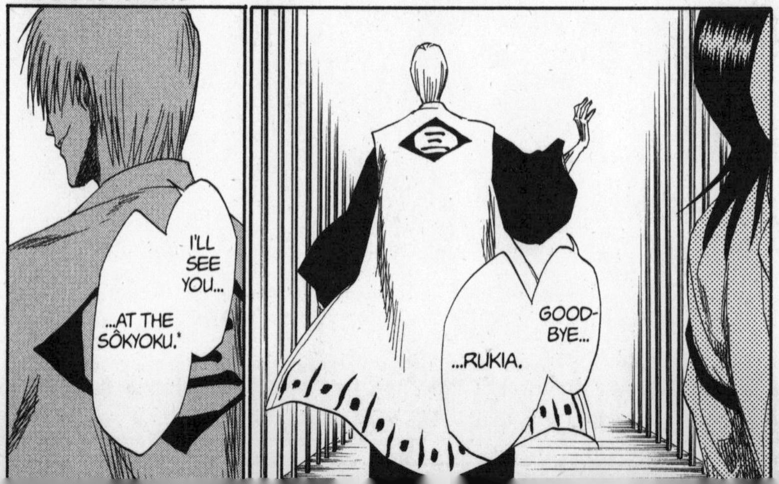
GOOD-BYE...
...RUKIA.
I'LL SEE YOU...
...AT THE SÔKYOKU.*

*THE EXECUTION SITE

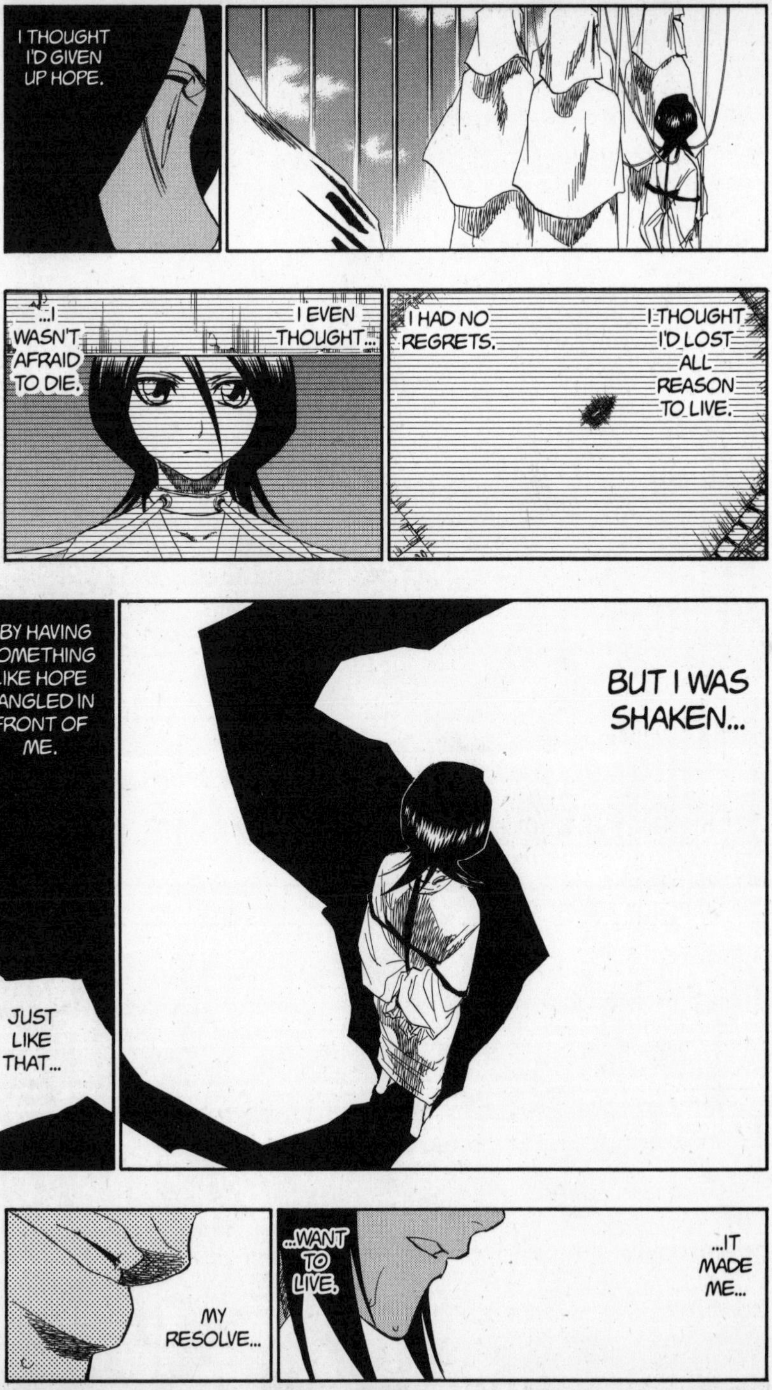
I THOUGHT I'D GIVEN UP HOPE.
I THOUGHT I'D LOST ALL REASON TO LIVE.
I HAD NO REGRETS.
I EVEN THOUGHT...
...I WASN'T AFRAID TO DIE.
BUT I WAS SHAKEN...
...BY HAVING SOMETHING LIKE HOPE DANGLED IN FRONT OF ME.
JUST LIKE THAT...
...IT MADE ME...
...WANT TO LIVE.
MY RESOLVE...

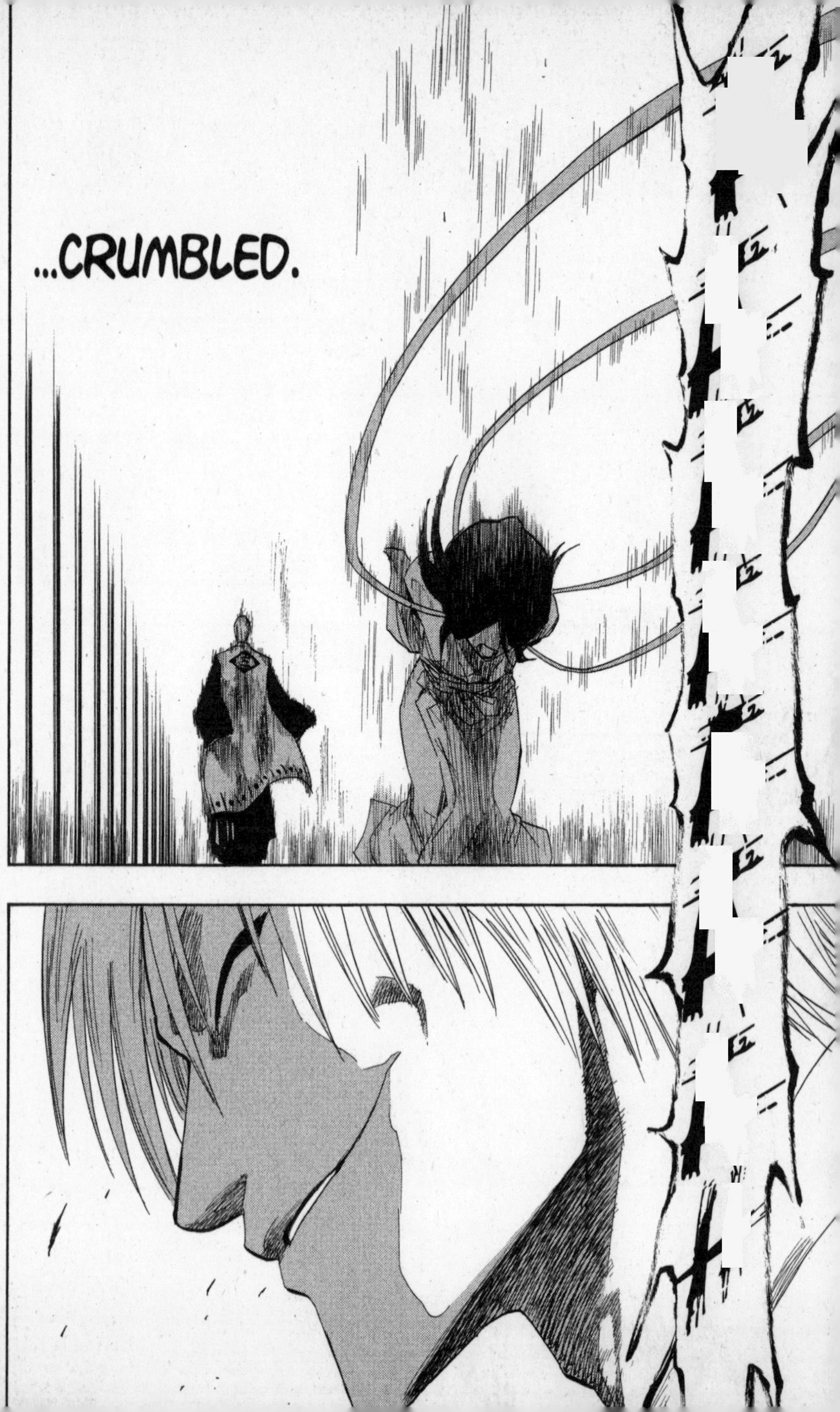
...CRUMBLED.

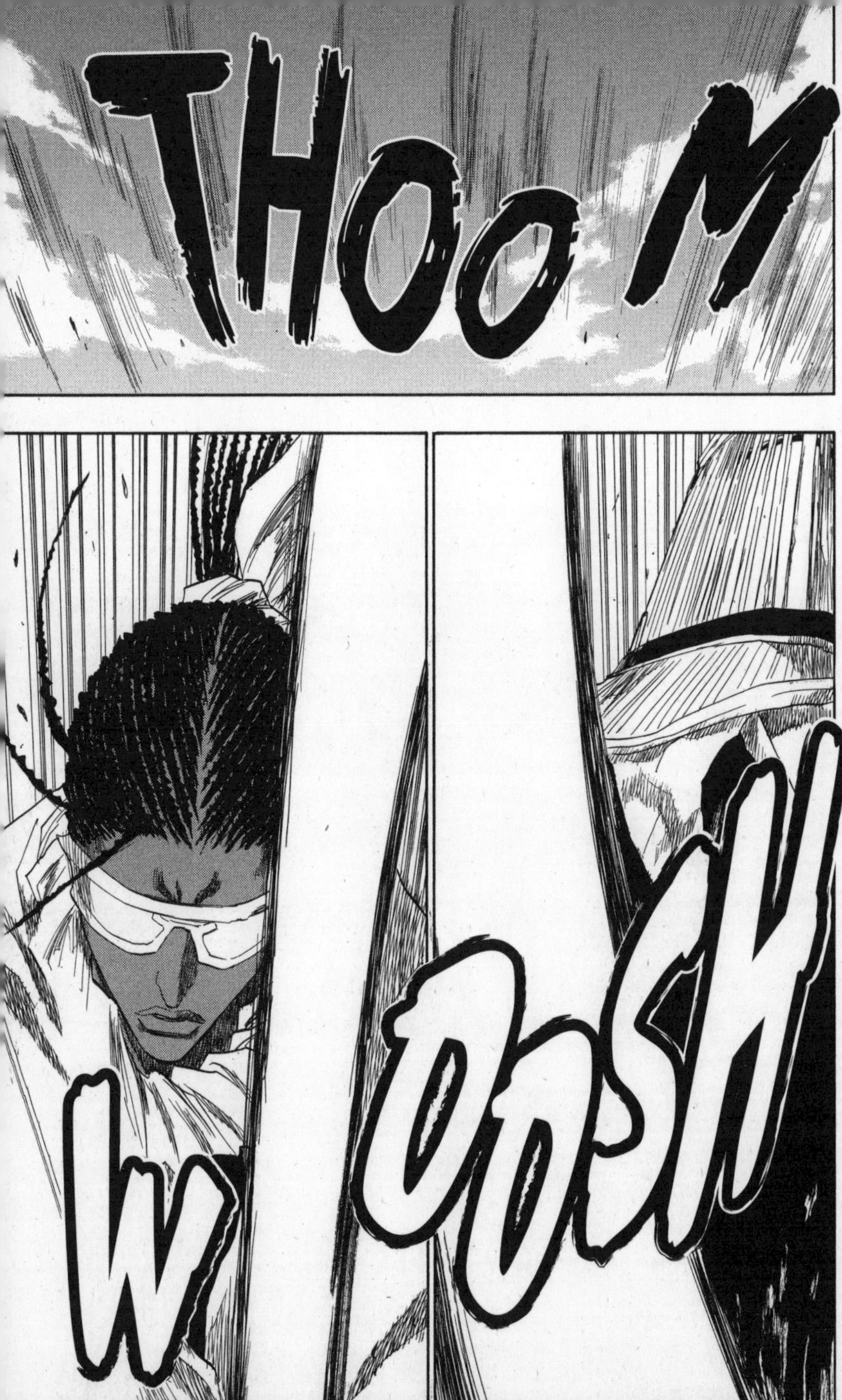
THOOM
WHOOSH

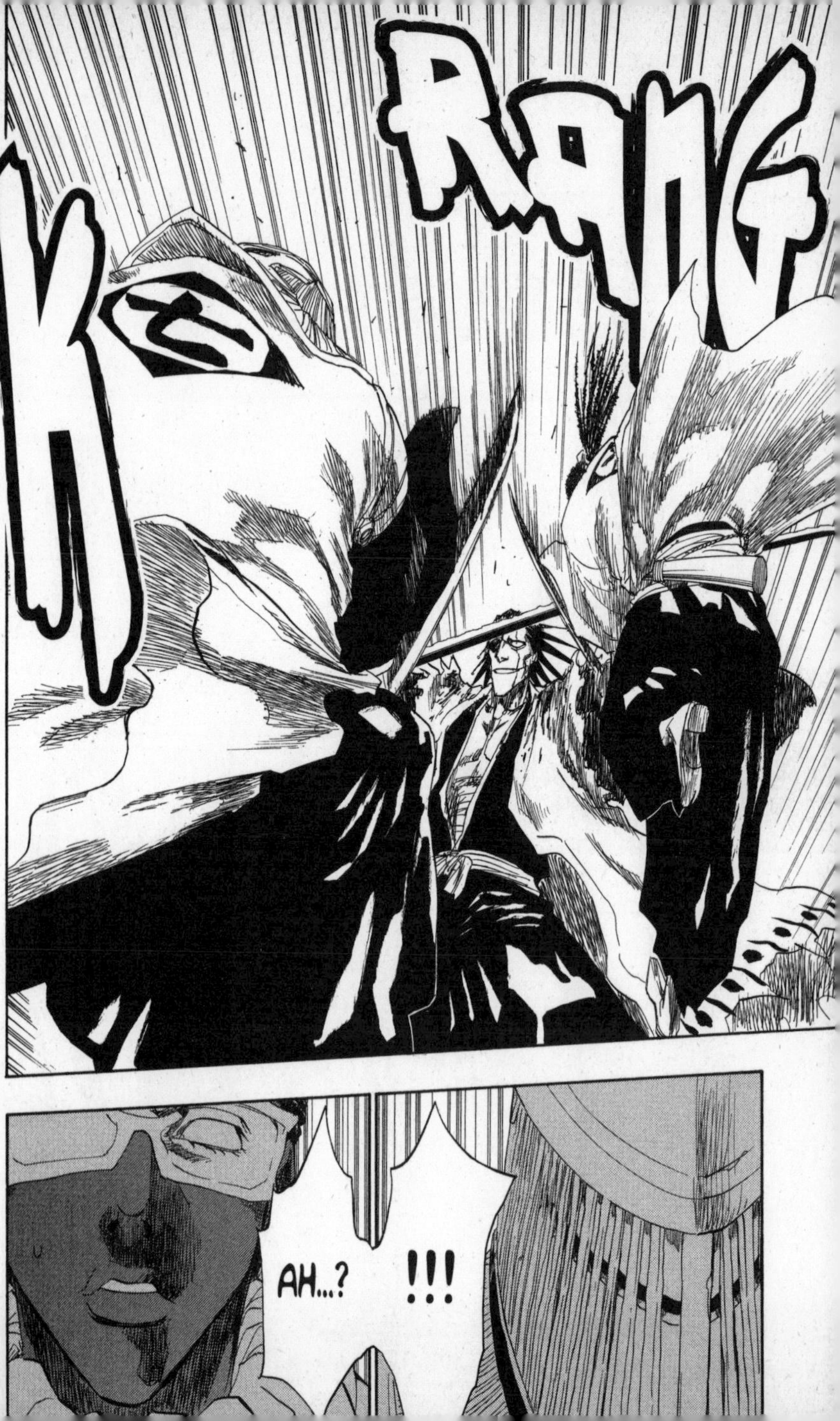
KRANG
!!!
AH...?

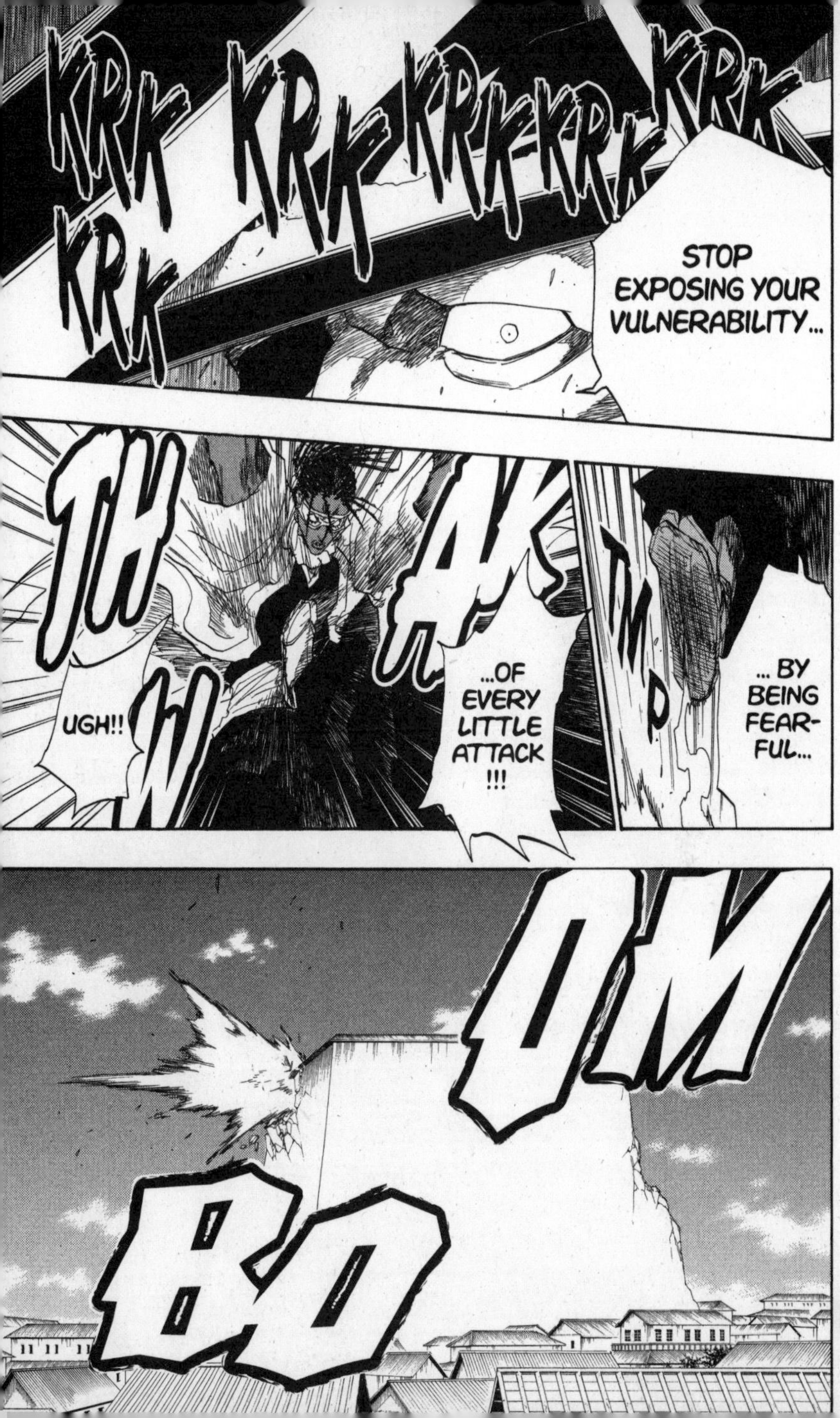
KRK KRK KRK KRK KRK KRK
STOP EXPOSING YOUR VULNERABILITY...
TMP
... BY BEING FEAR-FUL...
THWAK
...OF EVERY LITTLE ATTACK!!!
UGH!!
BO
OM

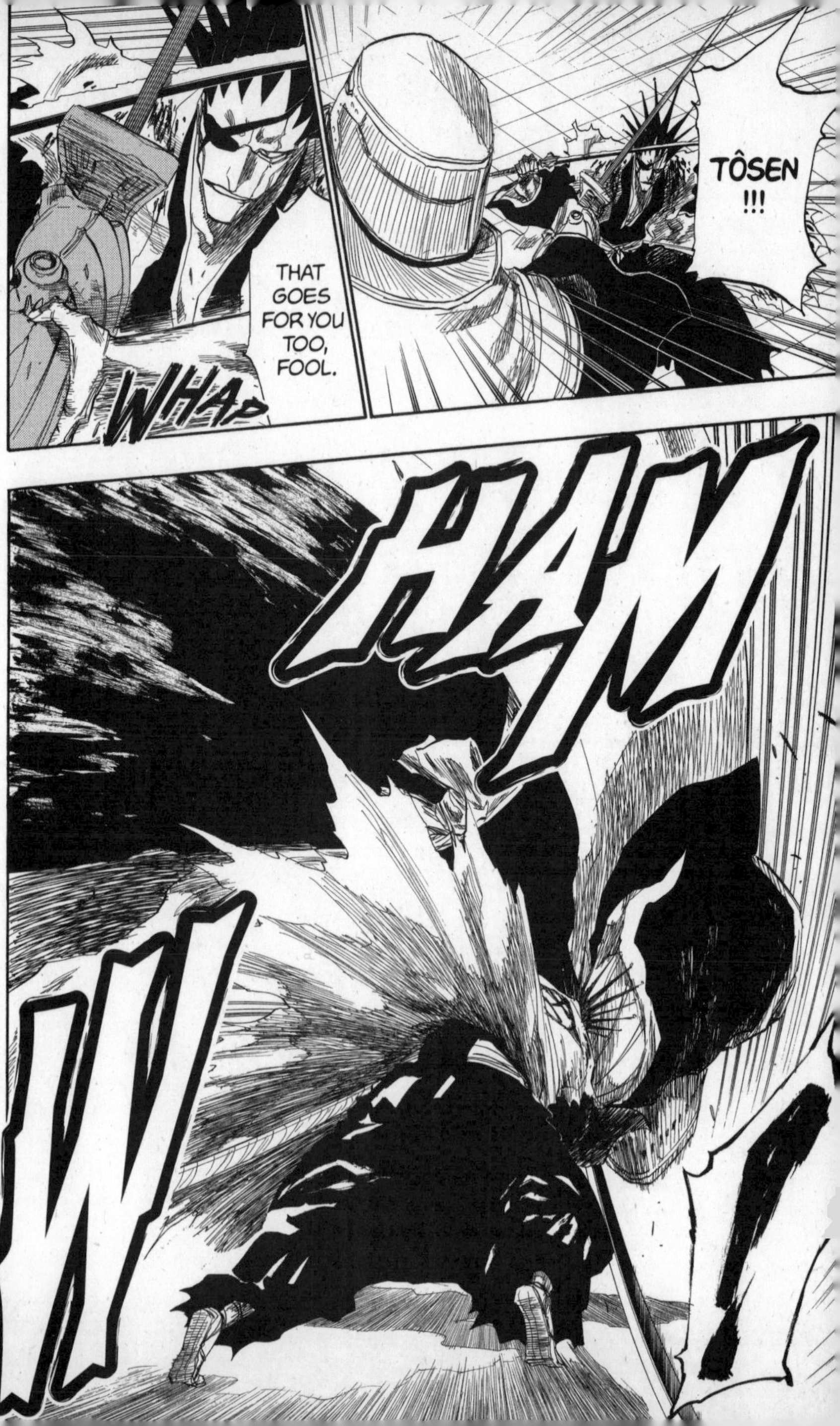
TÔSEN!!!
THAT GOES FOR YOU TOO, FOOL.
WHAP
WHAM!

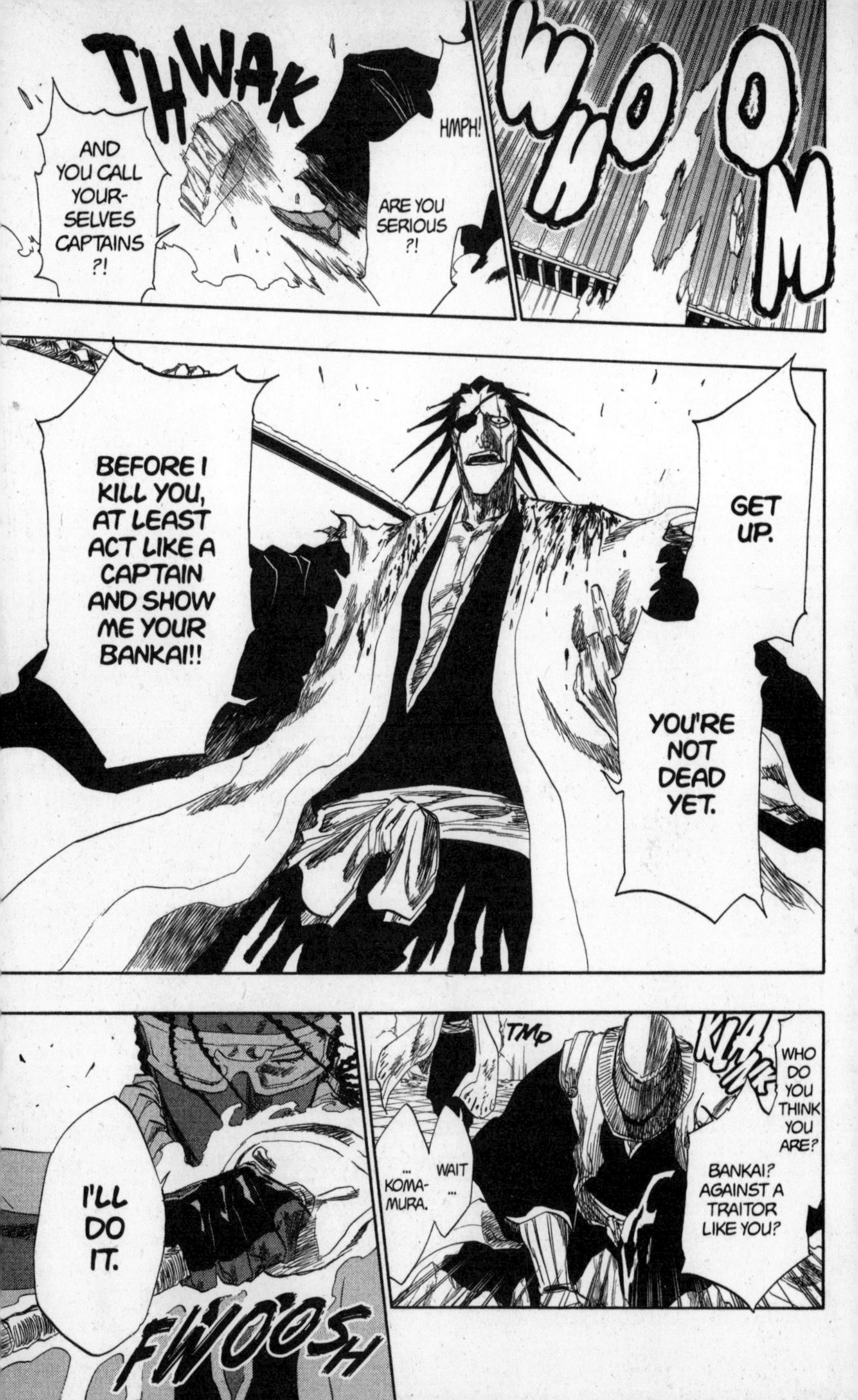
WHOOOM
HMPH!
THWAK
ARE YOU SERIOUS?!
AND YOU CALL YOURSELVES CAPTAINS?!
GET UP.
YOU'RE NOT DEAD YET.
BEFORE I KILL YOU, AT LEAST ACT LIKE A CAPTAIN AND SHOW ME YOUR BANKAI!!
KLANK
WHO DO YOU THINK YOU ARE?
TMP
BANKAI? AGAINST A TRAITOR LIKE YOU?
WAIT...
...KOMAMURA.
I'LL DO IT.
FWOOSH

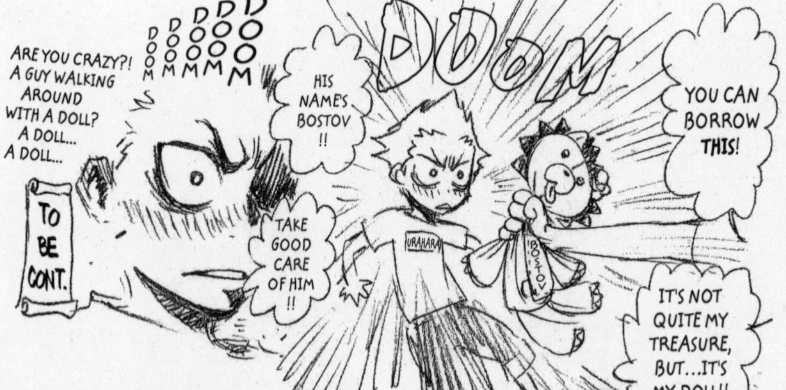
YOU CAN BORROW THIS!
IT'S NOT QUITE MY TREASURE, BUT…IT'S MY DOLL!!
DOOM
URAHARA
BOSTOV
HIS NAME'S BOSTOV!!
TAKE GOOD CARE OF HIM!!
DOOM DOOM DOOM DOOM DOOM
ARE YOU CRAZY?! A GUY WALKING AROUND WITH A DOLL? A DOLL... A DOLL...
TO BE CONT.

146. Demon Loves the Dark

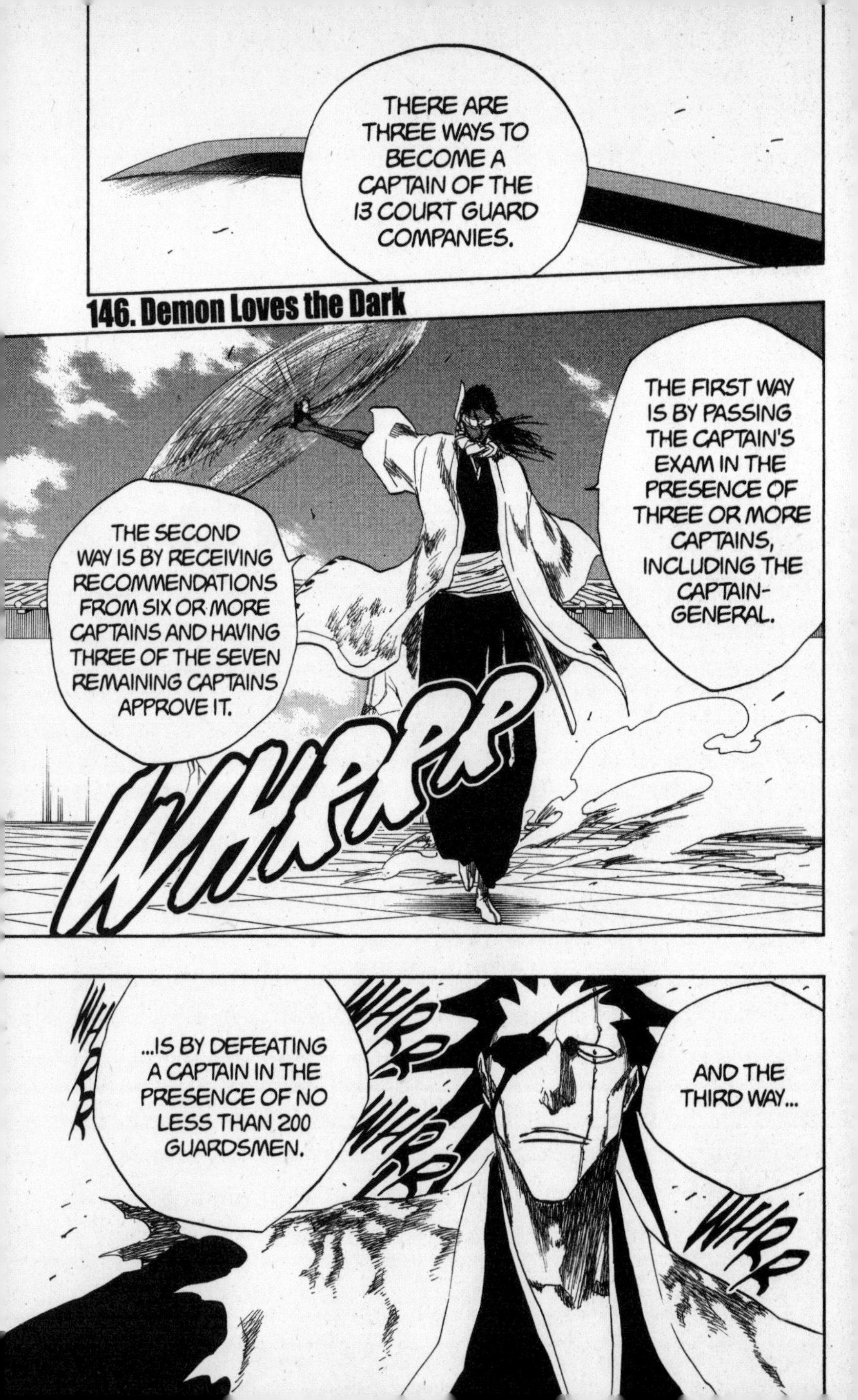
THERE ARE THREE WAYS TO BECOME A CAPTAIN OF THE 13 COURT GUARD COMPANIES.
THE FIRST WAY IS BY PASSING THE CAPTAIN'S EXAM IN THE PRESENCE OF THREE OR MORE CAPTAINS, INCLUDING THE CAPTAIN-GENERAL.
THE SECOND WAY IS BY RECEIVING RECOMMENDATIONS FROM SIX OR MORE CAPTAINS AND HAVING THREE OF THE SEVEN REMAINING CAPTAINS APPROVE IT.
WHRRR
AND THE THIRD WAY...
WHRR
WHRR
WHRR
...IS BY DEFEATING A CAPTAIN IN THE PRESENCE OF NO LESS THAN 200 GUARDSMEN.
WHRR

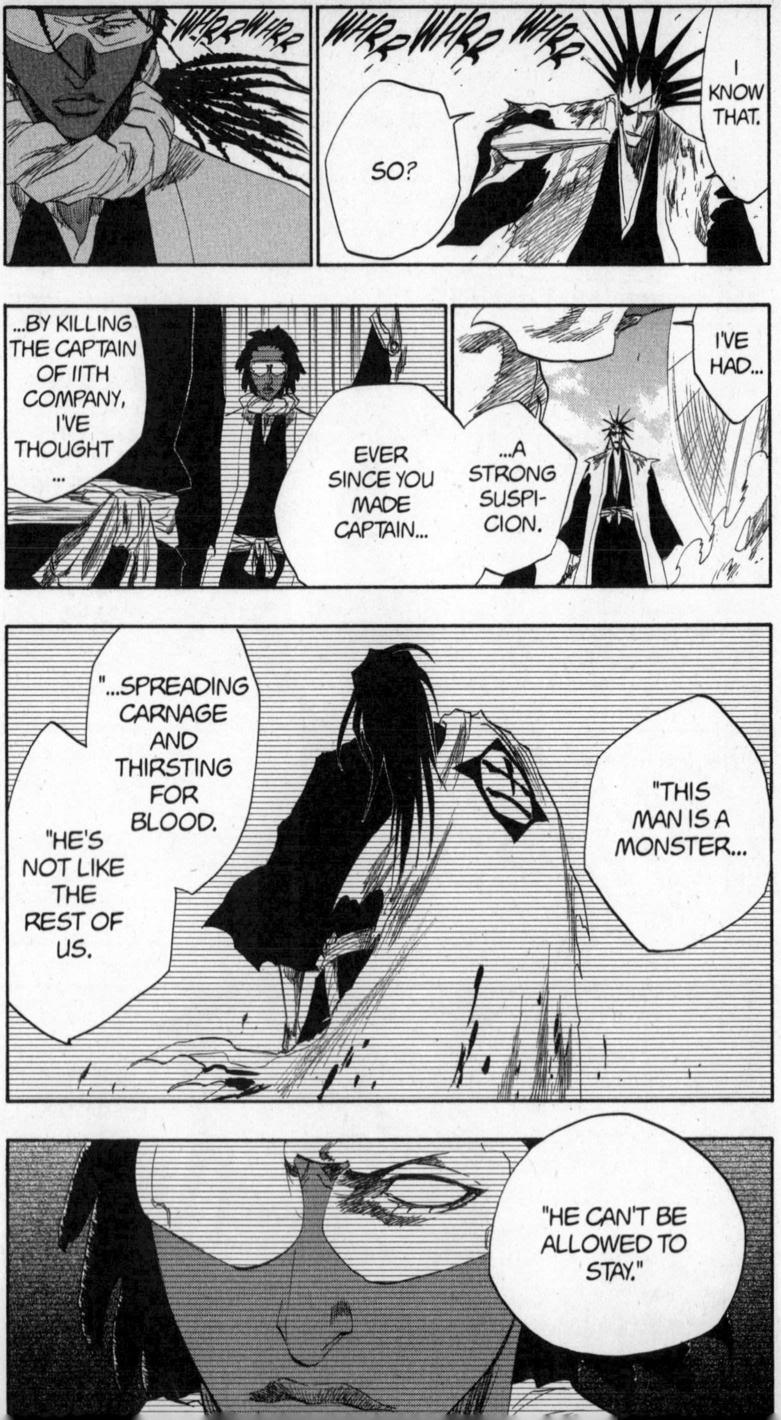
WHRR WHRR WHRR
I KNOW THAT.
SO?
WHRR WHRR
I'VE HAD...
...A STRONG SUSPI-CION.
EVER SINCE YOU MADE CAPTAIN...
...BY KILLING THE CAPTAIN OF 11TH COMPANY, I'VE THOUGHT ...
"THIS MAN IS A MONSTER...
"...SPREADING CARNAGE AND THIRSTING FOR BLOOD.
"HE'S NOT LIKE THE REST OF US.
"HE CAN'T BE ALLOWED TO STAY."

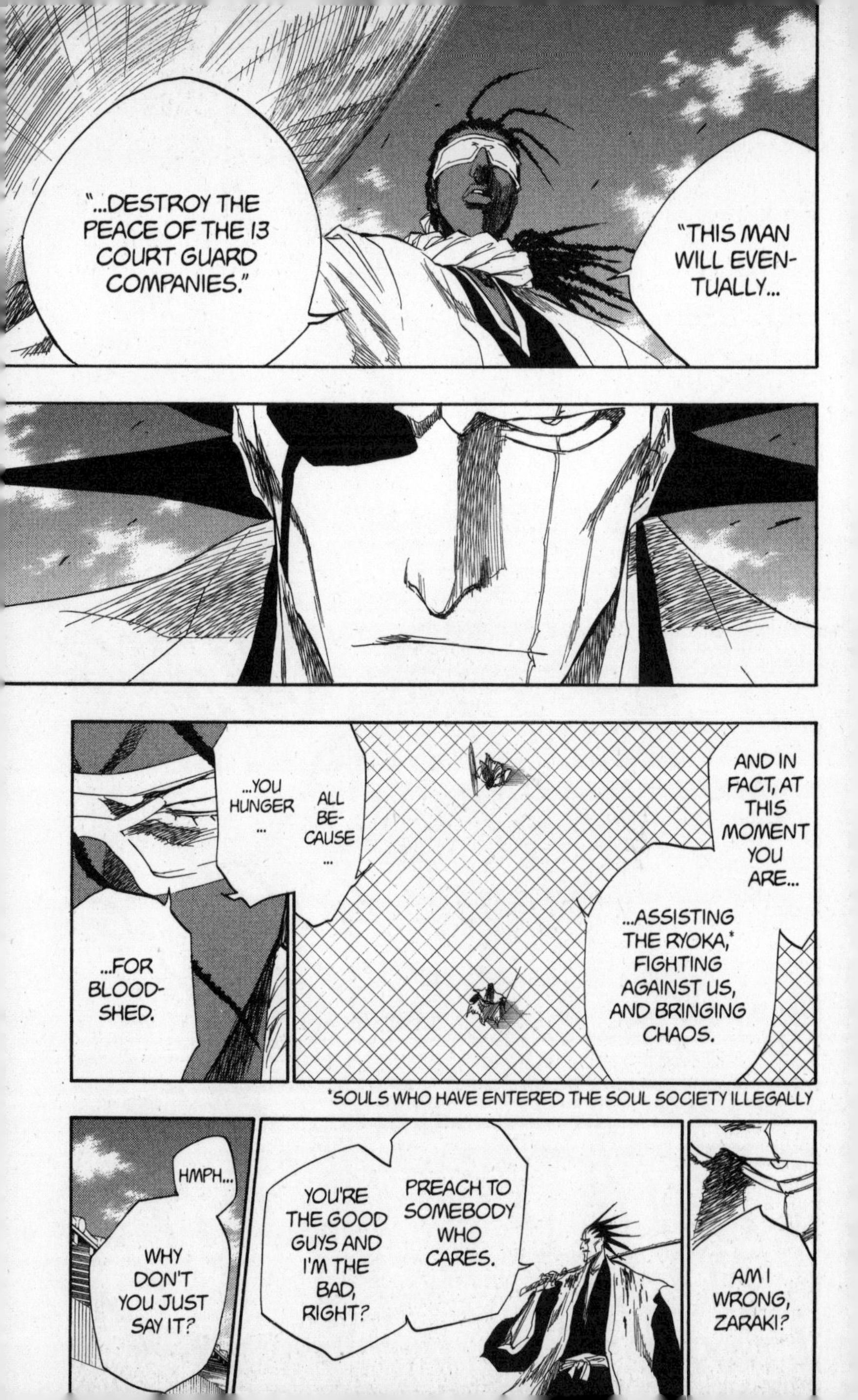
"THIS MAN WILL EVEN-TUALLY...
"...DESTROY THE PEACE OF THE 13 COURT GUARD COMPANIES."
AND IN FACT, AT THIS MOMENT YOU ARE...
...ASSISTING THE RYOKA,* FIGHTING AGAINST US, AND BRINGING CHAOS.
ALL BE-CAUSE ...
...YOU HUNGER ...
...FOR BLOOD-SHED.
AM I WRONG, ZARAKI?
PREACH TO SOMEBODY WHO CARES.
YOU'RE THE GOOD GUYS AND I'M THE BAD, RIGHT?
HMPH...
WHY DON'T YOU JUST SAY IT?

*SOULS WHO HAVE ENTERED THE SOUL SOCIETY ILLEGALLY

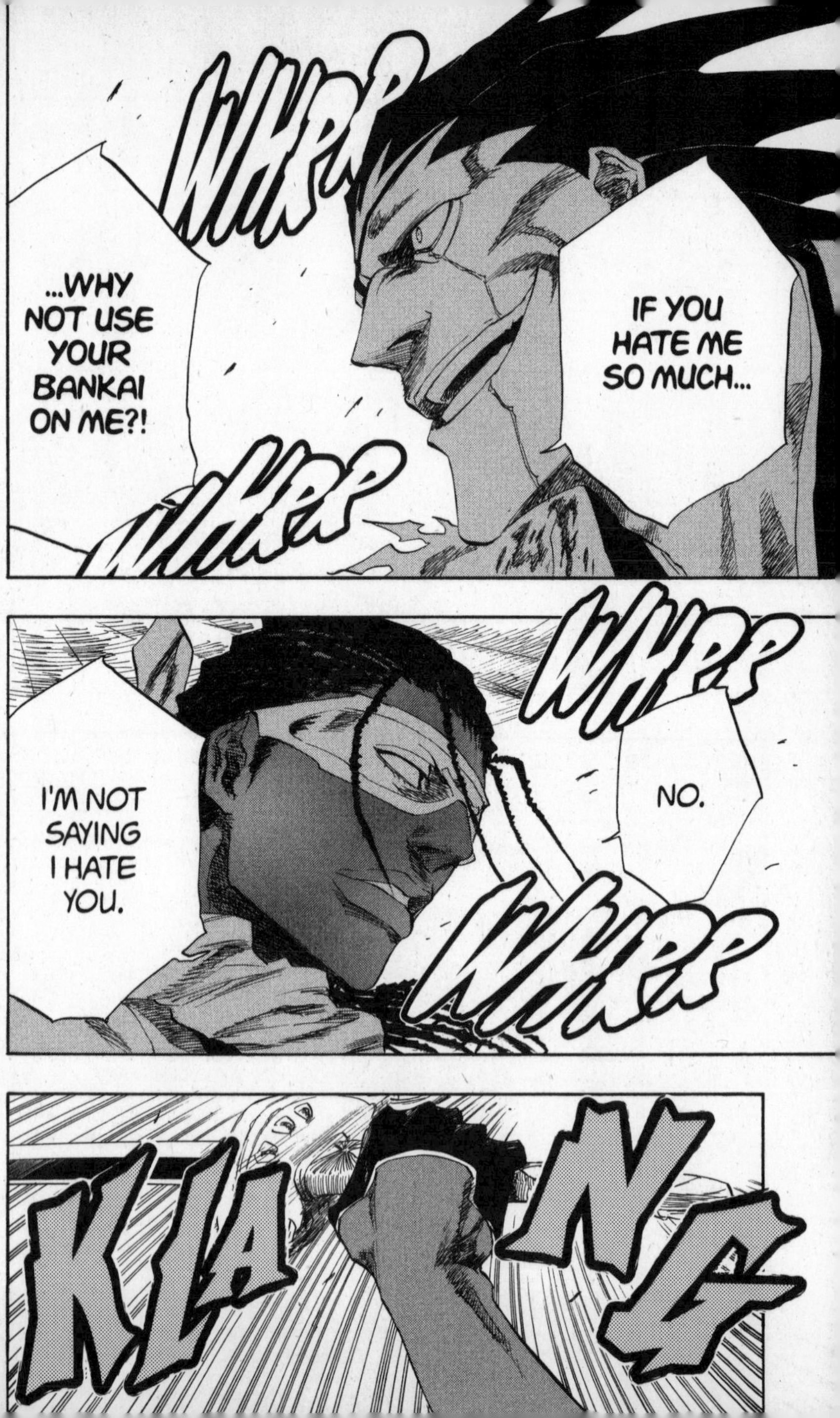
WHPP
IF YOU HATE ME SO MUCH...
...WHY NOT USE YOUR BANKAI ON ME?!
WHPP
WHPP
NO.
I'M NOT SAYING I HATE YOU.
WHPP
KLANG

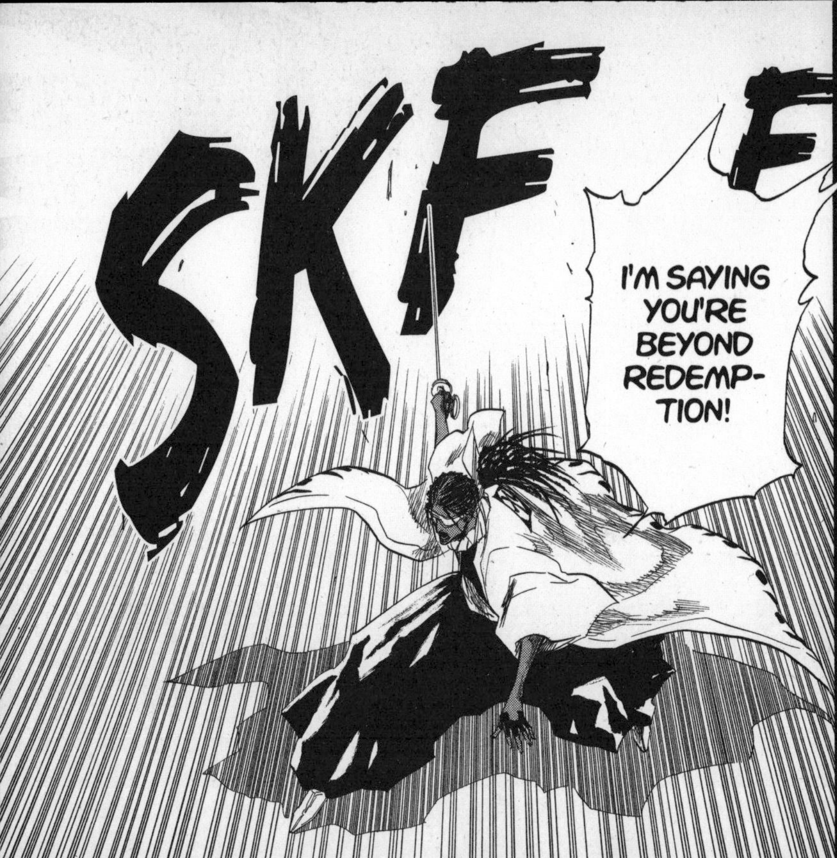
SKF
I'M SAYING YOU'RE BEYOND REDEMP-TION!

146. Demon Loves the Dark

BLEACH
-ブリーチ-

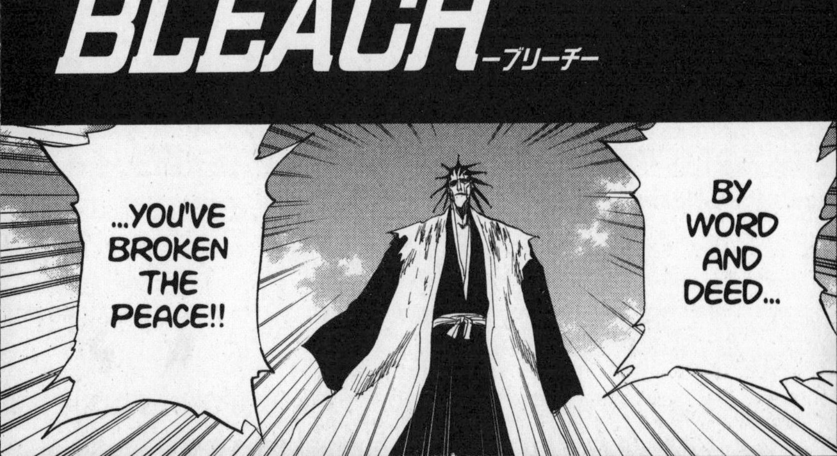
BY WORD AND DEED...
...YOU'VE BROKEN THE PEACE!!

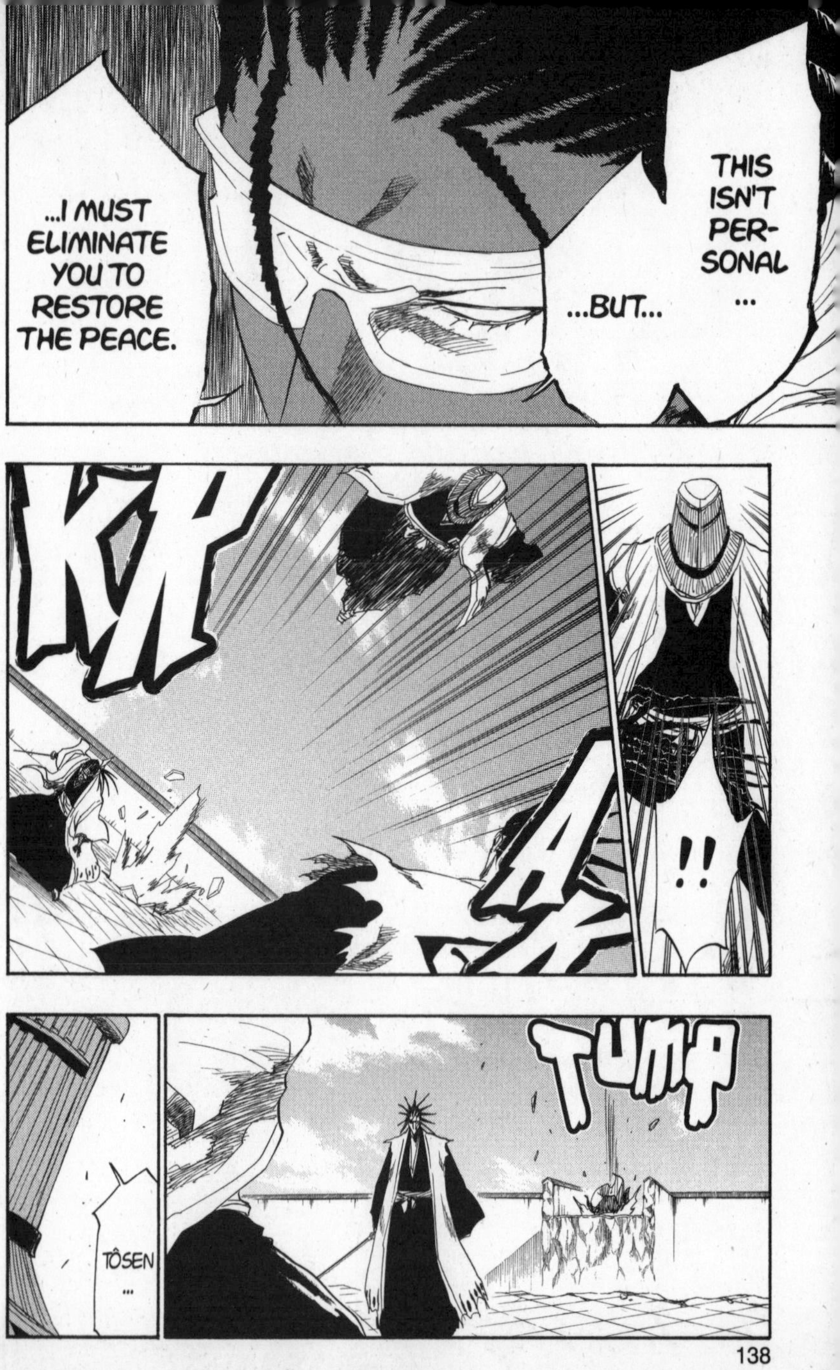
THIS ISN'T PERSONAL...
...BUT...
...I MUST ELIMINATE YOU TO RESTORE THE PEACE.
!!
TUMP
TÔSEN ...

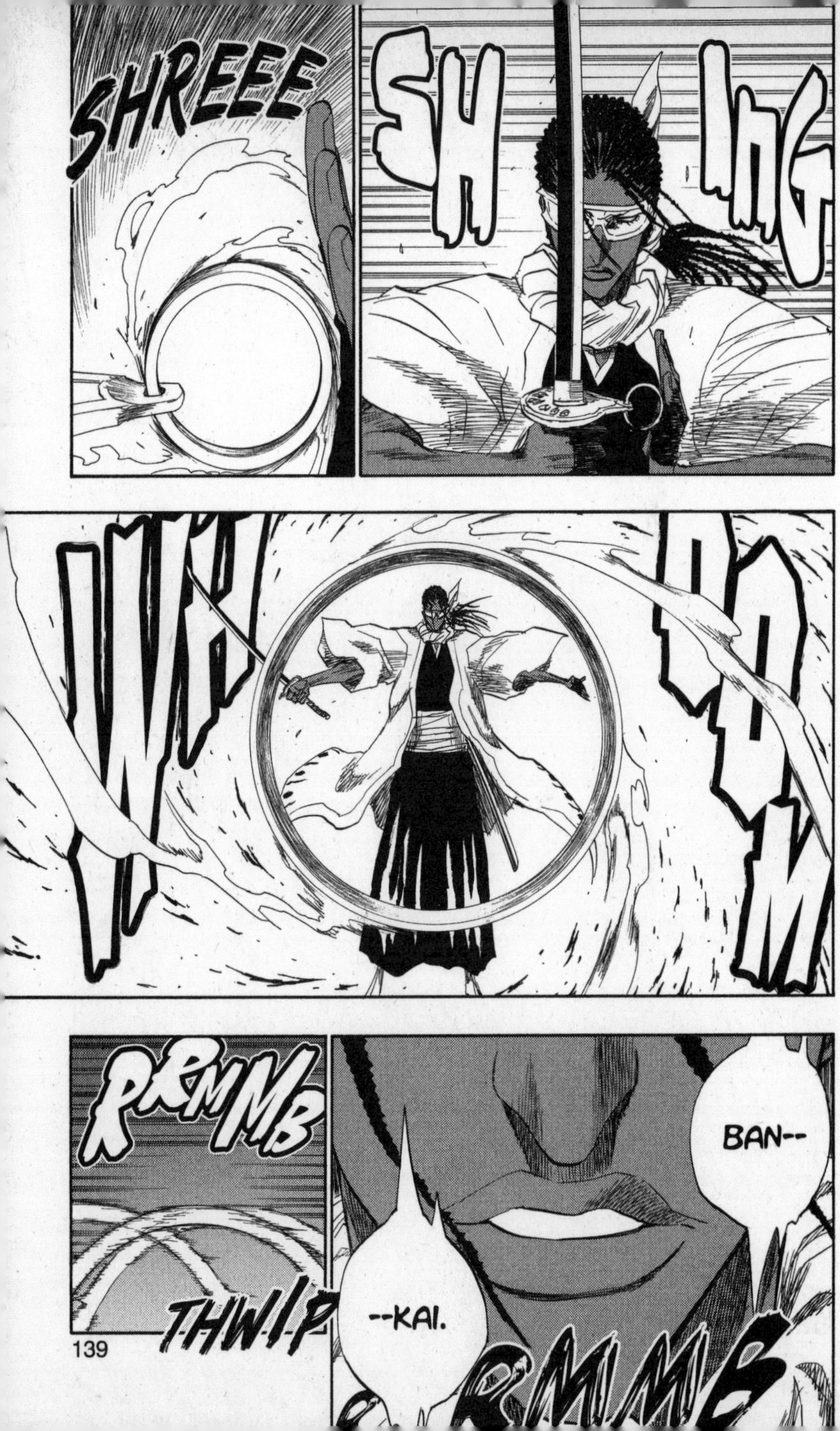
SH
ING
SHREEE
BAN--
--KAI.
RMMB
RRMMB
THWIP

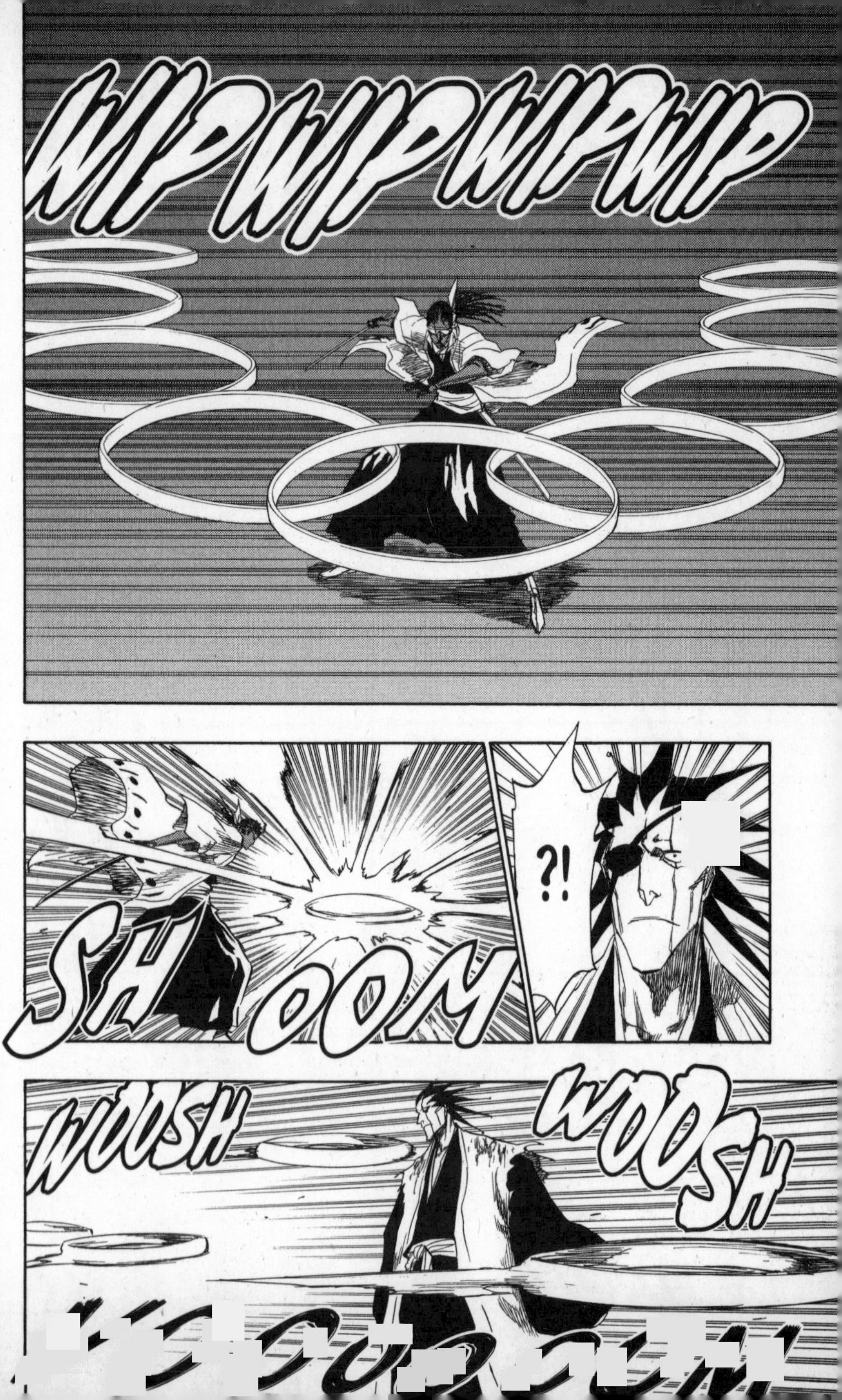
WIPWIPWIPWIP
?!
SHOOM
WOOSH
WOOSH

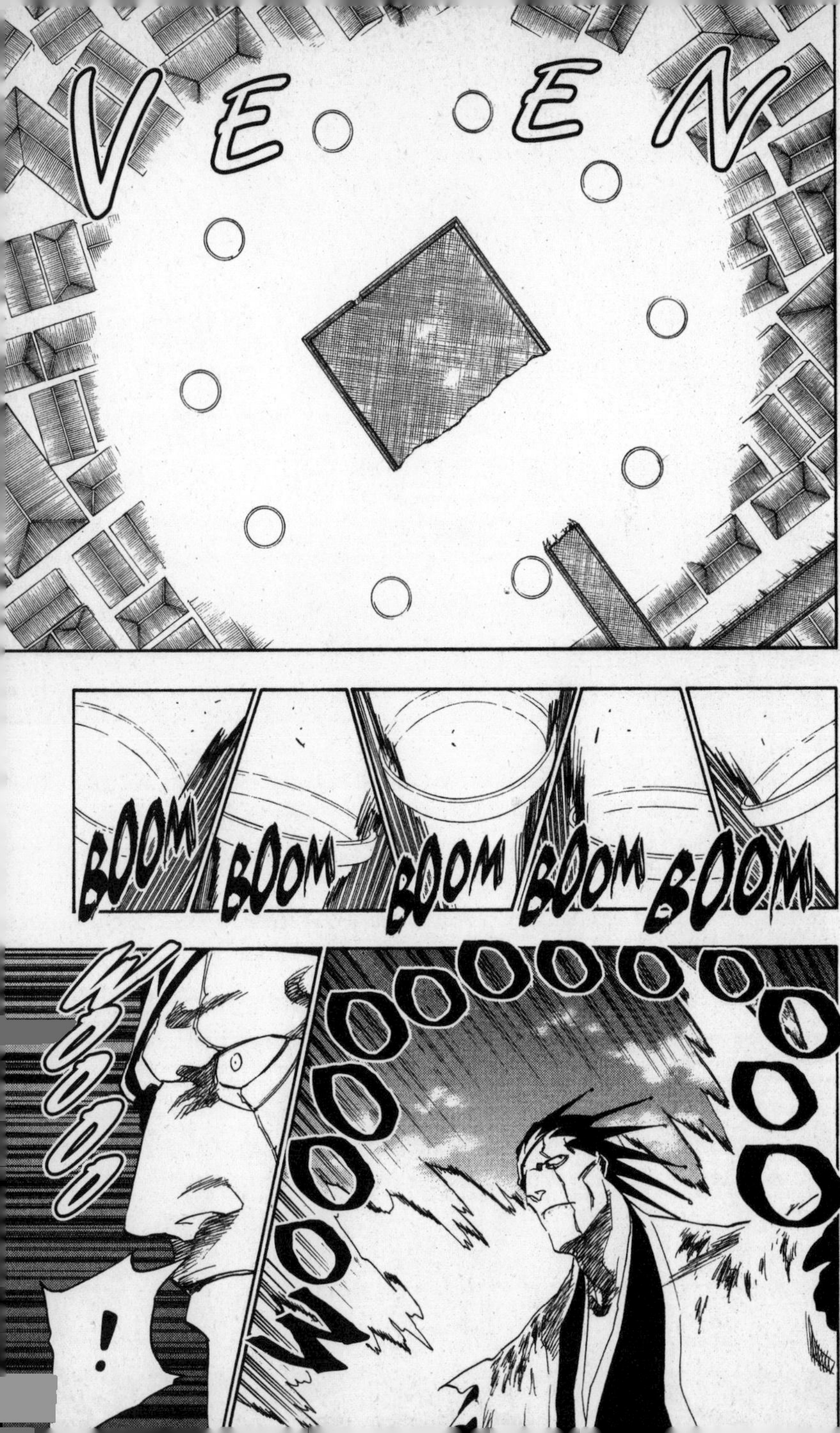
VEEN
BOOM BOOM BOOM BOOM BOOM
WOOOOOOOOOOOOOOM
WOOOOO
!

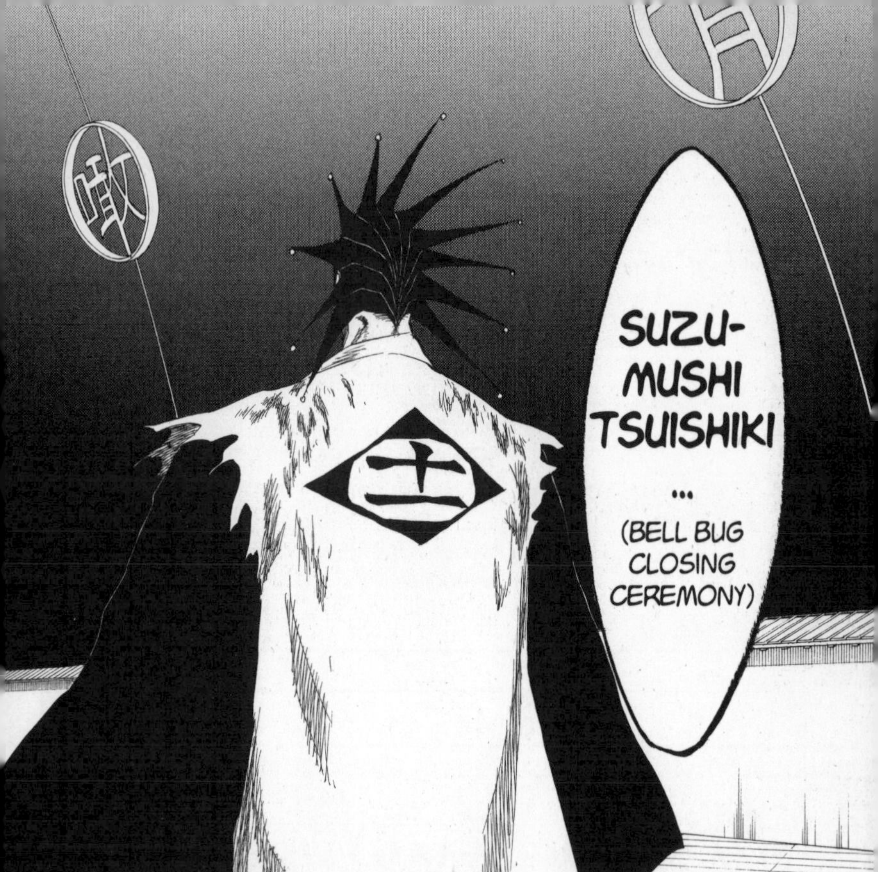
SUZU-MUSHI TSUISHIKI ... (BELL BUG CLOSING CEREMONY)
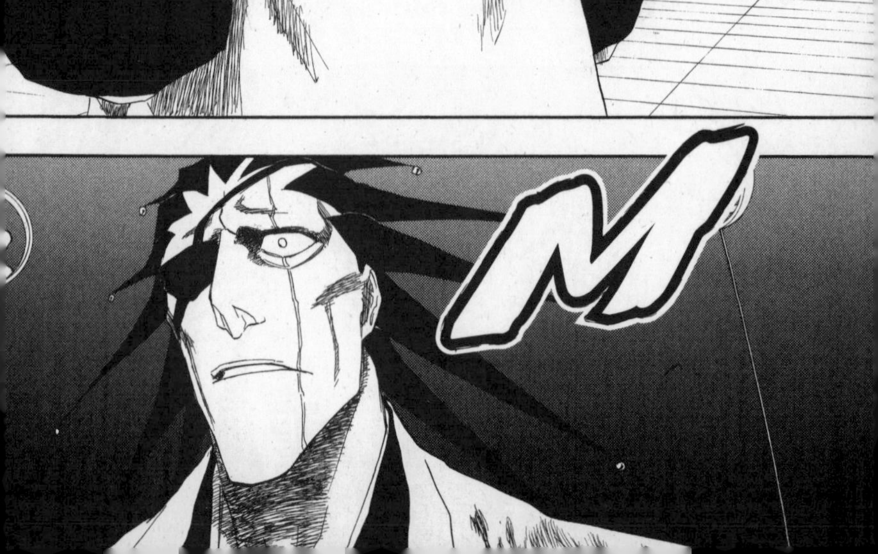
M

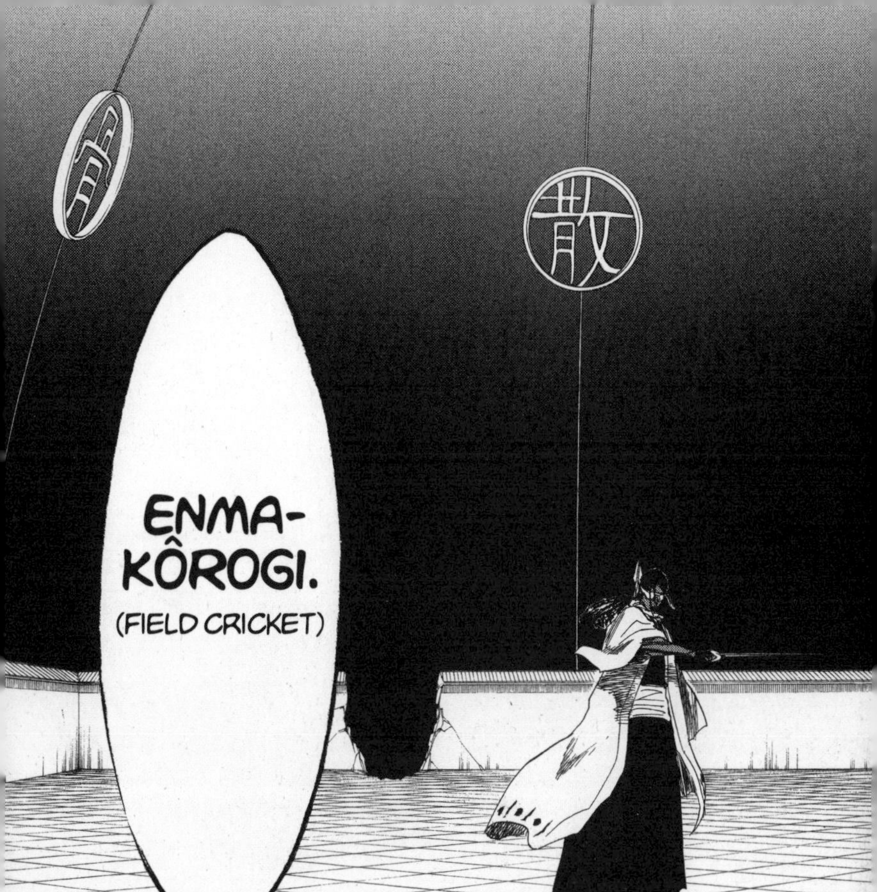
散
ENMA-
KÔROGI.
(FIELD CRICKET)
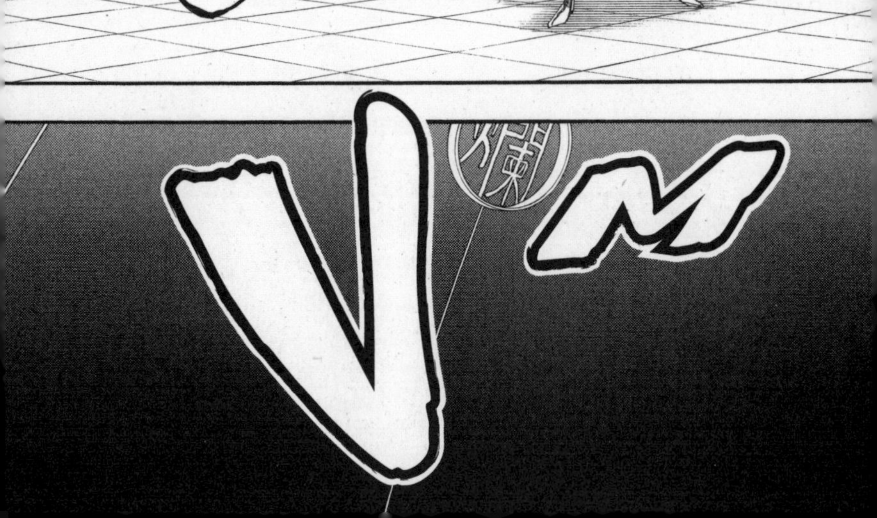
VM

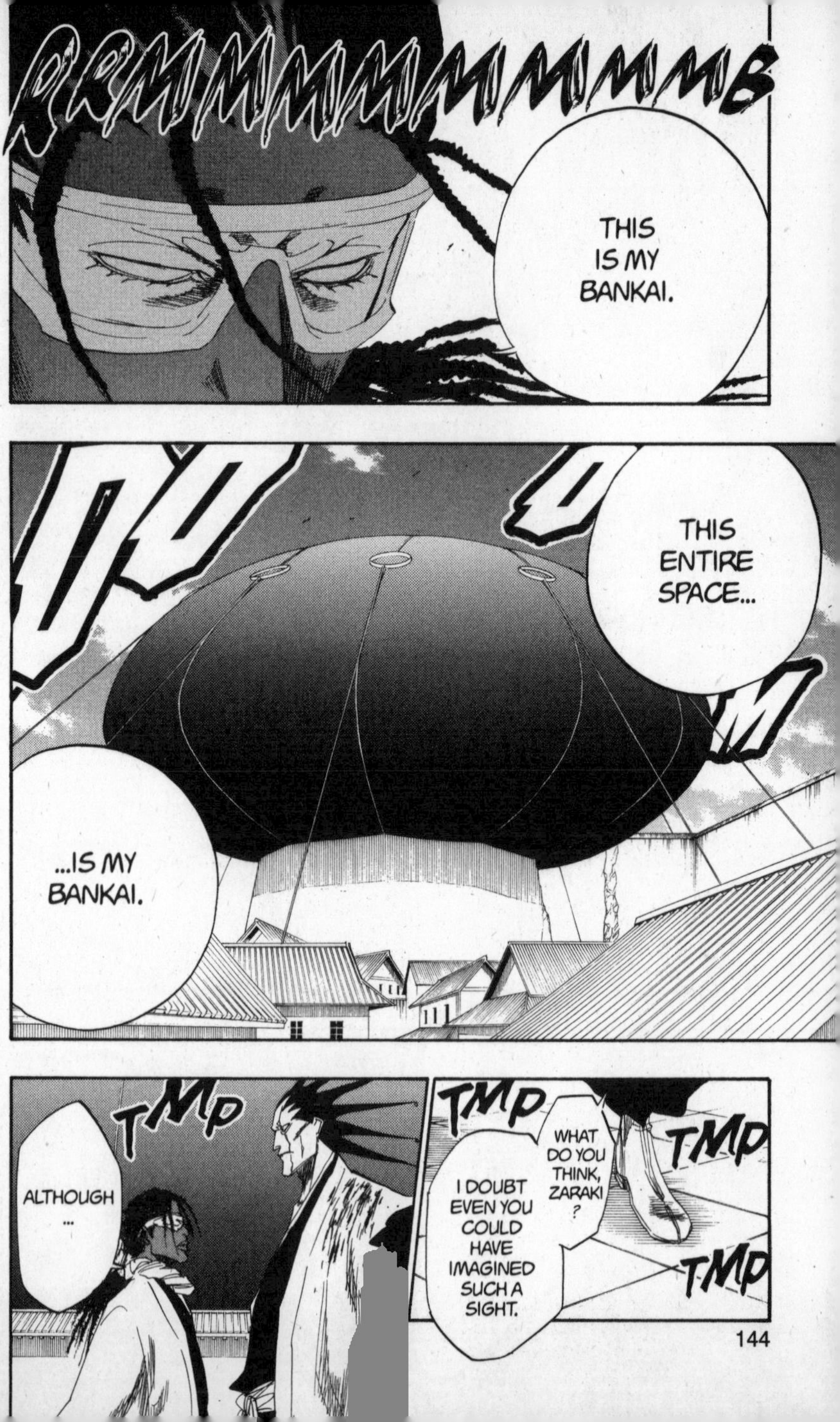
BRMMMMMMMMMMMMB
THIS IS MY BANKAI.
THIS ENTIRE SPACE...
...IS MY BANKAI.
TMP
WHAT DO YOU THINK, ZARAKI?
I DOUBT EVEN YOU COULD HAVE IMAGINED SUCH A SIGHT.
TMP
TMP
TMP
ALTHOUGH...

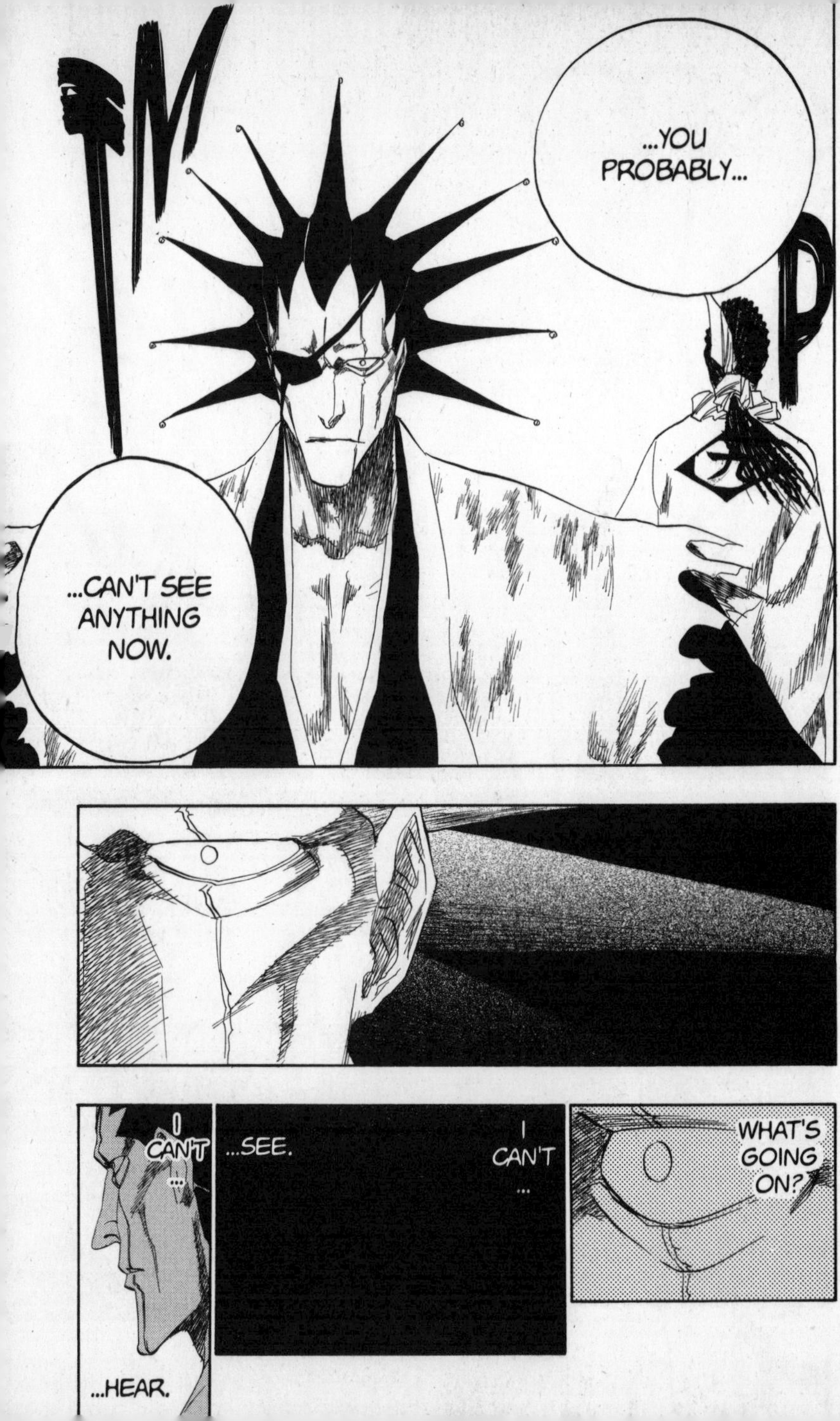
...YOU PROBABLY...
TMP
...CAN'T SEE ANYTHING NOW.
WHAT'S GOING ON?
I CAN'T ...
...SEE.
I CAN'T ...
...HEAR.

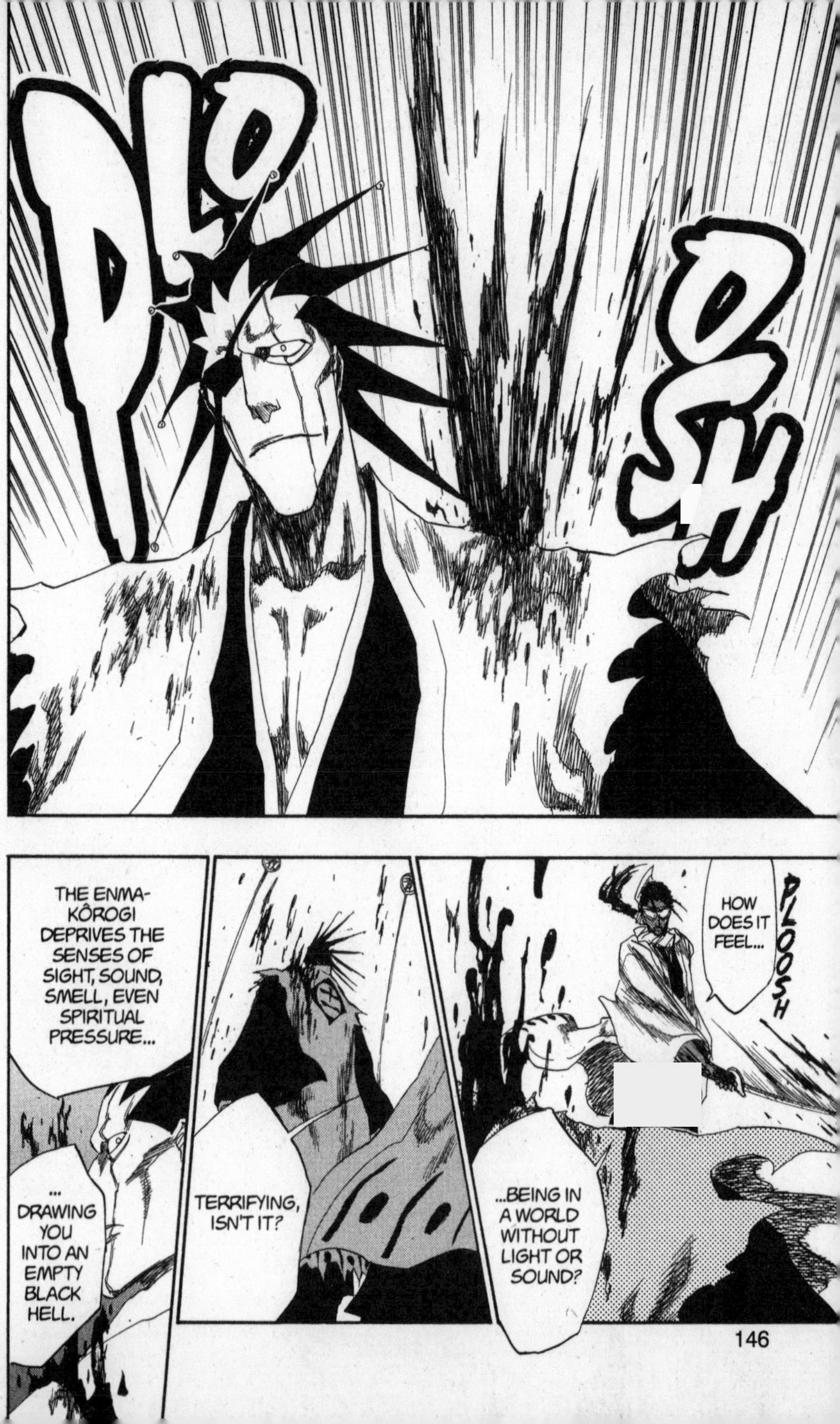
PLOOSH
PLOOSH
HOW DOES IT FEEL...
...BEING IN A WORLD WITHOUT LIGHT OR SOUND?
TERRIFYING, ISN'T IT?
THE ENMA-KÔROGI DEPRIVES THE SENSES OF SIGHT, SOUND, SMELL, EVEN SPIRITUAL PRESSURE...
...DRAWING YOU INTO AN EMPTY BLACK HELL.

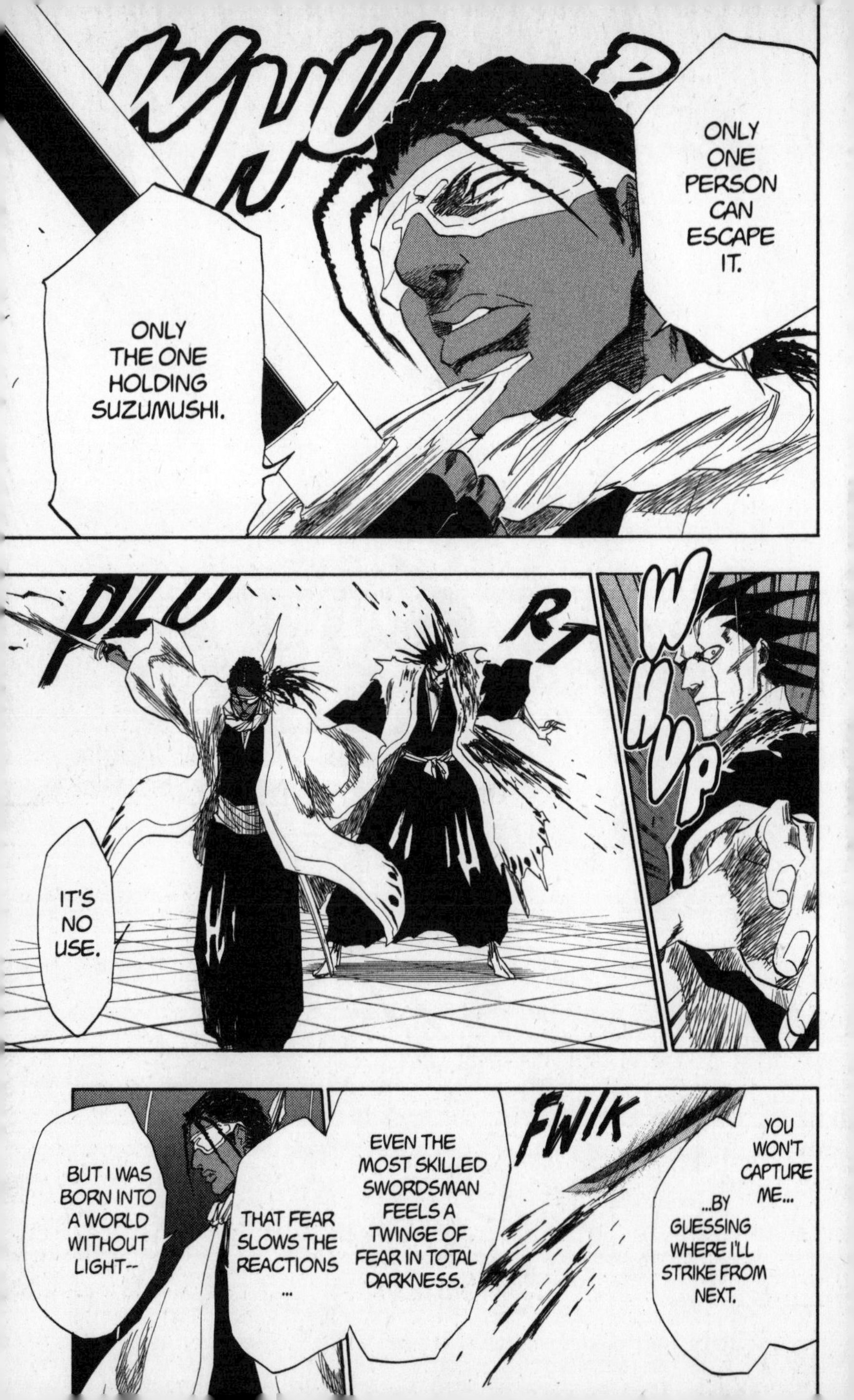
ONLY ONE PERSON CAN ESCAPE IT.
ONLY THE ONE HOLDING SUZUMUSHI.
WHUP
PLORT
IT'S NO USE.
YOU WON'T CAPTURE ME...
...BY GUESSING WHERE I'LL STRIKE FROM NEXT.
FWIK
EVEN THE MOST SKILLED SWORDSMAN FEELS A TWINGE OF FEAR IN TOTAL DARKNESS.
THAT FEAR SLOWS THE REACTIONS...
BUT I WAS BORN INTO A WORLD WITHOUT LIGHT--

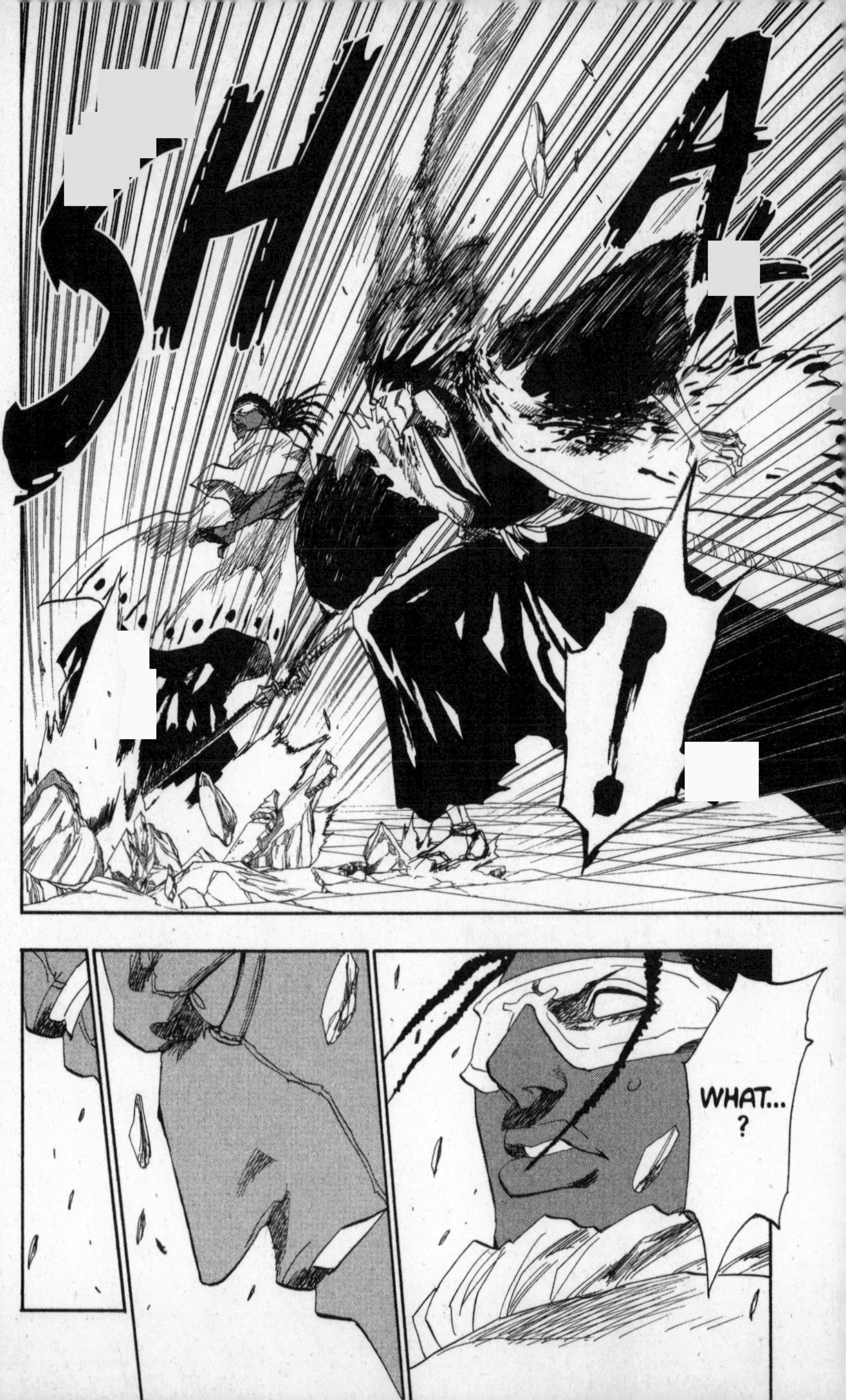
SHA
WHAT... ?

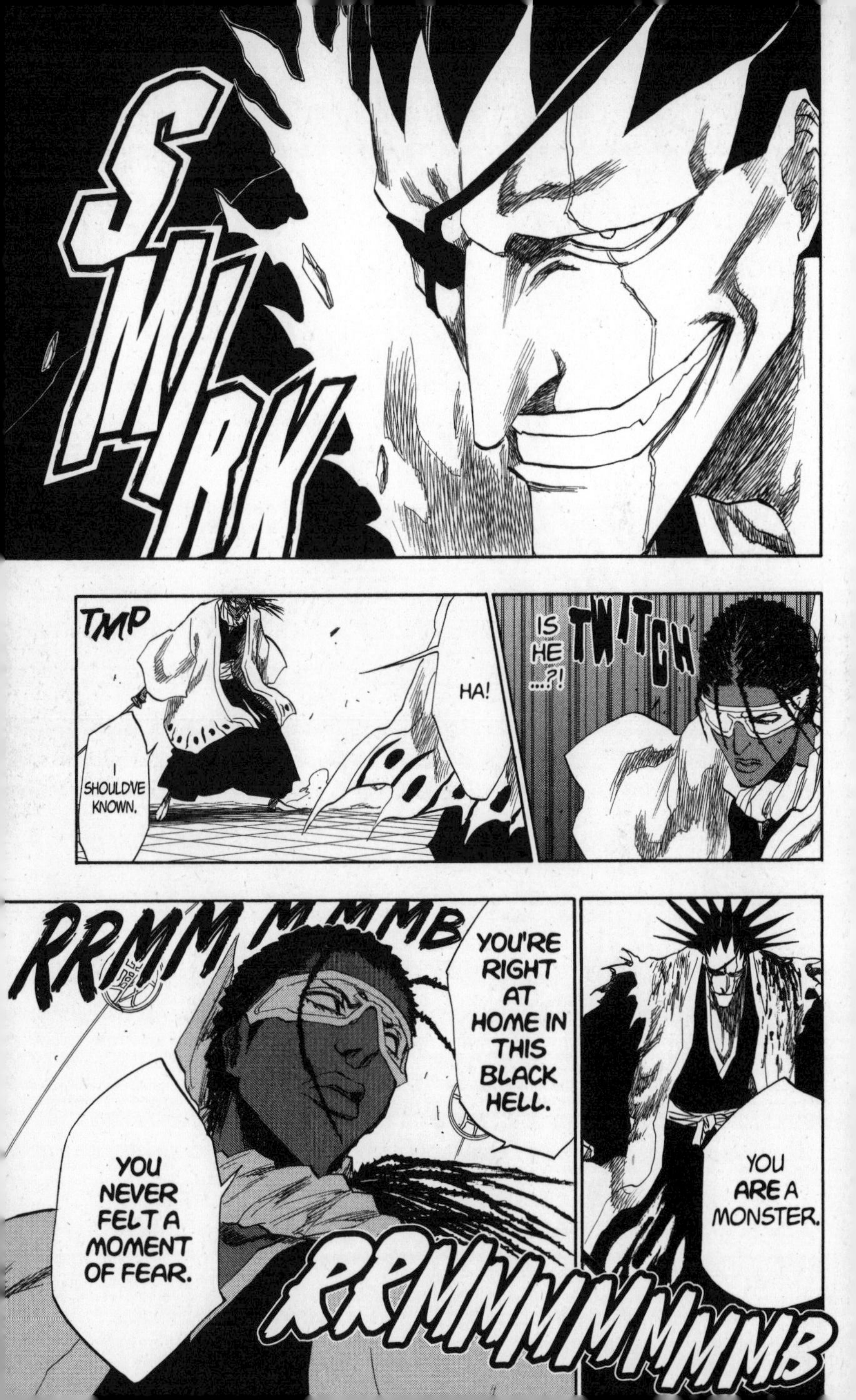
SMIRK
IS HE ...?!
TWITCH
TMP
HA!
I SHOULD'VE KNOWN.
YOU ARE A MONSTER.
RRMMMMMMMB
YOU'RE RIGHT AT HOME IN THIS BLACK HELL.
YOU NEVER FELT A MOMENT OF FEAR.
RRMMMMMMMMMB

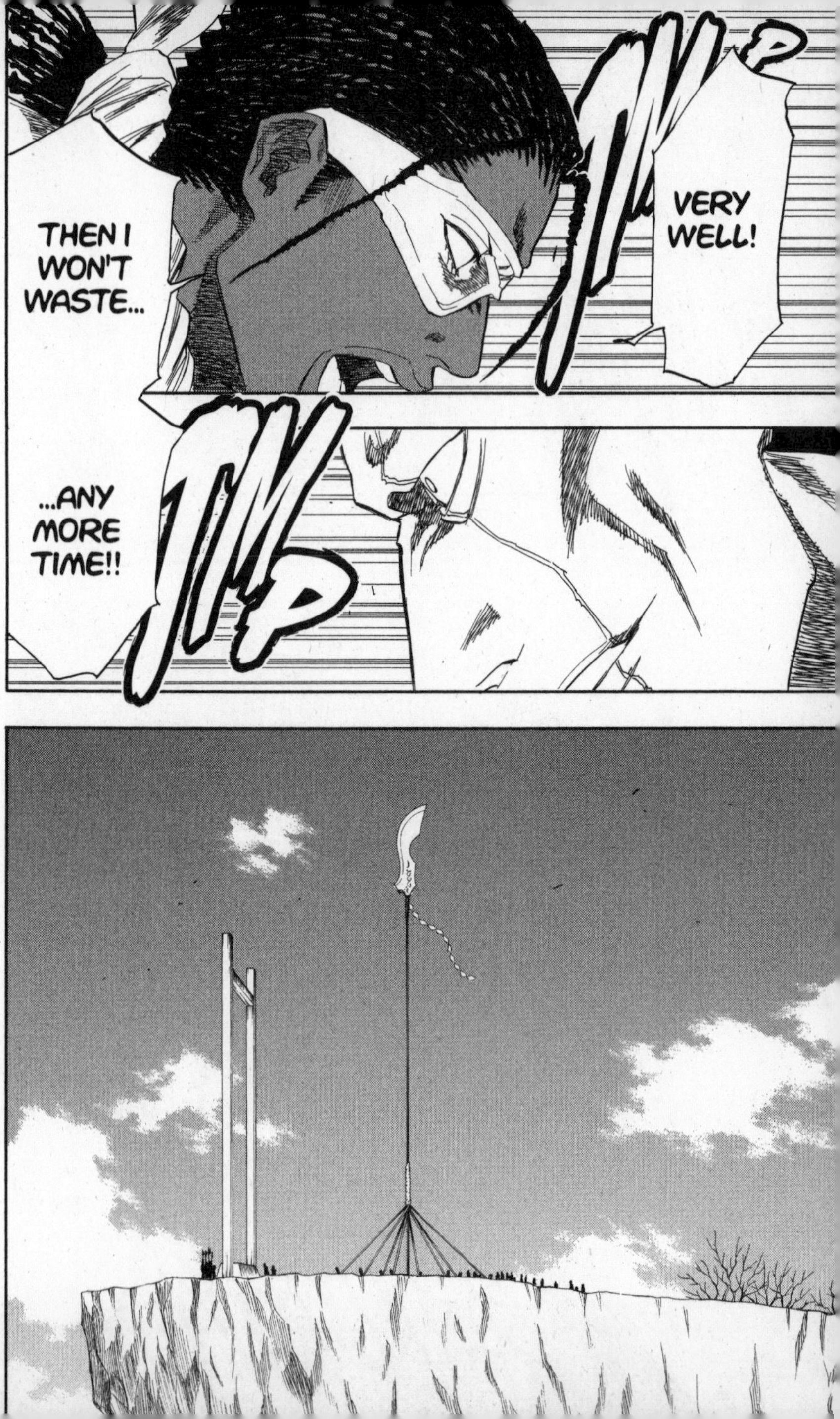
VERY WELL!
THEN I WON'T WASTE...
...ANY MORE TIME!!

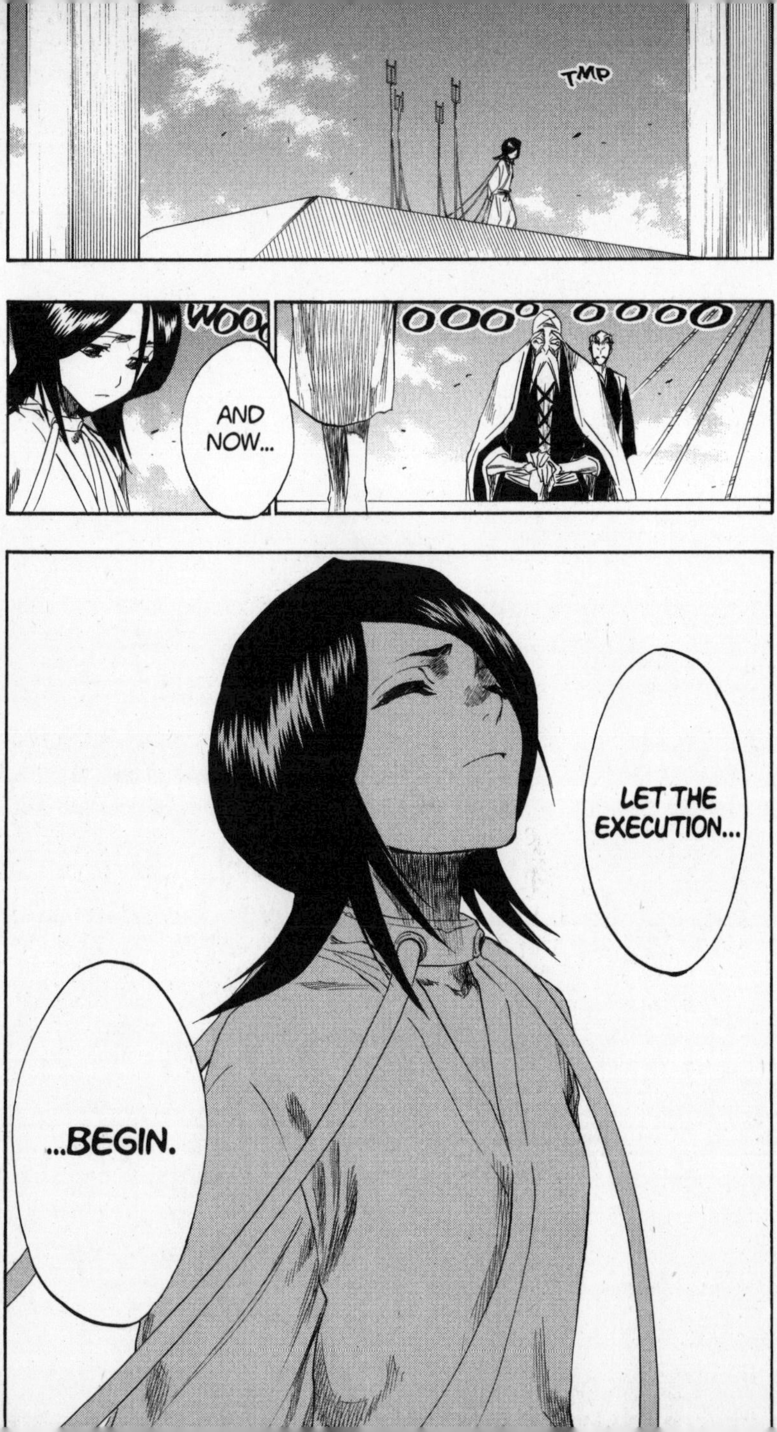
TMP
OOOO OOOO
WOOO
AND NOW...
LET THE EXECUTION...
...BEGIN.

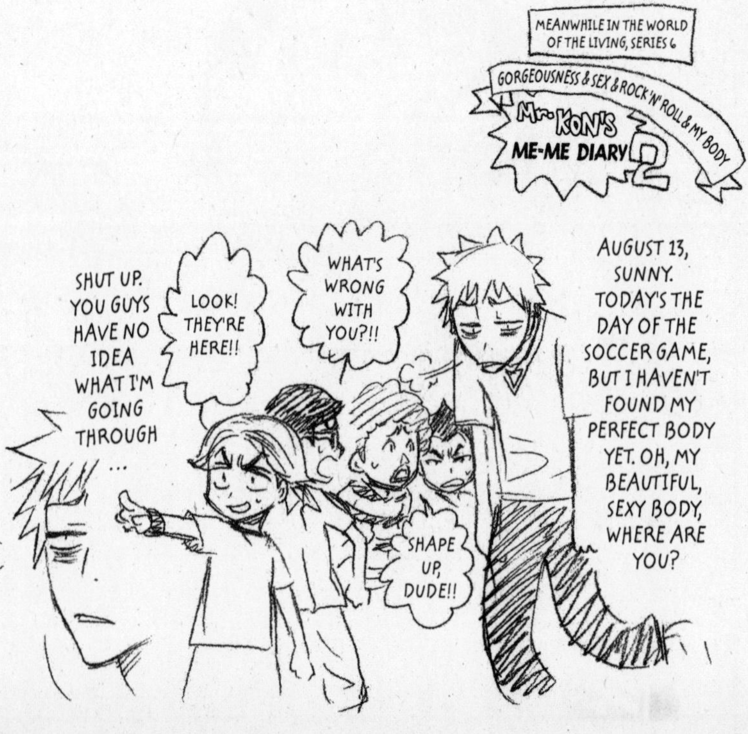
MEANWHILE IN THE WORLD OF THE LIVING, SERIES 6
GORGEOUSNESS & SEX & ROCK 'N' ROLL & MY BODY
Mr. KON'S ME-ME DIARY 2
AUGUST 13, SUNNY. TODAY'S THE DAY OF THE SOCCER GAME, BUT I HAVEN'T FOUND MY PERFECT BODY YET. OH, MY BEAUTIFUL, SEXY BODY, WHERE ARE YOU?
WHAT'S WRONG WITH YOU?!!
SHAPE UP, DUDE!!
LOOK! THEY'RE HERE!!
SHUT UP. YOU GUYS HAVE NO IDEA WHAT I'M GOING THROUGH...

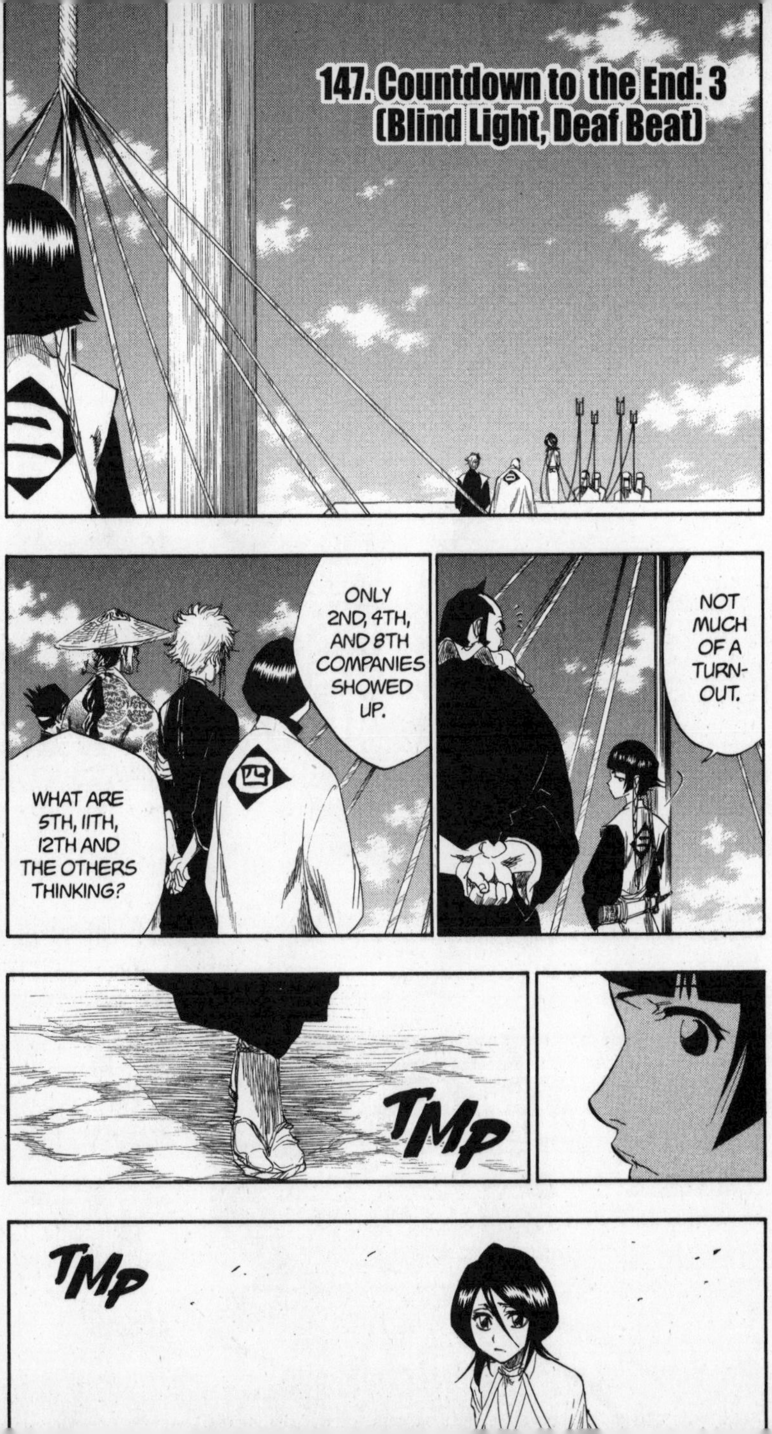
147. Countdown to the End: 3
(Blind Light, Deaf Beat)
NOT MUCH OF A TURN-OUT.
ONLY 2ND, 4TH, AND 8TH COMPANIES SHOWED UP.
WHAT ARE 5TH, 11TH, 12TH AND THE OTHERS THINKING?
TMP
TMP

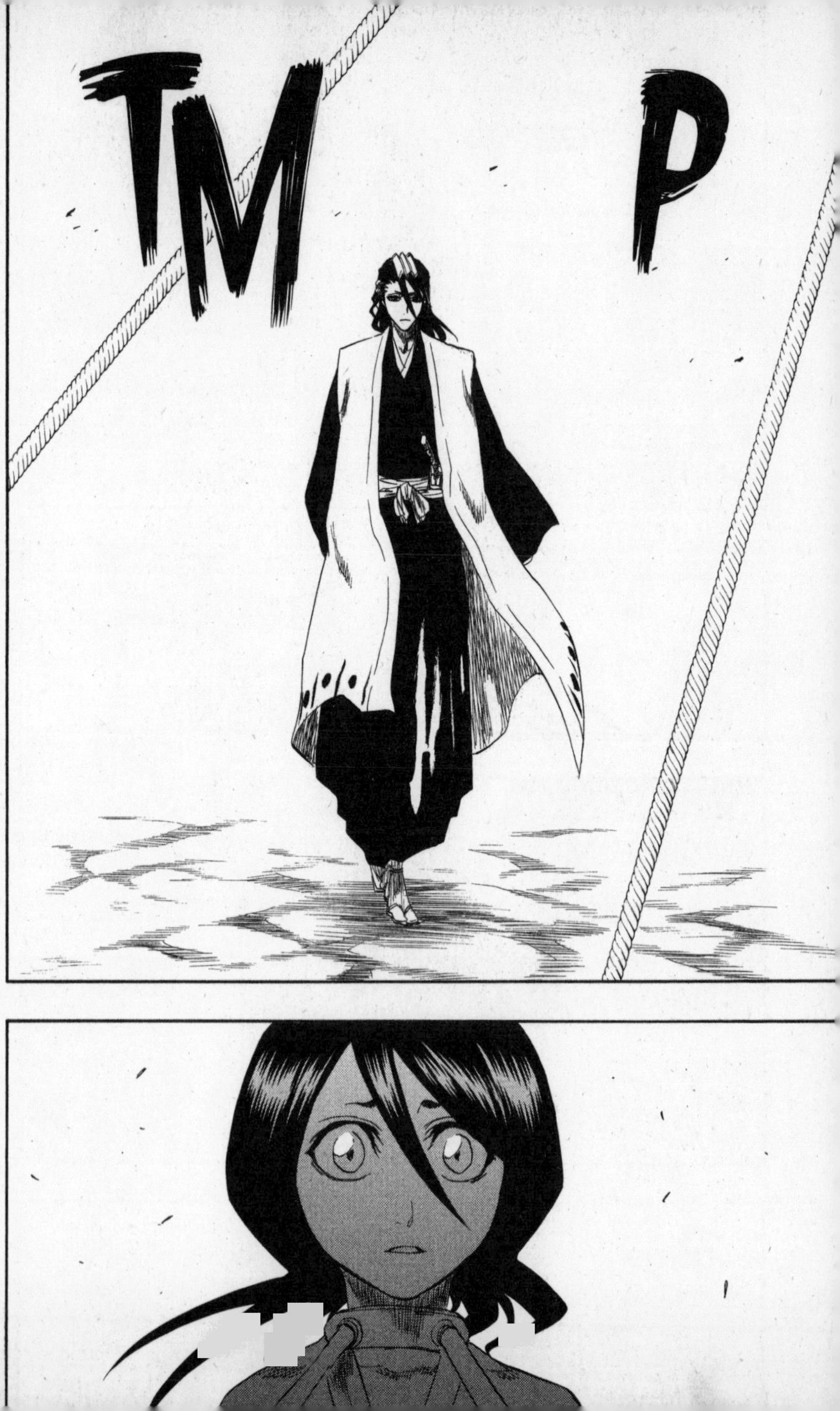
TMP

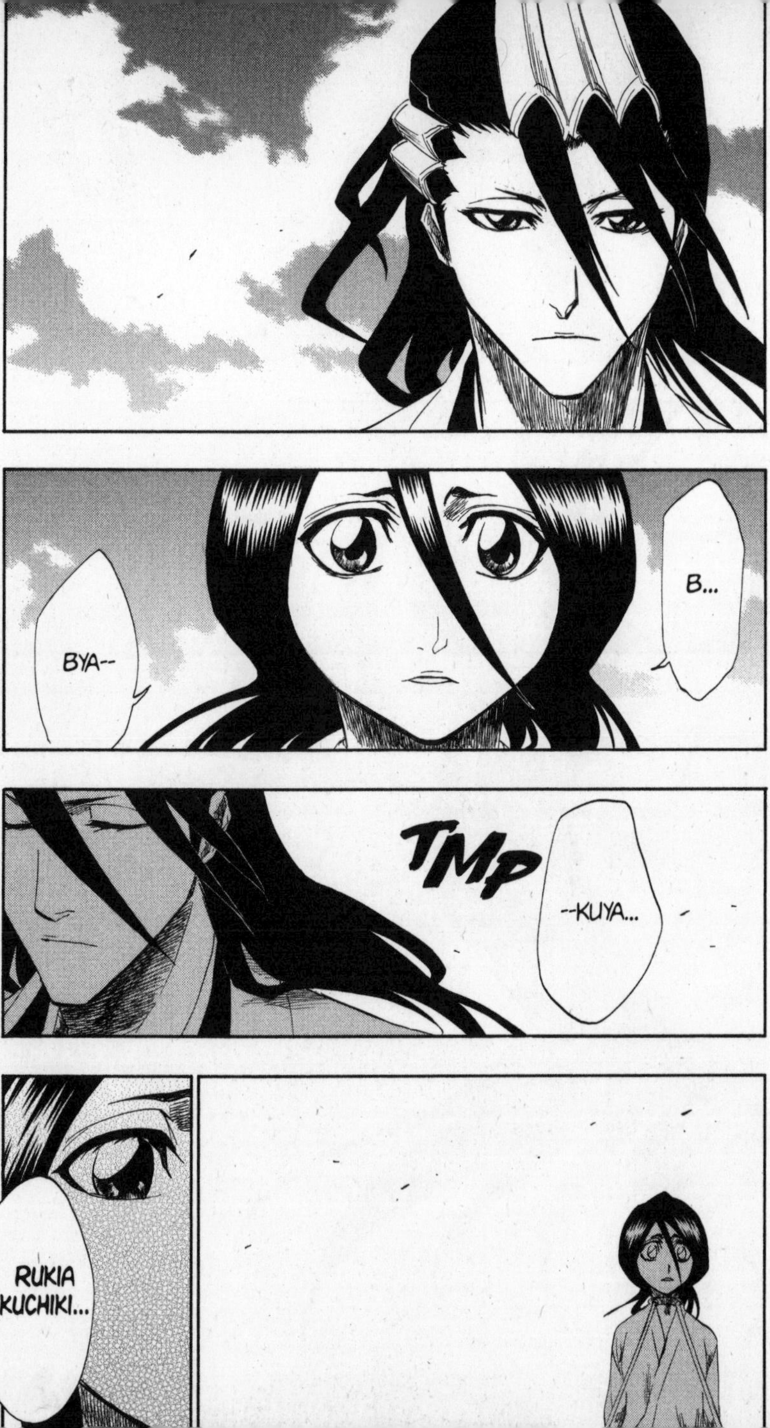
B...
BYA--
--KUYA...
TMP
RUKIA KUCHIKI...

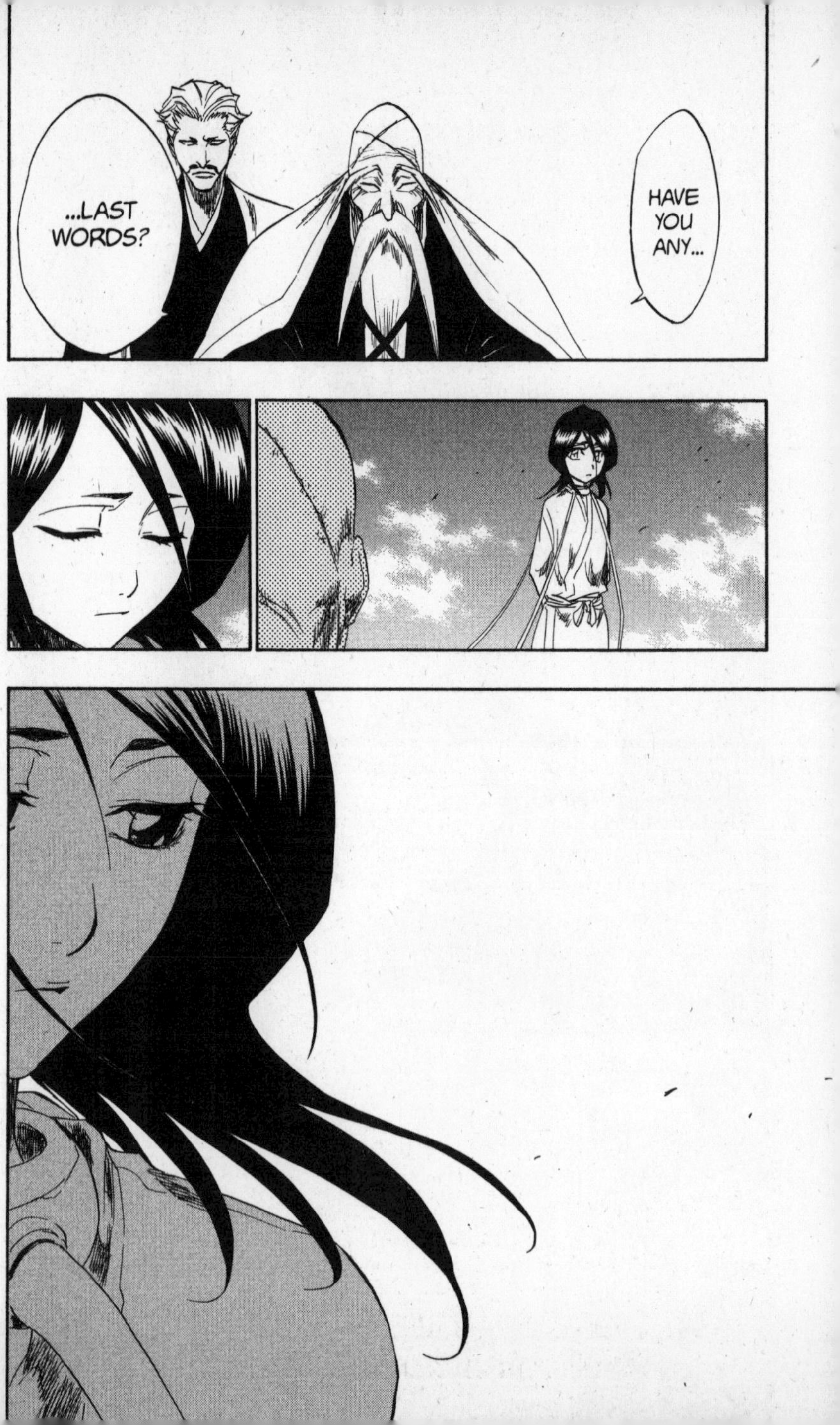
HAVE YOU ANY...
...LAST WORDS?

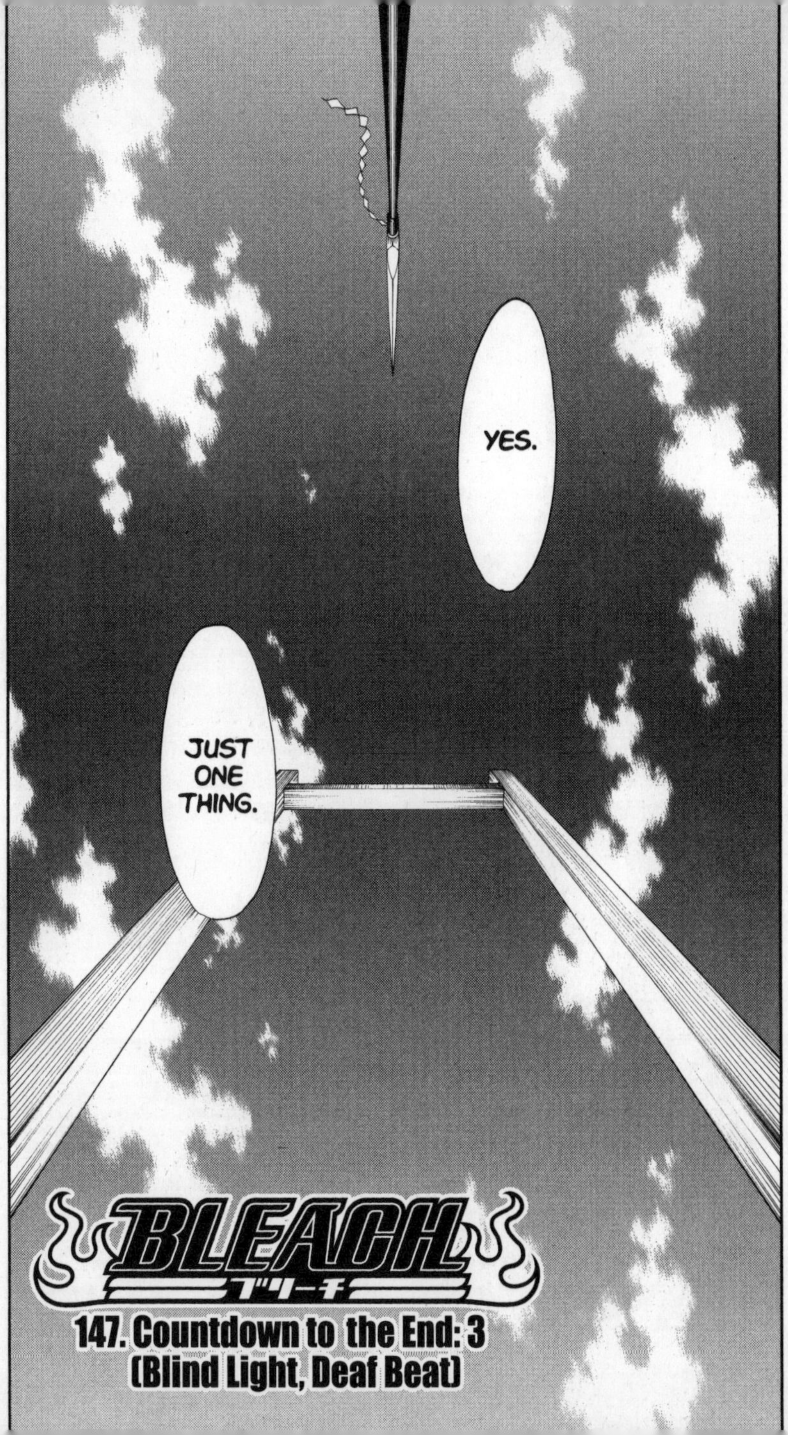
YES.
JUST ONE THING.
BLEACH
ブリーチ
147. Countdown to the End: 3
(Blind Light, Deaf Beat)

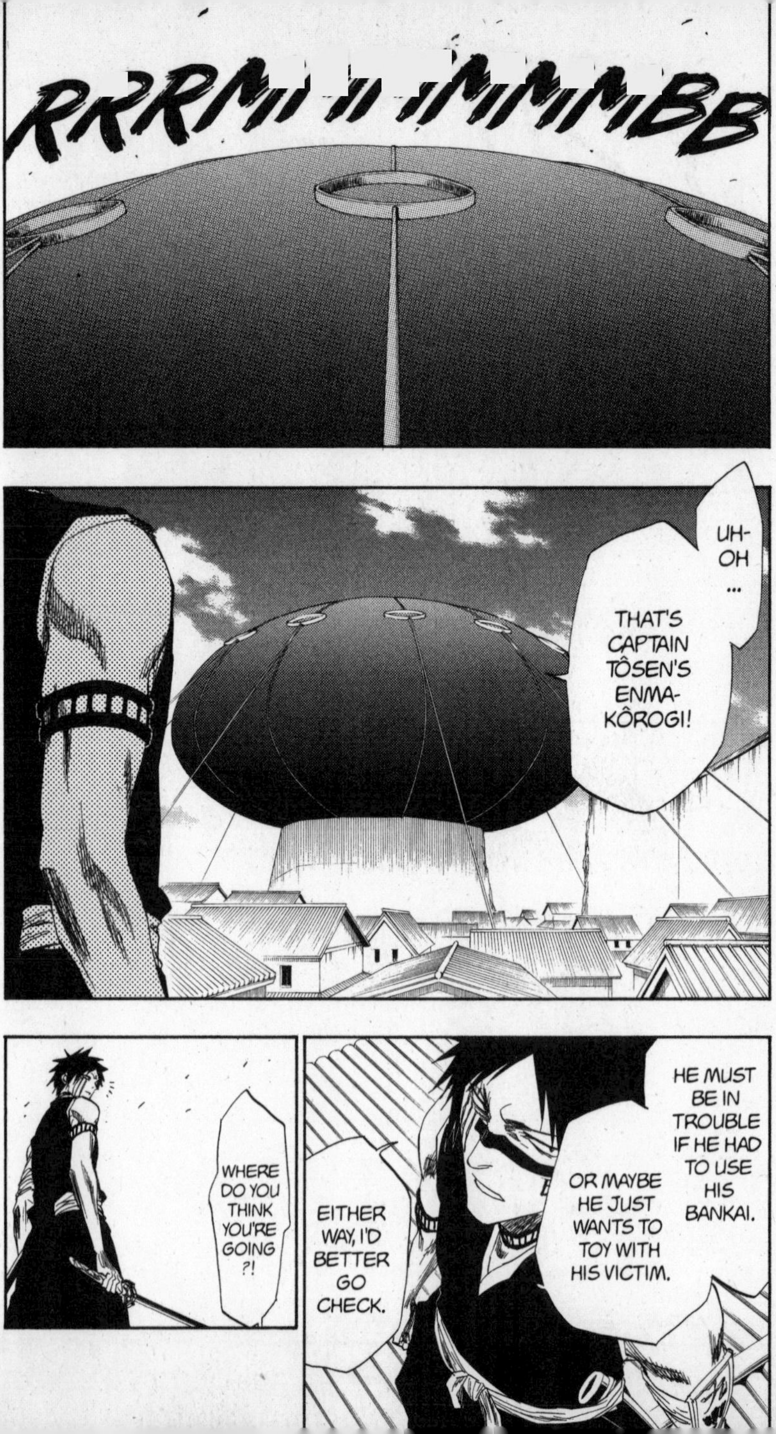
UH-OH ...
THAT'S CAPTAIN TÔSEN'S ENMA-KÔROGI!
HE MUST BE IN TROUBLE IF HE HAD TO USE HIS BANKAI.
OR MAYBE HE JUST WANTS TO TOY WITH HIS VICTIM.
EITHER WAY, I'D BETTER GO CHECK.
WHERE DO YOU THINK YOU'RE GOING?!

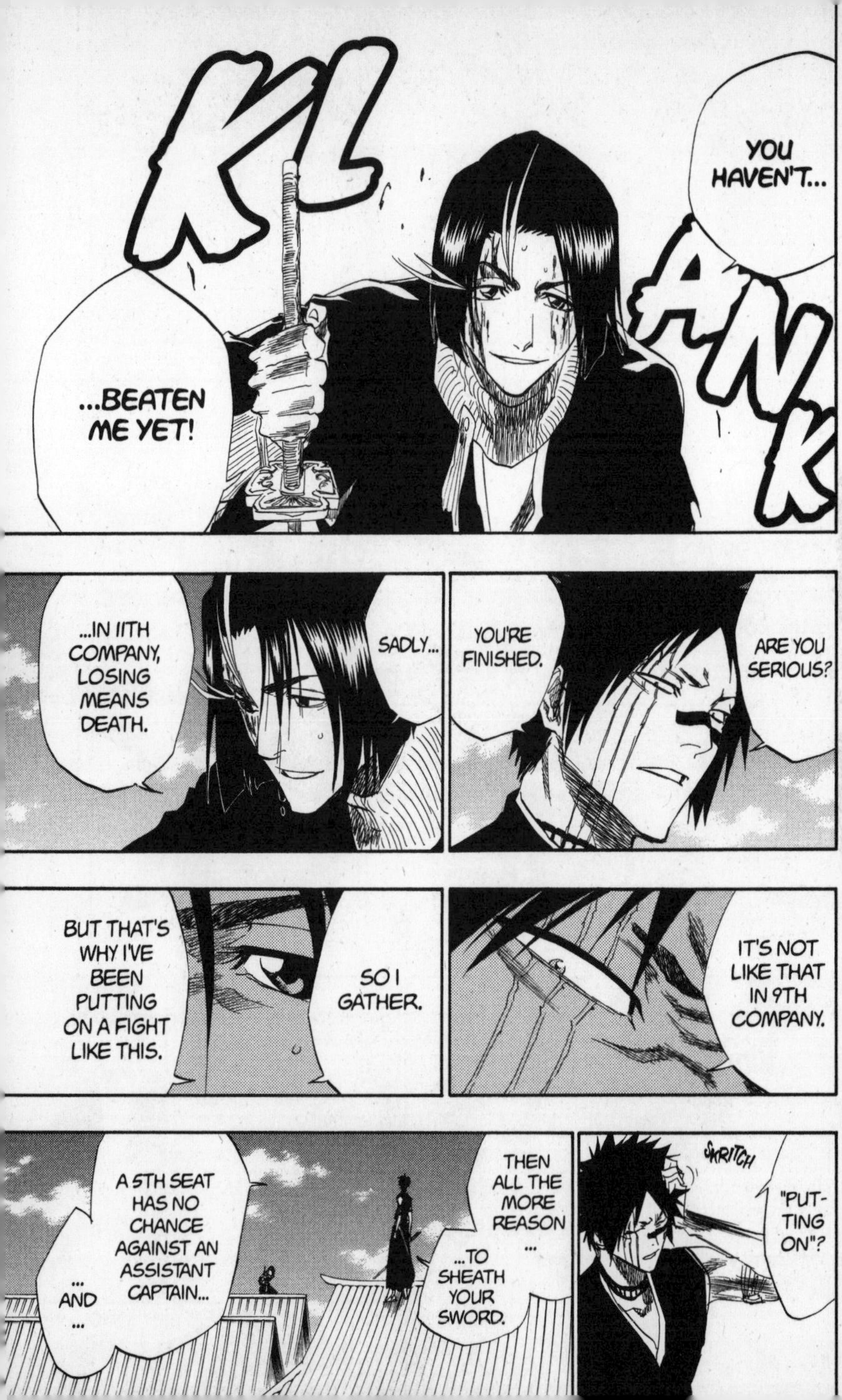
YOU HAVEN'T...
KLANK
...BEATEN ME YET!
ARE YOU SERIOUS?
YOU'RE FINISHED.
SADLY...
...IN 11TH COMPANY, LOSING MEANS DEATH.
IT'S NOT LIKE THAT IN 9TH COMPANY.
SO I GATHER.
BUT THAT'S WHY I'VE BEEN PUTTING ON A FIGHT LIKE THIS.
SKRITCH
"PUT-TING ON"?
THEN ALL THE MORE REASON ...
...TO SHEATH YOUR SWORD.
A 5TH SEAT HAS NO CHANCE AGAINST AN ASSISTANT CAPTAIN...
... AND ...

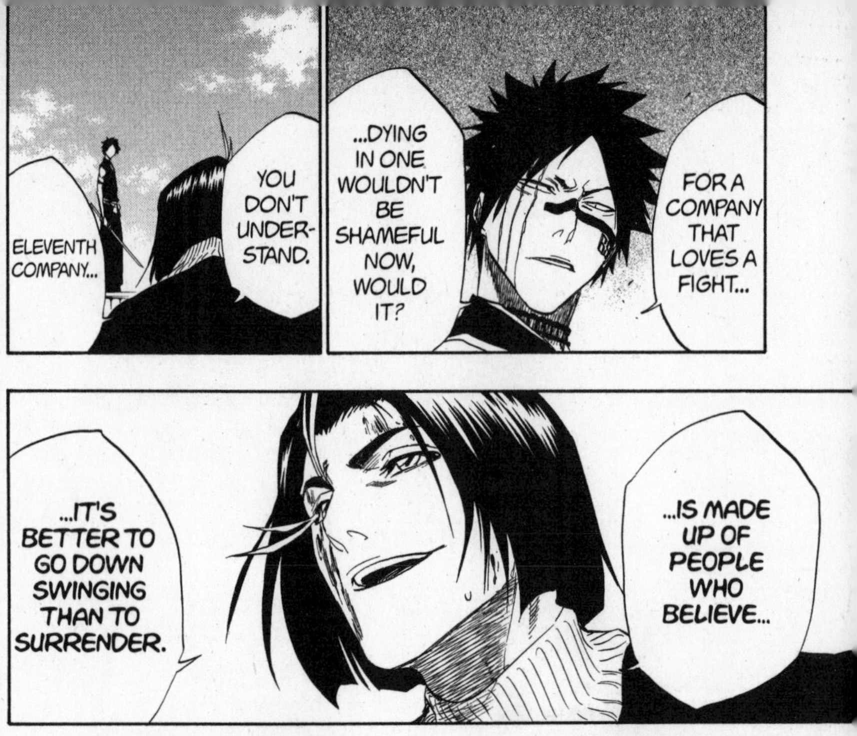
FOR A COMPANY THAT LOVES A FIGHT...
...DYING IN ONE WOULDN'T BE SHAMEFUL NOW, WOULD IT?
YOU DON'T UNDER-STAND.
ELEVENTH COMPANY...
...IS MADE UP OF PEOPLE WHO BELIEVE...
...IT'S BETTER TO GO DOWN SWINGING THAN TO SURRENDER.
WANNA KNOW A SECRET?
THE ONLY REASON I'M 5TH SEAT...
...IS BECAUSE I DON'T LIKE THE WAY "FOUR" LOOKS.*

*IN JAPANESE KANJI CHARACTERS, THREE IS 三, FOUR IS 四 AND FIVE IS 五.

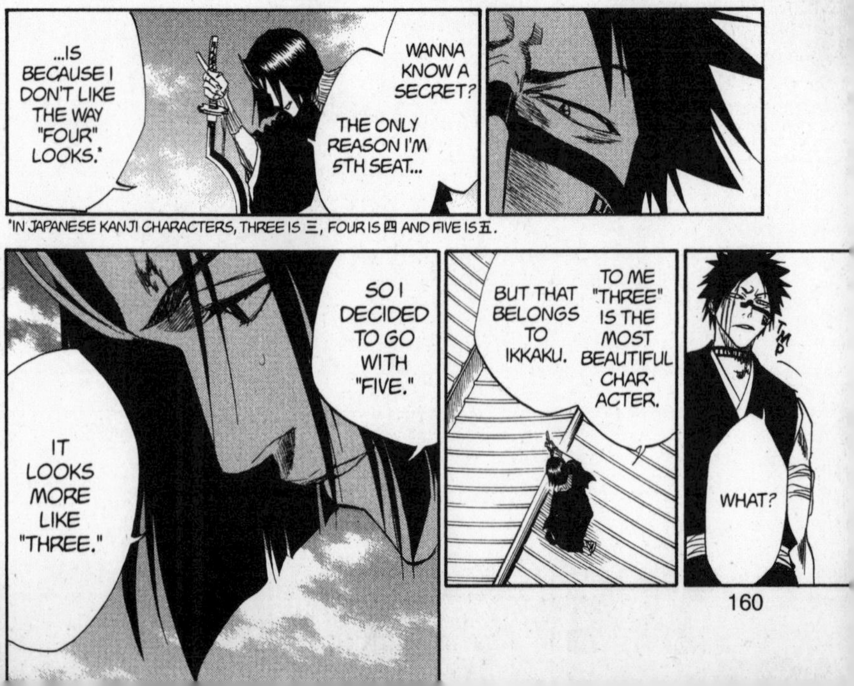
TMP
WHAT?
TO ME "THREE" IS THE MOST BEAUTIFUL CHAR-ACTER.
BUT THAT BELONGS TO IKKAKU.
SO I DECIDED TO GO WITH "FIVE."
IT LOOKS MORE LIKE "THREE."

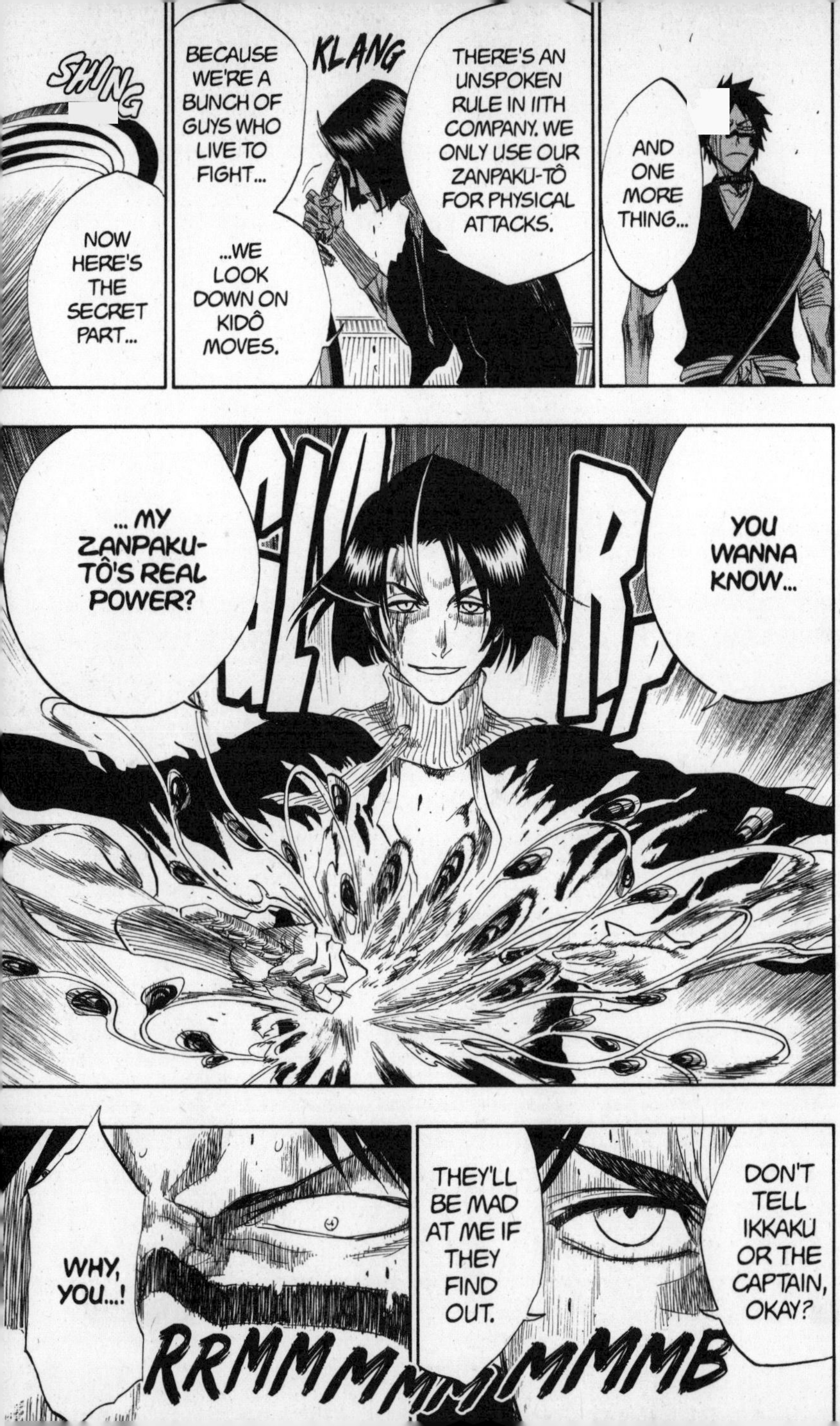
AND ONE MORE THING...
THERE'S AN UNSPOKEN RULE IN 11TH COMPANY. WE ONLY USE OUR ZANPAKU-TÔ FOR PHYSICAL ATTACKS.
KLANG
BECAUSE WE'RE A BUNCH OF GUYS WHO LIVE TO FIGHT...
...WE LOOK DOWN ON KIDÔ MOVES.
SHING
NOW HERE'S THE SECRET PART...
YOU WANNA KNOW...
... MY ZANPAKU-TÔ'S REAL POWER?
DON'T TELL IKKAKU OR THE CAPTAIN, OKAY?
THEY'LL BE MAD AT ME IF THEY FIND OUT.
WHY, YOU...!
RRMMMMMMMMMB

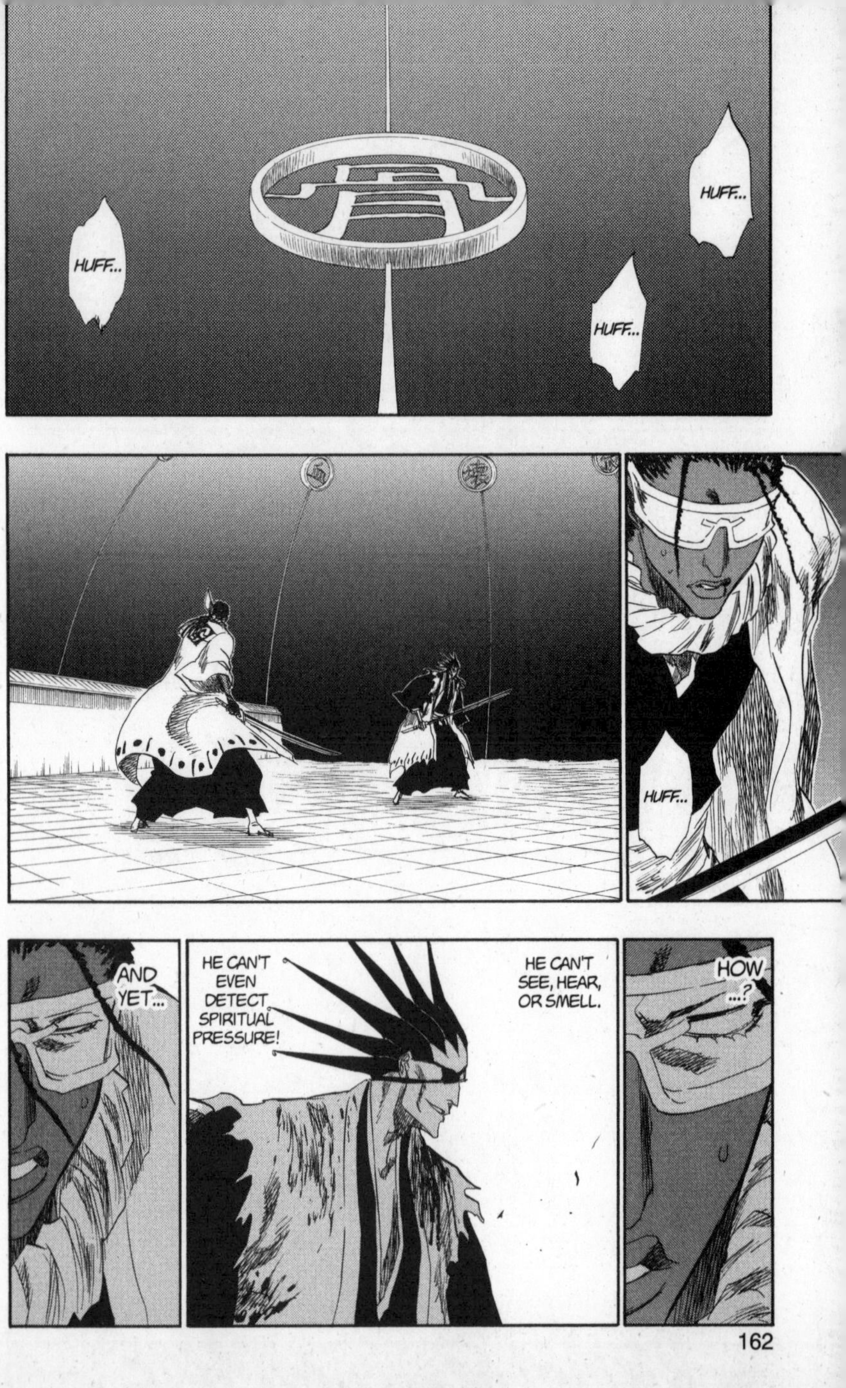
HUFF...
HUFF...
HUFF...
HUFF...
HOW ...?
HE CAN'T SEE, HEAR, OR SMELL.
HE CAN'T EVEN DETECT SPIRITUAL PRESSURE!
AND YET...

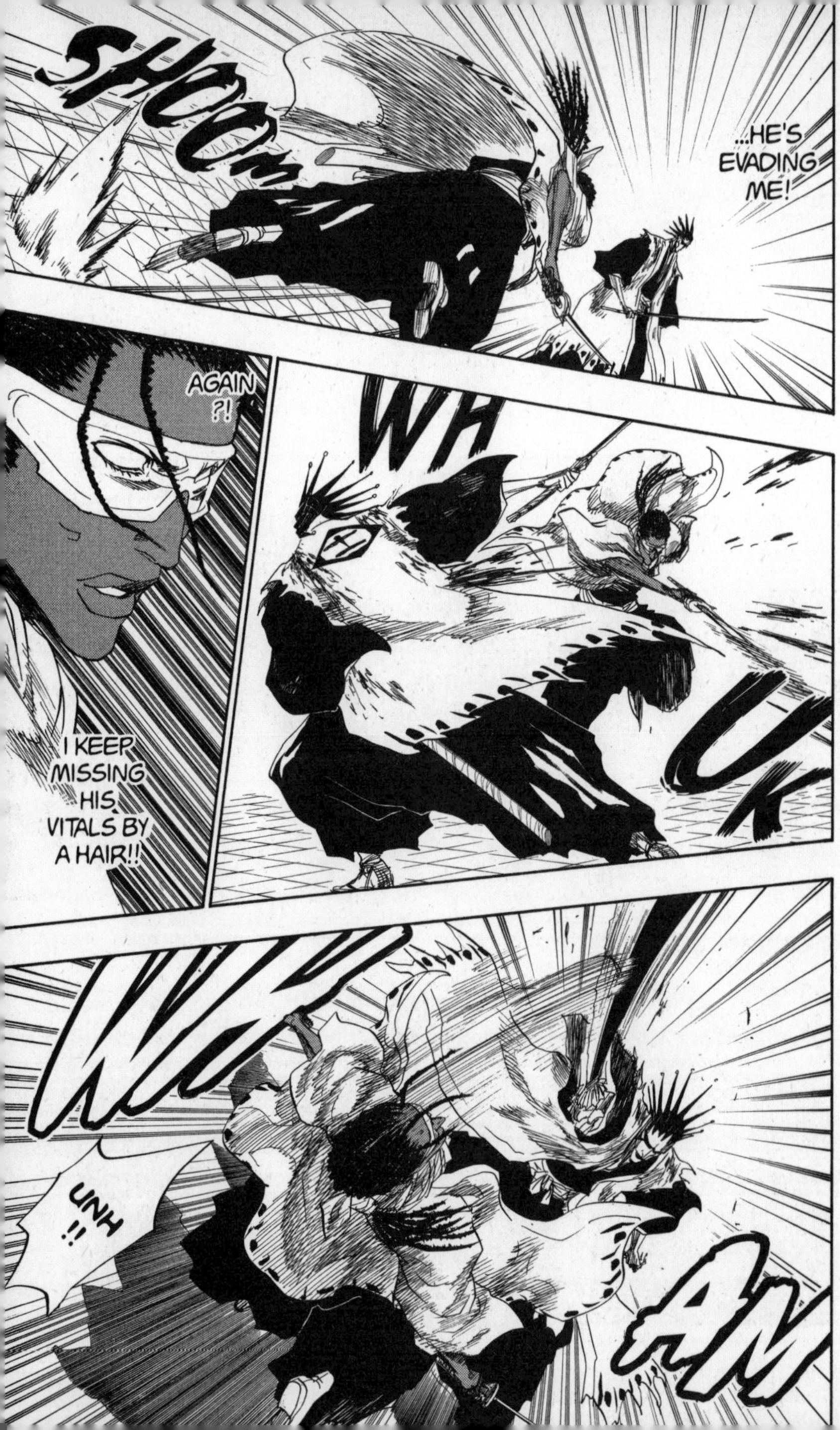
SHOOM
...HE'S EVADING ME!
WHUK
AGAIN?!
I KEEP MISSING HIS VITALS BY A HAIR!!
WHAM
UNH!!

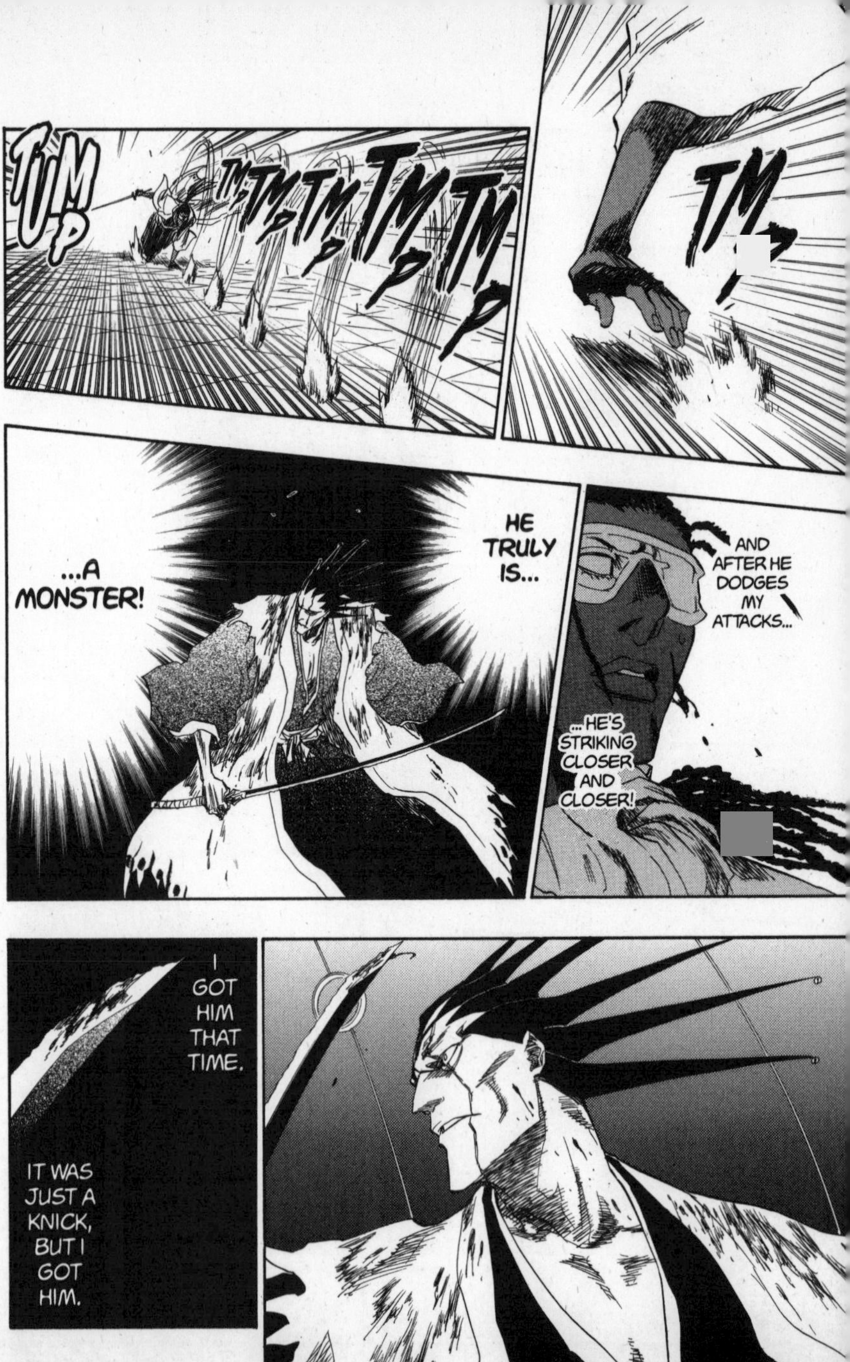
TMP
TUMP
TMP TMP TMP TMP TMP
AND AFTER HE DODGES MY ATTACKS...
...HE'S STRIKING CLOSER AND CLOSER!
HE TRULY IS...
...A MONSTER!
I GOT HIM THAT TIME.
IT WAS JUST A KNICK, BUT I GOT HIM.

READ THIS WAY

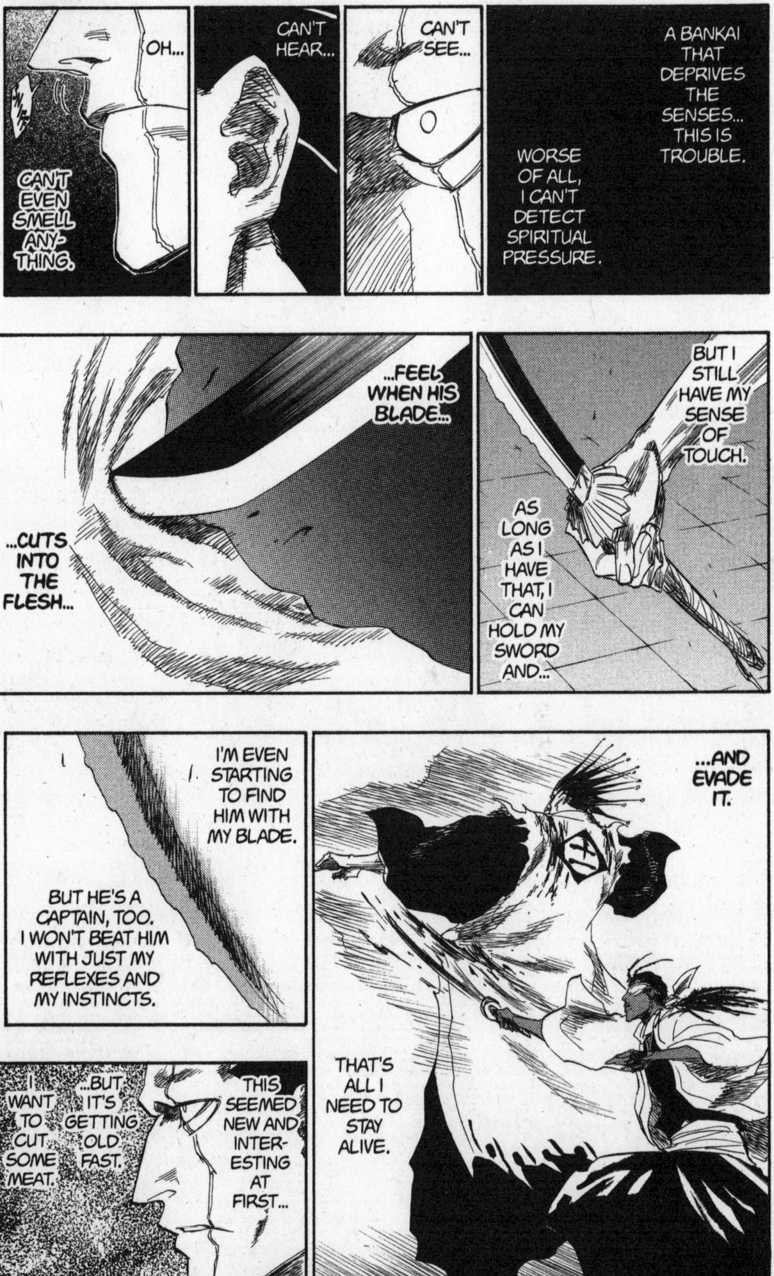
A BANKAI THAT DEPRIVES THE SENSES... THIS IS TROUBLE.
WORSE OF ALL, I CAN'T DETECT SPIRITUAL PRESSURE.
CAN'T SEE...
CAN'T HEAR...
OH...
CAN'T EVEN SMELL ANYTHING.
BUT I STILL HAVE MY SENSE OF TOUCH.
AS LONG AS I HAVE THAT, I CAN HOLD MY SWORD AND...
...FEEL WHEN HIS BLADE...
...CUTS INTO THE FLESH...
...AND EVADE IT.
THAT'S ALL I NEED TO STAY ALIVE.
I'M EVEN STARTING TO FIND HIM WITH MY BLADE.
BUT HE'S A CAPTAIN, TOO. I WON'T BEAT HIM WITH JUST MY REFLEXES AND MY INSTINCTS.
THIS SEEMED NEW AND INTERESTING AT FIRST...
...BUT IT'S GETTING OLD FAST.
I WANT TO CUT SOME MEAT.

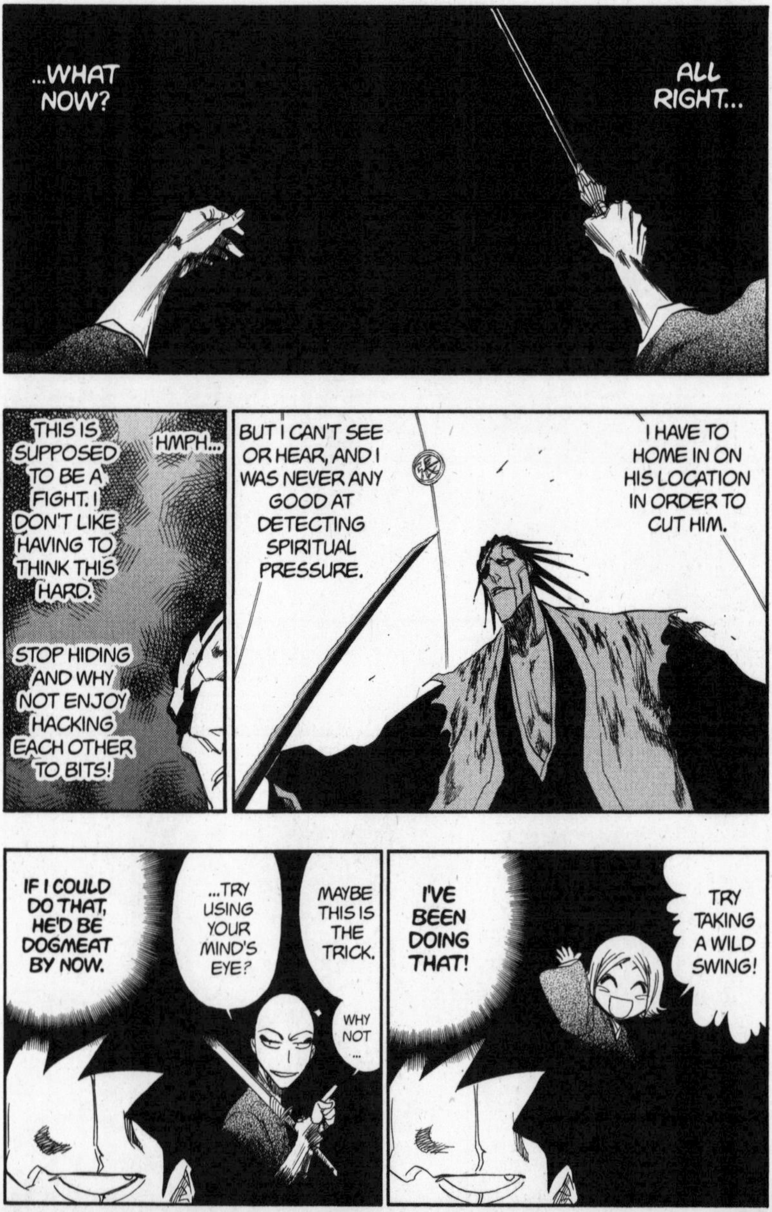
ALL RIGHT...
...WHAT NOW?
I HAVE TO HOME IN ON HIS LOCATION IN ORDER TO CUT HIM.
BUT I CAN'T SEE OR HEAR, AND I WAS NEVER ANY GOOD AT DETECTING SPIRITUAL PRESSURE.
HMPH...
THIS IS SUPPOSED TO BE A FIGHT. I DON'T LIKE HAVING TO THINK THIS HARD.
STOP HIDING AND WHY NOT ENJOY HACKING EACH OTHER TO BITS!
TRY TAKING A WILD SWING!
I'VE BEEN DOING THAT!
MAYBE THIS IS THE TRICK.
WHY NOT ...
...TRY USING YOUR MIND'S EYE?
IF I COULD DO THAT, HE'D BE DOGMEAT BY NOW.

READ THIS WAY

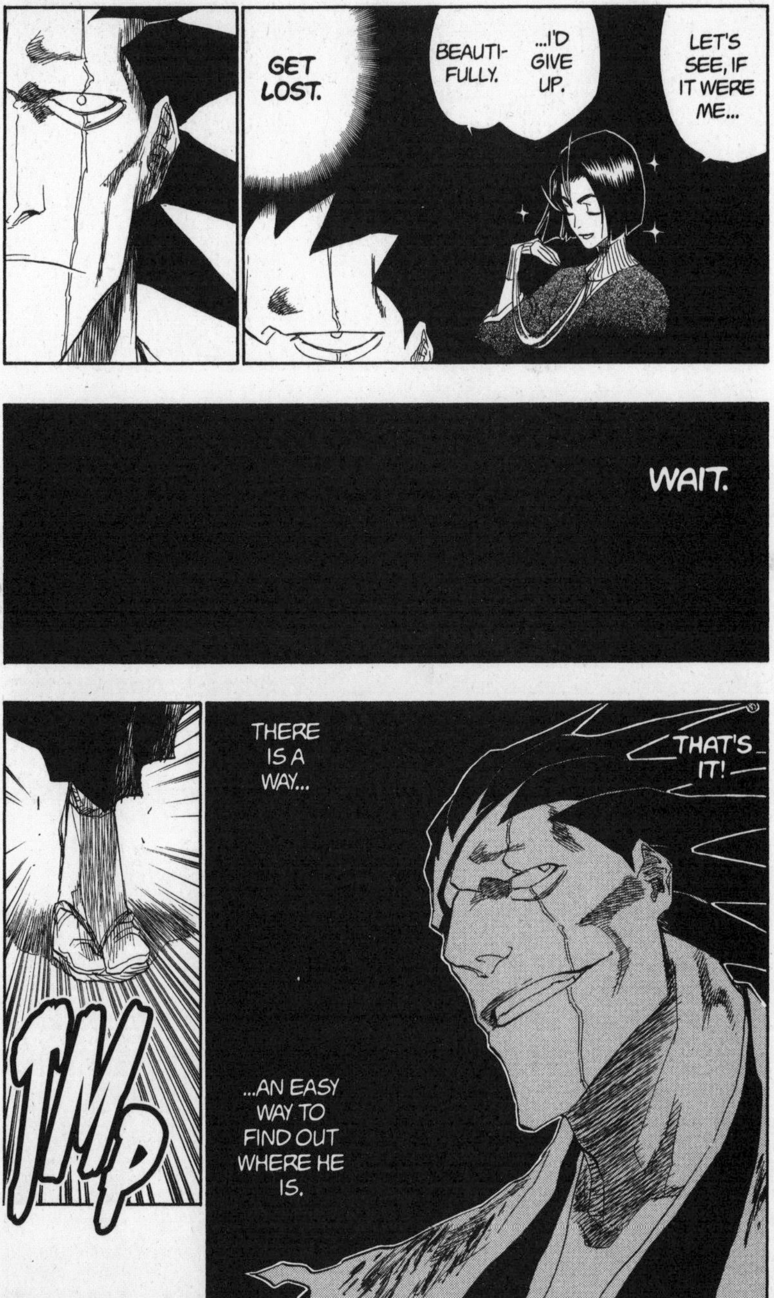
LET'S SEE, IF IT WERE ME...
...I'D GIVE UP.
BEAUTI-FULLY.
GET LOST.
WAIT.
THAT'S IT!
THERE IS A WAY...
...AN EASY WAY TO FIND OUT WHERE HE IS.
TMP

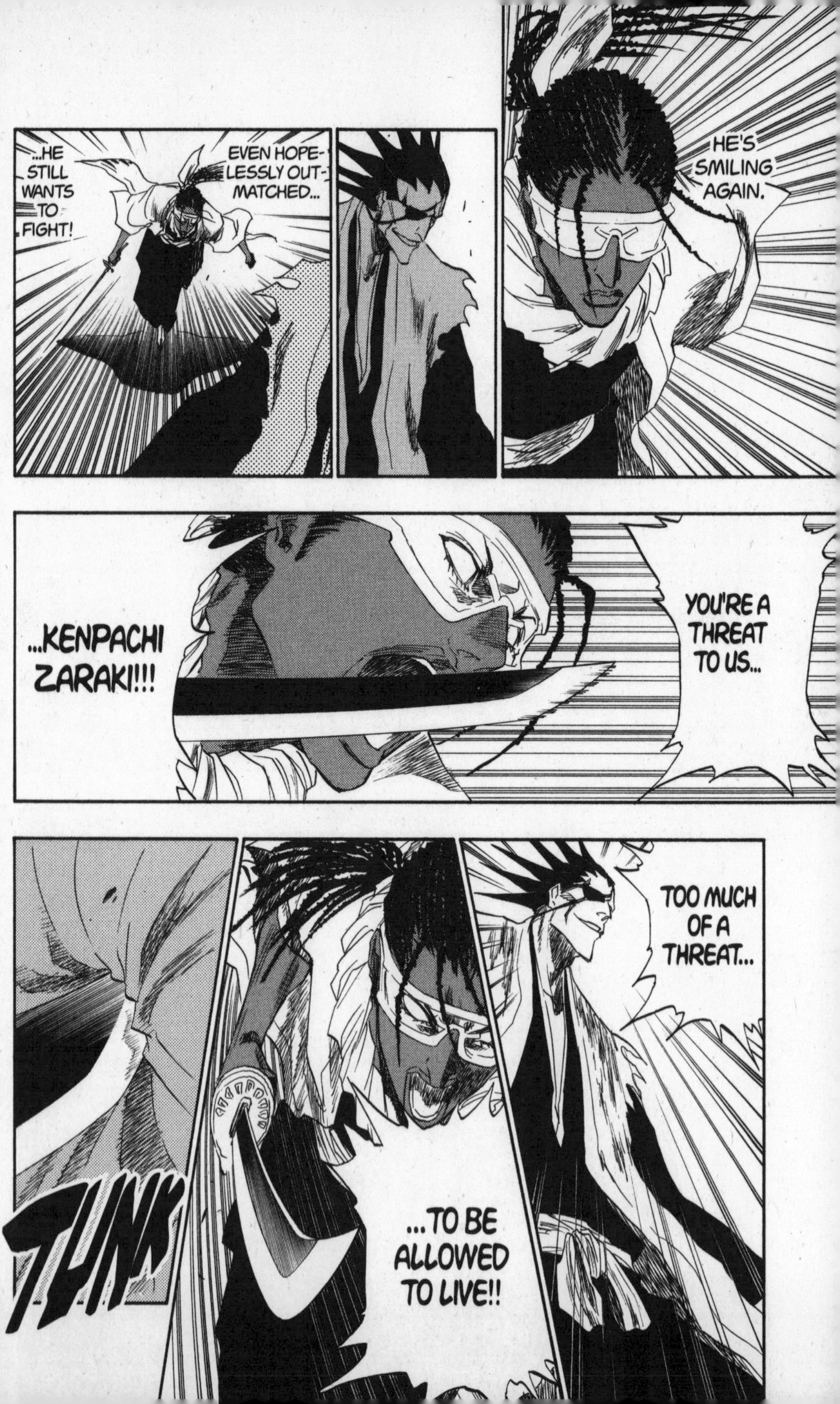
HE'S SMILING AGAIN.
EVEN HOPELESSLY OUTMATCHED...
...HE STILL WANTS TO FIGHT!
YOU'RE A THREAT TO US...
...KENPACHI ZARAKI!!!
TOO MUCH OF A THREAT...
...TO BE ALLOWED TO LIVE!!

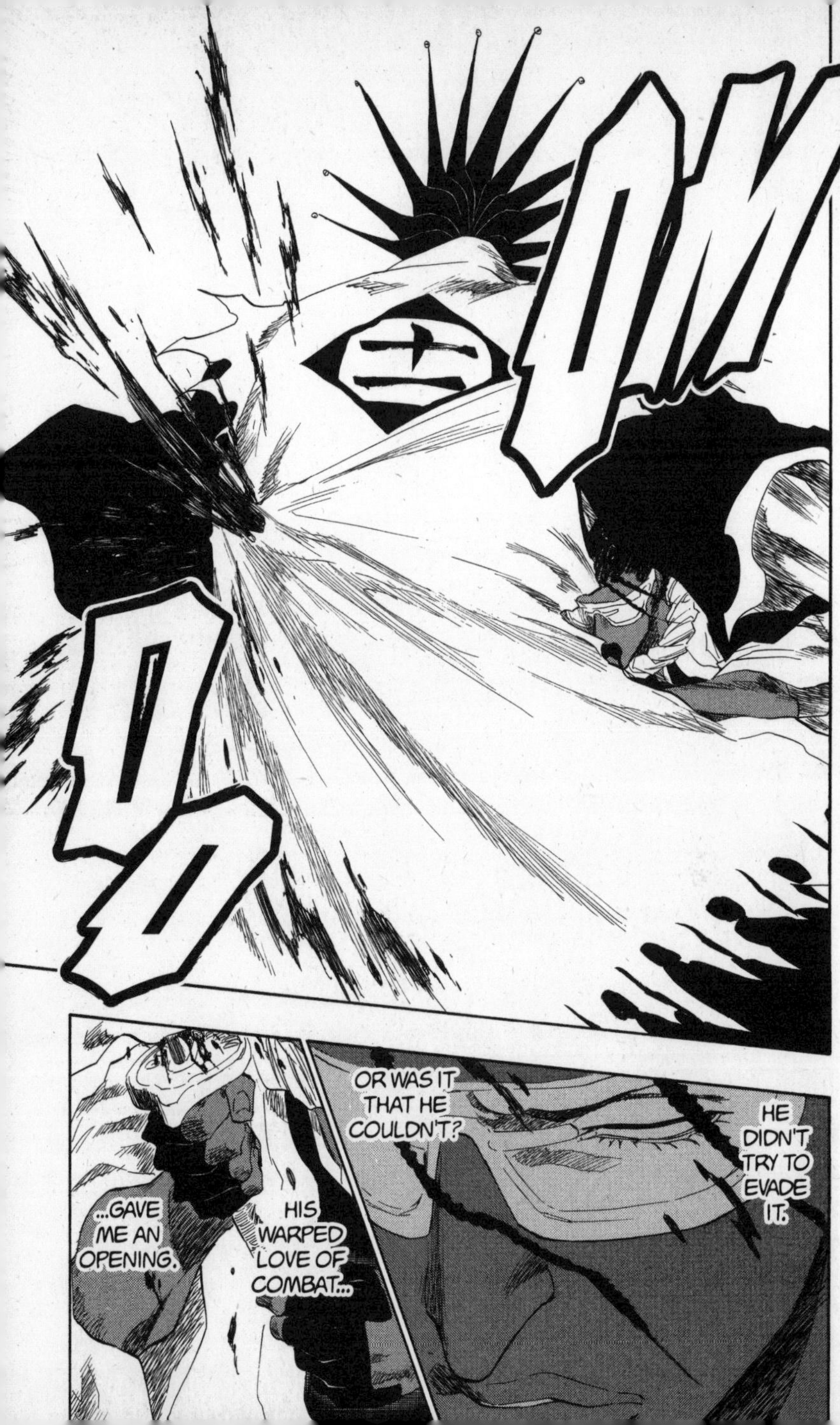
HE DIDN'T TRY TO EVADE IT.
OR WAS IT THAT HE COULDN'T?
HIS WARPED LOVE OF COMBAT...
...GAVE ME AN OPENING.

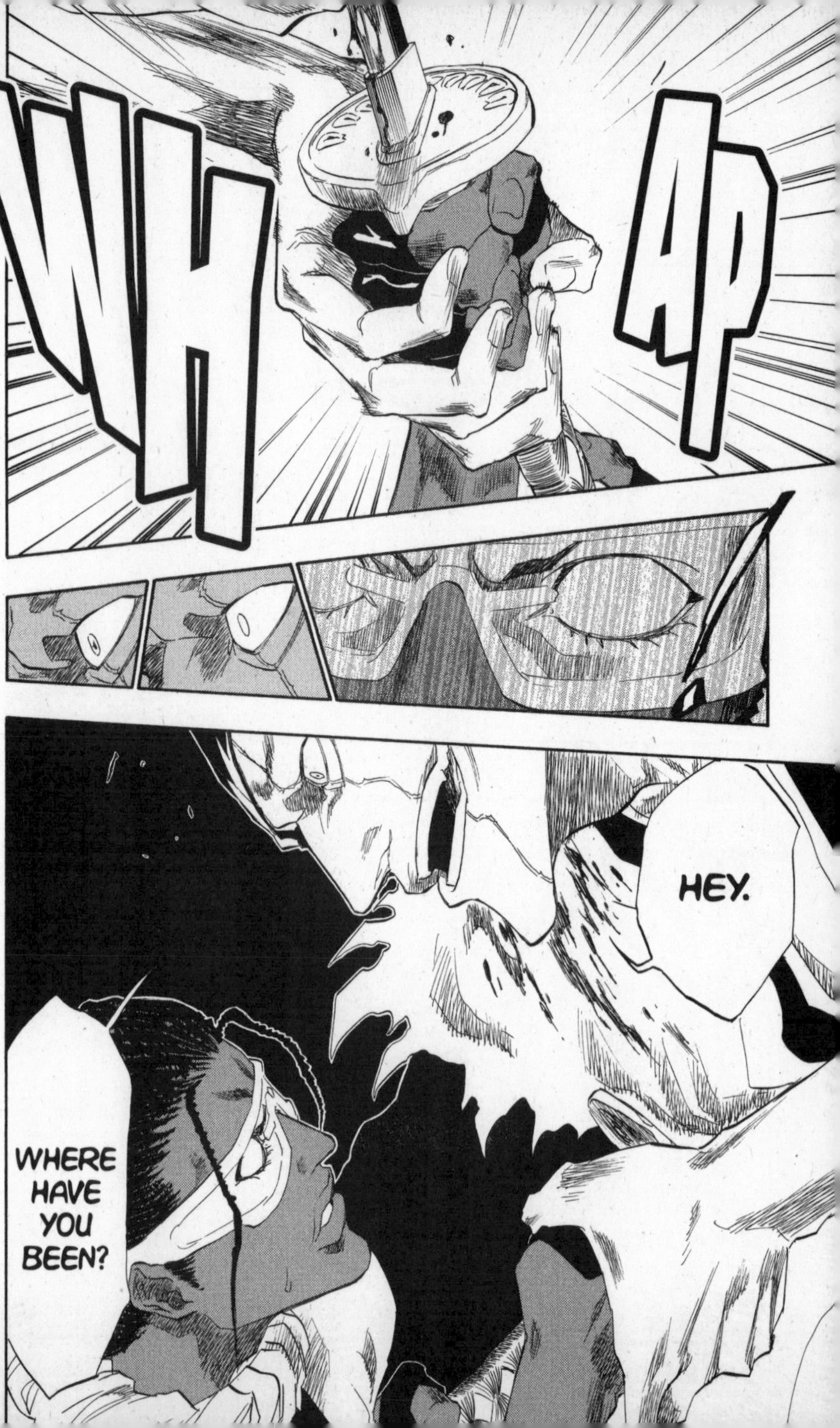
WHAP
HEY.
WHERE HAVE YOU BEEN?

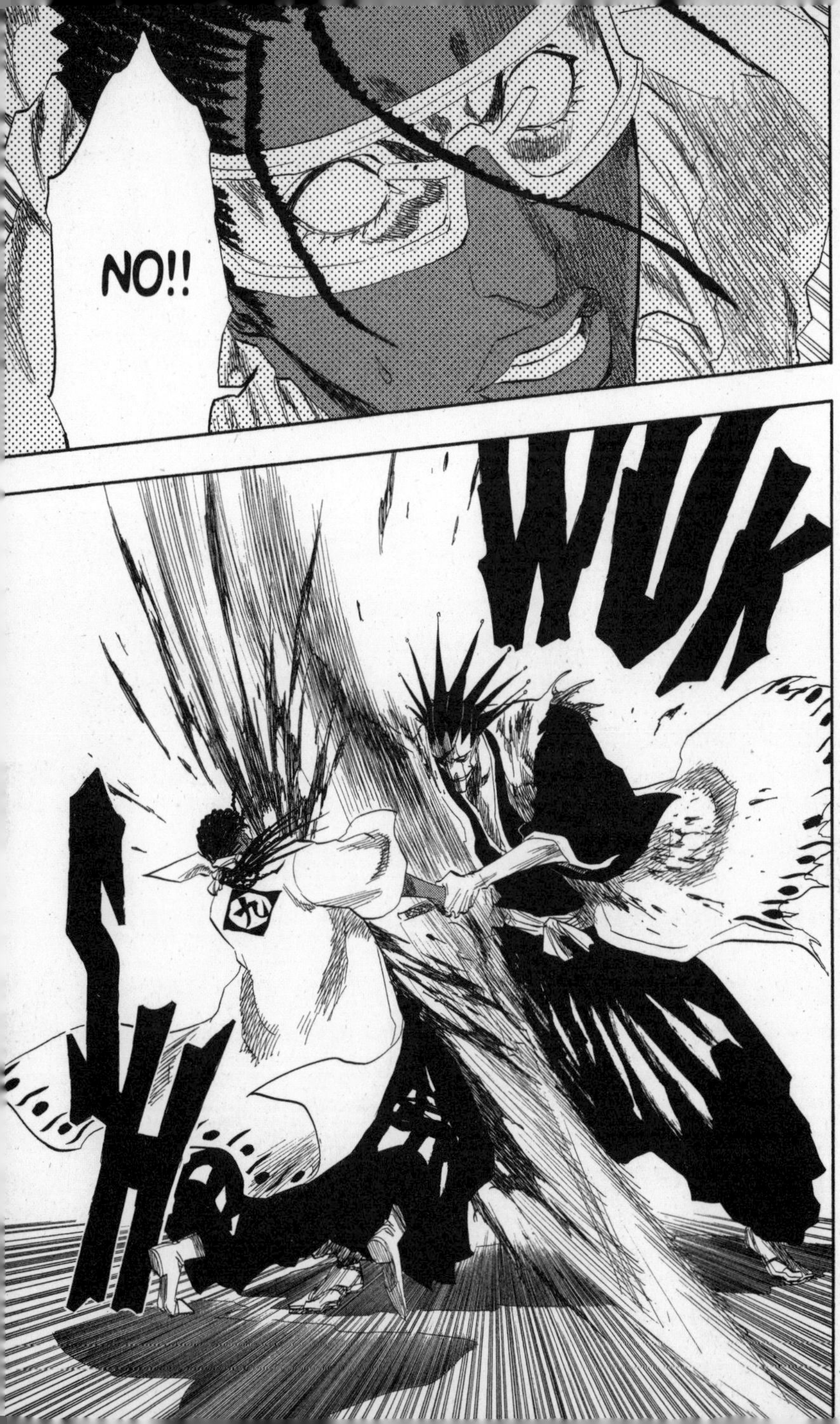
NO!!
WUK

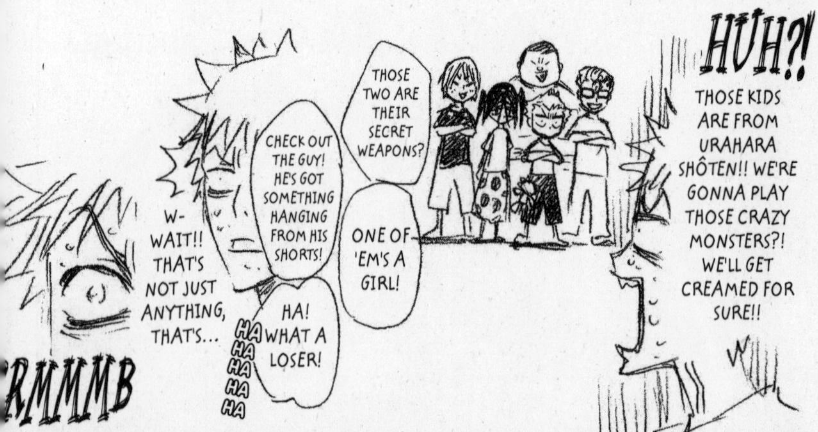
HUH?!
THOSE KIDS ARE FROM URAHARA SHÔTEN!! WE'RE GONNA PLAY THOSE CRAZY MONSTERS?! WE'LL GET CREAMED FOR SURE!!
THOSE TWO ARE THEIR SECRET WEAPONS?
ONE OF 'EM'S A GIRL!
CHECK OUT THE GUY! HE'S GOT SOMETHING HANGING FROM HIS SHORTS!
HA! WHAT A LOSER!
HA HA HA HA HA
W-WAIT!! THAT'S NOT JUST ANYTHING, THAT'S...
RMMMB

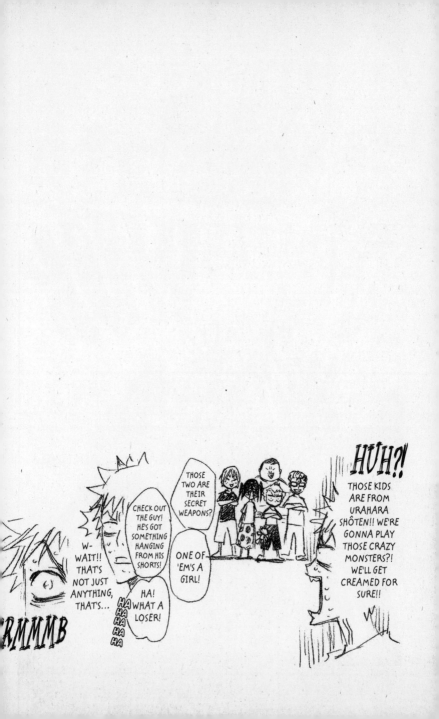

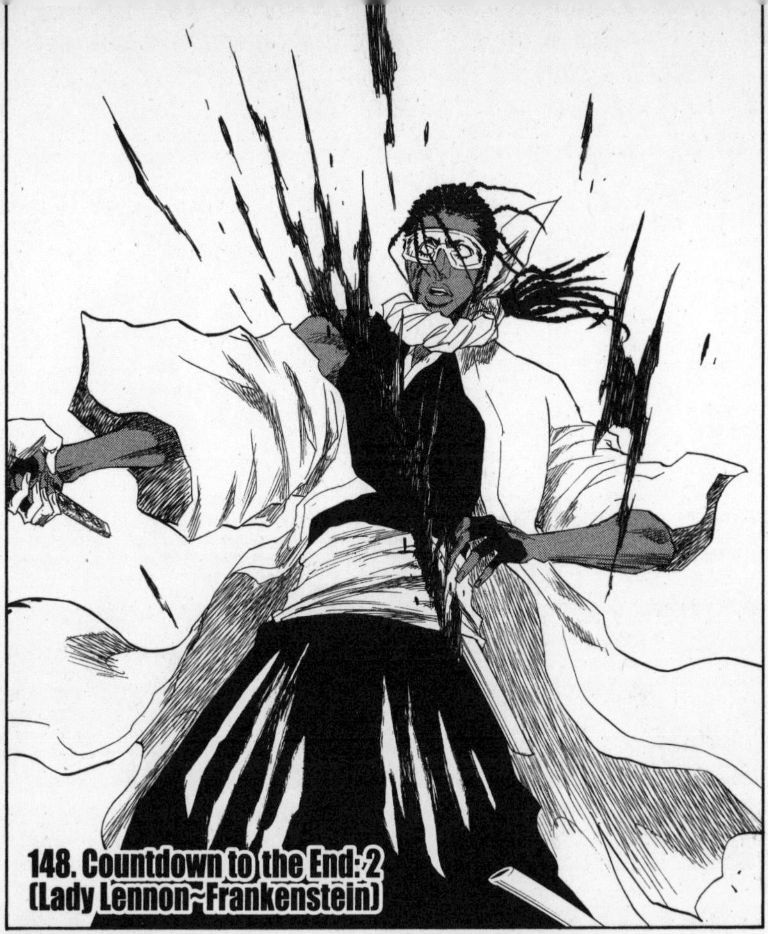

148. Countdown to the End: 2 (Lady Lennon~Frankenstein)

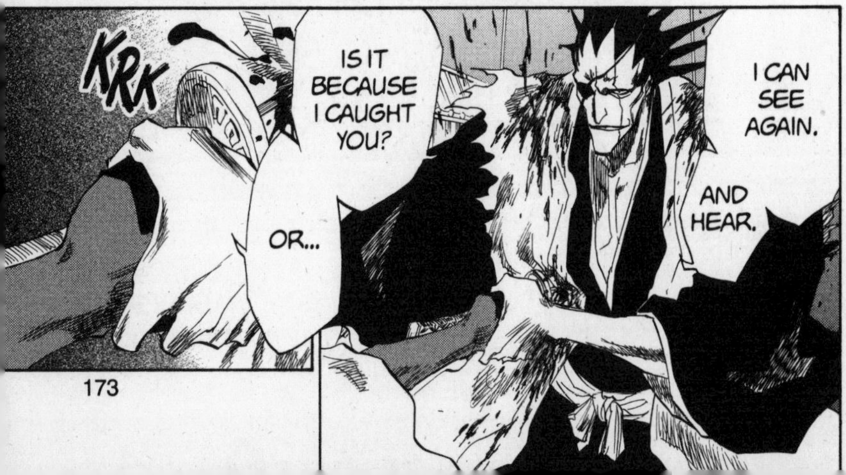
I CAN SEE AGAIN.
AND HEAR.
IS IT BECAUSE I CAUGHT YOU?
OR...
KRK

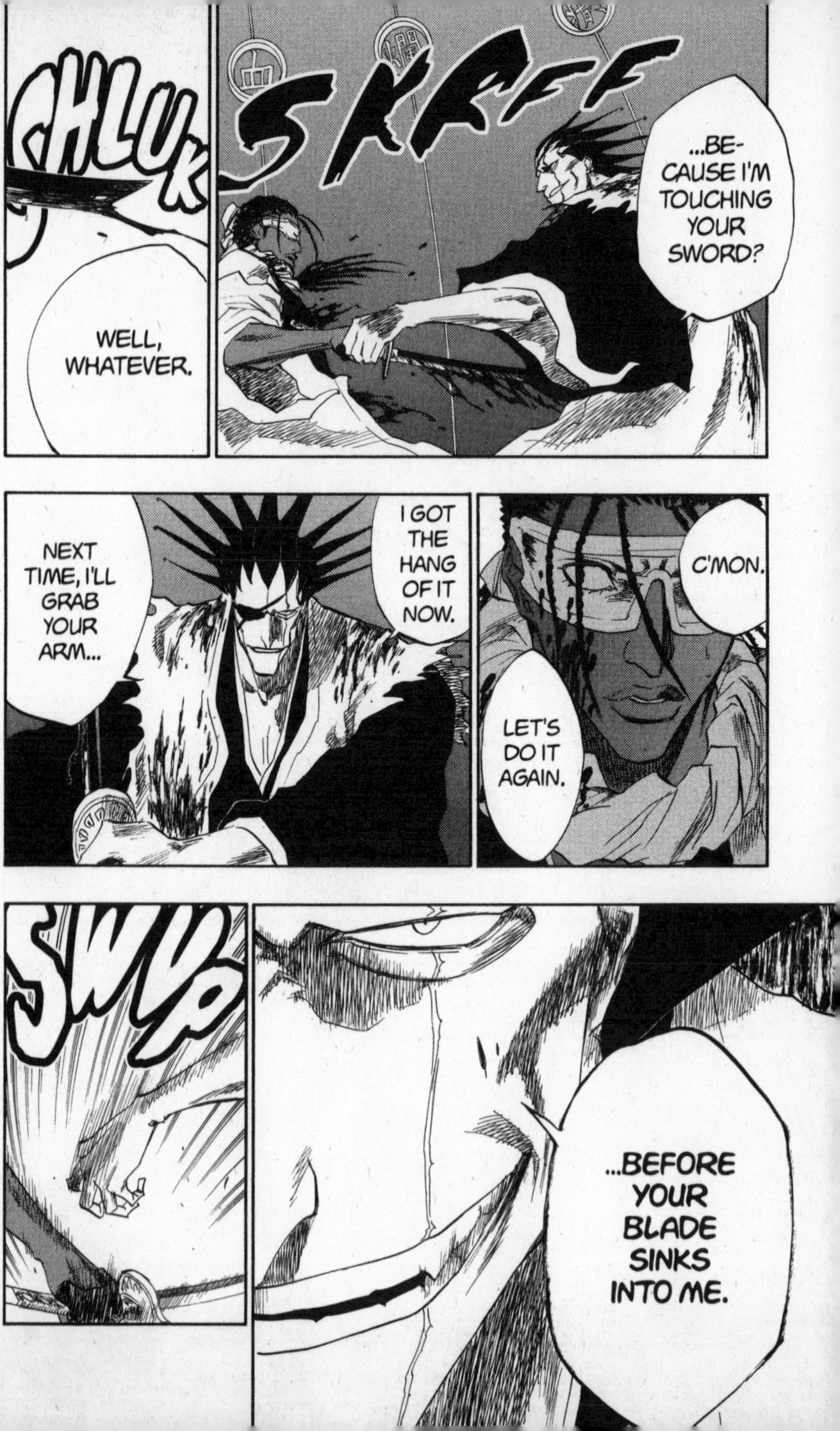
SKRFF
...BE-CAUSE I'M TOUCHING YOUR SWORD?
CHLUK
WELL, WHATEVER.
C'MON.
LET'S DO IT AGAIN.
I GOT THE HANG OF IT NOW.
NEXT TIME, I'LL GRAB YOUR ARM...
...BEFORE YOUR BLADE SINKS INTO ME.
SWIP

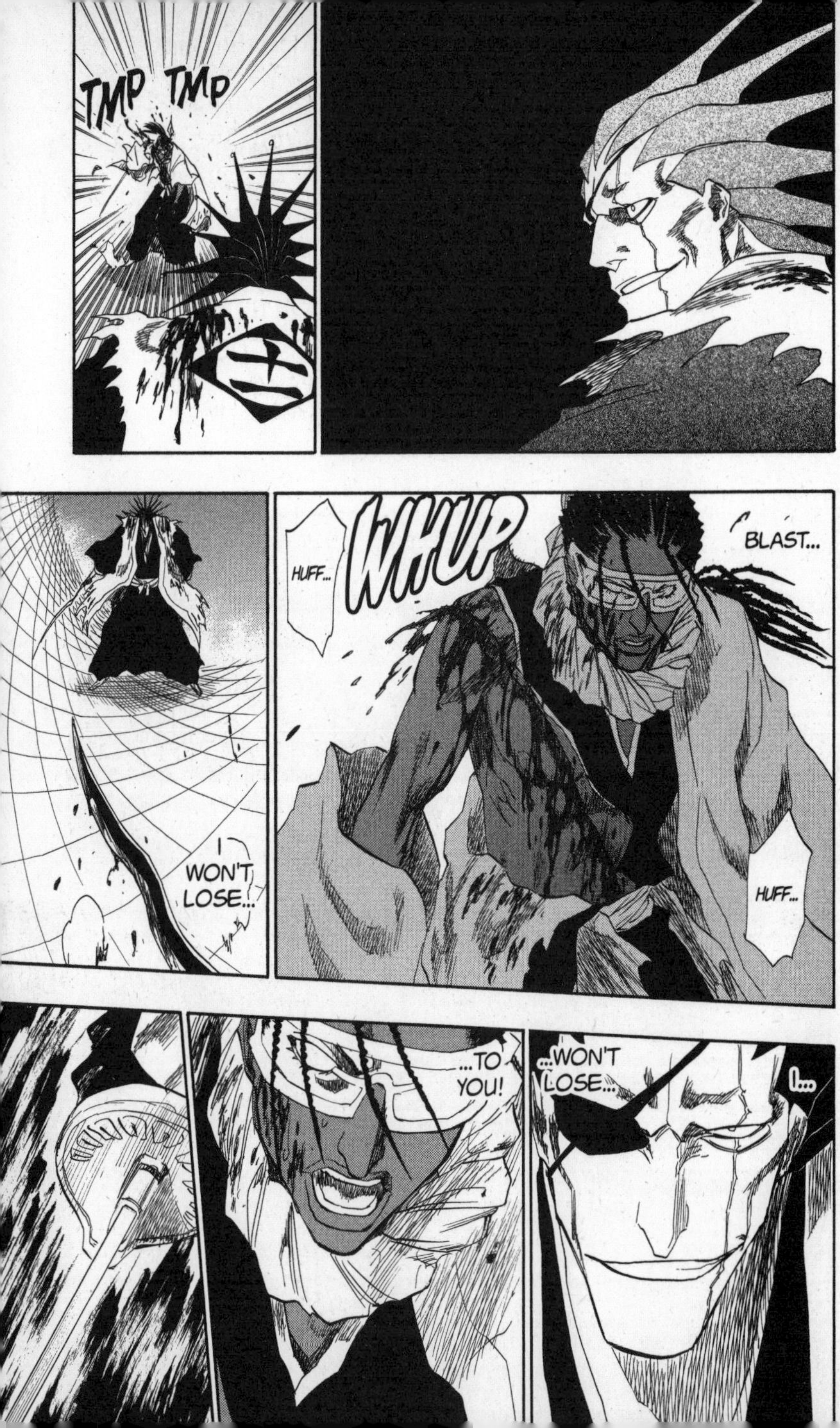
TMP TMP
BLAST...
WHUP
HUFF...
HUFF...
I WON'T LOSE...
I...
...WON'T LOSE...
...TO YOU!

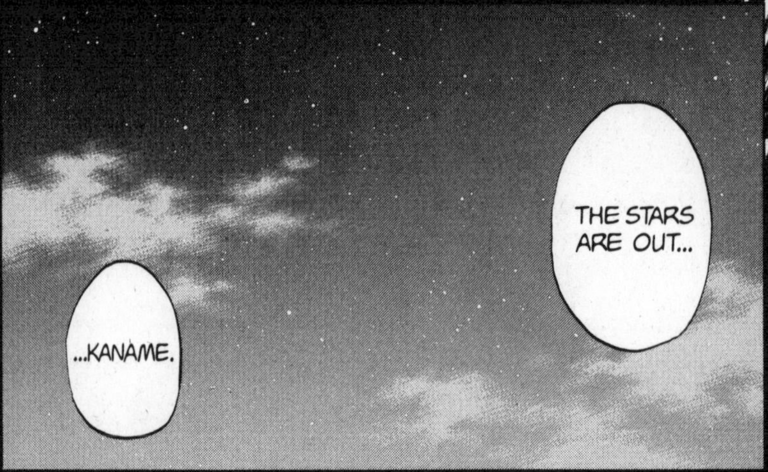
THE STARS ARE OUT...
...KANAME.

BLEACH —ブリーチ—

148. Countdown to the End: 2 (Lady Lennon~Frankenstein)

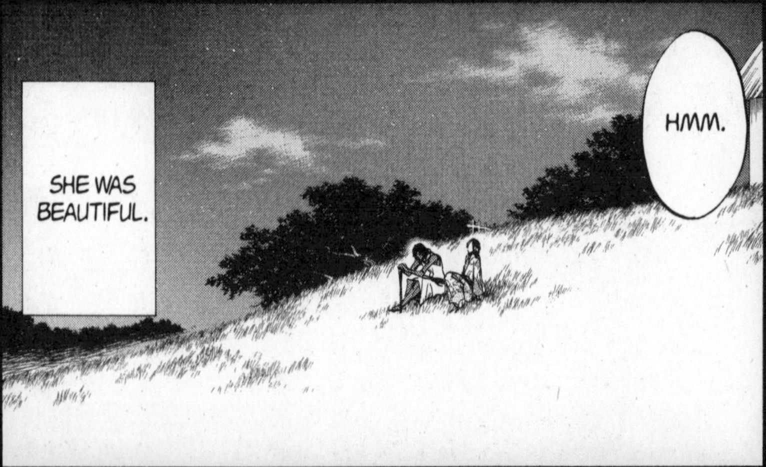
HMM.
SHE WAS BEAUTIFUL.

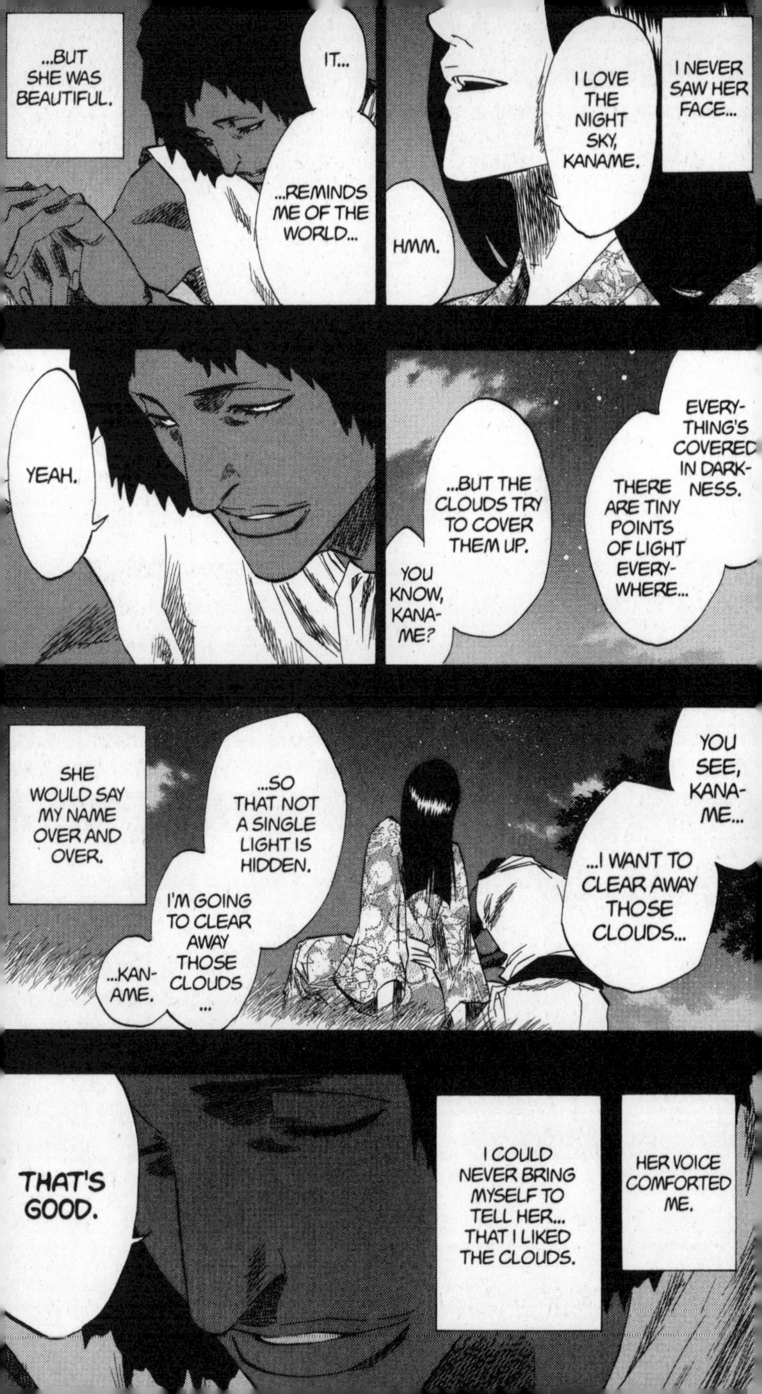
I NEVER SAW HER FACE...
I LOVE THE NIGHT SKY, KANAME.
HMM.
IT...
...REMINDS ME OF THE WORLD...
...BUT SHE WAS BEAUTIFUL.
EVERYTHING'S COVERED IN DARKNESS.
THERE ARE TINY POINTS OF LIGHT EVERYWHERE...
...BUT THE CLOUDS TRY TO COVER THEM UP.
YOU KNOW, KANAME?
YEAH.
YOU SEE, KANAME...
...I WANT TO CLEAR AWAY THOSE CLOUDS...
...SO THAT NOT A SINGLE LIGHT IS HIDDEN.
I'M GOING TO CLEAR AWAY THOSE CLOUDS...
...KANAME.
SHE WOULD SAY MY NAME OVER AND OVER.
HER VOICE COMFORTED ME.
I COULD NEVER BRING MYSELF TO TELL HER... THAT I LIKED THE CLOUDS.
THAT'S GOOD.

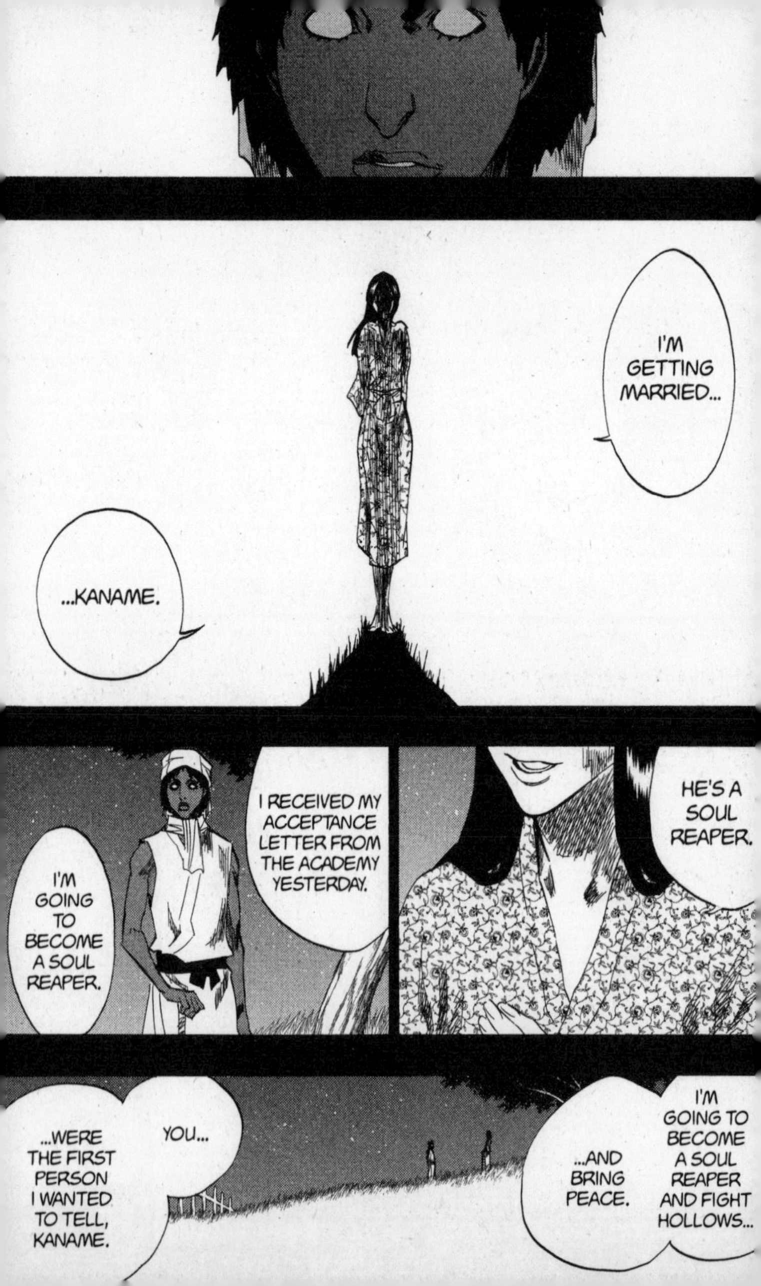
I'M GETTING MARRIED...
...KANAME.
HE'S A SOUL REAPER.
I RECEIVED MY ACCEPTANCE LETTER FROM THE ACADEMY YESTERDAY.
I'M GOING TO BECOME A SOUL REAPER.
I'M GOING TO BECOME A SOUL REAPER AND FIGHT HOLLOWS...
...AND BRING PEACE.
YOU...
...WERE THE FIRST PERSON I WANTED TO TELL, KANAME.

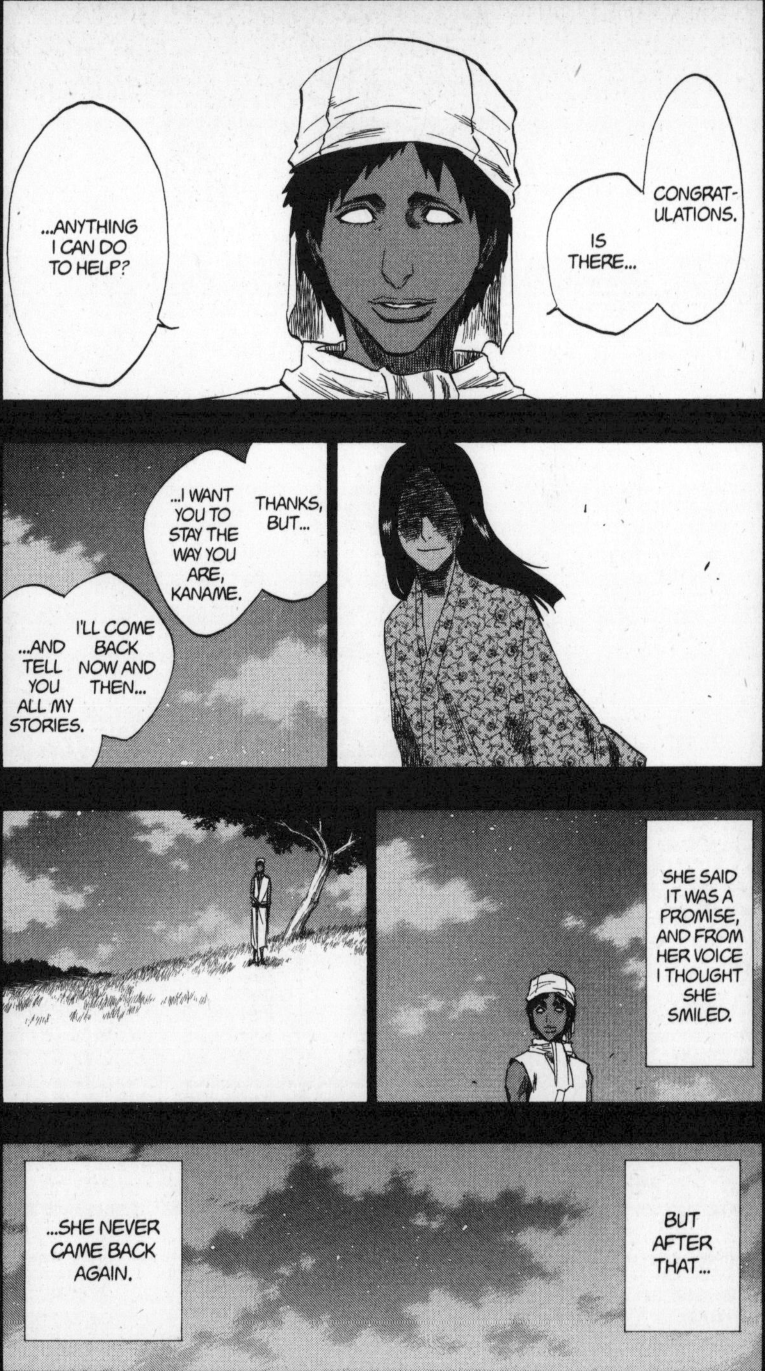
CONGRAT-ULATIONS.
IS THERE...
...ANYTHING I CAN DO TO HELP?
THANKS, BUT...
...I WANT YOU TO STAY THE WAY YOU ARE, KANAME.
I'LL COME BACK NOW AND THEN...
...AND TELL YOU ALL MY STORIES.
SHE SAID IT WAS A PROMISE, AND FROM HER VOICE I THOUGHT SHE SMILED.
BUT AFTER THAT...
...SHE NEVER CAME BACK AGAIN.

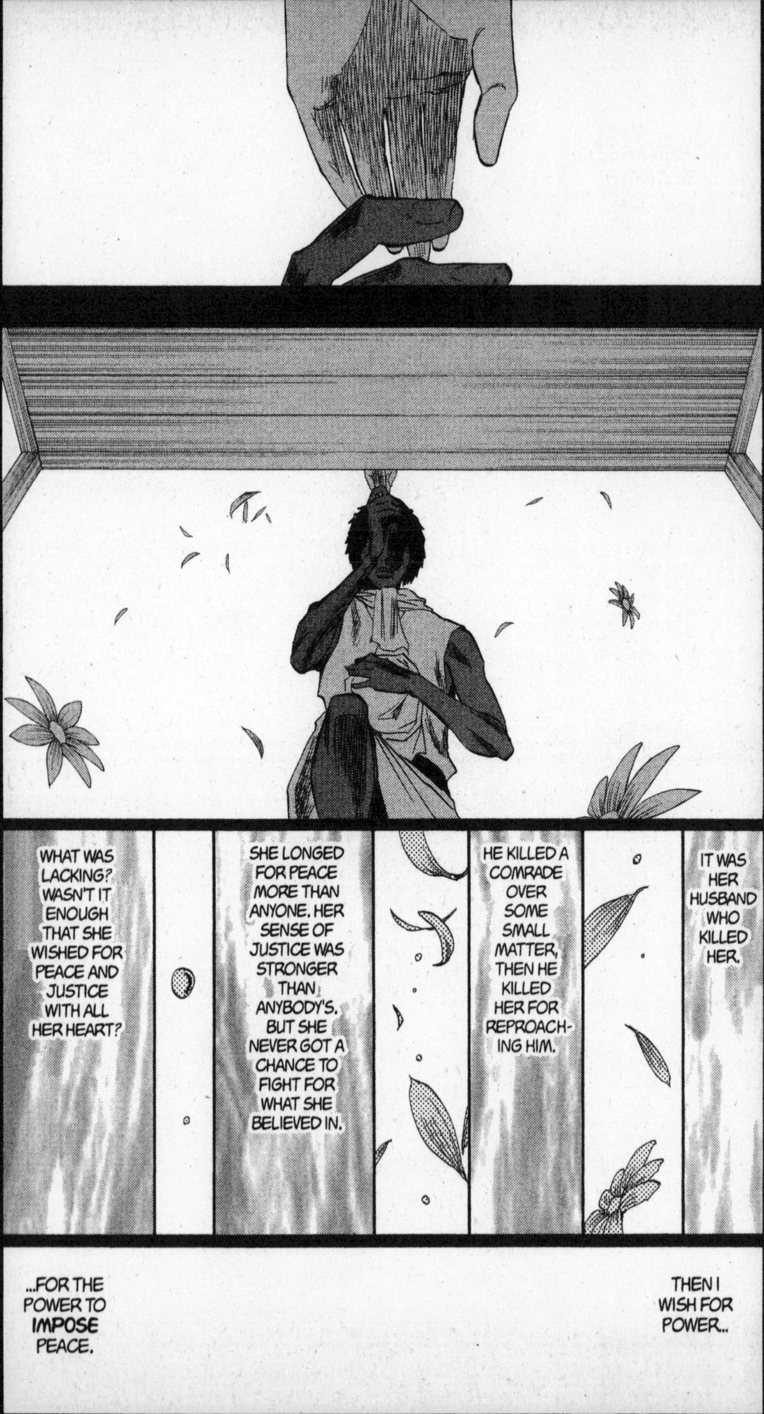
IT WAS HER HUSBAND WHO KILLED HER.
HE KILLED A COMRADE OVER SOME SMALL MATTER, THEN HE KILLED HER FOR REPROACHING HIM.
SHE LONGED FOR PEACE MORE THAN ANYONE. HER SENSE OF JUSTICE WAS STRONGER THAN ANYBODY'S. BUT SHE NEVER GOT A CHANCE TO FIGHT FOR WHAT SHE BELIEVED IN.
WHAT WAS LACKING? WASN'T IT ENOUGH THAT SHE WISHED FOR PEACE AND JUSTICE WITH ALL HER HEART?
THEN I WISH FOR POWER...
...FOR THE POWER TO **IMPOSE** PEACE.

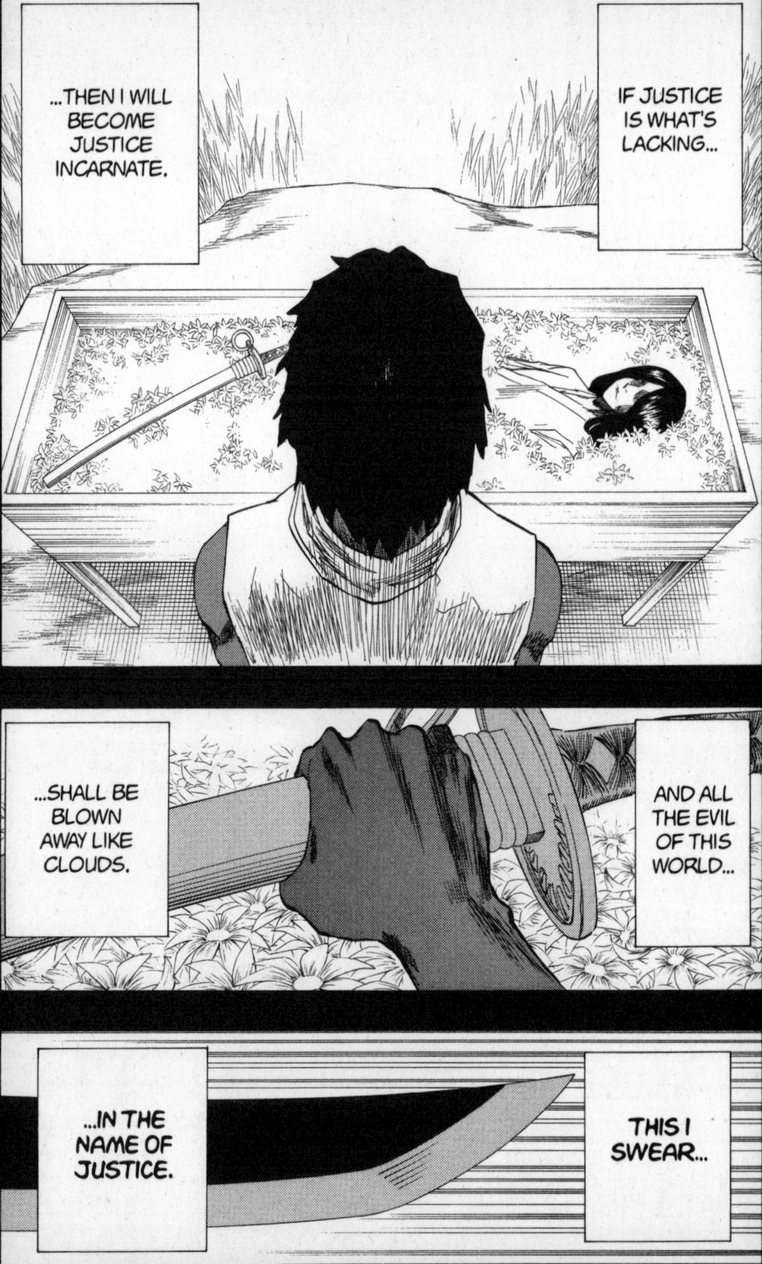
IF JUSTICE IS WHAT'S LACKING...
...THEN I WILL BECOME JUSTICE INCARNATE.
AND ALL THE EVIL OF THIS WORLD...
...SHALL BE BLOWN AWAY LIKE CLOUDS.
THIS I SWEAR...
...IN THE NAME OF JUSTICE.

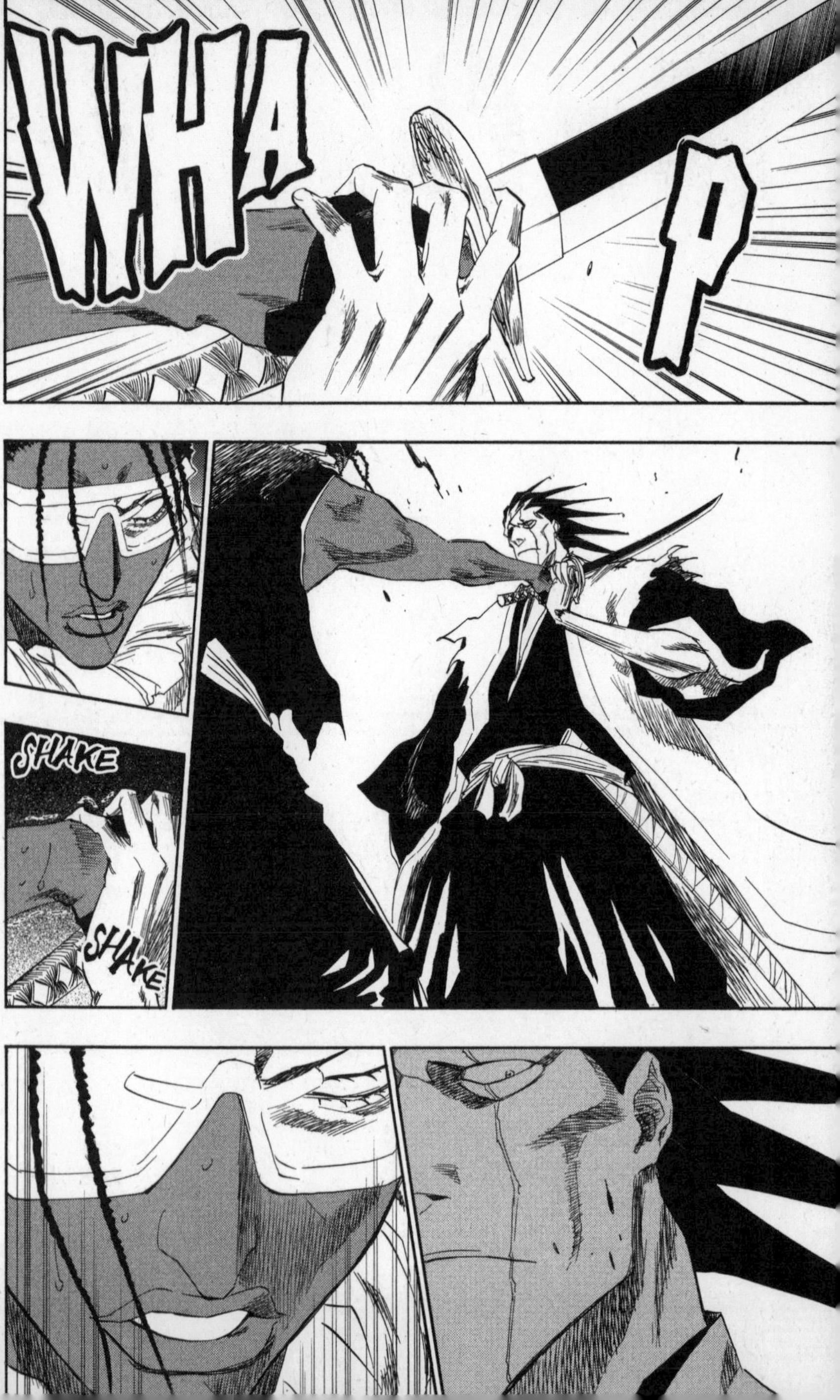
WHAP
SHAKE
SHAKE

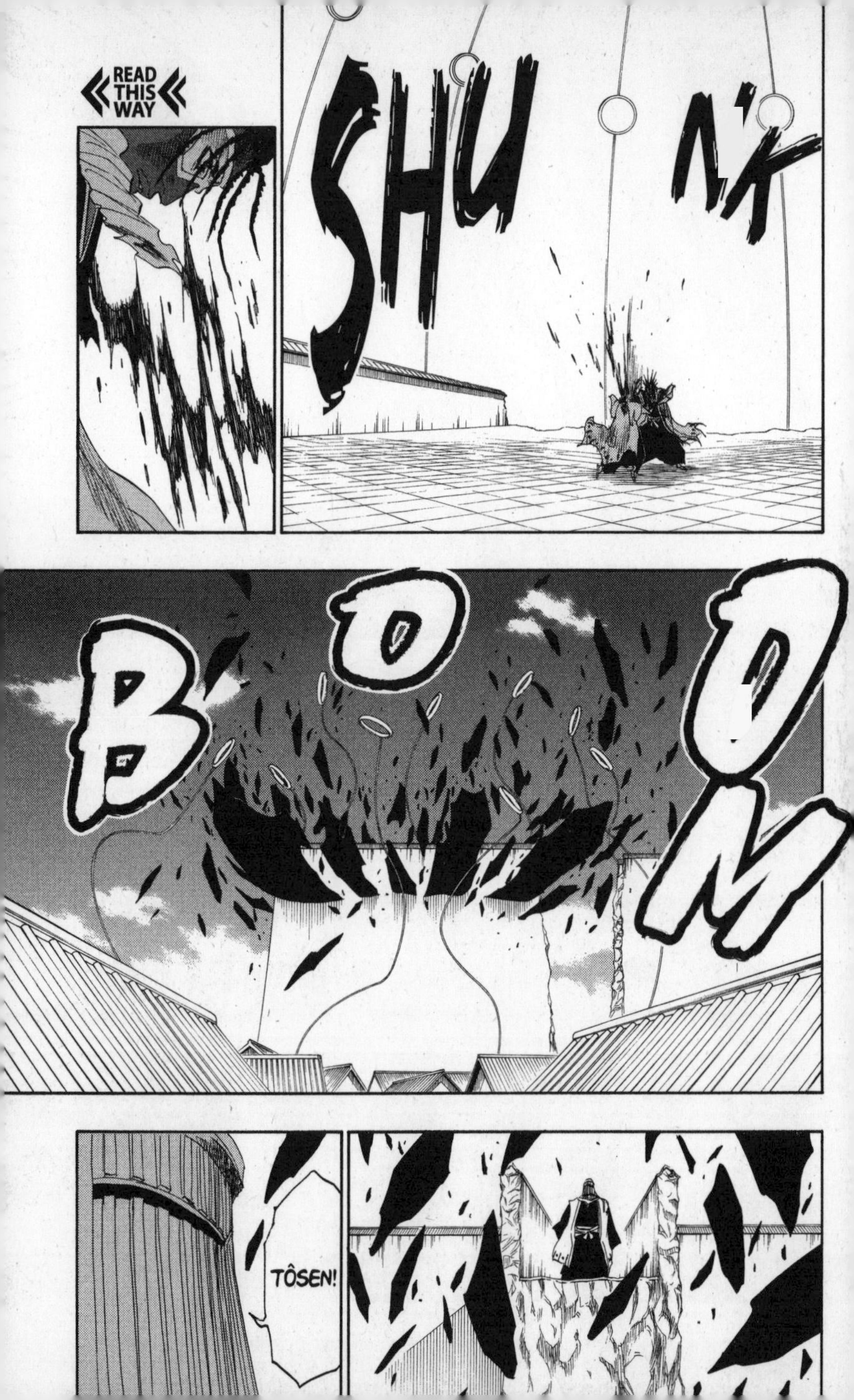
READ THIS WAY
SHUNK
BOOM
TÔSEN!

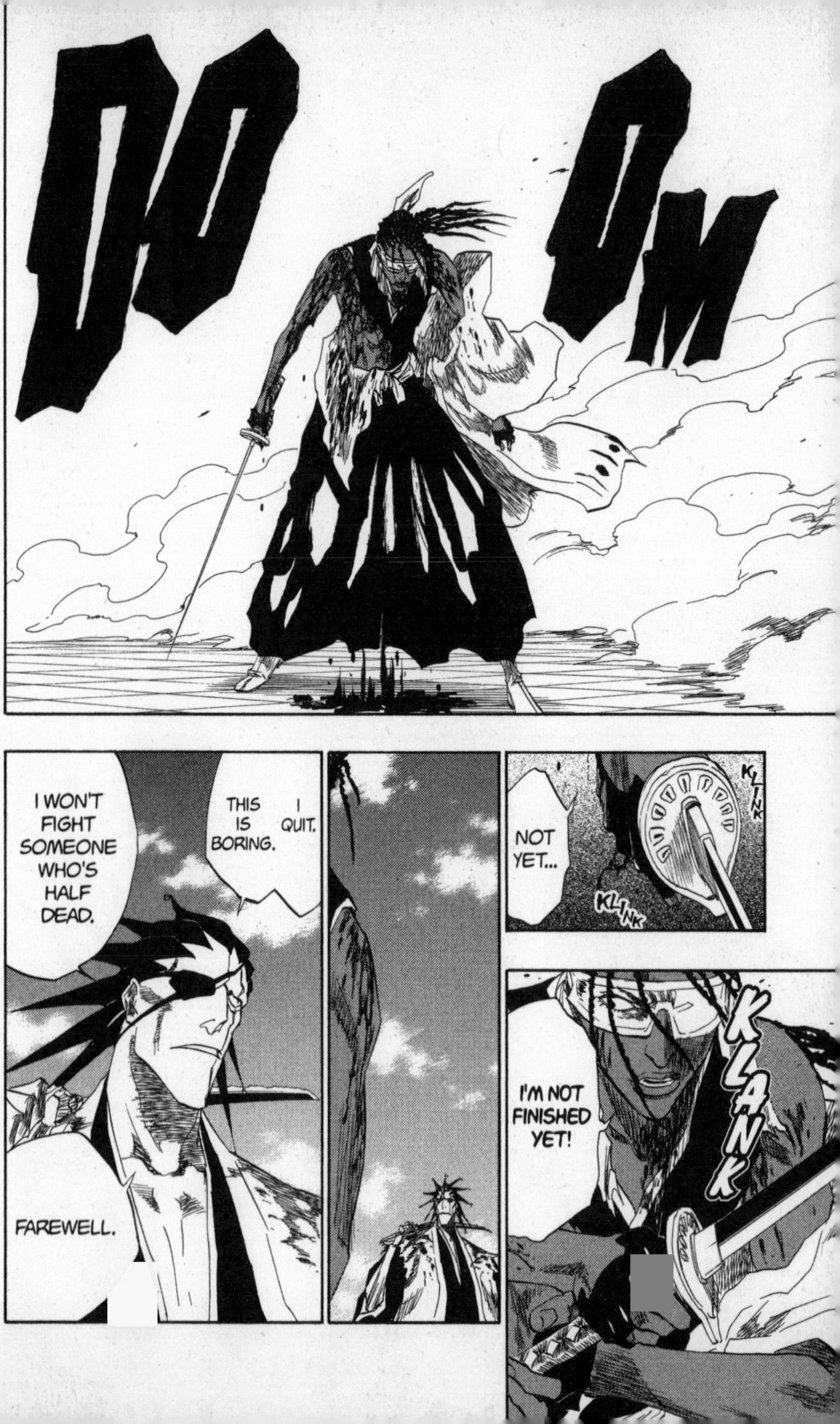
DOOM
NOT YET...
KLINK
KLINK
I'M NOT FINISHED YET!
KLANK
THIS IS BORING. I QUIT.
I WON'T FIGHT SOMEONE WHO'S HALF DEAD.
FAREWELL.

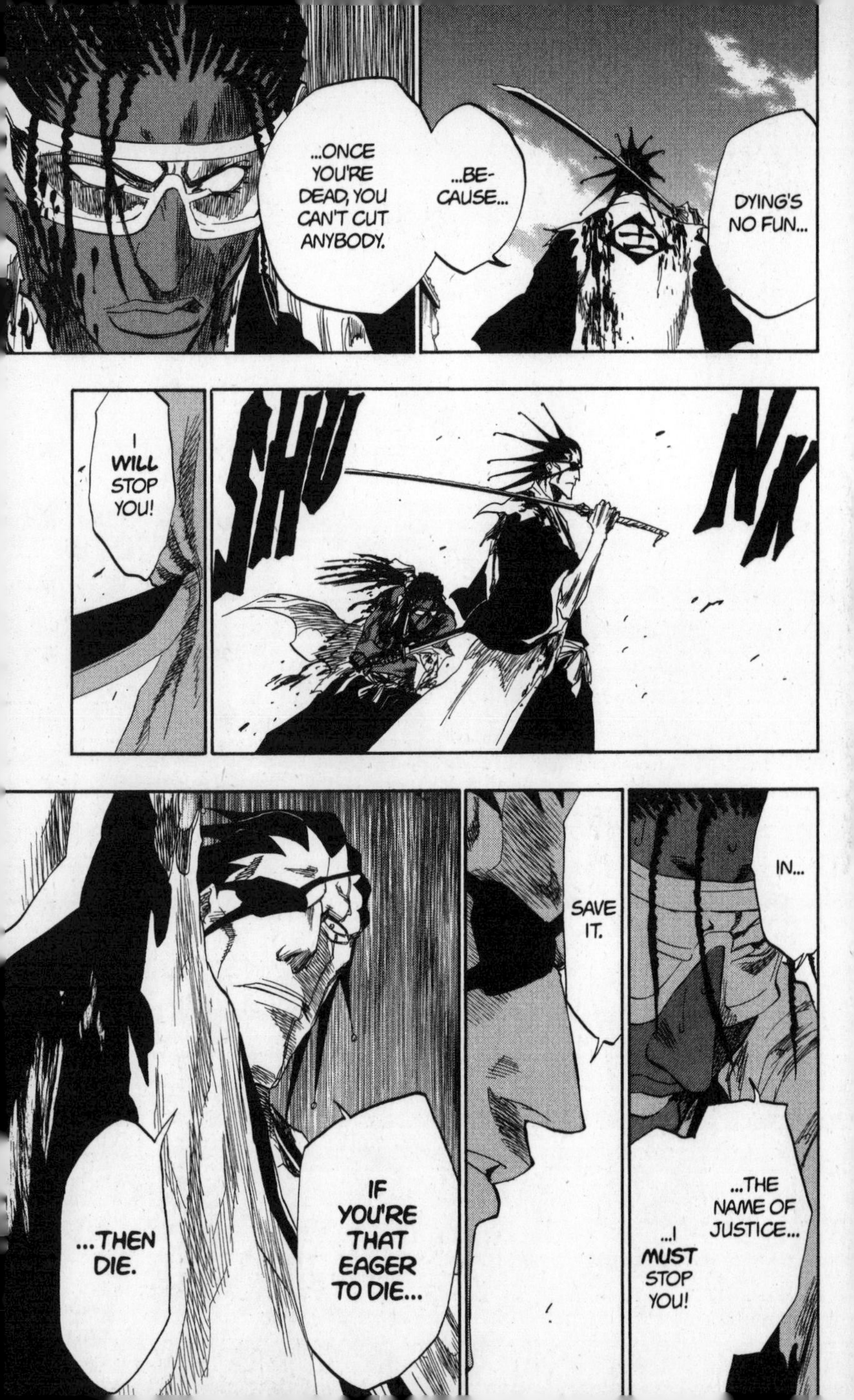
DYING'S NO FUN...
...BE-CAUSE...
...ONCE YOU'RE DEAD, YOU CAN'T CUT ANYBODY.
SHUNK
I WILL STOP YOU!
IN...
...THE NAME OF JUSTICE...
...I MUST STOP YOU!
SAVE IT.
IF YOU'RE THAT EAGER TO DIE...
...THEN DIE.

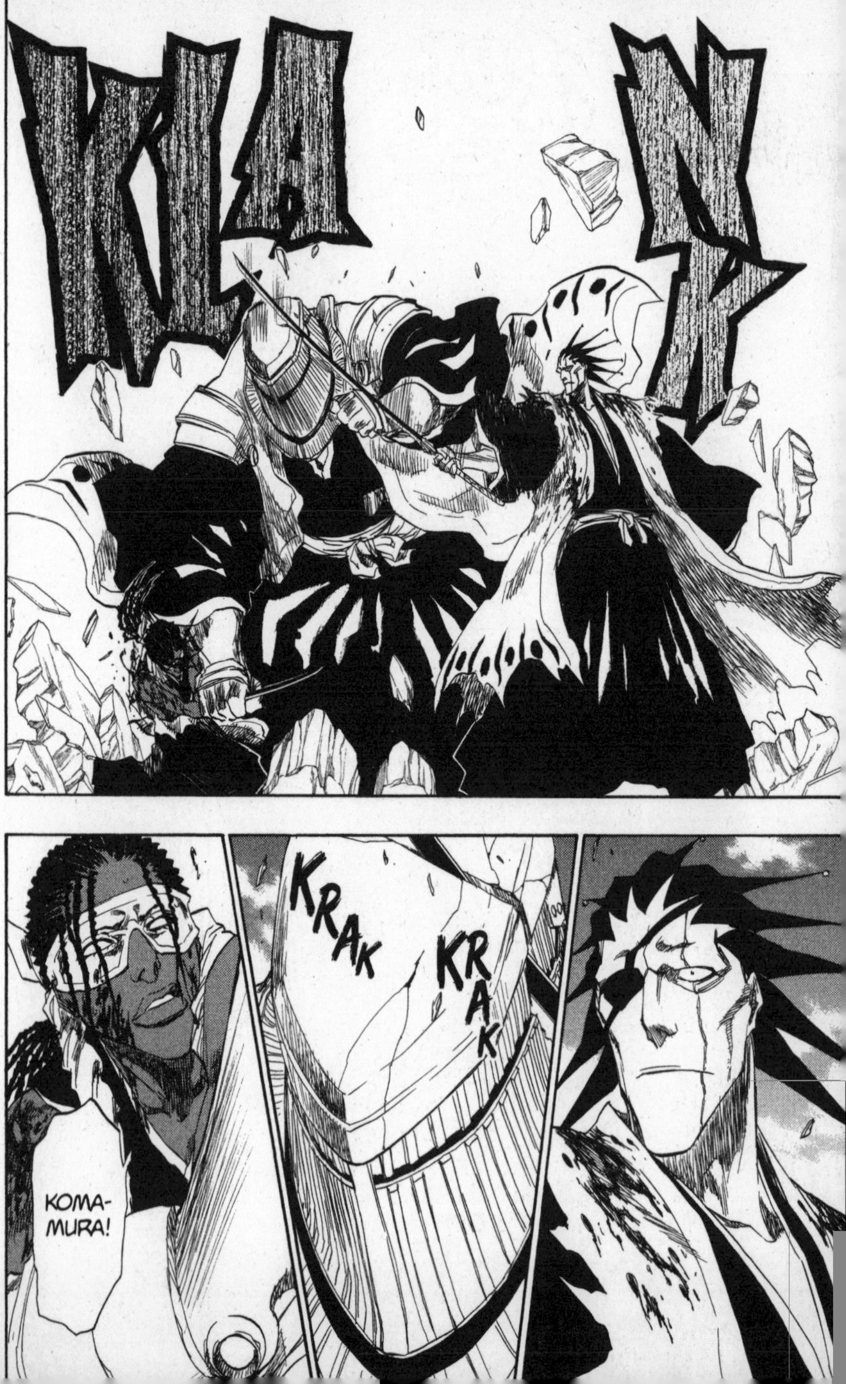
KLANK
KRAK KRAK
KOMA-MURA!

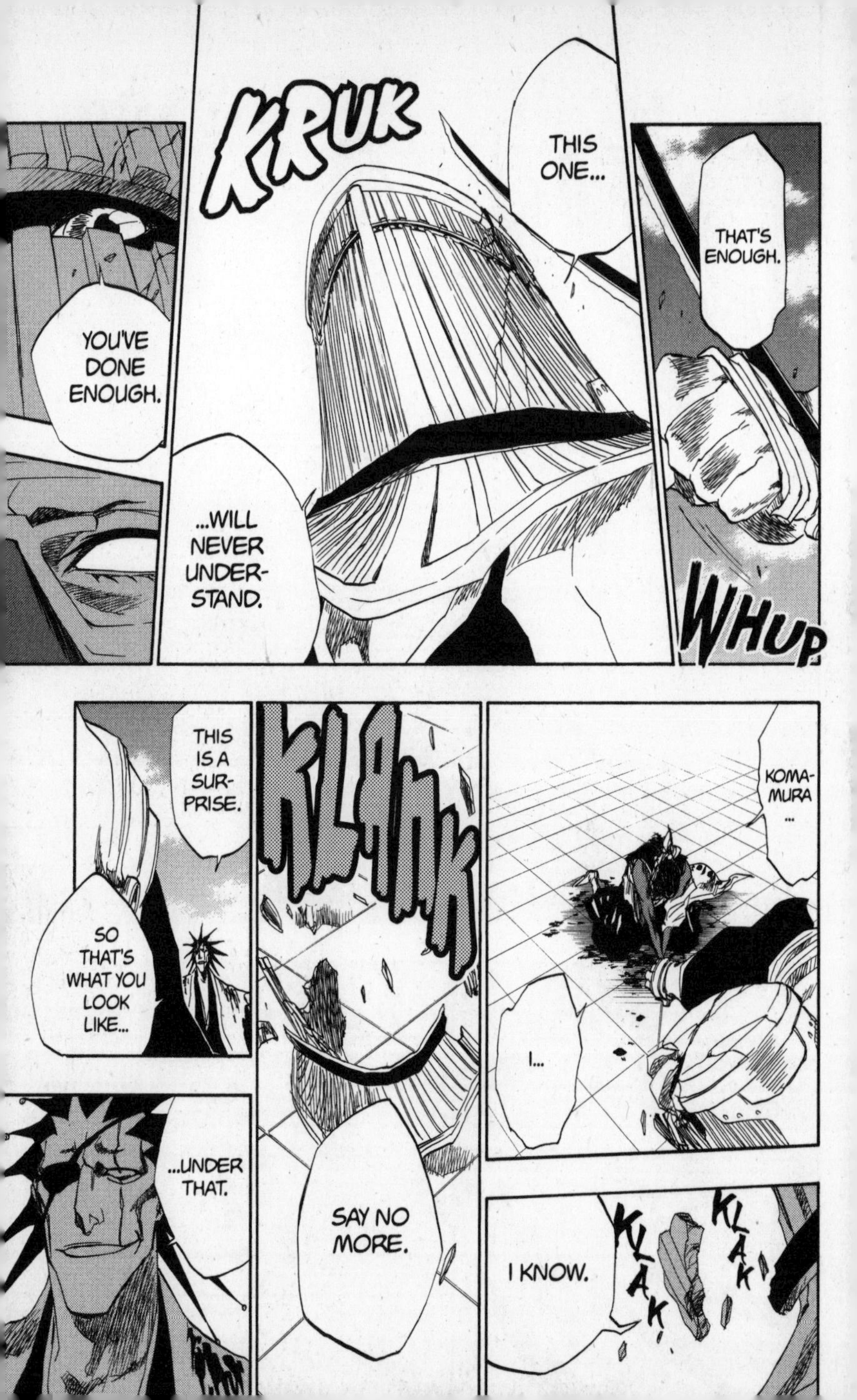
THAT'S ENOUGH.
WHUP
KRUK
THIS ONE...
...WILL NEVER UNDERSTAND.
YOU'VE DONE ENOUGH.
KOMAMURA...
I...
KLAK KLAK
I KNOW.
KLANK
SAY NO MORE.
THIS IS A SURPRISE.
SO THAT'S WHAT YOU LOOK LIKE...
...UNDER THAT.

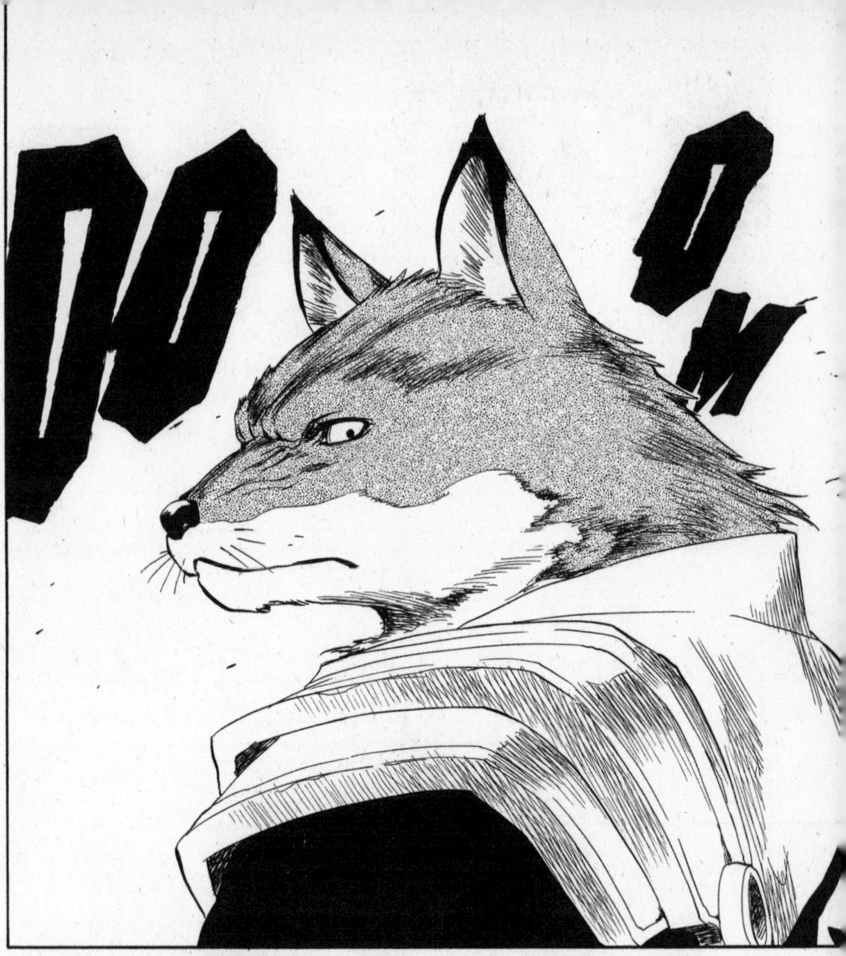
DOOM

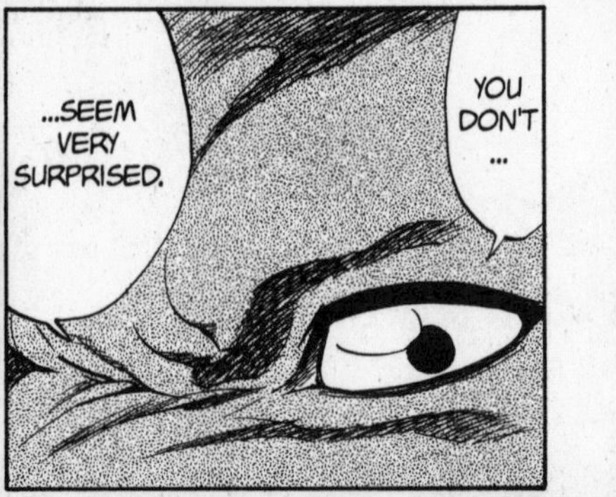
YOU DON'T ...
...SEEM VERY SURPRISED.

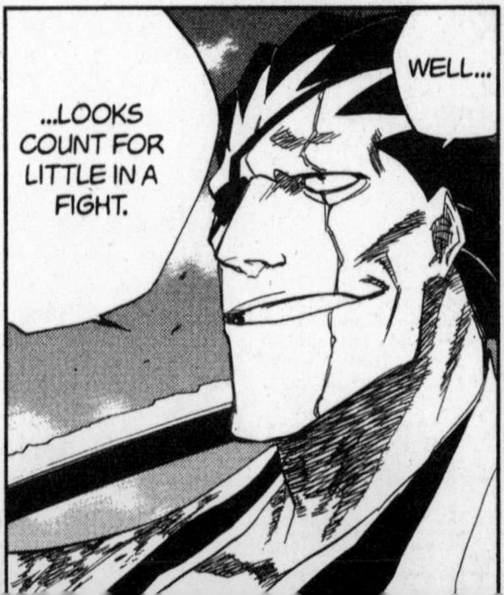
WELL...
...LOOKS COUNT FOR LITTLE IN A FIGHT.

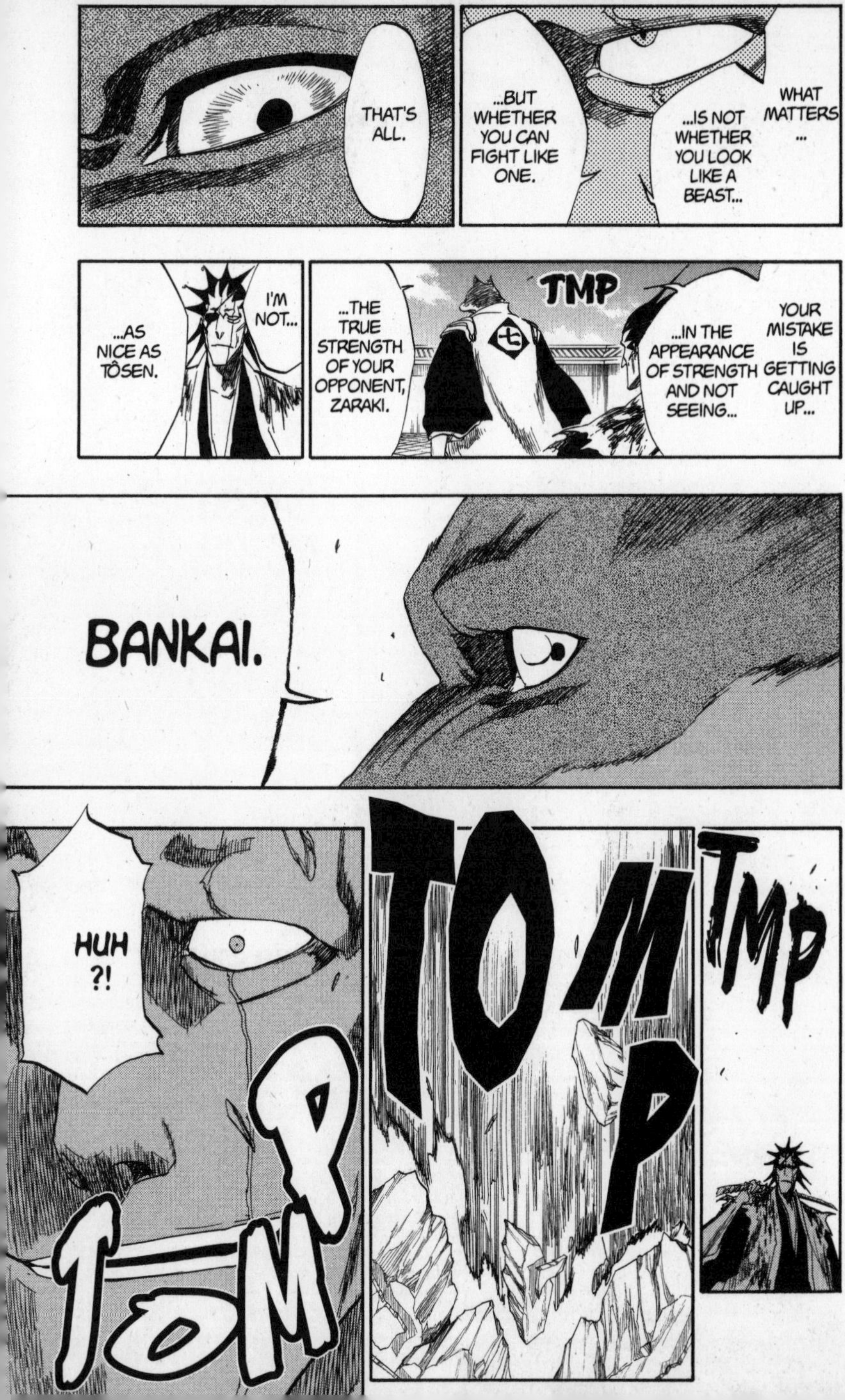
WHAT MATTERS ...
...IS NOT WHETHER YOU LOOK LIKE A BEAST...
...BUT WHETHER YOU CAN FIGHT LIKE ONE.
THAT'S ALL.
YOUR MISTAKE IS GETTING CAUGHT UP...
...IN THE APPEARANCE OF STRENGTH AND NOT SEEING...
TMP
...THE TRUE STRENGTH OF YOUR OPPONENT, ZARAKI.
I'M NOT...
...AS NICE AS TÔSEN.
BANKAI.
TMP
TOMP
HUH ?!
TOMP

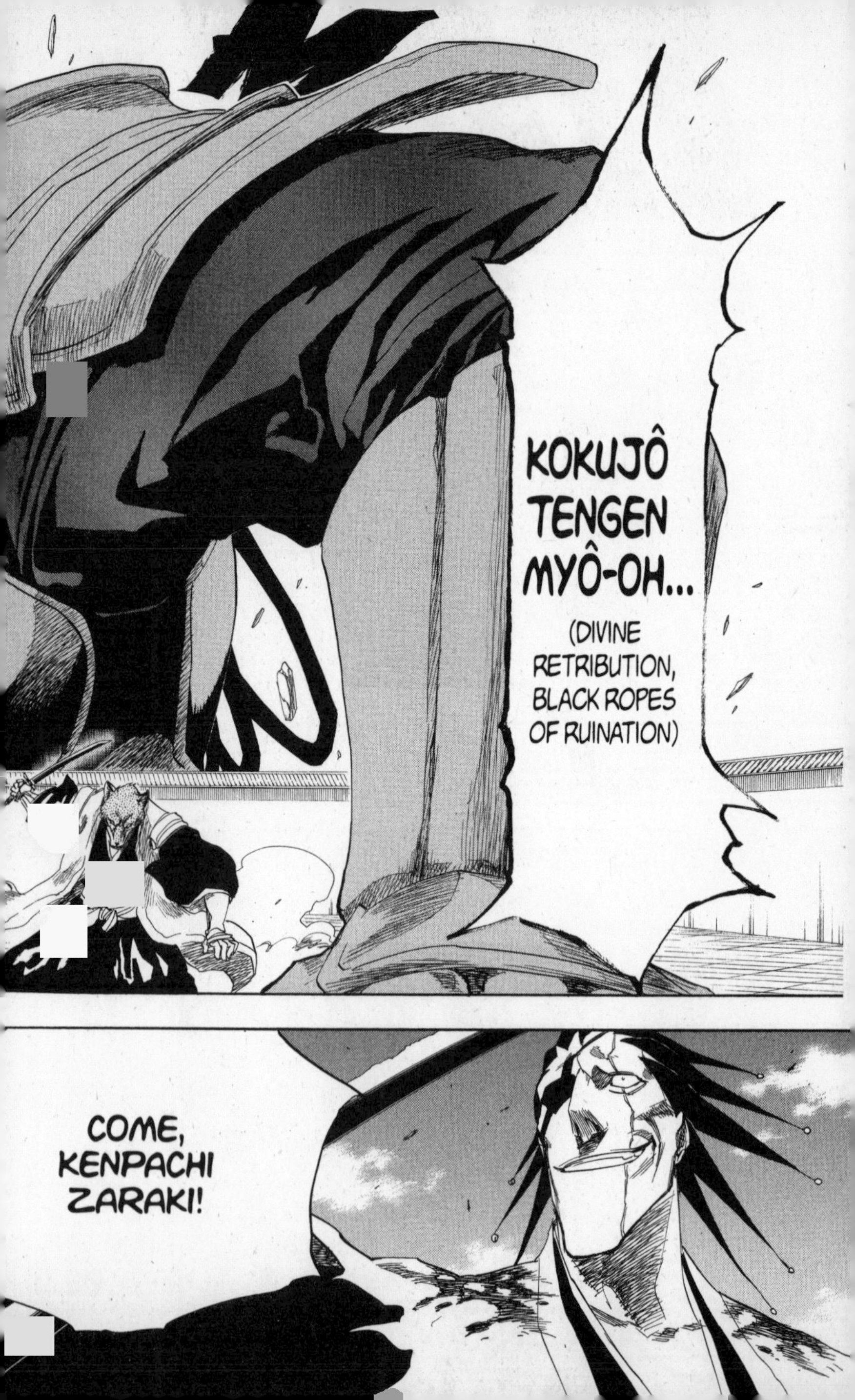
KOKUJÔ TENGEN MYÔ-OH...
(DIVINE RETRIBUTION, BLACK ROPES OF RUINATION)
COME, KENPACHI ZARAKI!

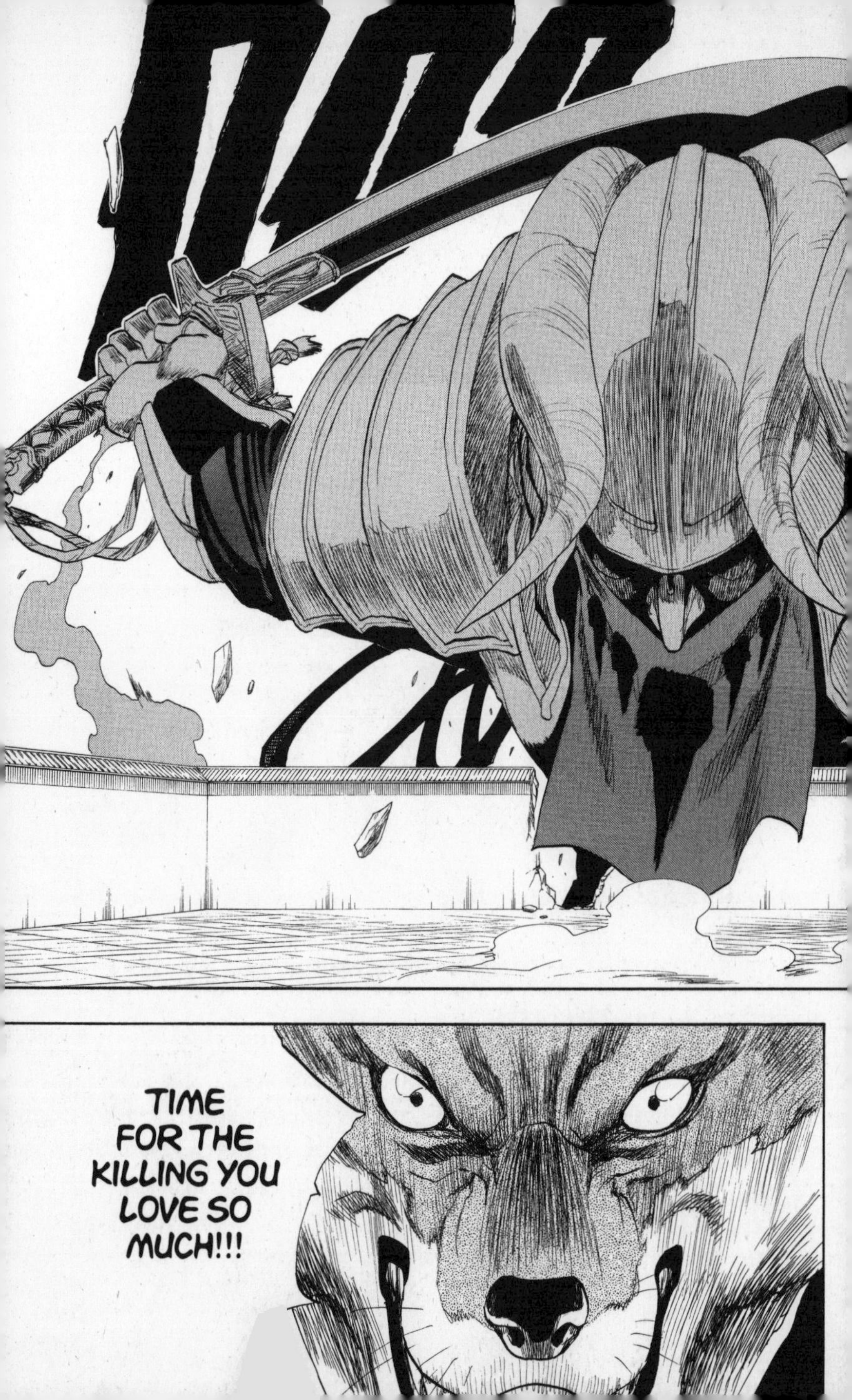
TIME FOR THE KILLING YOU LOVE SO MUCH!!!

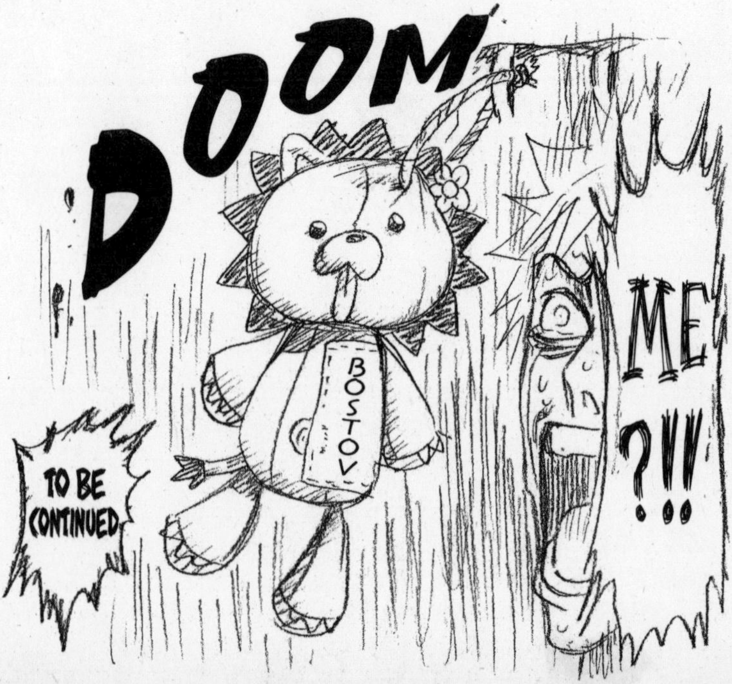
ME ?!!
DOOM
BOSTOV
TO BE CONTINUED

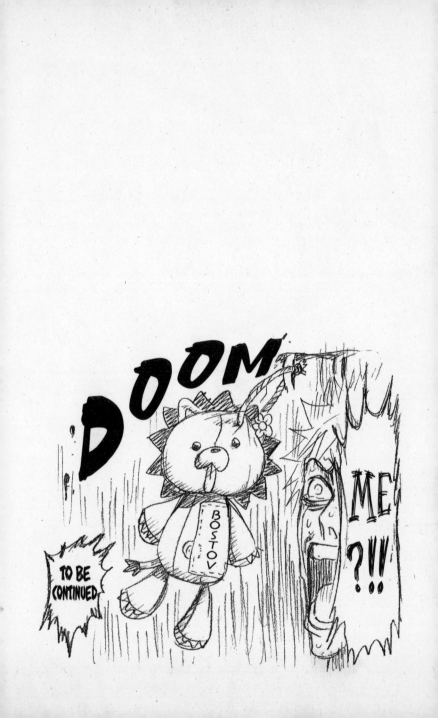

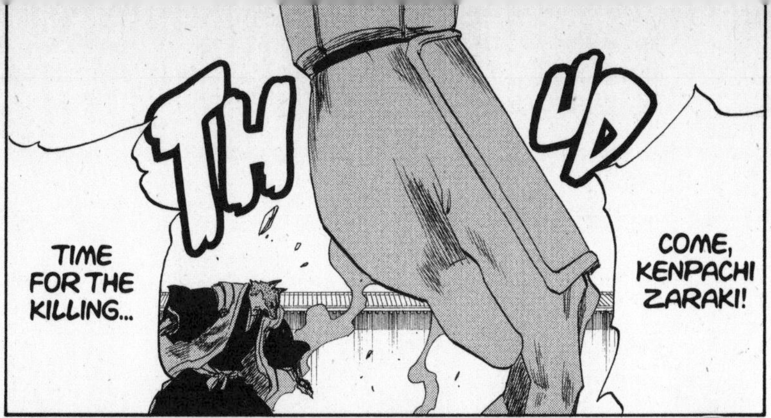
THUD
COME, KENPACHI ZARAKI!
TIME FOR THE KILLING...

149. COUNTDOWN TO THE END: 1 (ONLY MERCIFULLY)

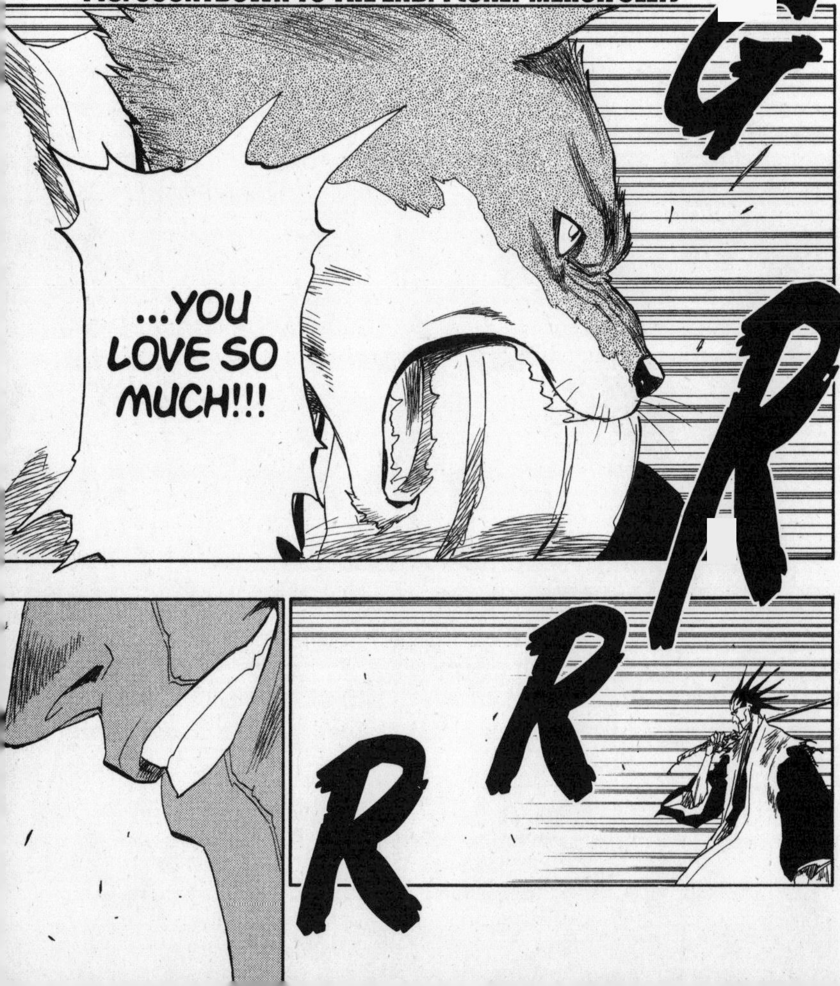
GRRRR
...YOU LOVE SO MUCH!!!

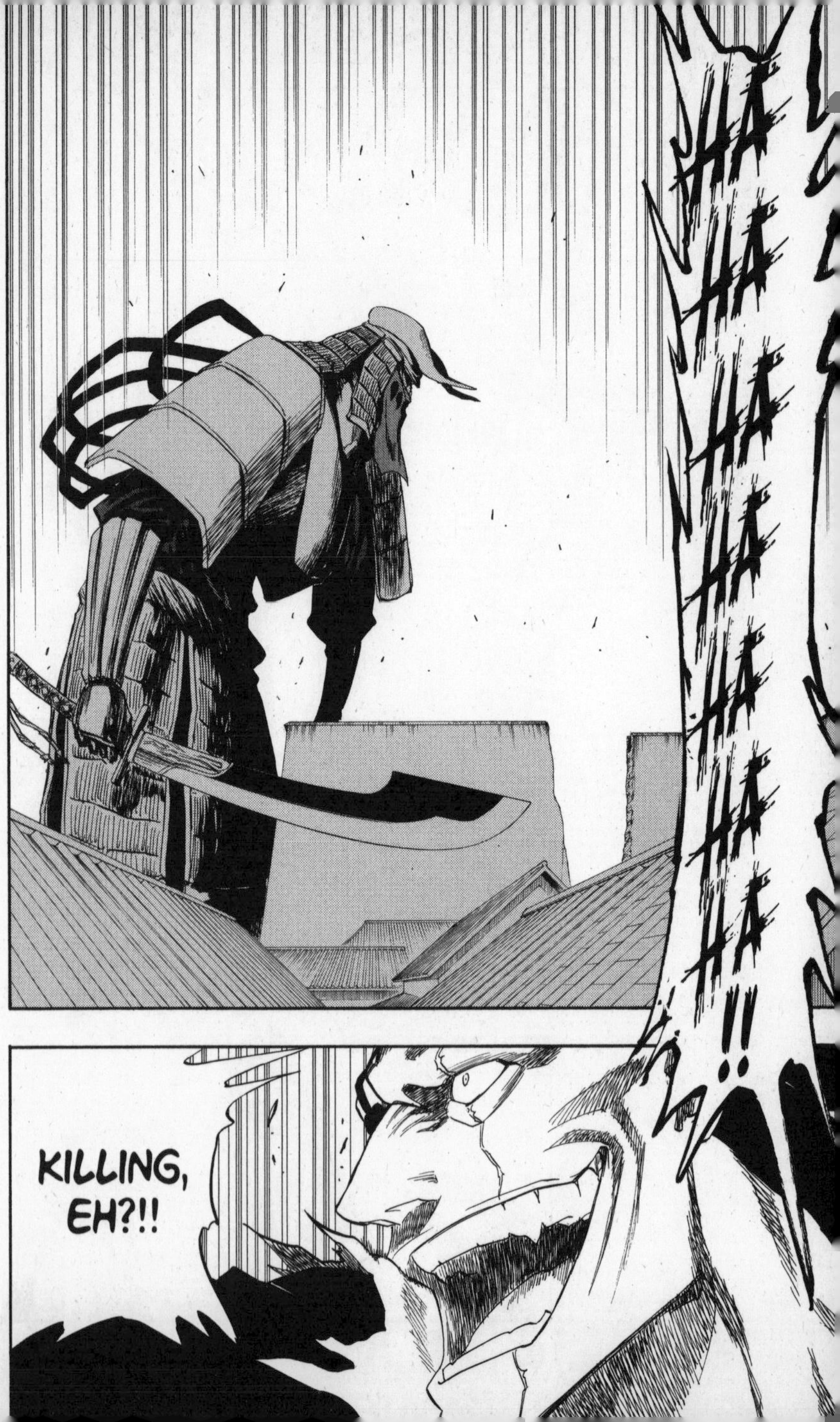
HAHAHAHAHAHAHAHA!!
KILLING, EH?!!

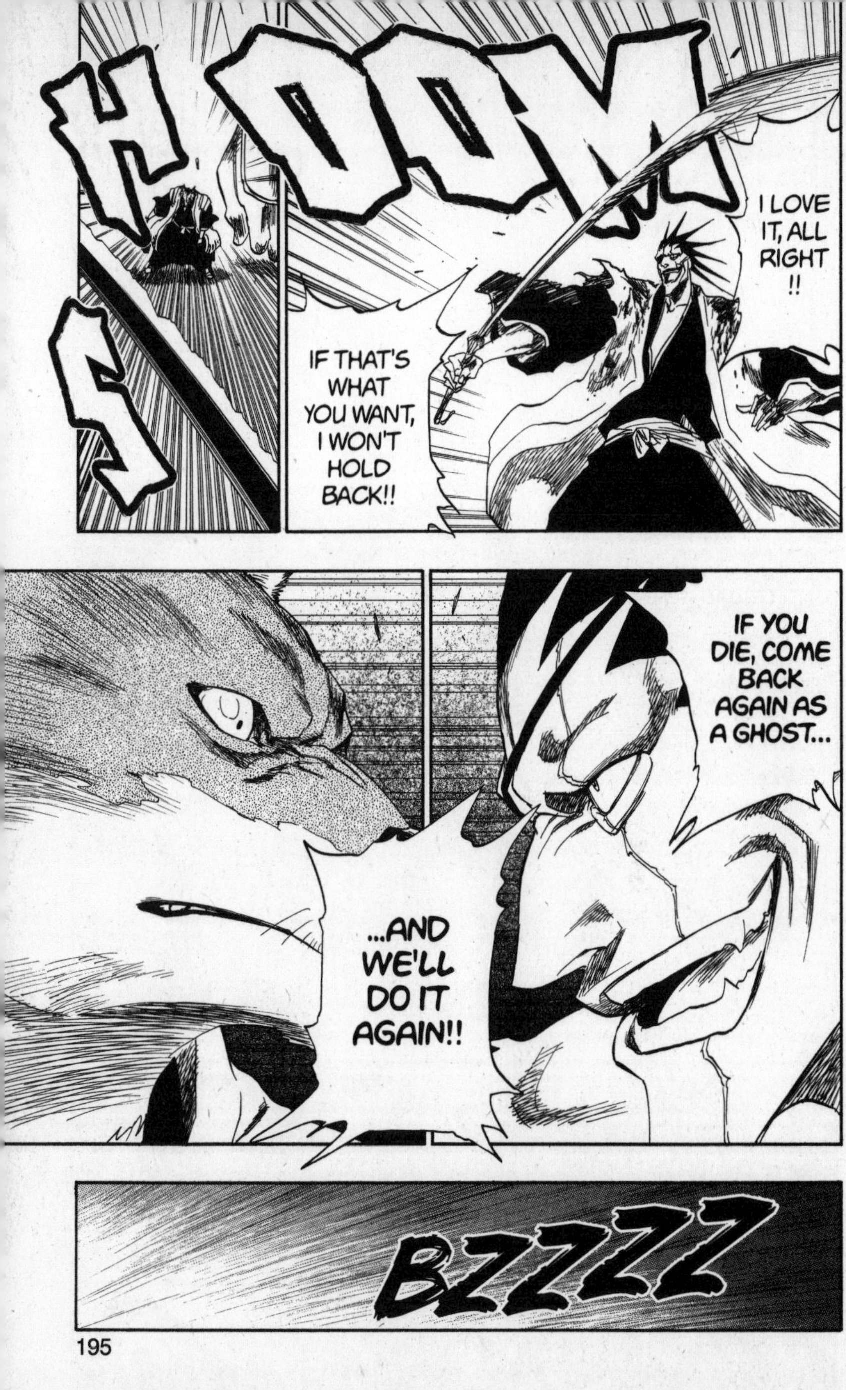
SHOOM
I LOVE IT, ALL RIGHT!!
IF THAT'S WHAT YOU WANT, I WON'T HOLD BACK!!
IF YOU DIE, COME BACK AGAIN AS A GHOST...
...AND WE'LL DO IT AGAIN!!
BZZZZ

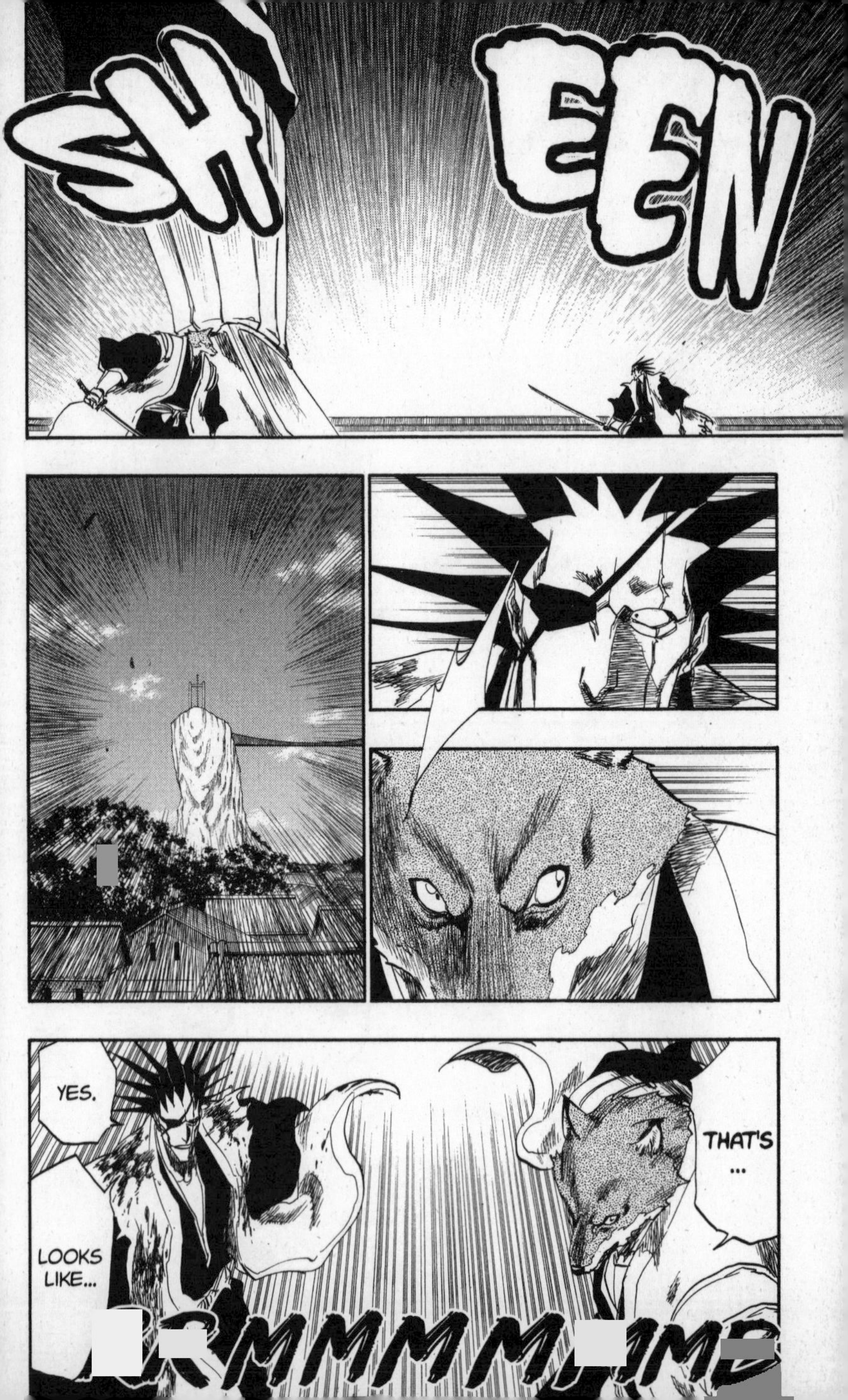
SH
EEN
THAT'S ...
YES.
LOOKS LIKE...

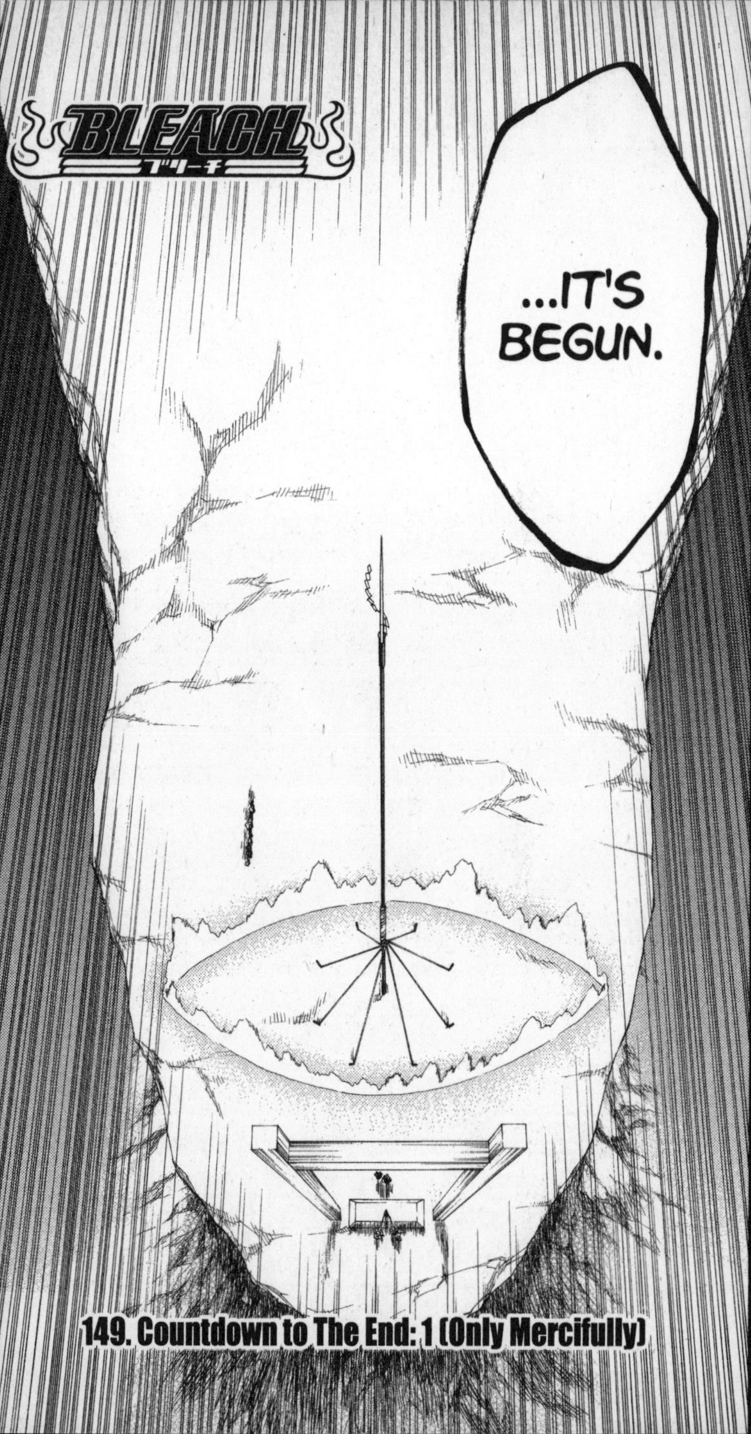
BLEACH
ブリーチ
...IT'S BEGUN.
149. Countdown to The End: 1 (Only Mercifully)

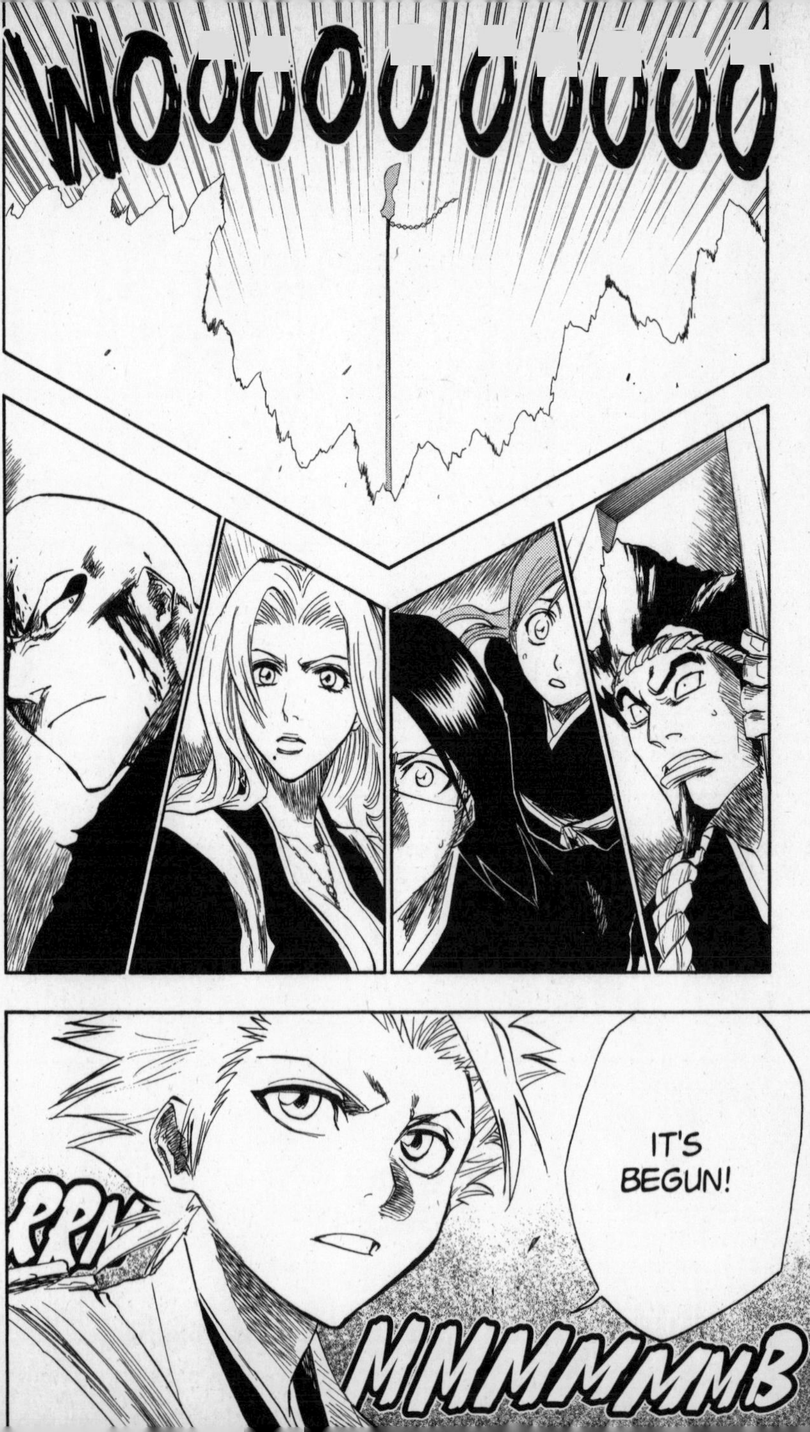
WOOOOOOOOOO
IT'S BEGUN!
MMMMMMB

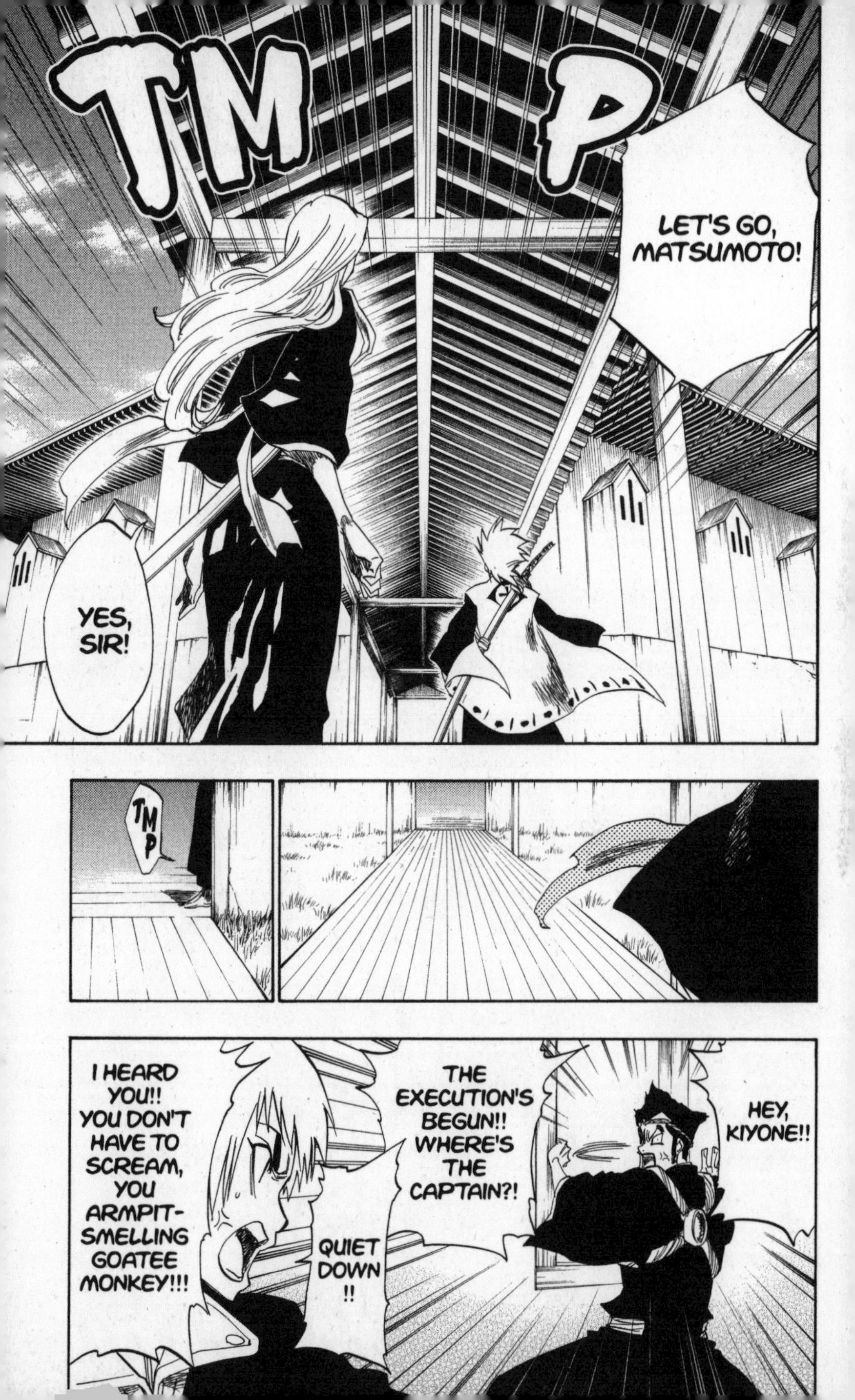

T'M P
LET'S GO, MATSUMOTO!
YES, SIR!
TMP
HEY, KIYONE!!
THE EXECUTION'S BEGUN!! WHERE'S THE CAPTAIN?!
I HEARD YOU!! YOU DON'T HAVE TO SCREAM, YOU ARMPIT-SMELLING GOATEE MONKEY!!!
QUIET DOWN !!

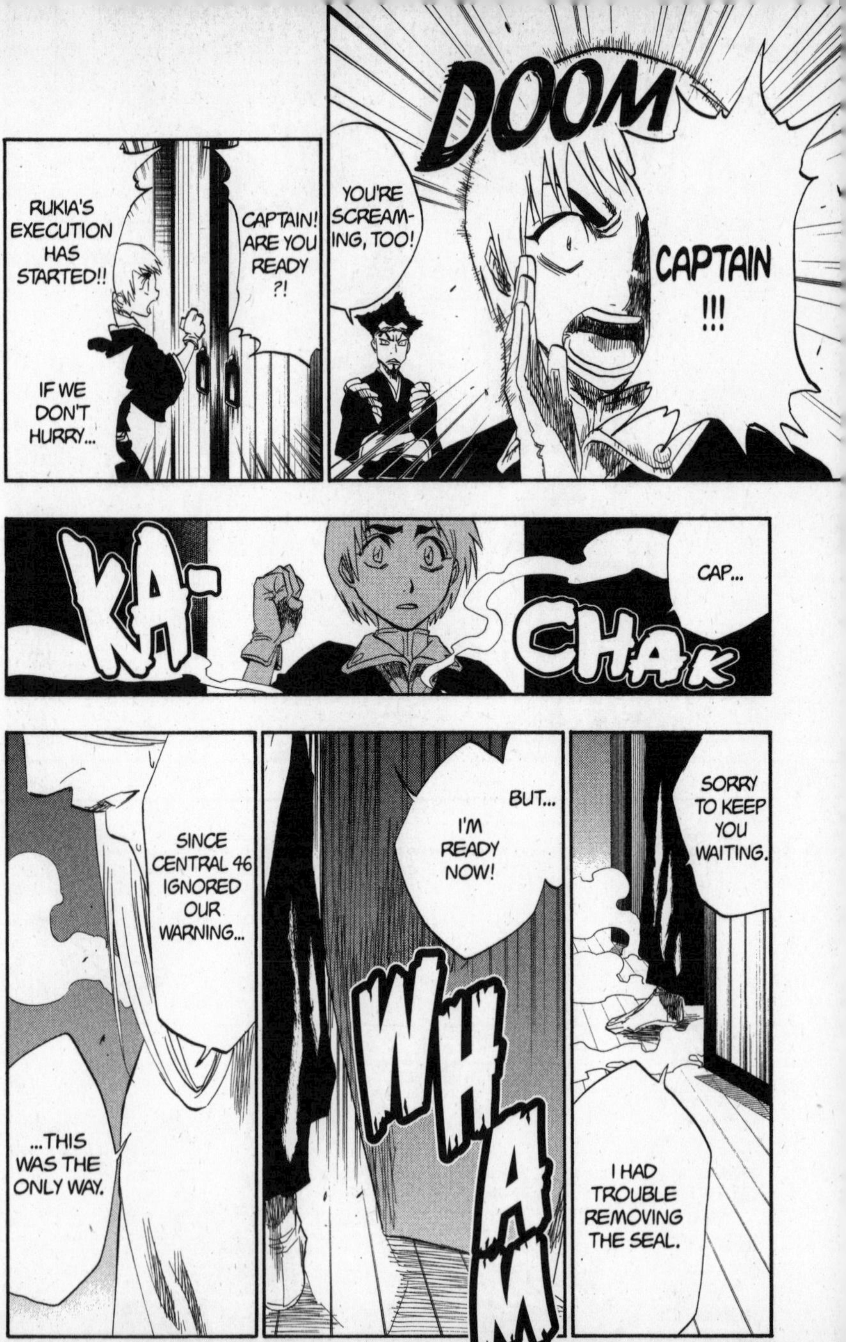
DOOM
CAPTAIN!!!
YOU'RE SCREAMING, TOO!
CAPTAIN! ARE YOU READY?!
RUKIA'S EXECUTION HAS STARTED!!
IF WE DON'T HURRY...
CAP...
KA-CHAK
SORRY TO KEEP YOU WAITING.
I HAD TROUBLE REMOVING THE SEAL.
BUT...
I'M READY NOW!
WHAM
SINCE CENTRAL 46 IGNORED OUR WARNING...
...THIS WAS THE ONLY WAY.

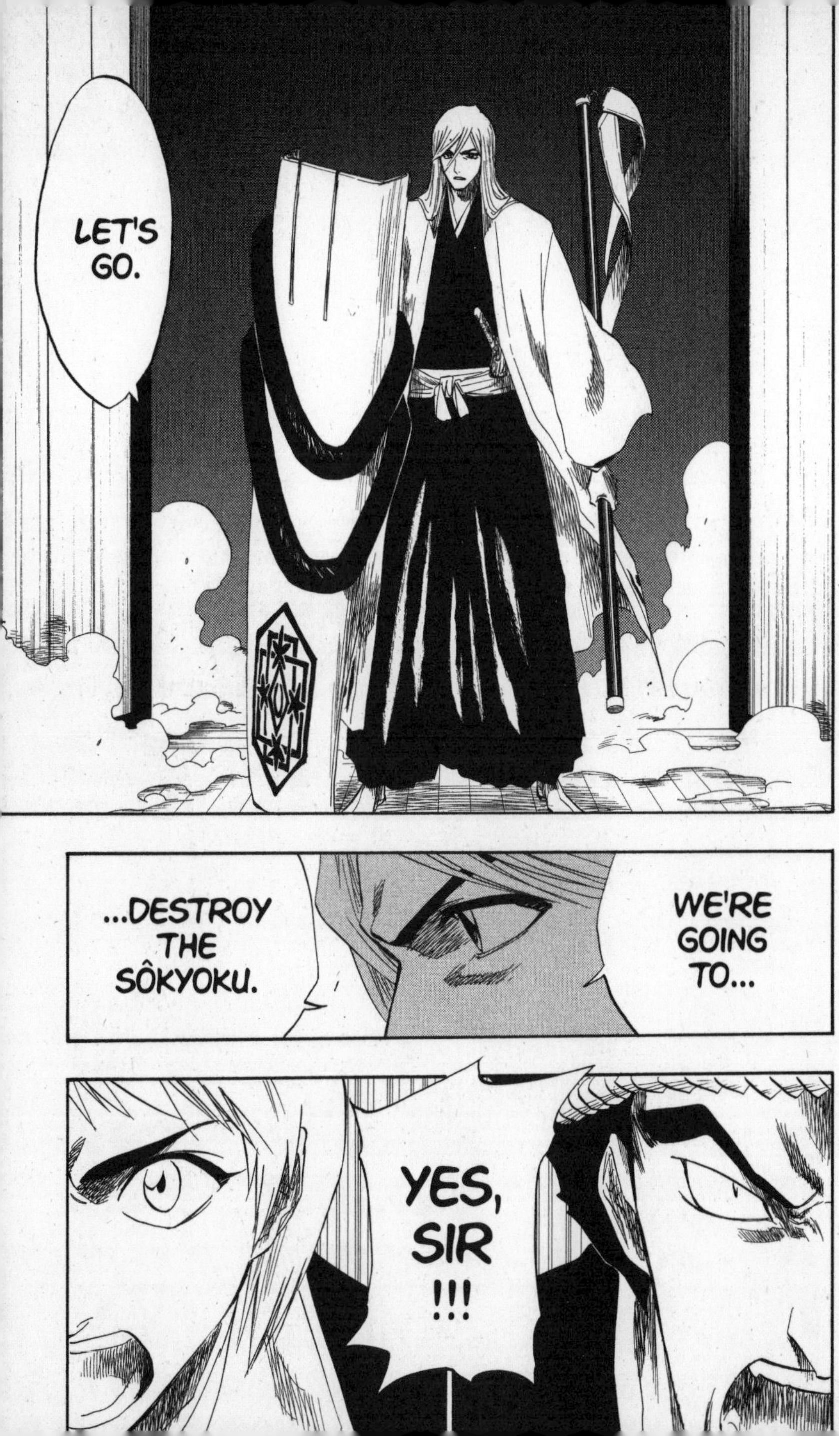
LET'S GO.
WE'RE GOING TO...
...DESTROY THE SÔKYOKU.
YES, SIR !!!

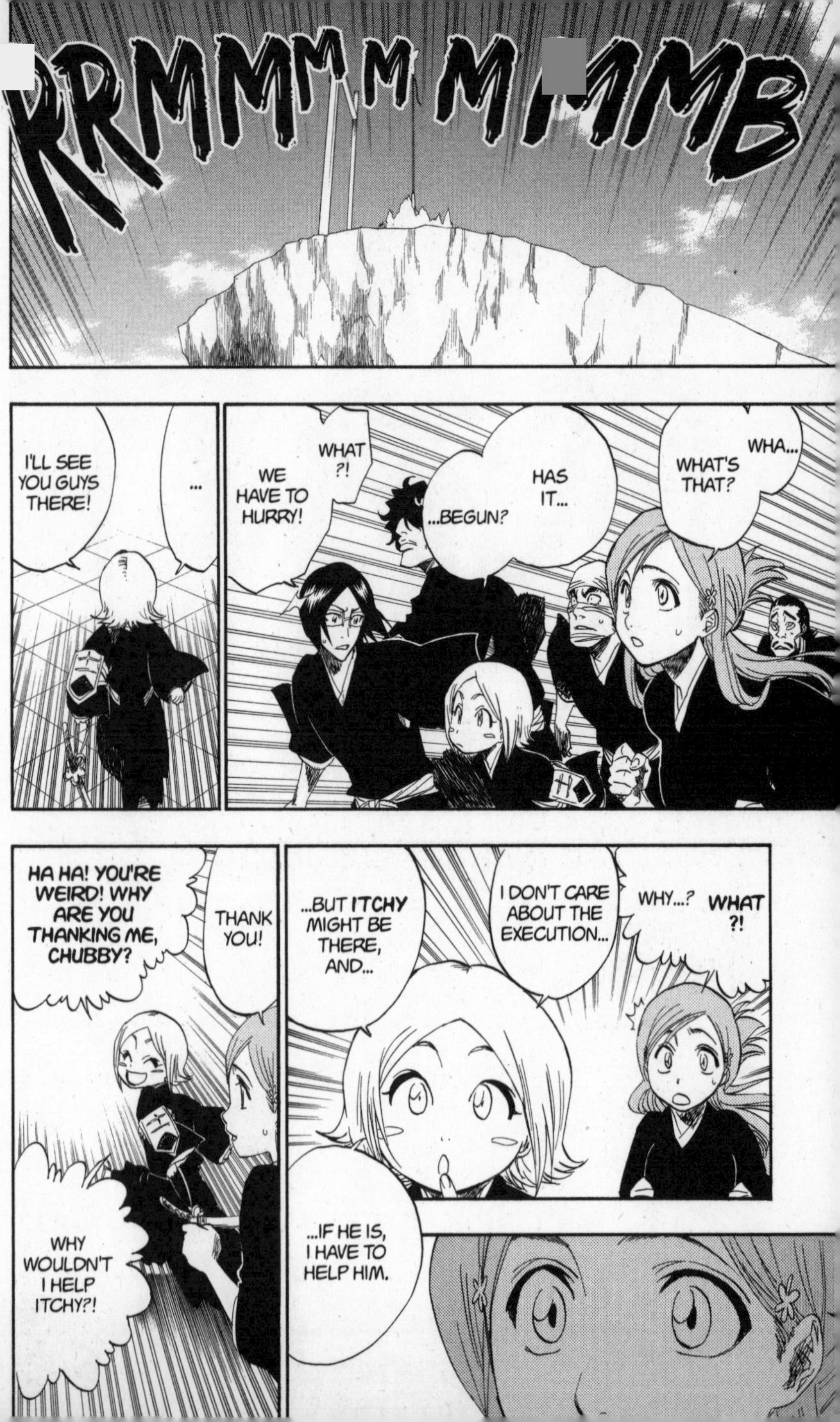
RRMMMMMMMMB
WHA... WHAT'S THAT?
HAS IT... ...BEGUN?
WHAT?!
WE HAVE TO HURRY!
...
I'LL SEE YOU GUYS THERE!
WHAT?!
WHY...?
I DON'T CARE ABOUT THE EXECUTION...
...BUT ITCHY MIGHT BE THERE, AND...
...IF HE IS, I HAVE TO HELP HIM.
THANK YOU!
HA HA! YOU'RE WEIRD! WHY ARE YOU THANKING ME, CHUBBY?
WHY WOULDN'T I HELP ITCHY?!

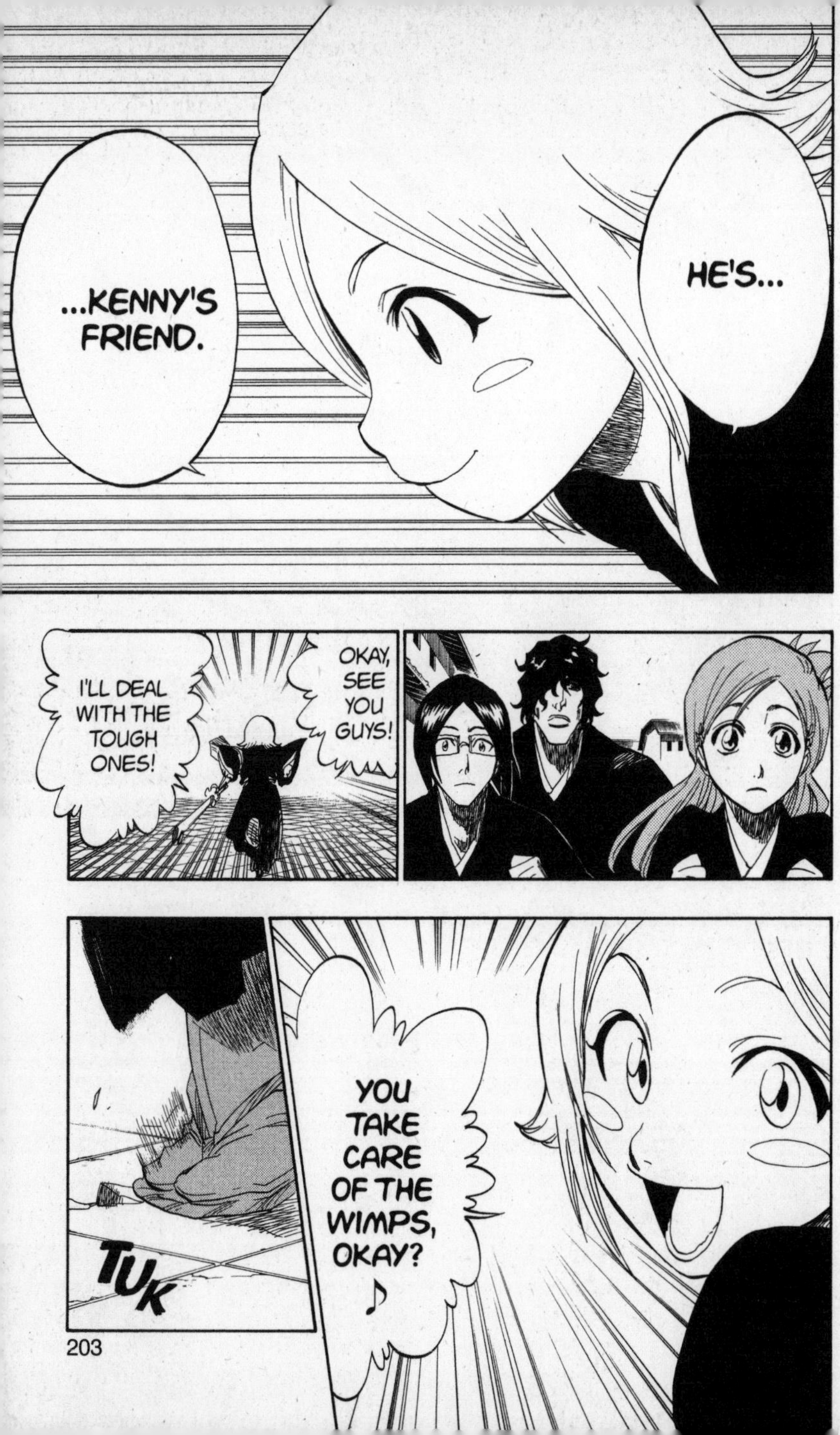
HE'S...
...KENNY'S FRIEND.
OKAY, SEE YOU GUYS!
I'LL DEAL WITH THE TOUGH ONES!
YOU TAKE CARE OF THE WIMPS, OKAY? ♪
TUK

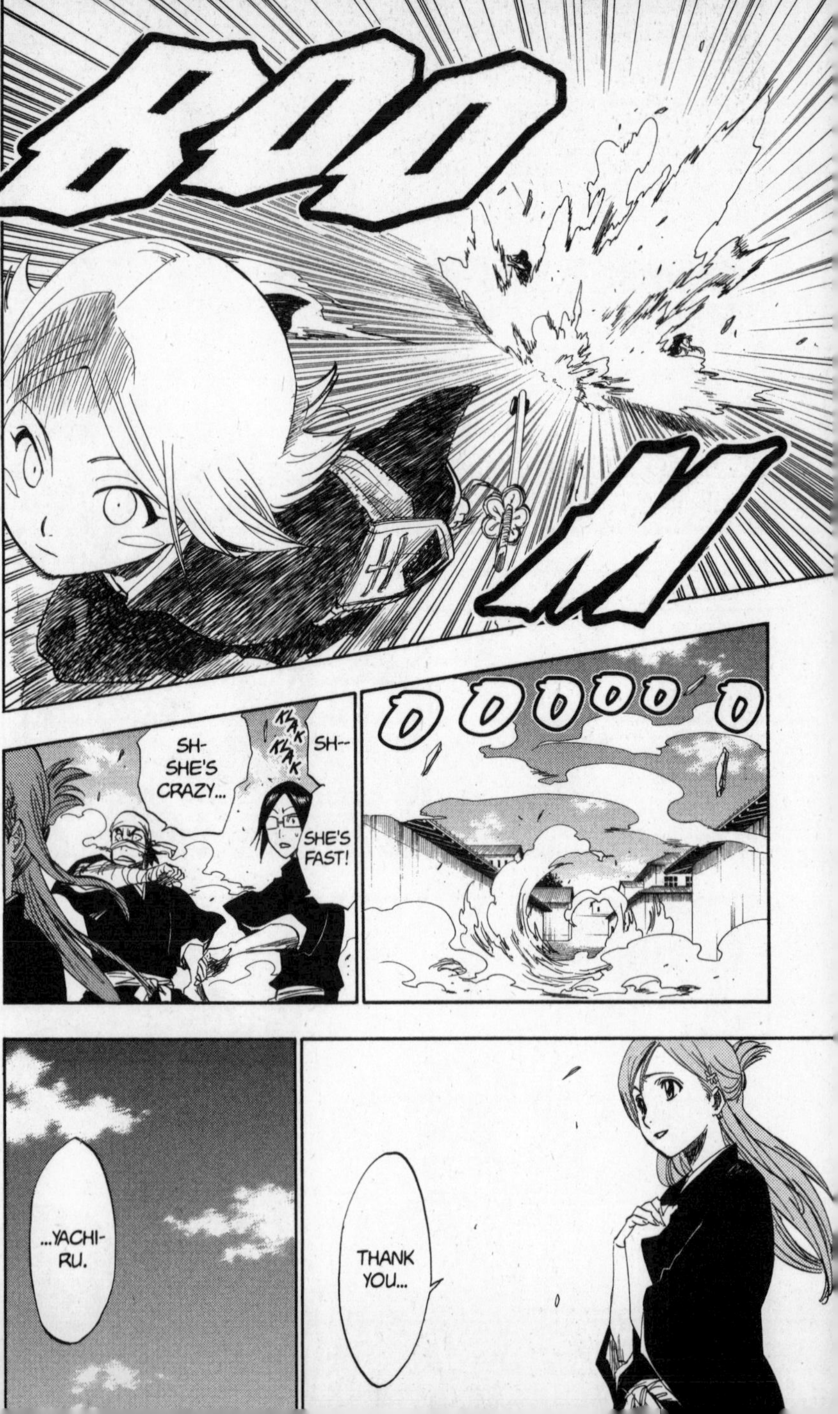
BOO
M
OOOOOO
SH-
SH-
SHE'S
CRAZY...
KLAK KLAK KLAK
SHE'S
FAST!
THANK
YOU...
...YACHI-
RU.

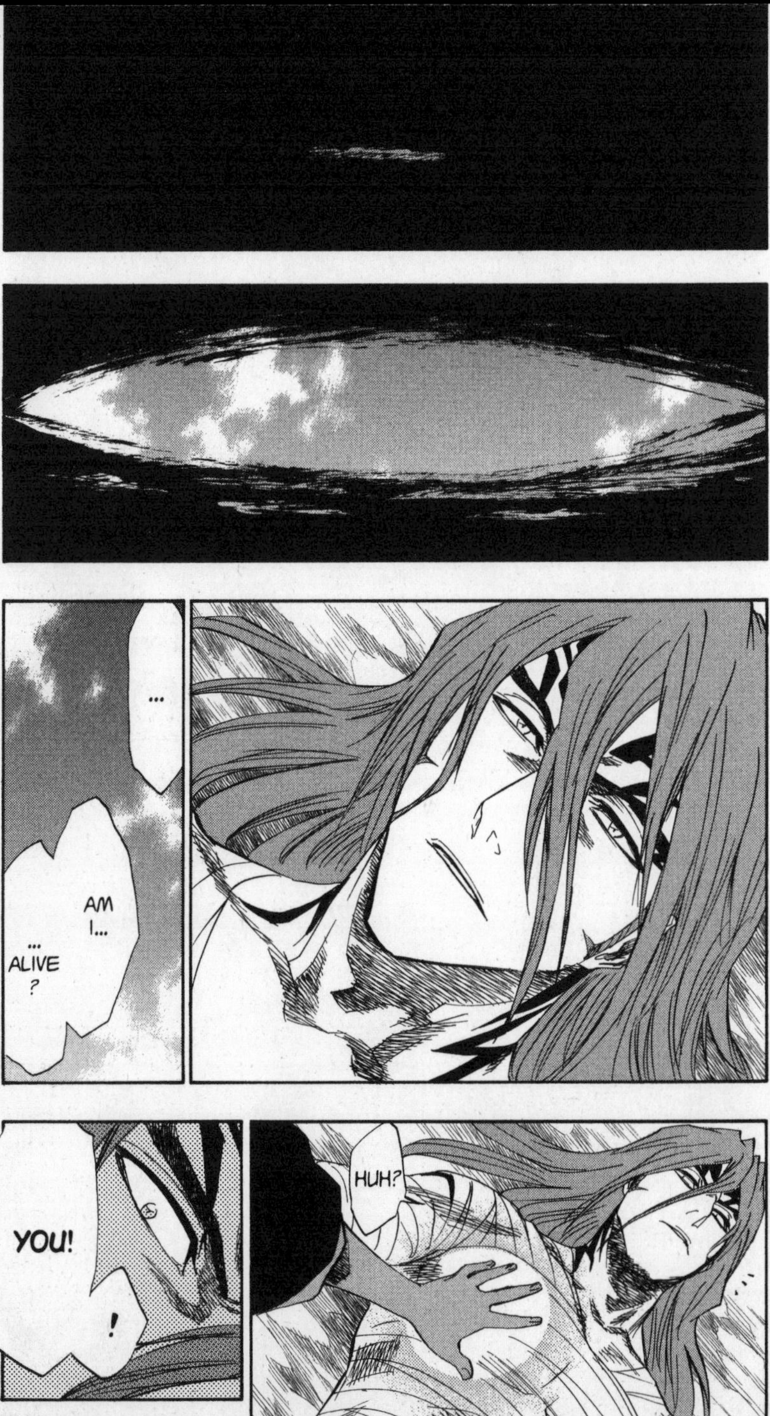
...
AM I... ...ALIVE?
HUH?
...
YOU!
!

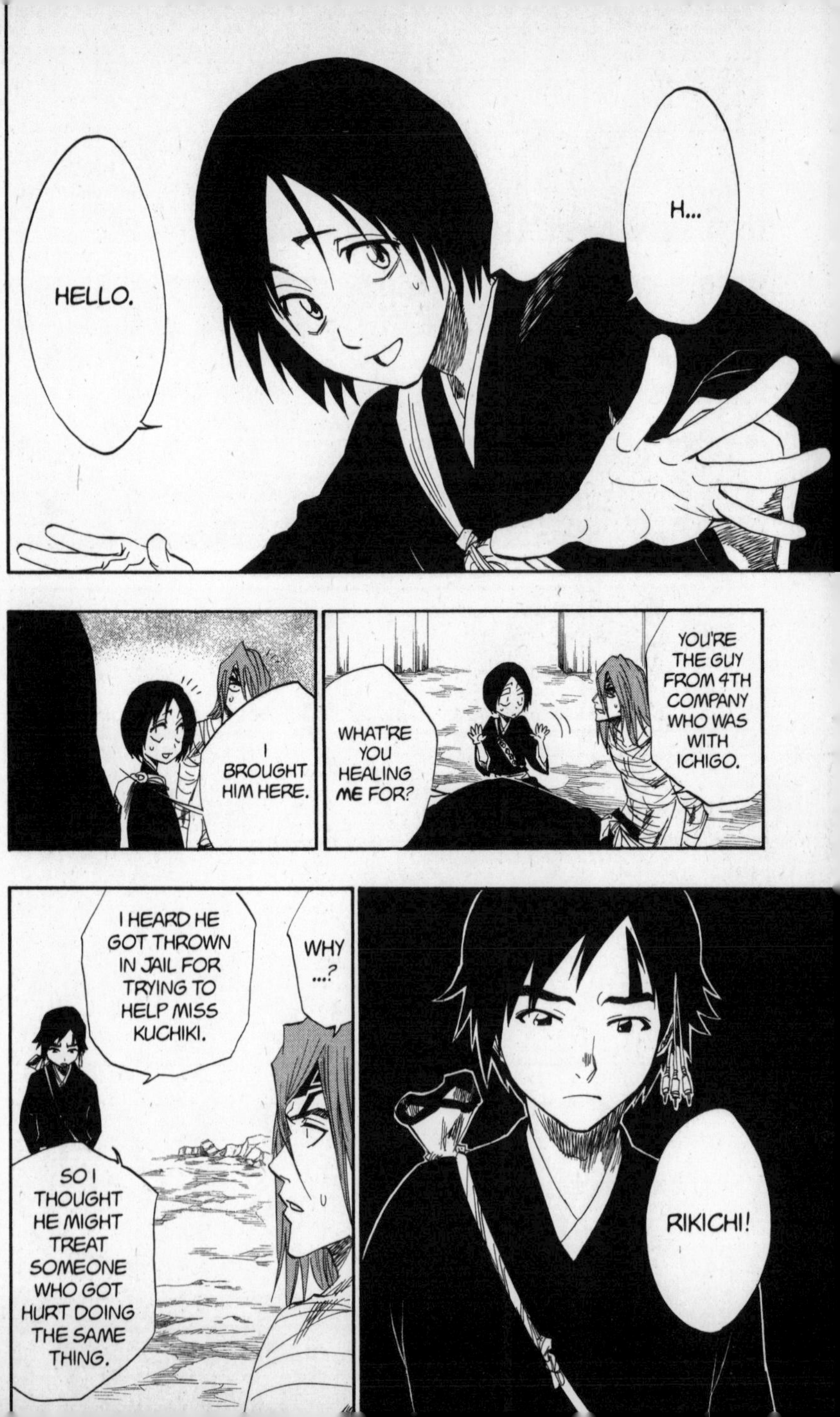
H...
HELLO.
YOU'RE THE GUY FROM 4TH COMPANY WHO WAS WITH ICHIGO.
WHAT'RE YOU HEALING ME FOR?
I BROUGHT HIM HERE.
RIKICHI!
WHY ...?
I HEARD HE GOT THROWN IN JAIL FOR TRYING TO HELP MISS KUCHIKI.
SO I THOUGHT HE MIGHT TREAT SOMEONE WHO GOT HURT DOING THE SAME THING.

READ THIS WAY

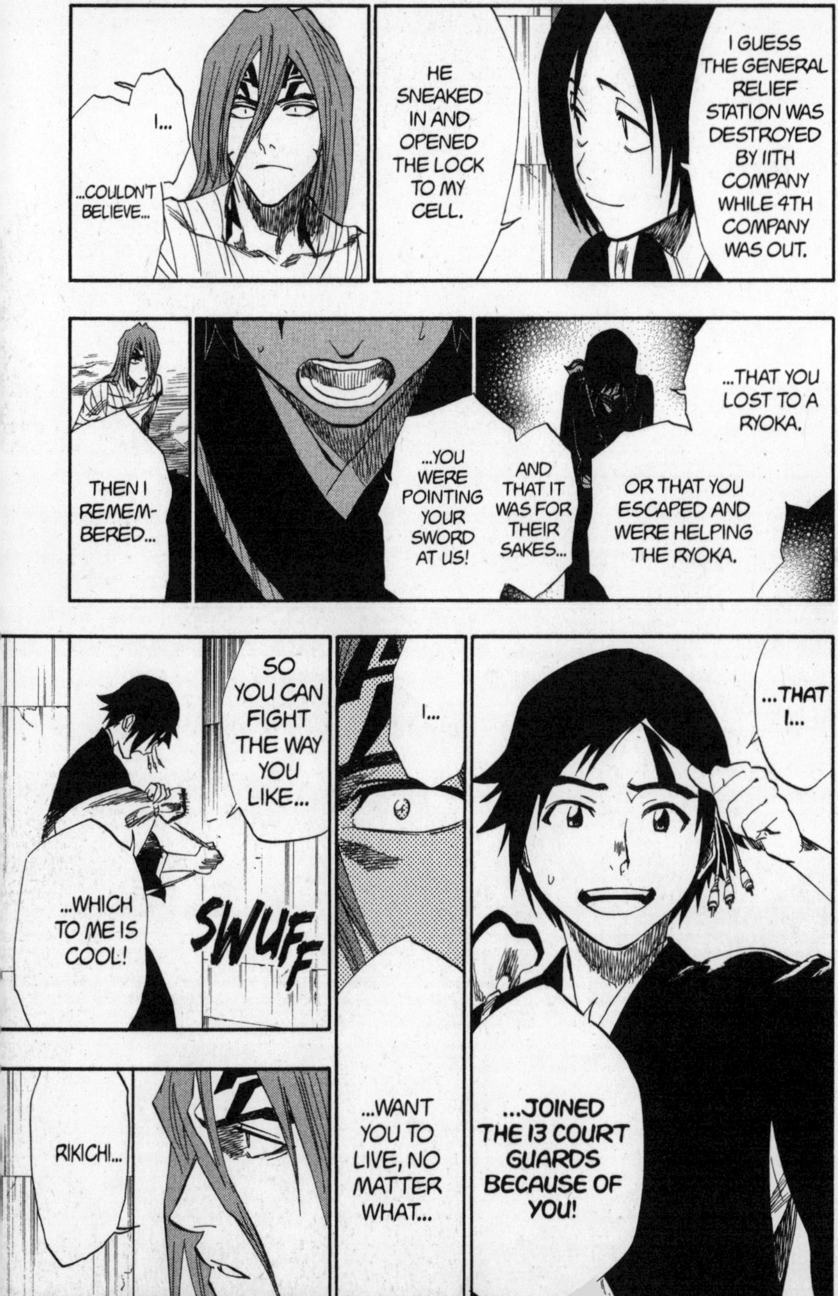
I GUESS THE GENERAL RELIEF STATION WAS DESTROYED BY 11TH COMPANY WHILE 4TH COMPANY WAS OUT.
HE SNEAKED IN AND OPENED THE LOCK TO MY CELL.
I...
...COULDN'T BELIEVE...
...THAT YOU LOST TO A RYOKA.
OR THAT YOU ESCAPED AND WERE HELPING THE RYOKA.
AND THAT IT WAS FOR THEIR SAKES...
...YOU WERE POINTING YOUR SWORD AT US!
THEN I REMEMBERED...
...THAT I...
...JOINED THE 13 COURT GUARDS BECAUSE OF YOU!
I...
...WANT YOU TO LIVE, NO MATTER WHAT...
SO YOU CAN FIGHT THE WAY YOU LIKE...
SWUFF
...WHICH TO ME IS COOL!
RIKICHI...

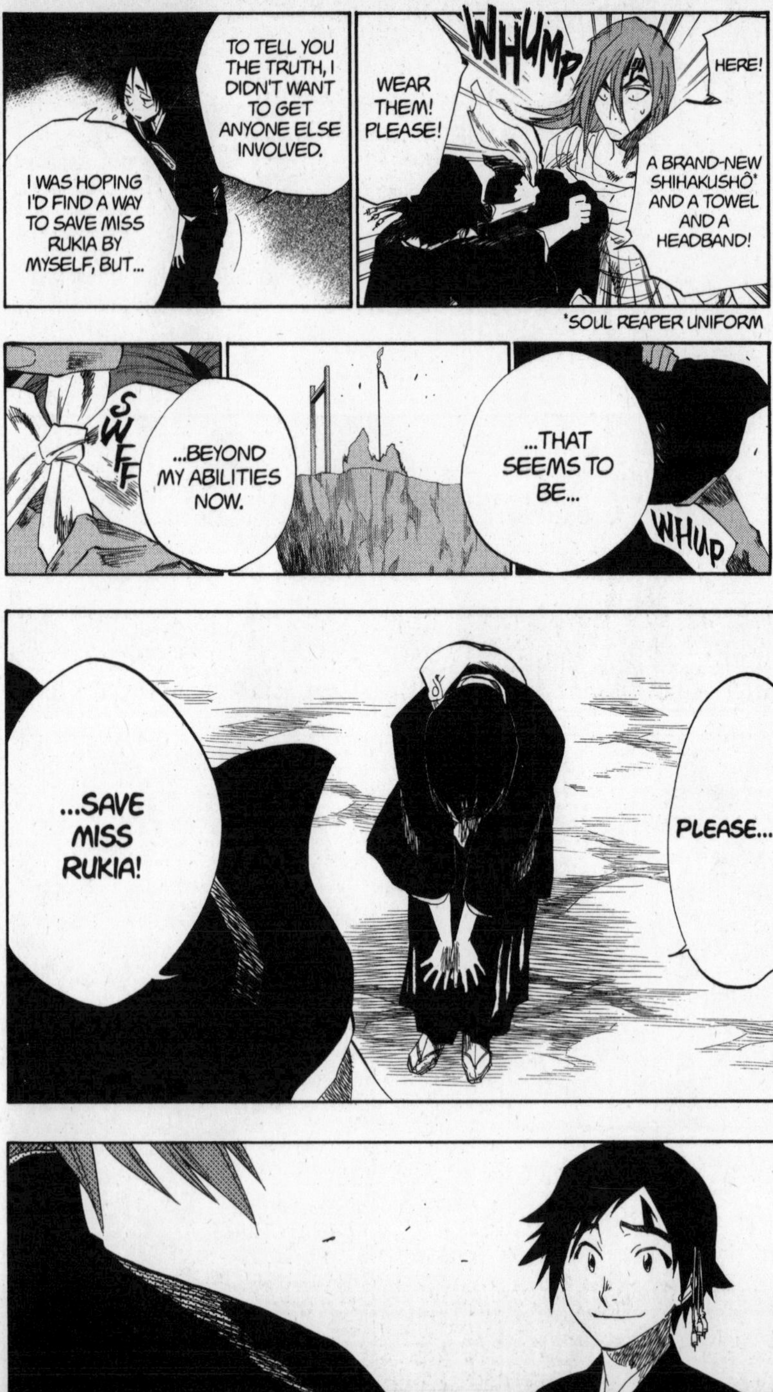
WHUMP
HERE!
A BRAND-NEW SHIHAKUSHÔ* AND A TOWEL AND A HEADBAND!
WEAR THEM! PLEASE!
TO TELL YOU THE TRUTH, I DIDN'T WANT TO GET ANYONE ELSE INVOLVED.
I WAS HOPING I'D FIND A WAY TO SAVE MISS RUKIA BY MYSELF, BUT...
...THAT SEEMS TO BE...
WHUP
...BEYOND MY ABILITIES NOW.
SWFF
PLEASE...
...SAVE MISS RUKIA!

*SOUL REAPER UNIFORM

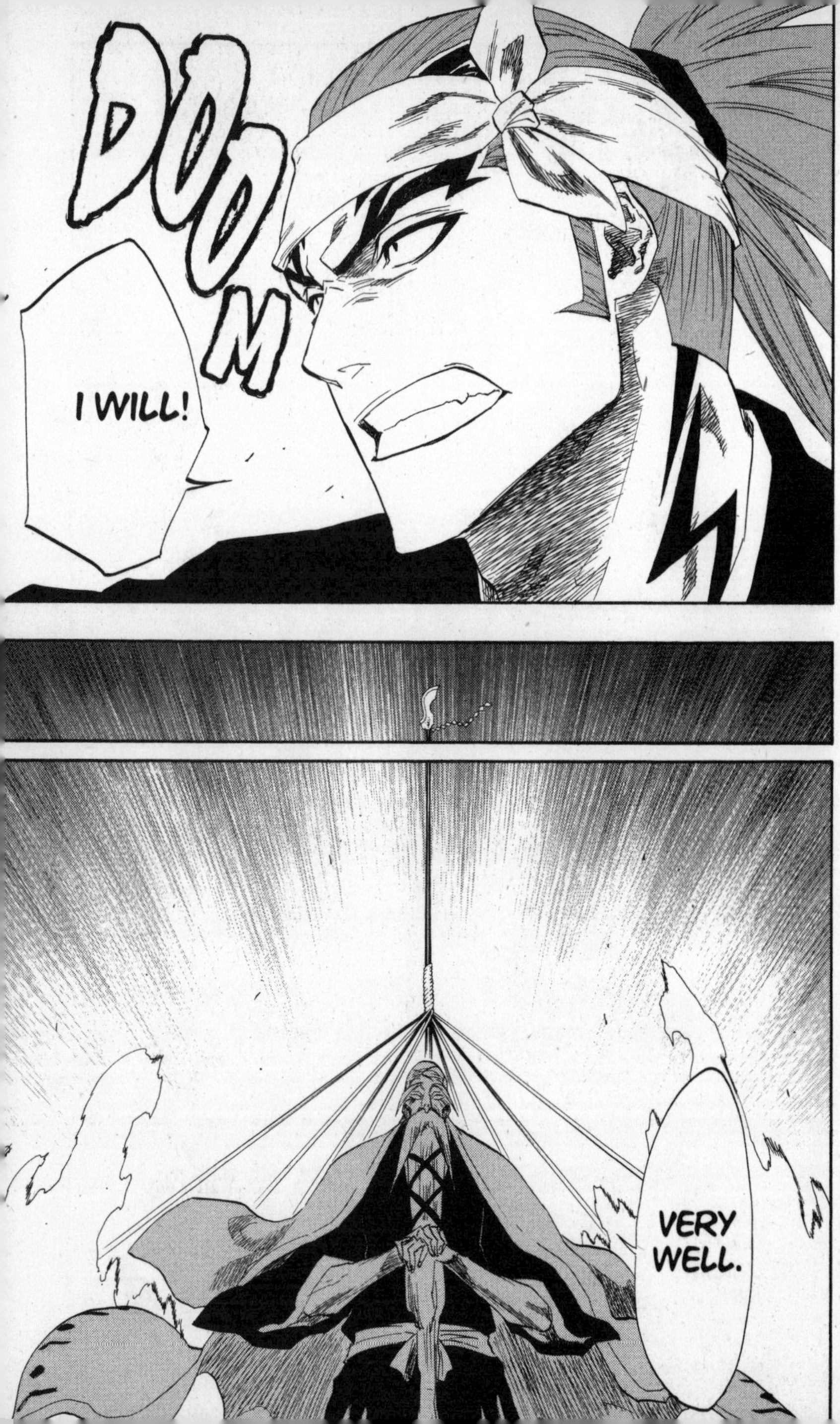
DOOOM
I WILL!
VERY WELL.

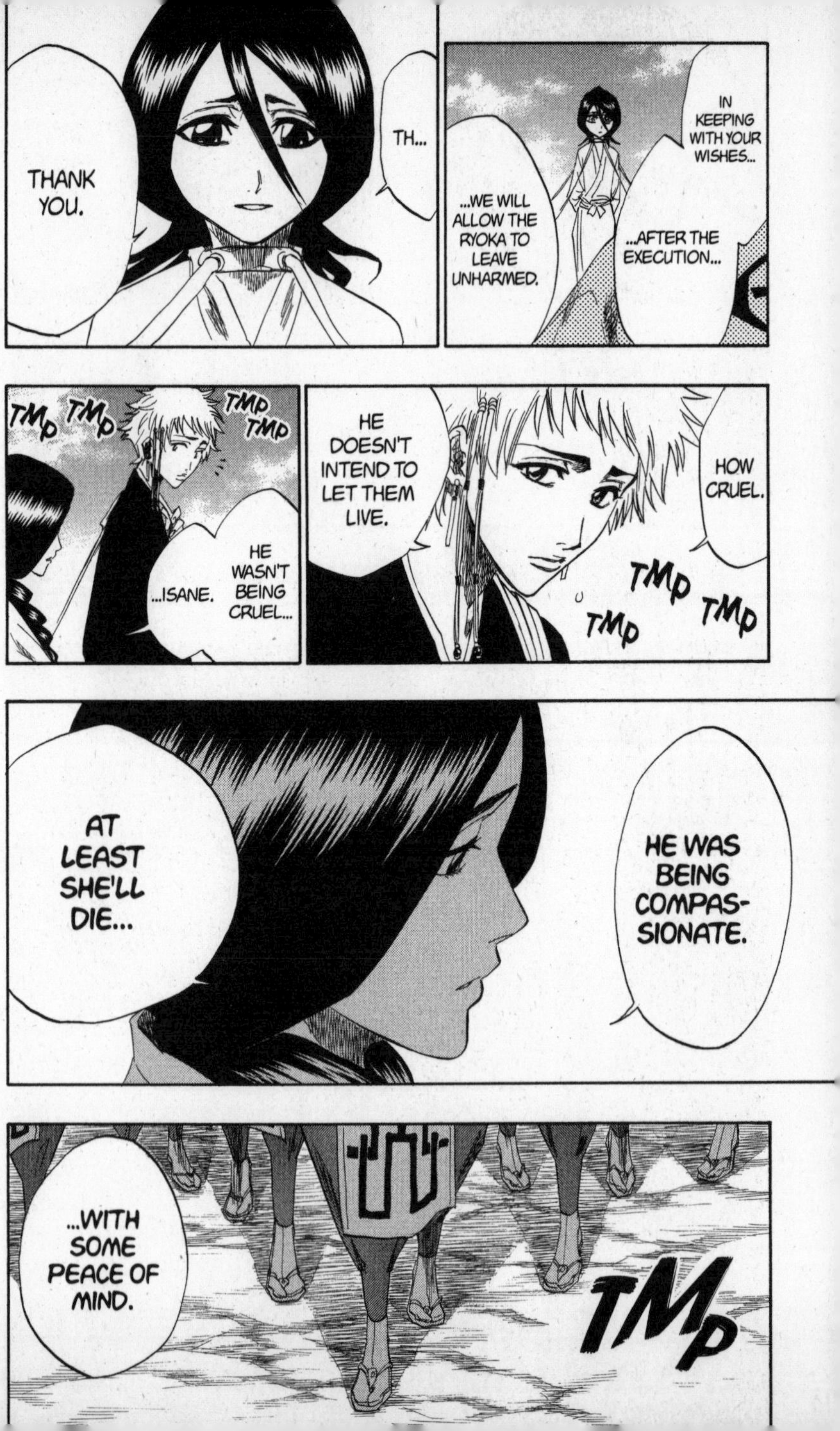

IN KEEPING WITH YOUR WISHES...
...AFTER THE EXECUTION...
...WE WILL ALLOW THE RYOKA TO LEAVE UNHARMED.
TH...
THANK YOU.
HOW CRUEL.
HE DOESN'T INTEND TO LET THEM LIVE.
TMP TMP TMP
TMP TMP TMP TMP
HE WASN'T BEING CRUEL...
...ISANE.
HE WAS BEING COMPAS-SIONATE.
AT LEAST SHE'LL DIE...
TMP
...WITH SOME PEACE OF MIND.

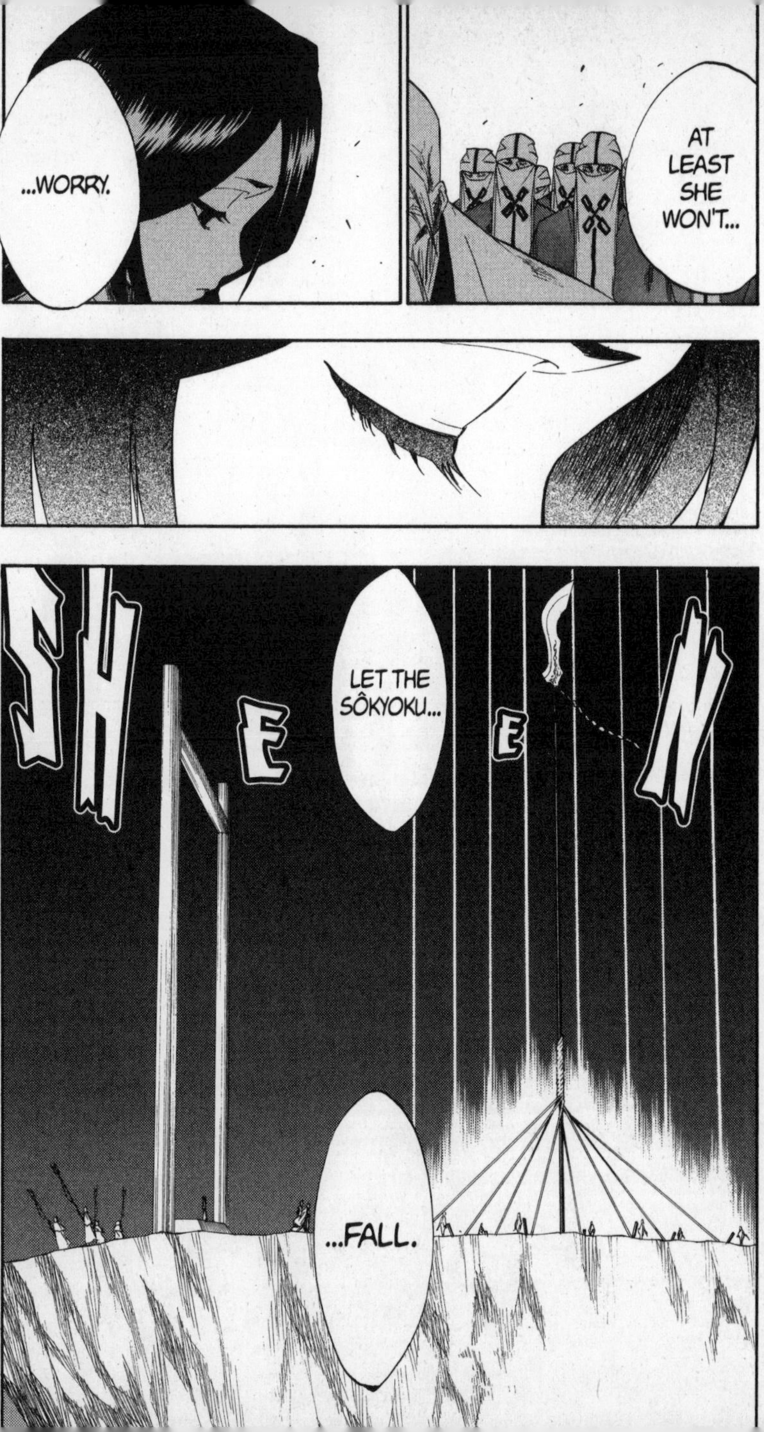
AT LEAST SHE WON'T...
...WORRY.
SHEEN
LET THE SÔKYOKU...
...FALL.

CONTI
NUED
IN
BLEACH
18

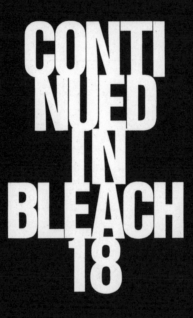

ラジコンベイビー

RADIO-KON★BABY!!

★4★

OPENING THEME MUSIC: "WE ARE RADIO-KON BABY!!"

YO! HOW YOU FOOLS DOING?!

IT'S BEEN TOO LONG! WAY TOO LONG!! YOU KNOW HOW LONG IT'S BEEN?! FIFTEEN MONTHS!! ONE YEAR AND THREE MONTHS!!! WHAT THE HECK'S A YEAR?! IT'S BEEN SO LONG, OUR LAST TAPING'S JUST A FOND MEMORY!!

SO TODAY, TO WORK OUT ALL THE FRUSTRATION THAT'S BUILT UP OVER THE LAST YEAR, I'M GONNA BE READING SOME OF YOUR LETTERS. THAT MEANS THERE WON'T BE MUCH TIME FOR CHITCHAT!! ALL RIGHT THEN, HERE'S "RADIO-KON 4"!! OUR GUEST IS... AW!! I KINDA HATE THIS GUY... KISUKE URAHARA!! SAY HELLO!!

HELLO. ♡

THANK YOU FOR YOUR PATIENCE, LADIES AND GENTLEMEN.♡ THIS IS URAHARA SHÔTEN'S SLIGHTLY SHADY BUT HANDSOME MANAGER, KISUKE URA--

Q DOES MR. URAHARA WEAR A TOUPEE? TAKASHI YAMASHITA--YAMAGUCHI

WOW, THAT WAS ABRUPT. C'MON, I WAITED A LONG TIME FOR THIS, SO GIVE ME TIME TO TALK. EVEN THAT QUESTION WAS TOO SHORT.

THAT'S WHY I SAID THERE WOULDN'T BE MUCH CHITCHAT! NOW ANSWER THE QUESTION!

IT'S A TOUPEE.

ALL RIGHT! WHAT'S NEXT?

HUH ?!

NOT REALLY.

...

Q THE OTHER DAY IN P.E., WE HAD TO RUN A 50-METER DASH. I SAID, "TAKE THE POWER OF JUSTICE! THE ARMOR AND HEAD-BAND OF JUSTICE!!"

THEN I PUT MY HEADBAND ON. I RAN .75 SECONDS FASTER THAN I EVER HAVE BEFORE. WAS THAT SOME KIND OF MAGIC, OR DID I JUST HAVE A GOOD DAY?
TSUBASA YAMAMOTO--TOYAMA

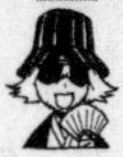

IT WAS 100 PERCENT MAGIC.

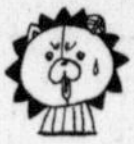

DUDE, ARE YOU GONNA ANSWER THESE QUESTIONS SERIOUSLY, OR NOT?

Q

MR. URAHARA! I LOVE YOU!! MARRY ME!!
AYAKA--WAKAYAMA

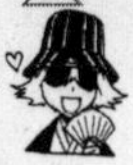

OKAY. ♡

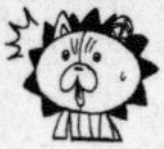

HEY! DON'T BE TAKING QUESTIONS WHEN I'M TALKING!!

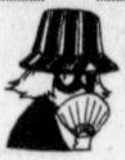

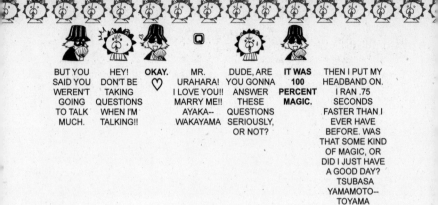

BUT YOU SAID YOU WEREN'T GOING TO TALK MUCH.

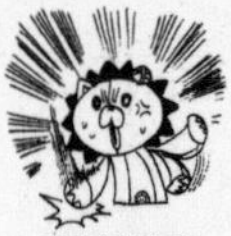

SHUT UP!! I GET TO TALK AS MUCH AS I WANT!! I'M THE HOST HERE!

Q

THERE WAS A SCENE IN VOLUME TWO WHERE YOU HUGGED URURU! I'M JEALOUS. WOULD YOU HUG ME, TOO?
MAKIKO NAKAMURA--HOKKAIDO

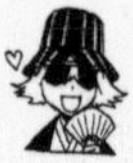

SURE! ♡

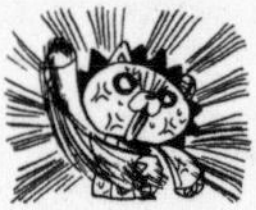

HEY!! DON'T CUT ME OFF LIKE THAT!! AND THAT QUESTION TICKS ME OFF, TOO!!

Q

AT THE END OF ICHIGO'S TRAINING, THE HAT THAT YOU WORE (AND THAT ICHIGO CUT) WAS FIXED. WHO FIXED IT? OR DO YOU KEEP SPARES, LIKE URYÛ?
TANAKA--NAGANO

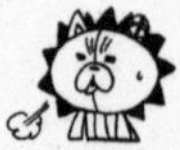

SO WE FINALLY ARRIVE AT THIS, THE MOST COMMONLY ASKED QUESTION. WELL? WHAT'S THE DEAL?

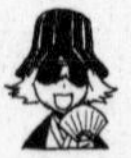

I HAVE A LOT OF THOSE HATS, MAYBE A HUNDRED OF THEM. BY THE WAY, I HAVE A LOT OF IDENTICAL ROBES AND CLOGS AND *JINBEI* (SUMMER CASUAL WEAR) TOO. ♪

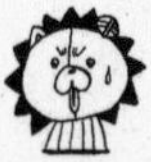

WOW... IF I WERE A DRAWER AND HAD A BUNCH OF IDENTICAL THINGS STUFFED INTO ME, I'D GO NUTS.

Q

WHAT KIND OF PEOPLE SHOP AT URAHARA SHÔTEN AND WHAT DO THEY BUY?
JUN KAMATA--FUKUSHIMA

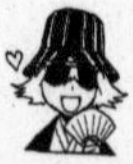

EVERYONE FROM LITTLE GIRLS TO HOUSEWIVES WITH TOO MUCH TIME ON THEIR HANDS SHOPS THERE. THEY BUY THINGS THAT I CAN'T EVEN MENTION IN MIXED COMPANY.

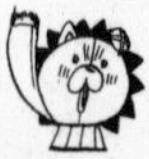

ARE YOU SERIOUS?! I TOTALLY WANNA GO THERE!!!

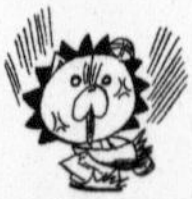

NO!! WHAT THE HECK?! YOU'VE ONLY ANSWERED ONE QUESTION SERIOUSLY SO FAR!!

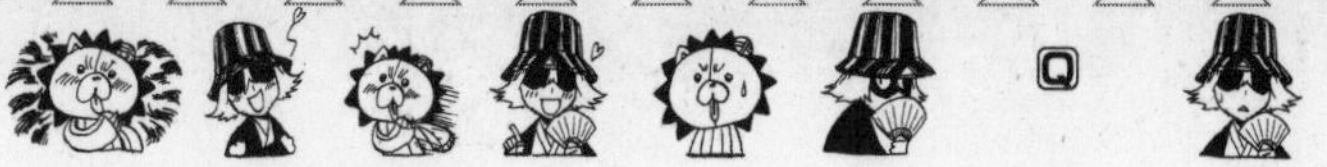

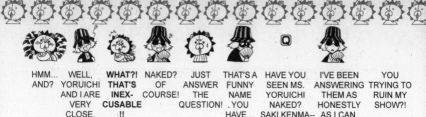

YOU TRYING TO RUIN MY SHOW?!

I'VE BEEN ANSWERING THEM AS HONESTLY AS I CAN.

Q HAVE YOU SEEN MS. YORUICHI NAKED? SAKI KENMA--OKAYAMA

THAT'S A FUNNY NAME YOU HAVE...

JUST ANSWER THE QUESTION!

NAKED? OF COURSE!

WHAT?! THAT'S INEXCUSABLE!!

WELL, YORUICHI AND I ARE VERY CLOSE. I REALLY CAN'T SAY ANY MORE.

HMM... AND?

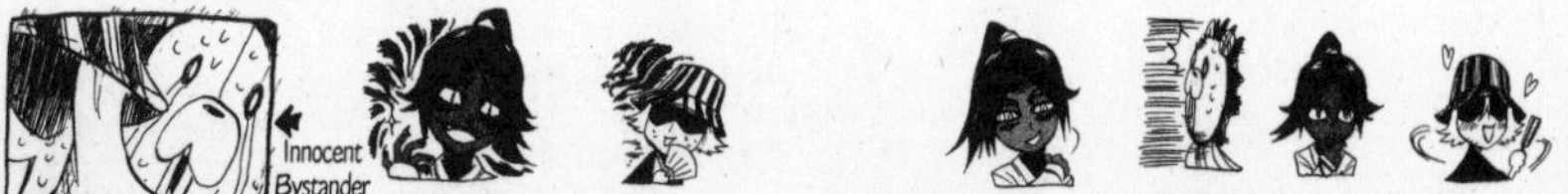
Innocent Bystander

I'VE SEEN PARTS OF HER BEYOND NAKED!!

HMM...

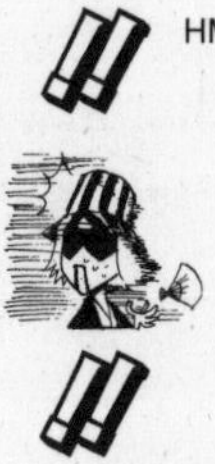
!!
!!

I SEE. I DIDN'T KNOW WE WERE SO INTIMATE. WOULD YOU CARE TO ELABORATE?

AW, C'MON, YORUICHI. NOT HERE...

DON'T BE SHY. "BEYOND NAKED," HUH? LET'S START BY CHECKING OUT YOUR BONES.

N-N-NOOOOOOOOOOOOOO...

NOW ACCEPTING LETTERS!!

ANY QUESTION IS OKAY!!
WE'RE ACCEPTING SUGGESTIONS FOR ENDING THEME MUSIC AS WELL AS QUESTIONS!! WRITE DOWN THE TITLE OF A SONG OR THE NAME OF AN ARTIST THAT INCLUDES THE WORD "LION," AND STUFF IT IN THE NEAREST MAILBOX!! OUR NEXT GUEST WILL BE HANATARO YAMADA (CONFIRMED)!! INCLUDE YOUR QUESTION, NAME, ADDRESS, AGE, AND TELEPHONE NUMBER AND SEND TO THE ADDRESS BELOW!!
SHONEN JUMP C/O VIZ MEDIA, LLC
P.O. BOX 77010, SAN FRANCISCO, CA 94107
ATTN: "BLEACH" RADIO-KON BABY!!

SINGLE: "GOODNIGHT RADIO-KON BABY!" ENDING THEME MUSIC: "CAN YOU FEEL THE LOVE TONIGHT" FROM *THE LION KING*, REQUESTED BY KANAGAWA (WHO LOVES CAPTAIN AIZEN)

Next Volume Preview

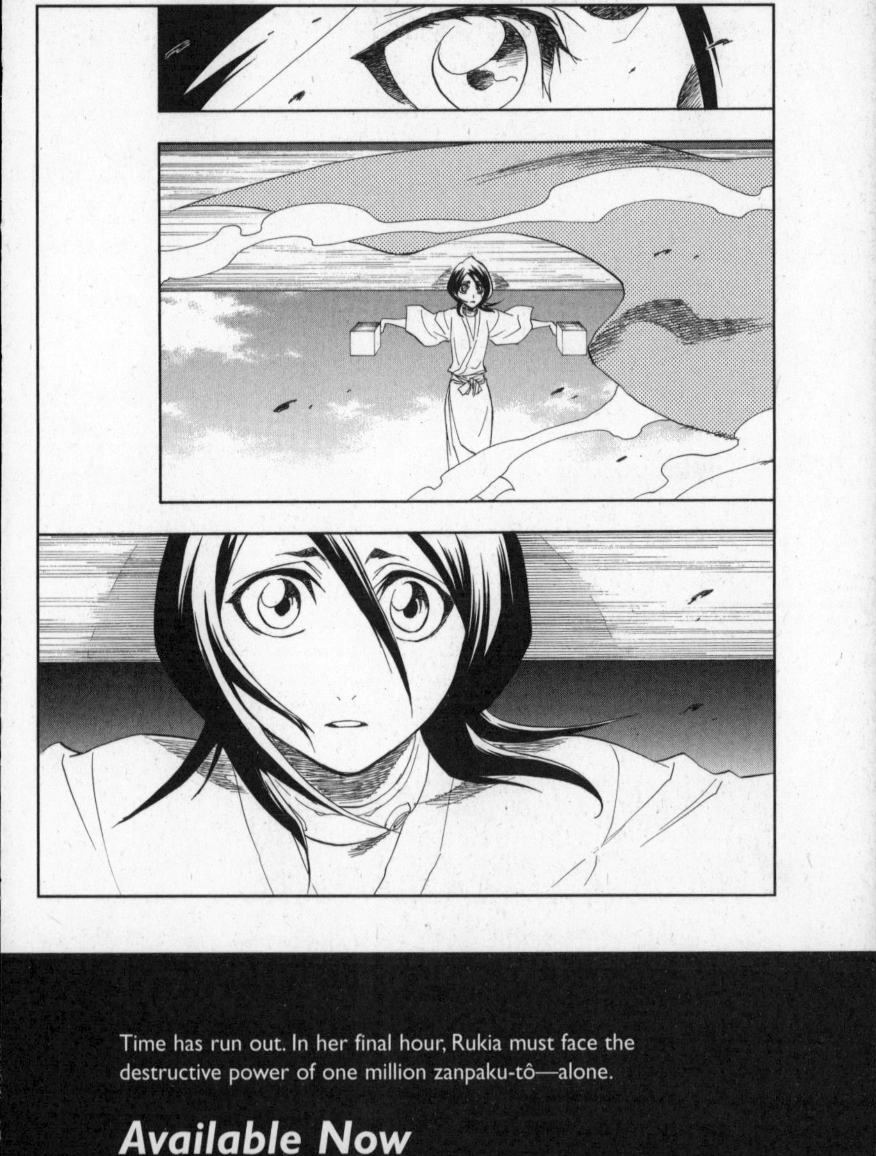

Time has run out. In her final hour, Rukia must face the destructive power of one million zanpaku-tô—alone.

Available Now

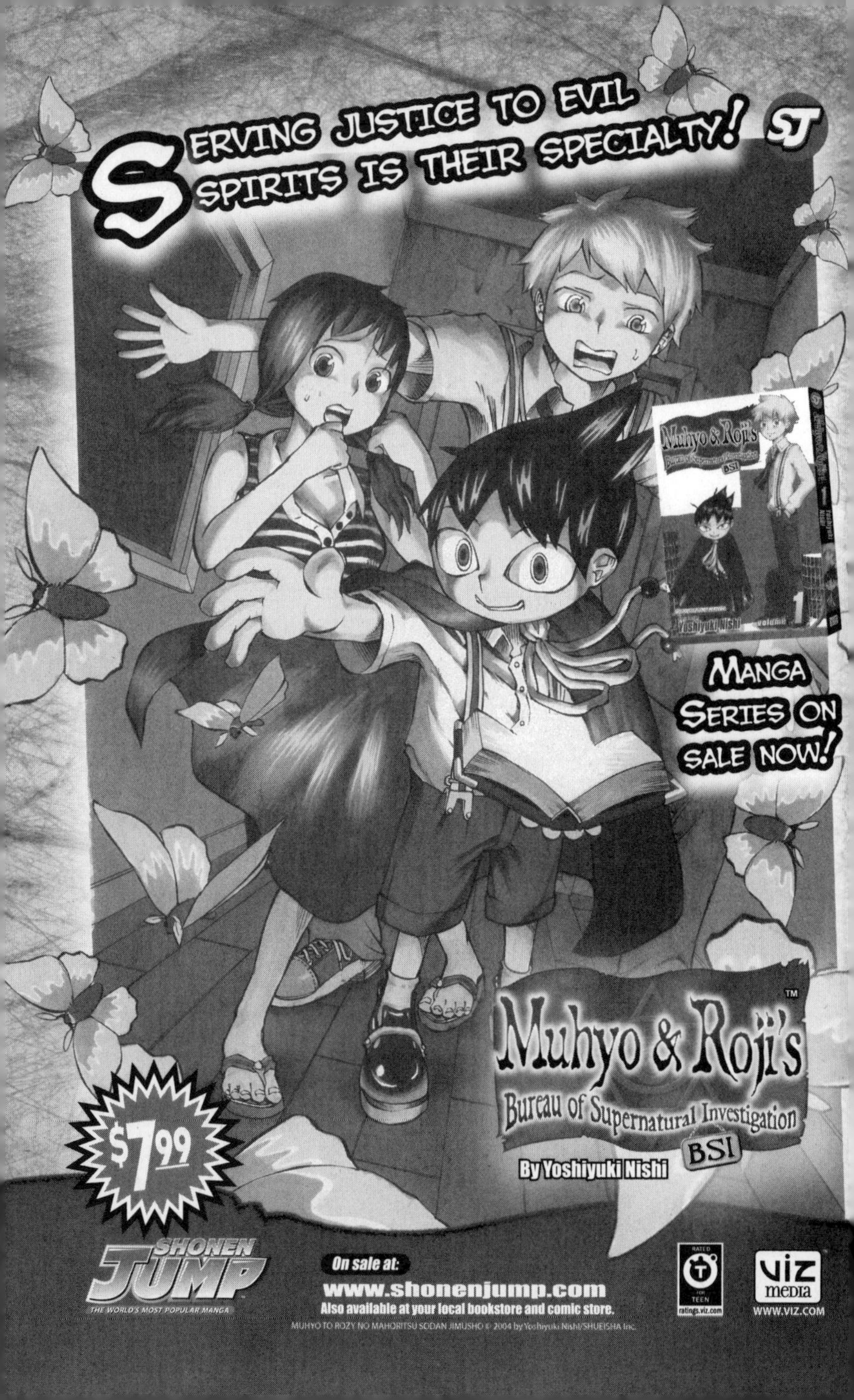
SERVING JUSTICE TO EVIL SPIRITS IS THEIR SPECIALTY!
SJ
MANGA SERIES ON SALE NOW!
Muhyo & Roji's
Bureau of Supernatural Investigation
BSI
By Yoshiyuki Nishi
$7.99
SHONEN JUMP
THE WORLD'S MOST POPULAR MANGA
On sale at:
www.shonenjump.com
Also available at your local bookstore and comic store.
MUHYO TO ROZY NO MAHORITSU SODAN JIMUSHO © 2004 by Yoshiyuki Nishi/SHUEISHA Inc.
RATED T FOR TEEN
ratings.viz.com
VIZ media
WWW.VIZ.COM

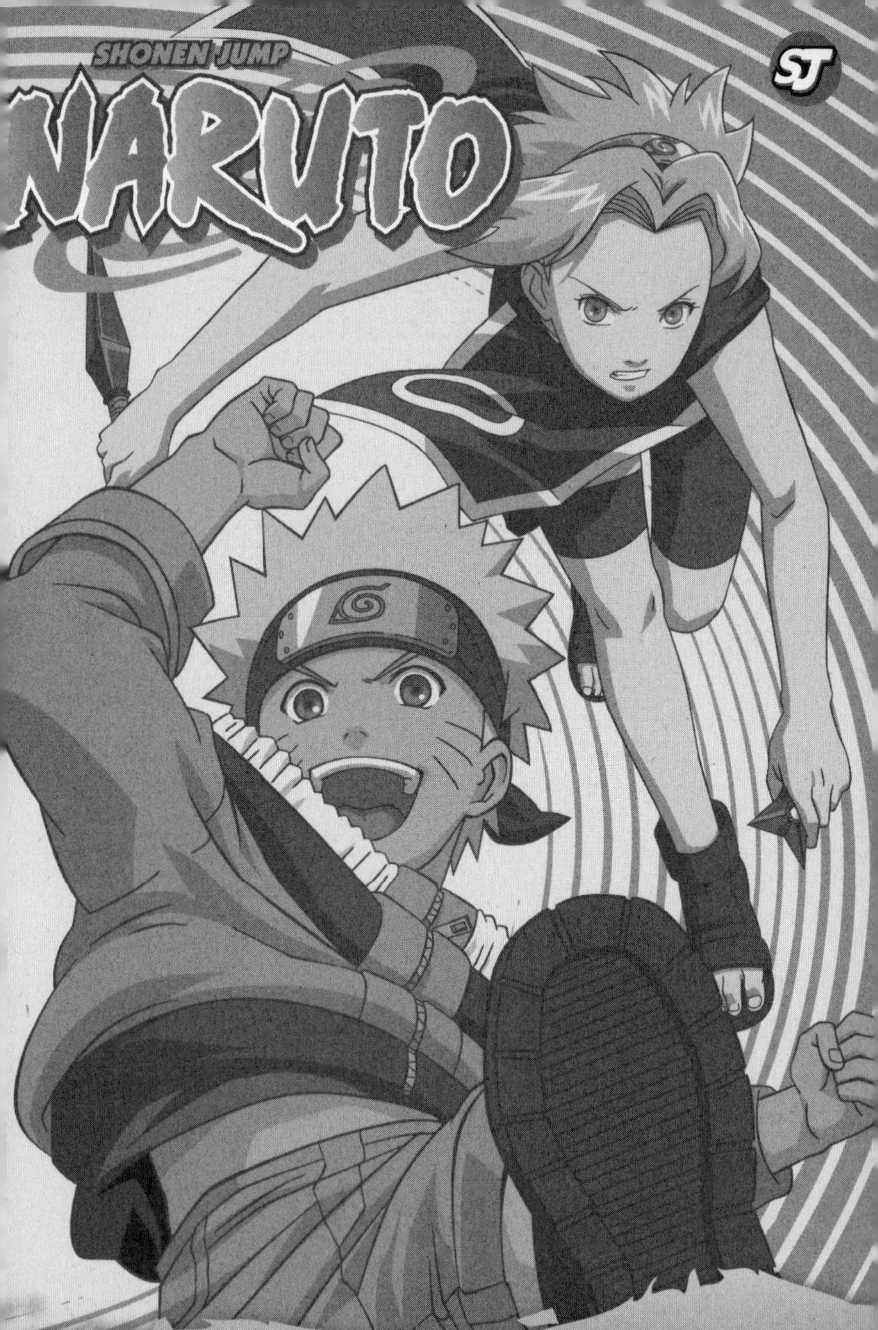
SHONEN JUMP
NARUTO
SJ

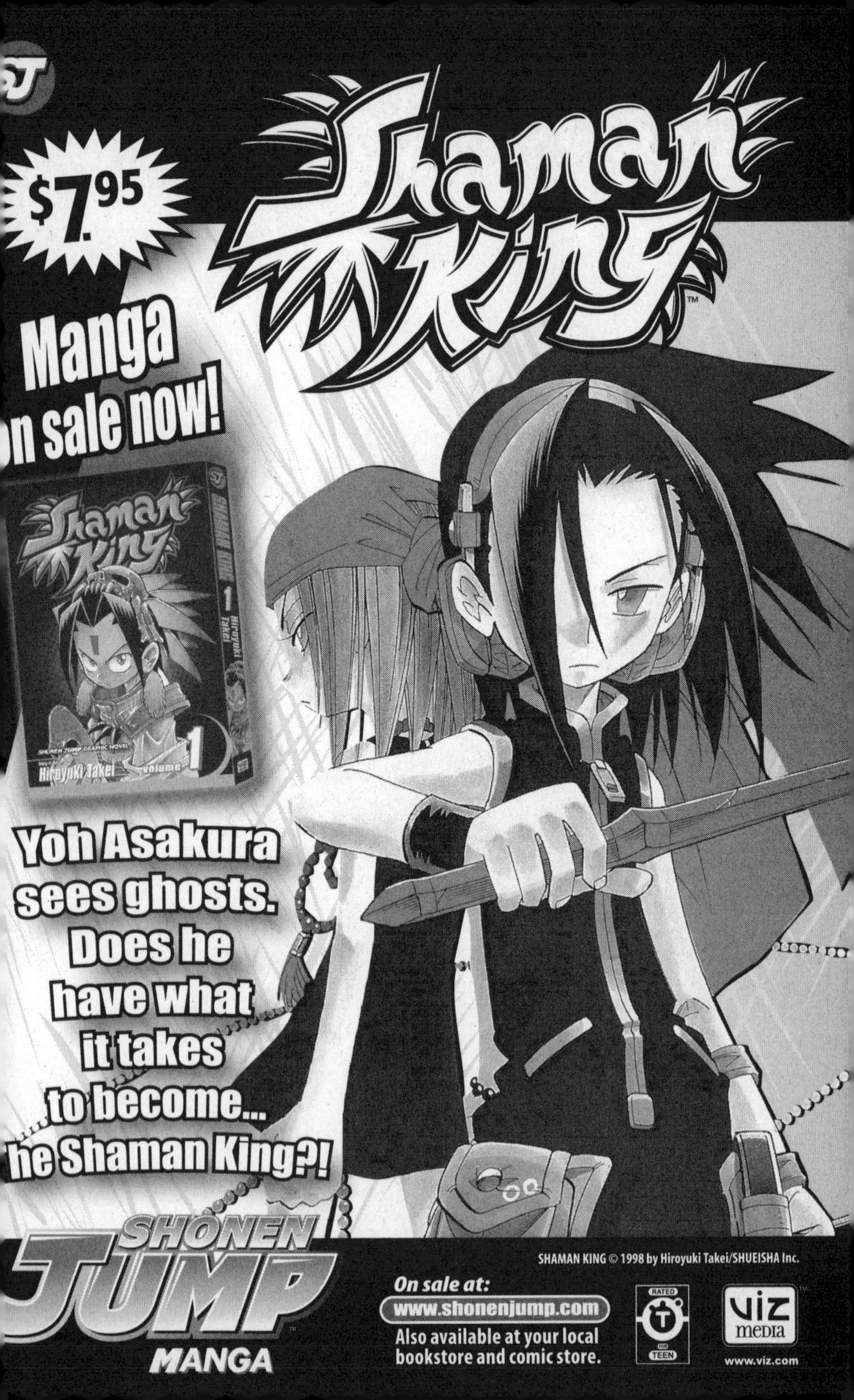
SJ
$7.95
Shaman King™
Manga
on sale now!
Shaman King
1
Hiroyuki Takei
SHONEN JUMP GRAPHIC NOVEL
Hiroyuki Takei volume 1
Yoh Asakura
sees ghosts.
Does he
have what
it takes
to become...
the Shaman King?!
SHONEN JUMP™
MANGA
SHAMAN KING © 1998 by Hiroyuki Takei/SHUEISHA Inc.
On sale at:
www.shonenjump.com
Also available at your local
bookstore and comic store.
RATED T FOR TEEN
viz media
www.viz.com

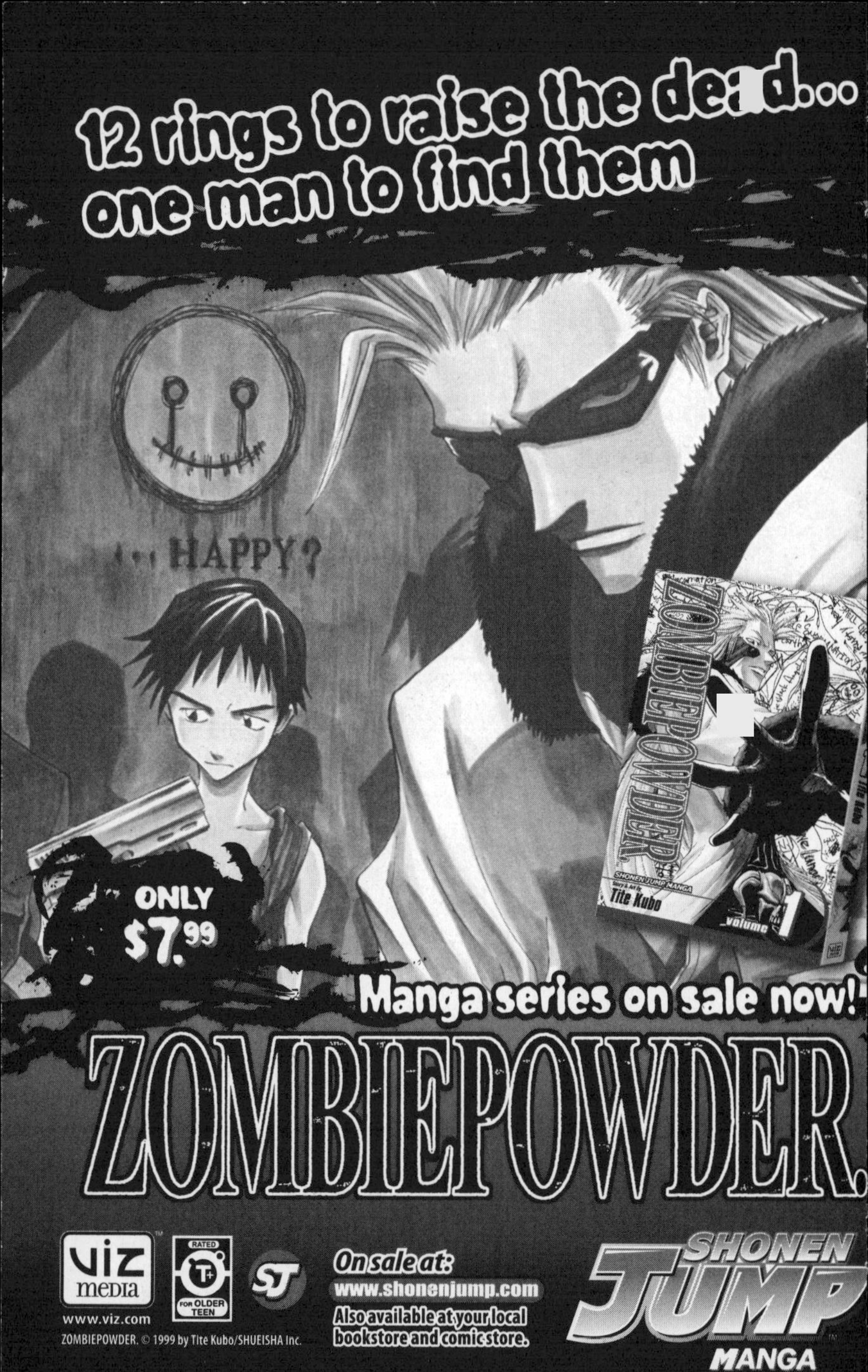
12 rings to raise the dead...
one man to find them
...HAPPY?
ZOMBIEPOWDER.
SHONEN JUMP MANGA
Tite Kubo
volume 1
ONLY
$7.99
Manga series on sale now!
ZOMBIEPOWDER.
viz media
www.viz.com
RATED
T+
FOR OLDER TEEN
SJ
On sale at:
www.shonenjump.com
Also available at your local bookstore and comic store.
SHONEN JUMP
MANGA
ZOMBIEPOWDER. © 1999 by Tite Kubo/SHUEISHA Inc.

Tell us what you think about SHONEN JUMP manga!

Our survey is now available online.
Go to: www.SHONENJUMP.com/mangasurvey

Help us make our product offering better!

Save **50% OFF** the cover price!

SHONEN JUMP

THE WORLD'S MOST POPULAR MANGA

Over **300 pages** per issue!

Each issue of SHONEN JUMP contains the coolest manga available in the U.S., anime news, and info on video & card games, toys AND more!

☑ **YES!** Please enter my one-year subscription (12 HUGE issues) to **SHONEN JUMP** at the LOW SUBSCRIPTION RATE of **$29.95!**

NAME

ADDRESS

CITY   STATE   ZIP

E-MAIL ADDRESS   P7GNC1

☐ MY CHECK IS ENCLOSED (PAYABLE TO SHONEN JUMP)   ☐ BILL ME LATER

CREDIT CARD: ☐ VISA   ☐ MASTERCARD

ACCOUNT #   EXP. DATE

SIGNATURE

CLIP AND MAIL TO

SHONEN JUMP
Subscriptions Service Dept.
P.O. Box 515
Mount Morris, IL 61054-0515

Make checks payable to: **SHONEN JUMP**. Canada price for 12 issues: $41.95 USD, including GST, HST and QST. US/CAN orders only. Allow 6-8 weeks for delivery.

RATED **T** FOR TEEN
ratings.viz.com

BLEACH © 2001 by Tite Kubo/SHUEISHA Inc. NARUTO © 1999 by Masashi Kishimoto/SHUEISHA Inc.
ONE PIECE © 1997 by Eiichiro Oda/SHUEISHA Inc.